John Bidwell and California

JOHN BIDWELL, ca. 1858.
Reprinted with permission by Special Collections,
Meriam Library, California State University, Chico

# John Bidwell
## and
# California

The Life and Writings
of a Pioneer
1841–1900

by
Michael J. Gillis
and
Michael F. Magliari

THE ARTHUR H. CLARK COMPANY
Spokane, Washington
2003

Copyright 2003 by
Michael J. Gillis and Michael F. Magliari

All rights reserved including the rights
to translate or reproduce this work or parts
thereof in any form or by any media.

Arthur H. Clark Company
P.O. Box 14707
Spokane, WA 99214

LIBRARY OF CONGRESS CATALOG CARD NUMBER 2002019281
ISBN-0-87062-316-8

Library of Congress Cataloging-in-Publication Data
Bidwell, John, 1819-1900.
  John Bidwell and California: the life and writings of a pioneer, 1841-1900 / [edited] by Michael J. Gillis, and Michael F. Magliari
    p. cm.—(Western frontiersman series; 30)
  Includes bibliographical references.
  ISBN 0-87062-316-8
  1. Bidwell, John, 1819-1900. 2. Pioneers—California—Biography. 3. Frontier and pioneer life—California. 4. California—History—1846-1850. 5. California—History—1850-1950. 6. Bidwell, John, 1819-1900—Quotations. 7. California—History—Sources. I. Gillis, Michael J. II. Magliari, Michaelf F. III. Title. IV. Western frontiersmen series; 30.
F864 .B5935 2002
979.4'04'092—dc21
[B]                                                               2002019281

The authors and publisher gratefully acknowledge the assistance of The California Historical Society, San Francisco, and California State University, Chico, in providing supporting grants to aid in the publication of this work.

for Jeanette, Karen, Monica and Dante

# Contents

| | |
|---|---:|
| Acknowledgments | 13 |
| Introduction: John Bidwell and the Historians | 17 |
| Prologue: John Bidwell, 1819–1841 | 27 |
| 1. First Emigrants on the California Trail | 31 |
|     *Recollections of the California Trail* | 41 |
| 2. Mexican California and the American Conquest, 1841–1848 | 73 |
|     *Remarks on Mexican California, the Bear Flag Revolt, and the Mexican War* | 81 |
| 3. Bidwell and California Gold | 115 |
|     *Remarks on the Gold Rush and Gold Mining* | 119 |
| 4. Rancho Chico and the Development of California Agriculture | 129 |
|     *Bidwell on California Agriculture* | 151 |
|     *Growing and Marketing "Bonanza Wheat"* | 155 |
|     *Specialty Crops and Diversification* | 162 |
|     *Mechanization* | 166 |
|     *Livestock and Dairy Production* | 170 |
|     *Irrigation and Reclamation* | 173 |
|     *Promoting Scientific Agriculture* | 177 |
|     *Fences and Fence Laws* | 178 |
|     *Financial Hazards of Farming* | 180 |
| 5. A Career in California Politics | 185 |
|     *Bidwell on His Political Beliefs and Career* | 205 |
| 6. Bidwell and the California Indians | 249 |
|     *Remarks on the California Indians* | 283 |

7. Bidwell and the California Chinese . . . . . . 311
    *Bidwell's Remarks on the Chinese* . . . . . . . 332
A Bidwell Bibliography . . . . . . . . . . 343
Index . . . . . . . . . . . . 358

# Illustrations

| | |
|---|---|
| John Bidwell, ca. 1858 | *frontispiece* |
| Rancho del Arroyo Chico *diseño* drawn by John Bidwell | 128 |
| John Bidwell's adobe and store | 130 |
| Chico Roller Flouring Mills | 138 |
| Annie Ellicott Kennedy Bidwell, ca. 1868 | 141 |
| John and Annie Bidwell on mansion grounds in Chico | 142 |
| Drying fruit on Rancho Chico | 142 |
| John Bidwell's office at 1st St. and Broadway, ca. 1895 | 143 |
| Rancho Chico cannery | 143 |
| Combined harvester at work on Rancho Chico, ca. 1890 | 169 |
| Wheat sacks ready for shipment from Chico landing | 169 |
| Indian workers shelling almonds on Rancho Chico | 181 |
| President Fillmore and Bidwell | 184 |
| Chico store and Post Office | 196 |
| John Bidwell, ca. 1880 | 205 |
| John Bidwell, ca. 1866 | 214 |
| Chinese New Year Procession in Chico | 316 |

# List of Maps

| | |
|---|---|
| 1. Bidwell-Bartleson Overland Route | 30 |
| 2. Bidwell-Bartleson 1841 Route Through the Sierra Nevada | 36 |
| 3. Chico-to-Humboldt Wagon Road and Idaho Stage Routes | 195 |
| 4. Butte and Tehama Counties, 1850–1865 | 263 |

## List of Tables

1. Rancho Chico Field Crops, Livestock and Produce . . 134
2. Growth of Rancho Chico's Orchards . . . . . . 140
3. 1875 California Gubernatorial Election Returns . . . 203

# List of Abbreviations

| | |
|---|---|
| AB | Annie E. K. Bidwell |
| ABD | Annie E. K. Bidwell's Diary, California State Library, Sacramento |
| ANCRR | Association for Northern California Records and Research |
| BANC | Bancroft Library, University of California, Berkeley |
| b. | Box |
| BFP | Bidwell Family Papers, Bancroft Library, University of California, Berkeley |
| *Colusa* | Justus H. Rogers. *Colusa County: Its History* (Orland, California, n.p. 1891). |
| CSAS | Transactions of the California State Agricultural Society |
| CSL | California State Library, Sacramento |
| CSUC | California State University, Chico |
| *f.* | *Folder* |
| *General* | Linda Rawlings, ed., *Dear General: The Private Letters of Annie E. Kennedy and John Bidwell, 1866–1868* (Sacramento: California Department of Parks and Recreation, 1993). |
| JB | John Bidwell |
| JBD | John Bidwell Diary, 1864–1900, California State Library, Sacramento |
| JB-77 | John Bidwell. "California 1841–1848: An Immigrant's Recollections of a Trip Across the Plains and of Men and Events in Early Days, Including the Bear Flag Revolution." Dictation to Seth Sprague Boynton for Hubert H. Bancroft, 1877. Bancroft Library, University of California, Berkeley. |
| JB-91 | John Bidwell. "Dictation from General John Bidwell: An Autobiography." Dictation for Hubert H. Bancroft Collections with some corrections in Bidwell's handwriting, 1891. Bancroft Library, University of California, Berkeley. |
| JB-CSL | John Bidwell Papers, California State Library, Sacramento |

JB-CSUC   John Bidwell Papers, Meriam Library Special Collections, California State University, Chico
HUNT      Henry Huntington Library, San Marino, California
*Journey*  John Bidwell. *A Journey to California, With Observations about the Country, Climate, and the Route to this Country.* Introduction by Herbert I. Priestly. San Francisco: John H. Nash, 1937.
*Pioneers* John Bidwell. "Address of John Bidwell to the Members of the Society of California Pioneers, November 1, 1897." Edited by Henry L. Byrne. *Quarterly of the Society of California Pioneers,* 3 (March 31, 1926): 9–29.

# Acknowledgments

We have accumulated numerous debts during the eight years it has taken to research and write this book. The kind support of many people deserves recognition here. First of all, we wish to thank Theodore 'Ted' Meriam for his enthusiastic backing of our project. A lifelong Chicoan and Bidwell enthusiast, Ted was instrumental in helping us to secure a research grant from the Bidwell Mansion Association. A former Chico mayor and President of the California State University Board of Trustees, Ted used his great political skills to engineer our subsequent appointments to the Association's board of directors, *after* we had demonstrated an ability to spend our grant monies wisely. To the board we wish to once again express our appreciation for its willingness to provide us with such a generous endorsement. Along with Ted, two other members of the board, John Nopel and Lois H. McDonald, aided us by reading and correcting early drafts of several chapters.

Parts of our manuscript also received careful and helpful readings from Lisa Emmerich, John Boyle, and Jeffery Livingston, three of our colleagues in the History Department at California State University, Chico. Jessica Herrick, our overworked but cheerful graduate student assistant for one very valuable semester, spent untold hours scanning through National Archives microfilms for us, risking her eyesight to preserve ours. Meanwhile, across campus in Political Science, Professor Michele Shover provided a number of beneficial suggestions regarding our chapter on John Bidwell's use of Chinese labor. We have also benefited tremendously from Michele's insightful work on Bidwell's complex interactions with Native American peoples. We especially appreciate her willingness to share several of her essays prior to their publication. Generous and greatly appreciated financial support for our project was rendered in the early goings by Provost Scott McNall of CSU, Chico and Professor Laird Easton of The University Press at Chico.

Our gathering of Bidwell materials took us all over California and required the assistance of many helpful archivists, librarians, and curators. We are particularly indebted to manuscripts curator Peter Blodgett of the Huntington Library in San Marino, and to the helpful staffs of the Bancroft Library at the University of California, Berkeley, and the special collections department of the University Research Library at UCLA. Craig D. Bates, Curator of Ethnography at Yosemite National Park, provided some very helpful information regarding Maidu and Mechoopda Indian history. Two individuals in San Francisco also deserve special mention here: Stanleigh Bry, Library Director for the Society of California Pioneers, who helped us mine that organization's valuable collections, and Michael McCone, the Executive Director of the California Historical Society. Mike, who delivered a memorable banquet address to the 1997 annual meeting of the Bidwell Mansion Association, became an enthusiastic supporter of our efforts. To him we owe our appreciation for the society's decision to join The Arthur H. Clark Company as our co-publisher. Speaking of publishers, we also must thank Robert Clark of The Arthur H. Clark Company in Spokane, Washington, for his help in transforming our bulky manuscript into a manageable book.

We are especially grateful for the never-failing assistance of two very valuable friends in Sacramento: Gary Kurutz, Director of Special Collections at the California State Library, and archivist Joseph Samora of the California State Archives. Closer to home, Butte County Clerk-Recorder Candace Grubbs and Assistant County Recorder Rosemary Dickson deserve a special commendation for making the historic public records of Butte County so conveniently accessible. In addition, we owe special notes of appreciation to Larry Williams and Tim Krane, our cartographers at the CSU Chico Department of Geography and Planning, and many, many thanks to the secretaries of the CSU Chico Department of History: Claudia Beaty, Nancy Riley, and Mary Bock.

For the ultimate success of our research efforts, we must acknowledge those individuals at CSU Chico's Meriam Library who rendered invaluable and continuous service on our behalf. At Interlibrary Loan, Jo Ann Bradley, George Thompson, Lorraine Mosley, and Karen Seaman saved us countless hours by retrieving all sorts of obscure items located far beyond the confines of Butte County. Meanwhile, it is safe to say that completing this book would have been impossible without the help of William Jones and his dedicated staff at the Meriam Library's Special Collections department. We therefore extend our many thanks to Bill and archivists Mary Ellen Bailey, Deborah Besnard, and Pam Herman Bush, along with their hardworking student assistants.

Finally, we extend our appreciation to Jeanette Alosi for all the techical assistance cheerfully rendered, and to Professor Ian Tyrrell of the University of New South Wales in Sydney, Australia. Tyrrell generously provided us with a copy of the long out-of-print description of Rancho Chico published at Melbourne by Thomas K. Dow in 1884. Like Dow before him, Tyrrell eventually made the journey from Down Under to visit Chico, where he delivered the keynote address to the Bidwell Mansion Association's annual meeting in January 2002.

Our heartfelt apologies to anyone we have omitted.

MICHAEL GILLIS and MICHAEL MAGLIARI
Chico, California

# INTRODUCTION:
# John Bidwell and the Historians

On November 1, 1897, an elderly but still vigorous gentleman addressed the annual meeting of the Society of California Pioneers in San Francisco. A member of the society since its inception in 1850, the distinguished speaker was shortly to mark the fifty-sixth anniversary of his arrival in California at the head of the first overland party of American settlers bound for what was then still Mexican territory. Many great changes had taken place in the golden state since November 4, 1841, and the society's keynote speaker had been instrumental in shaping many of those changes. It was therefore with only slight exaggeration that John Bidwell could now, at the venerable age of seventy-eight, truthfully declare to his audience that "The history of California lies like a map before me. Somewhat confused it may be, but I have seen it all, and if I had been a writer, which I am not, I could have written history."[1]

If anything, Bidwell's claim was overly modest. To a degree unmatched by any among his fellow pioneers, Bidwell could fairly claim to "have seen it all." And, his humble denial notwithstanding, he did in fact write history. Just seven years earlier, Bidwell had composed a three-part memoir that appeared in *The Century Illustrated Monthly Magazine*. Covering the years 1841–1848, these vivid firsthand accounts of the overland trek, Mexican California, the American conquest, and the discovery of gold have been republished in various formats at least eleven times since Bidwell's death in 1900. The *Century* essays, together with Bidwell's overland trail journal and the lengthy dictations and manuscripts given to historians Seth Boynton, Hubert Howe Bancroft, Justus Rogers, and O. B.

---
[1] John Bidwell, "Address of John Bidwell to the Members of the Society of California Pioneers, November 1, 1897," *Quarterly of the Society of California Pioneers*, 3 (March 31, 1926), pp. 9-29. Bidwell was elected vice president of the Society of California Pioneers in 1854 and had also served as president of the Old Settlers' Association of California. See Marcus Benjamin, *John Bidwell, Pioneer: A Sketch of His Career* (Washington, D.C.: 1907), p. 46 and Rockwell D. Hunt, *John Bidwell, Prince of California Pioneers* (Caldwell, Idaho: Caxton Printers, 1942), pp. 199-201.

Parkinson, guaranteed Bidwell's place among the important original interpreters of the late Mexican and early American periods of California history.[2]

These overtly historical writings, moreover, comprise only a small portion of the written legacy that Bidwell bequeathed to subsequent generations of historians. Again, despite his claim to the contrary, Bidwell *was* a writer, and a prolific one at that. Throughout his long and active life, Bidwell produced a voluminous body of published and unpublished work treating just about every imaginable aspect of life in California between 1841 and the turn of the century. Like the deliberate and meticulous man he was, Bidwell faithfully maintained a diary from 1864 until the week of his death thirty-six years later.

He also wrote hundreds of letters to correspondents all over the state and nation, as well as in Europe. These included John Muir; John Sutter; Susan B. Anthony; Frances Willard; William Tecumseh Sherman; President Rutherford B. Hayes; Sir Joseph Hooker, England's premier botanist during the late nineteenth century; and Asa Gray, the Harvard botanist who was proclaimed the "Columbus" of his field. Most important among Bidwell's correspondents was his wife Annie. To her he wrote daily whenever they were separated, either by his frequent business trips away from home, or by her annual visits with her family in Washington, D.C.[3]

In addition to his torrential outpouring of letters, Bidwell often penned essays for publication in newspapers, farm journals, and government documents. Like his personal and commercial correspondence, these covered a remarkable array of topics that ran the gamut from hydraulic mining and scientific farming to women's suffrage and Chinese immigration. Taken altogether, Bidwell's writings reflect an active and curious

---

[2] Bidwell's overland journal, first published in Missouri in 1842, has seen at least three reprintings. The recollections he recorded for Rogers were published in the latter's *Colusa County: Its History* (Orland, CA: n.p., 1891), pp. 35–37. The edited transcripts of Parkinson's interviews with Bidwell appeared as "Early California Reminiscences," an eight-part article in *Out West* magazine that ran from January through August 1904. See bibliography for a complete listing of Bidwell's publications and unpublished dictations.

[3] Try as she might, Annie could rarely keep pace with John's daily missives, which often consumed five or six pages of their well-used stationery. For some intimate excerpts of John and Annie's courtship correspondence, see Chad Hoopes, ed., *What Makes A Man: The Annie Kennedy-John Bidwell Letters, 1866–1868* (Fresno, CA: Valley Publishers, 1973) and Linda Rawlings, ed., *Dear General: The Private Letters of Annie E. Kennedy and John Bidwell, 1866–1868* (Sacramento: California Department of Parks and Recreation, 1993).

intellect that pondered nearly every important public issue in its day. They show Bidwell to have been a thoughtful and even visionary man of deep convictions balanced by practical common sense, a man blessed with keen powers of observation and a gift for the often florid and hyperbolic prose so highly prized by Gilded Age Americans.

Given its sheer size, as well as its remarkable provenance and chronological sweep, the Bidwell literary corpus would have tremendous historical value even if its author had been just a minor figure in the development of California. John Bidwell, however, was no supporting actor. From the moment he began organizing the wagon train that became known as the Bidwell-Bartleson Party, Bidwell assumed a permanent and leading role in the history of California and the American West. Indeed, of all the American pioneers who settled in California before the gold rush, none enjoyed more subsequent fame and success than John Bidwell, and none made as great a contribution to the state's economic, political, and cultural development during the late nineteenth century.

On the eve of his death in April 1900, Bidwell could look back with pride on a lifetime of great accomplishments. A veteran of the Bear Flag Revolt and the Mexican War, Bidwell was among the first of the fortunate few who struck it rich in the California gold rush. The pastoral empire he went on to establish at Rancho Chico, the chief and constant labor of his life, served for decades as a model farm that made numerous contributions to the spectacular development of California agriculture between 1850 and 1900. All the while, steeped in classical republican notions of civic duty and fired by powerful personal ambitions, Bidwell pursued a career of public service capped by his famous but largely ceremonial campaign for the Presidency in 1892 at the head of the Prohibition party ticket. Before that, he had served in the California state senate and the United States House of Representatives; run four times for governor; held three important gubernatorial appointments; laid out the city of Chico; and founded the state normal school's northern campus, today's California State University, Chico.

Despite this impressive record of achievement, Bidwell has received remarkably little attention from historians. In light of the wealth of written records he left behind, this neglect is rather astounding. Nevertheless, the small shelf of Bidwelliana remains dominated by three aging books written during the first half of the twentieth century.

The earliest of these works was Colonel Charles C. Royce's *John Bidwell: Pioneer, Statesman, Philanthropist*, published in 1906. Hardly an objective source, Royce had been a close companion of Bidwell's since 1886. In 1888, he became Rancho Chico's general superintendent, a post he held until 1914. As a family friend and trusted employee, Royce could not have been expected to produce anything of a critical nature, and he did not. Consequently, his brief work is more properly regarded as an extended eulogy or commemoration rather than a genuine biography.

Much the same can be said of Dr. Marcus Benjamin's *John Bidwell, Pioneer*, published just one year after Royce's book. An editor of medical and technical journals, Benjamin had a deep interest in American history and served on the staff of *Appleton's Cyclopedia of American Biography*. As he stated in his foreword, Benjamin took up the Bidwell project at the behest of the California State Association of the District of Columbia and with the expressed purpose of "doing homage to the memory of John Bidwell...."[4] Thus, while it is clearly written and provides an excellent overview of Bidwell's life, Benjamin's slender volume clearly belongs next to Royce's in what might be called the celebratory school of Bidwell studies.[5]

The grand master craftsman of this school was not, however, either of its two cofounders. That title belongs without question to Dr. Rockwell D. Hunt. A native of Sacramento and a lifelong Californian, Hunt carved out a distinguished academic career as a professor and administrator at the University of Southern California and the College (now University) of the Pacific. By the time of his death in 1966, the ninety-eight-year-old Hunt had written or edited twenty-four books on various aspects of California history and had been officially proclaimed "Mr. California" by Governor Goodwin J. Knight.

Easily the most enduring of his many works is *John Bidwell: Prince of California Pioneers*, the only full-length biography ever written about its understudied subject. This well-worn book has been enormously influ-

---

[4] *Who Was Who in America, I, 1897–1942* (Chicago: A.N. Marquis Co., 1942), p. 83; Benjamin, *John Bidwell, Pioneer*, foreword.

[5] Other early and influential contributors to this school include Bidwell's longtime friend Will S. Green, the editor of the *Colusa Sun*, and California historian George Wharton James. See Green, "John Bidwell: A Character Study," *Out West*, 19 (December 1903), pp. 625–634; and James, *Heroes of California: The Story of Founders of the Golden State* (Boston: Little, Brown, and Co., 1910), pp. 45–55.

ential in shaping the images of John Bidwell that appear so frequently in textbooks and other histories devoted to California and the American West. Published in 1942, *Prince of California Pioneers* emerged out of the close friendship Hunt struck with John and Annie Bidwell shortly after he began corresponding with them in 1895.[6] At the time, Hunt was a twenty-seven-year-old student at Johns Hopkins who had returned home to conduct research for his doctoral dissertation on California's first constitution. Subsequent work brought him to Rancho Chico for the first time in 1897. There, Hunt made such a favorable impression on his hosts that he received an invitation to return the following summer and go camping with them in the Sierra Nevada mountains. For the rest of his life, Hunt treasured the visits and letters he shared with the Bidwells. It is clear from his later recollections that the young historian felt extremely honored and privileged by the warm attentions paid to him by these still-living figures from California's pioneer past. A deep sense of gratitude undoubtedly helped motivate Hunt to become John Bidwell's biographer in the decades following Annie's death in 1918. So too did the fundamental values he shared with the Bidwells. Like them, Hunt was a devout Protestant and Prohibitionist who had cast two of his earliest ballots for John Bidwell in the gubernatorial campaign of 1890 and the Presidential election of 1892. A Bidwell biography was thus a natural for "Mr. California."[7]

Preoccupied as he was by numerous other projects and responsibilities, however, it took Hunt years to finally bring forth *Prince of California Pioneers*. The product of prodigious research, the strengths of Hunt's book are readily apparent, and all stem from two key advantages enjoyed by its author. As the first scholar to gain access to the Bidwells' private papers, Hunt, unlike Royce and Benjamin, had at his disposal a tremendously rich collection of primary source materials. Similarly, as the last scholar to claim a personal acquaintance with his now deceased subject, Hunt occupied a unique vantage point for interpreting these sources. A

---

[6] *Who's Who in the West* (Chicago: Marquis-Who's Who, 1960), p. 344; Hunt, *Personal Sketches of California Pioneers I Have Known* (Stockton: University of the Pacific, 1962), pp. 1–2; Hunt, *"Mr. California": Autobiography of Rockwell D. Hunt* (San Francisco: Fearon Publishers, 1956), pp. 257–261.

[7] A church-going Methodist all his life, Hunt belonged to the Prohibition Party until his defection to the Republicans during Theodore Roosevelt's presidency. See Hunt, *Personal Sketches*, pp. 2–5; and Hunt, *"Mr. California,"* pp. 27–30, 55–61, 109–113, 148–152, 236, 240–241.

true professional, Mr. California did not squander his assets. On the contrary, he produced a highly accurate and richly detailed book that has endured for over half a century.

Unfortunately, time has taken its inevitable toll, and *Prince of California Pioneers* is now badly out of step with the concerns and style of contemporary historical scholarship. Moreover, despite its many strengths, Hunt's book was, from the very outset, marred by serious shortcomings. As his subtitle suggests, Hunt was anything but objective regarding his subject. Though generally filled with useful information, too many passages in his book contain little more than eulogistic puffery. Indeed, Hunt's prose often calls to mind the triumphal bombast of late nineteenth century local histories and pioneer "mugbooks." In his concluding peroration, Hunt claimed that "John Bidwell has long been known as a prince among California pioneers." Such an exalted reputation, however, was deemed insufficient by Hunt, who argued that Bidwell deserved even greater recognition. "By virtue of what he was and what he did," decreed Hunt, "he is adjudged worthy of the distinguishing title, 'Premier among Princes.' In all the galaxy of characters assembled in California's stately Hall of Fame there is none that can be likened unto him."[8] Because he made absolutely no effort to contain his overflowing admiration of John Bidwell, Hunt created a book that is more hagiography than biography. In this respect, *Prince of California Pioneers* made no improvement whatsoever over its predecessors.[9]

Worse, Hunt subscribed to a crude racism that allowed him to attribute much of the greatness he perceived in Bidwell to their shared English ancestry. Bidwell's strength of character was, according to Hunt, largely the inheritance of a "robust race," while his ample reserves of courage and fortitude were continuously replenished by "the blood of the Saxon war

---

[8] Hunt, *John Bidwell*, p. 431. The passing of time did nothing to cool Hunt's ardor. Writing eight years later, he echoed his previous judgment in the same overblown prose. "Take him all in all— his splendid physique, his seasoned knowledge and experience of the American frontier, his alert mind, expansive vision, affluence and abounding hospitality, his unswerving devotion to high political and moral principle, his unassuming Christian character—adventurer, agriculturist, politician, philanthropist, nature lover, gentle, imperious man, I do not hesitate to designate John Bidwell prince among the aristocracy of California pioneers." See Hunt, *California's Stately Hall of Fame* (Stockton: College of the Pacific, 1950), p. 174.

[9] For serious scholars, Hunt's book also proved disappointing due to its complete lack of footnotes and bibliography. Instead, Hunt simply offered a three-page essay on sources entitled "Bibliographic Notes." See Hunt, *John Bidwell*, pp. 437–39.

wolf" that supposedly coursed through his veins.[10] Hunt's racial notions also colored his portrayal of Rancho Chico's resident Mechoopda Indians, whom he depicted as the "simple-minded" and credulous "children of nature." In Hunt's account, the ignorant and superstitious Mechoopda were extremely fortunate to find in John Bidwell an "unselfish" protector and, in Annie, a "patron saint."[11]

Surprisingly, the biased and one-sided views of Hunt and his two predecessors have only recently begun to attract challengers. Between 1942 and 1978, most of what was published on John Bidwell said little that was new. Article-length biographies written by George Stewart and Richard Dillon, for examples, were essentially secondhand derivatives that echoed the laudatory paeans of Benjamin, Royce, and Hunt.[12] Within the last twenty years, however, an outpouring of new research has at last begun to undermine the marble edifice erected by Bidwell's canonizers.

Butte County historian Lois McDonald, for instance, has reexamined the critical decade of the 1840s to discover a more troubled and complex John Bidwell. In her revealing account, McDonald finds the confident son of the Saxon war wolf plagued by self-doubt, depression, and "near paranoia" during the difficult gold rush winter of 1848–1849.[13]

Meanwhile, Ohio State University professor Barbara Edmonson has offered a fresh reappraisal of Bidwell's half-century on Rancho Chico. Drawing from a wide array of primary and secondary sources, Edmonson's well-researched essay adds rich detail to previous accounts of Bidwell's achievements in agriculture. To a far greater extent than Hunt, however, Edmonson balances the familiar story of Rancho Chico's triumphs with a careful accounting of its failures. As her study makes clear, fifty years of daring innovation and experimentation did not result in an uninterrupted string of successes. Bidwell risked and suffered a number

---

[10] Ibid., p. 23.
[11] Ibid., pp. 133–41.
[12] George Stewart, *Good Lives: The Stories of Six Men and the Good Life That Each Won for Himself* (Boston: Houghton Mifflin, 1967), pp. 244–88; Richard Dillon, *Humbugs and Heroes: A Gallery of California Pioneers* (Garden City, NY: Doubleday and Co., 1970), pp. 43–49. Much the same can be said of the recent sketch of Bidwell that appeared in Donovan Lewis, *Pioneers of California: True Stories of Early Settlers in the Golden State* (San Francisco: Scottwall Associates, 1993), pp. 62–74.
[13] Lois H. McDonald, "Decade of Decision: John Bidwell's First Ten Years in California," in *Ripples Along Chico Creek: Perspectives on People and Times* (Chico: Butte County Branch, National League of American Pen Women, 1992), pp. 13, 25–27.

of costly setbacks that, when combined with the instability of late nineteenth century farm prices, kept him hopelessly in debt for over thirty years and led to the swift breakup of Rancho Chico after his death.[14]

The most direct challenge to the celebratory school has come from Michele Shover, a professor of political science at California State University, Chico. In a provocative essay first published in 1990, Shover took issue with Hunt's portrayal of John Bidwell as the beloved founder and "Patron Saint of Chico." Rather than being appreciated and revered by grateful local townspeople, Shover argued that Bidwell endured a tense and rocky relationship with many Chico denizens who envied his wealth, feared his power, deprecated his philanthropy, resented his aloof personality, and scorned his moral rigidity. Conflicts over Civil War loyalties, municipal incorporation, and water diversions from Chico Creek aggravated tensions between Bidwell and his neighbors. So too did Bidwell's protection of the Mechoopda Indians and his employment of Chinese laborers. Indeed, Bidwell's patronage of these two marginalized groups subjected him to death threats and violent acts against his property each time Chico's constantly simmering race relations reached the boiling point. This occurred at least once every decade after Bidwell laid out the town in 1860. As Shover observes, the founder of Chico often "must have felt like Dr. Frankenstein confronting his creature."[15]

In dealing with the local community, the Prince of California Pioneers frequently became his own worst enemy. Much of the goodwill earned by his civic generosity was offset by an outward demeanor that appeared cold and arrogant on most occasions, and hot-tempered on others. Bidwell alienated public opinion even further by distancing himself from town society. Aside from the elders of the Presbyterian Church, he did not associate with many community residents and developed a close personal friendship with only one, his attorney Franklin C. Lusk. Bidwell deepened this social gulf after 1865 by constructing his ornate mansion, the largest and grandest residence in nineteenth-century Chico. In contrast to the romantic legend perpetuated by Hunt, Shover argued persuasively that Bidwell did not erect his elegant new home as a gift for his fash-

---

[14] Barbara T. Edmonson, "John Bidwell's Fifty Years on Rancho del Arroyo Chico," in *Ripples Along Chico Creek*, pp. 47–48, 52–55, 62.

[15] Michele Shover, "John Bidwell: A Reconsideration," in *Ripples Along Chico Creek*, pp. 105–117. An abbreviated version of Shover's essay first appeared under the same title in the CSUC *University Journal*, 35 (Winter 1990), pp. 11–22.

ionable East Coast bride Annie Kennedy. Instead, she interprets the construction of Bidwell's mansion, and the simultaneous demolition of his spacious but rustic "Old Adobe," as deliberate declarations of elitist separatism. It therefore comes as no surprise when Shover asserts that "John Bidwell's funeral was the first time ... the community celebrated him."[16]

The dramatic recasting of Bidwell's reputation effected by Shover, McDonald, and Edmonson has been augmented by others focusing on what have become the most controversial aspects of Bidwell's career: his relationships with ethnic and religious minorities. While his ambivalent attitudes toward Roman Catholics, Jews, and immigrants have yet to receive much scholarly attention,[17] Bidwell's significant dealings with Native Americans and Chinese workers have attracted very intense, and often critical, scrutiny. The details of these studies will be taken up here in succeeding chapters. For the moment it is only necessary to observe that modern artists are unlikely to ever again paint a nimbus around John Bidwell's head. That distorting feature of Hunt's original portrait has been permanently removed.

This work shall make no attempt at restoration, since the authors believe that the desanctified John Bidwell is a much more plausible and fascinating character. Moreover, as we hope to show, he retains most of the virtues and strengths of character so carefully catalogued by his admirers. Wary readers sensing yet another New West deconstruction of an Old Western hero can therefore remain calm. Still, the revised John Bidwell now looks different enough to warrant a fresh introduction to students of California and the American West. This study, the first book-length survey of Bidwell to appear since Hunt's *Prince of California Pioneers*, is designed to reintroduce Bidwell in two important roles: as a major historical figure and as a vital historical source. Consequently, it has been designed as a hybrid of two genres: biography and anthology.

Employing a topical arrangement rather than a single continuous and comprehensive narrative, this "biographical anthology" is divided into distinct chapters, each focusing on an important event or theme in the life of John Bidwell and the history of California. Each chapter is subdivided

---

[16] Ibid., pp. 111–113, 116; Hunt, *John Bidwell*, pp. 275–276.
[17] For two important exceptions, see Rosaline Levenson, "Chico's Jewish Residents and the Bidwells: Interactions and Relationships," Butte County Historical Society *Diggin's*, 33 (Summer 1989), pp. 27–53; and Levenson, "Bidwell's Relationships with Minorities: The Altruistic-Pragmatic Mix," in *Ripples Along Chico Creek*, pp. 75–104.

into two sections. The first in each instance is a biographical essay intended to synthesize the available secondary literature, both old and new, regarding Bidwell and the topic at hand, and to place them clearly in the larger historical context of nineteenth century California. Chapters dealing with very familiar and well-worn themes like the overland trail or the gold rush have been kept as brief as possible. However, in chapters covering controversial or understudied topics such as the development of California agriculture or Bidwell's interactions with the Indians or Chinese, a great deal of original research has been added to help shed new light on Bidwell's motivations and accomplishments. In either case, the biographical essays should provide readers with sufficient background for interpreting the second halves of each chapter, which contain pertinent passages excerpted from Bidwell's own writing.

Taken as a whole, these latter sections in the present volume comprise a topically arranged "Bidwell Reader" that, for the first time, brings together generous samples of his voluminous but widely scattered literary legacy. As previously noted, historians have been slow to mine this rich vein of published and unpublished primary source material, and it is among the goals of this book to serve as a starting point and guide for those interested in pursuing Bidwell's lengthy paper trail. To further aid the pursuers, a comprehensive and long overdue Bidwell bibliography is also presented here.

One final note about authorship. Michael Gillis served as chief composer of the Overland Trail and Gold Rush chapters, while Michael Magliari bears primary responsibility for the Introduction and Prologue, as well as the essays concerning Mexican California, Rancho Chico and California agriculture, Bidwell's political career, Bidwell's use of Chinese labor, and Bidwell's relationship with the California Indians. In each case, however, the quality of the final product should reflect equally on both authors.

# Prologue:
# John Bidwell, 1819–1841

To judge from his own writings, John Bidwell was born at the age of twenty when he left his parents and siblings behind in Ohio and headed west to the Iowa and Missouri frontiers. Whether he was fleeing something other than poverty, or whether he was seeking something greater than cheap land or youthful adventure, are questions that so far remain unanswered. Though he wrote prolifically about his experiences after 1839, Bidwell maintained a curious silence regarding the first two decades of his life. Whatever the reasons for his reticence, Bidwell provided historians with only a bare outline of his boyhood years.

Born near Ripley in Chautauqua County, New York, on August 5, 1819, John Bidwell was the second child and first son of Abraham (or Abram) and Clarissa Griggs Bidwell. Natives, respectively, of Connecticut and Massachusetts, the elder Bidwells eventually had five children, all of whom were born on their isolated farmstead of forty-eight acres, located four miles from the southern shore of Lake Erie. Bidwell, who never met any of his grandparents, fondly recalled his mother as a mild-mannered, kind, and hardworking woman, a devout Baptist and well-versed reader of the Bible. It was she who evidently fashioned Bidwell's strong moral compass, and first stirred the spiritual yearnings that Annie Kennedy would later find so attractive in him.

Bidwell's father was a different matter. An industrious but uneducated man who could never seem to get ahead, Abram Bidwell was remembered by his famous son as a strong-willed individual with a "pretty severe" disposition. He had once been well off and had prospered as a lumberman after moving to Canada just prior to the War of 1812. Together with his first wife, Abigail Benedict, Abram raised and successfully supported a large family of seven children until the war brought him permanent ruin. Drafted into the British army along with his eldest son, Abram soon deserted and made his escape to New York while Canadian authorities confiscated his property. Returning to recover his family and free his son, Abram was taken prisoner but escaped once again, this time with his family in tow. Unfortunately, Abigail died shortly upon their return to New York and, without any funds to provide for his children, Abram was forced to bind them all out as indentured servants.

As Bidwell later recalled, it became the great burden of his father's life to reunite his scattered first family, a forlorn quest that he doggedly pursued all the while he was raising a second family with Clarissa Griggs, whom he had met and married in Vermont in 1816.[1] Poor and discontented, Abram would keep his new bride and family constantly on the move for the next two decades, steadily heading west in a fruitless effort to recover from his personal and financial losses. In 1829, the Bidwells left upstate New York and moved the short distance to Erie, Pennsylvania. Two years later, their westward migration resumed with a move to Ashtabula in northeastern Ohio. In 1834, the Bidwells crossed Ohio and settled around Greenville in Drake County, just east of the Indiana state line. Then, in 1836, they pulled up stakes one more time and relocated to Centerville, a small town outside Dayton.

Despite all these moves, young John Bidwell managed to receive a common school education that inspired him to continue his studies on his own. In 1837, he set out alone and on foot for the Kingsville Academy, three hundred miles away back in Ashtabula County. Before he could commence with his studies, however, Bidwell first had to earn some money, which he did by hiring out as a teamster hauling logs and cut lumber. He also worked briefly as a sawmill tender in nearby Geauga County, and occasionally helped ferry logs to Toledo on small schooners plying Lake Erie. Meanwhile, having finally reentered school, Bidwell acquitted himself well in the classroom. By completing just one term at Kingsville, he learned enough to pass the teacher's exam and begin a brief career as a

---

[1] JB-91, pp. 1–6; Rockwell Hunt, *John Bidwell: Prince of California Pioneers* (Caldwell, Idaho: Caxton Printers, 1942), pp. 18–21. During his life, Bidwell met only one of his seven older half-siblings. In 1854 Daniel, the youngest of them, followed his adult son Henry to California and settled in Chico, eventually starting a farm on 700 acres that John gave to him on the north bank of Sandy Gulch, known today as Lindo Channel. Subsequently, three more Bidwells arrived from back east to take up residence in Chico. Thomas, Bidwell's brother, arrived in 1856; Abram, the son of Bidwell's half-brother Elias, in 1871; and George, the son of Bidwell's brother Alpheus, in 1886. See Lois McDonald, "The Bidwell Family," in *Ripples Along Chico Creek* (Chico: Butte County Branch, National League of American Pen Women, 1991), pp. 175–88.

rural schoolmaster. Taking his first post at Greenville, Bidwell soon decided to leave Ohio and move further west.²

Not quite twenty years old, Bidwell headed off for the frontier in the spring of 1839, carrying a knapsack and his savings of $75. Starting out on foot once again, he soon hitched a ride on a wagon that carried him most of the ninety miles south to Cincinnati where he boarded a steamboat. Following the Ohio and Mississippi rivers, he paused briefly at Burlington to meet with Governor Robert Lucas and sound out opportunities in the Iowa Territory. After taking up and quickly abandoning a 160-acre claim on the Iowa River, he then journeyed overland by foot, heading south and west across central Iowa and Missouri until he struck the north bank of the Missouri River near Keytesville. Then, following the river westward, Bidwell finally arrived at the pale of American settlement: Platte County, Missouri. There he preempted another 160 acres of recently opened public land across the water from Fort Leavenworth, Kansas. With his savings completely spent Bidwell began teaching school near Weston, Missouri, hoping to raise the capital necessary to develop his new farmstead. During the following summer of 1840, Bidwell departed for St. Louis to buy books and farm supplies. When he returned one month later, he found himself confronted by a defiant squatter who had occupied his claim during his absence. The squatter, who had a violent reputation, refused to budge or even consider a proposal to divide the claim into halves. His resolve placed Bidwell in an untenable situation. Bidwell had never actually resided on the property, nor had he reached the minimum age of twenty-one required for land ownership by single men. With no legal recourse for compelling his rival's eviction, Bidwell had little choice but to surrender without a fight. His claim had been legally jumped!³

This early and hard lesson in frontier land law was not wasted on Bidwell, who would deal with squatters much more effectively the next time he ran into them. In the meantime, however, the landless young schoolteacher was in a quandary. Fortunately, it was at this very low point in his life that Bidwell first heard about California and the rich opportunities it offered. Though vague and lacking in detail, the news was more than enough to inspire the dispirited Bidwell to leave Missouri and head west once again, this time for the Pacific Coast of northern Mexico.

---
² Hunt, pp. 25–29; JB-91, p. 7.
³ John Bidwell, "The First Emigrant Train to California," *Century Illustrated Monthly Magazine*, 41 (November 1890), pp. 106–109.

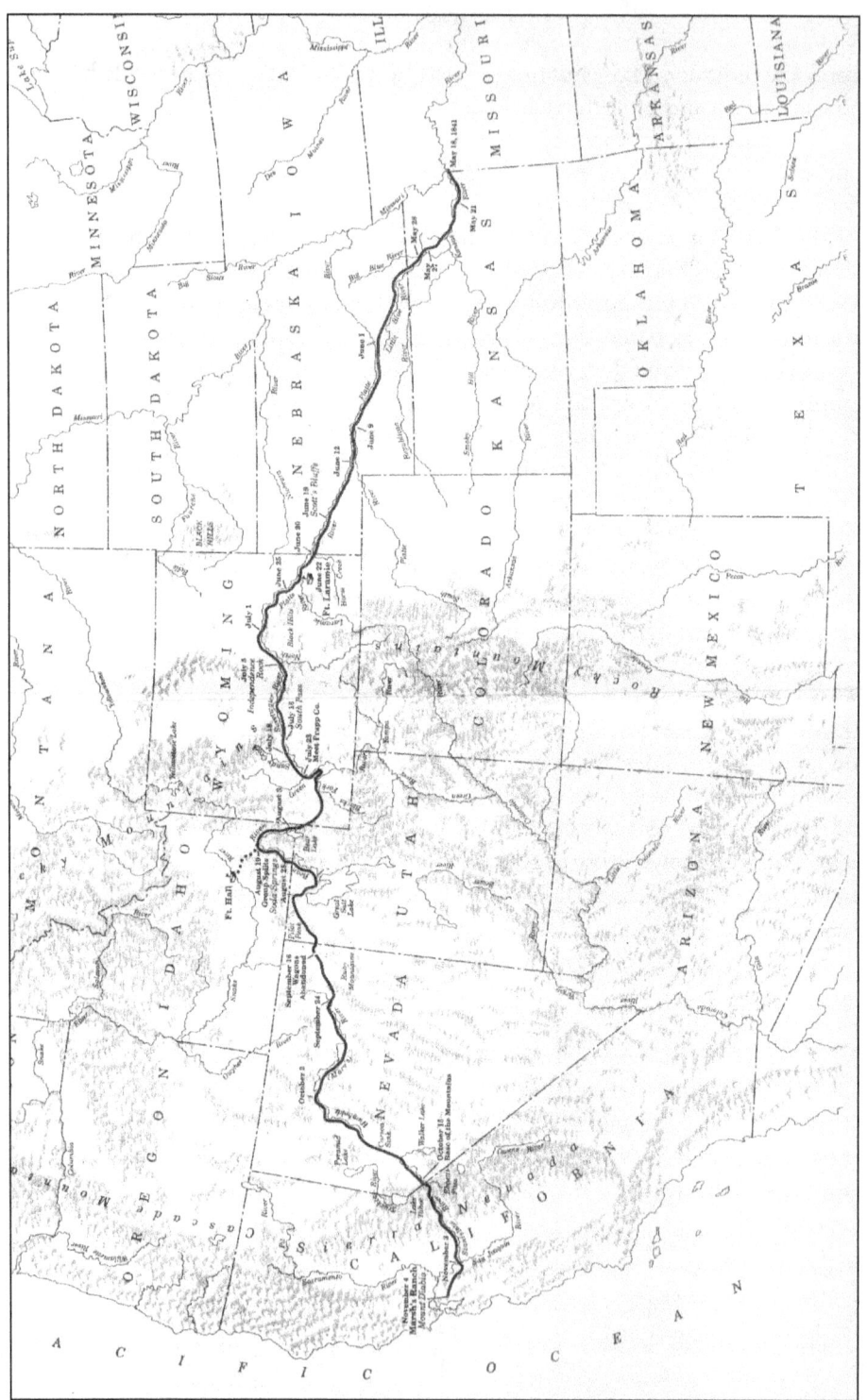

Bidwell-Bartleson Overland Route.
Permission to reprint courtesy of Doyce B. Nunis, Jr.

# I
# First Emigrants on the California Trail

While living in Missouri in 1840, John Bidwell met Rocky Mountain fur trader Antoine Robidoux, who had just returned from California. Robidoux raved about the remote Mexican territory which he described as a veritable paradise featuring a mild climate, fertile soil, and abundant natural resources. Bidwell also heard of California's richness from a family in Missouri that had recently received letters from John Marsh, an American emigrant who had settled in northern California in 1836. These two sources convinced him that California was a land of opportunity and a place where he could start over again.

The local excitement created by Robidoux's description of California "took like wildfire." Within a month over five hundred people, including Bidwell, had joined together and formed the Western Emigration Society, each signing a pledge "to purchase a suitable outfit, and to rendezvous at Sapling Grove . . . on the 9th of the following May, armed and equipped to cross the Rocky mountains to California."[1] Their California fever cooled quickly, however, when a letter written by a lawyer from New York who had recently returned from the Pacific Coast was published in a Missouri newspaper describing how dangerous it was for Americans to go there. Membership in the Society plummeted and the enthusiasm for moving west was soon dampened further by Platte County merchants who criticized and ridiculed the idea in an attempt to keep their customers at home. When Bidwell arrived at Sapling Grove in early May of 1841, he found only one other wagon waiting at the rendezvous site. Over the next several days, however, more people and wagons appeared, including a group of eight men headed by

---

[1] John Bidwell, "The First Emigrant Train to California," The Century Illustrated Monthly Magazine, XLI (Nov. 1890), p. 109. Located in what later became the territory and state of Kansas, Sapling Grove lay near the banks of the Kansas River, just twenty miles west of Independence and Westport (now Kansas City), Missouri, on the Santa Fe Trail.

John Bartleson of nearby Jackson County. Bartleson made it clear that if he wasn't elected captain of the emerging wagon train then neither he nor his men would go. Unwilling to risk the loss of so many potential companions, the anxious emigrants chose Bartleson as their leader.

What later became known as the Bidwell-Bartleson Party, the first group of American settlers to travel overland to California, left Sapling Grove on May 19, 1841.[2] Setting out on the Oregon Trail, they were guided by Thomas "Broken Hand" Fitzpatrick, an experienced fur trader and mountain man. Fitzpatrick's familiarity with the Oregon Trail and his knowledge and skill in dealing with the various Indian tribes made him indispensable. The original party consisted of sixty-one people, including a complement of six Jesuit missionaries led by Father Pierre Jean De Smet.[3] Their trek along the Oregon route took them from western Missouri to the Kansas River which they followed west for a week and a half before turning north to trace the Little Blue River into Nebraska. On June 1, the party reached the Platte River and, for the next month, they advanced in a northwesterly direction, following the course of the river across Nebraska and into central Wyoming. On July 5, they reached Independence Rock, and then, following the Sweetwater River, they began their ascent into the Rockies. Eleven days later, the emigrants crossed the continental divide via South Pass, and descended southwest across the Green River, arriving at Bear Lake on August 3. From there, they followed the Bear River north to Soda Springs, which they reached on August 10, 1841.

At Soda Springs the wagon train split into three separate groups. Father De Smet and the Jesuits linked up with a small contingent of Flathead Indians who guided them on to Fort Hall on Idaho's Snake River, and then to a site south of present-day Missoula, Montana, where the priests established St. Mary's Mission. On August 11, the day after the Jesuits' departure, the remaining party separated into two companies, one bound for Oregon, the other for California. The former followed Fitzpatrick to Fort Hall, while the latter, including Bidwell, Bartleson, and thirty-two others, headed south and west towards the Great Salt Lake.

---

[2]The Bidwell-Bartleson Party is so named because John Bidwell was one of the founders of the original Western Emigration Society and was instrumental in organizing the trek. Bartleson's name is used because he was elected captain of the party.

[3]Doyce B. Nunis, Jr., ed., *The Bidwell-Bartleson Party, 1841: California Emigrant Adventure* (Santa Cruz, Ca.: Western Tanager Press, 1991), p. 254. On Fitzpatrick see LeRoy R. Hafen and Ann W. Hafen, "Thomas Fitzpatrick," in LeRoy R. Hafen and Harvey L. Carter, eds., *Mountain Men and Fur Traders of the Far West: Eighteen Biographical Sketches* (Lincoln: University of Nebraska Press, 1982), pp. 236–51.

*First Emigrants on the California Trail*

The success of the first leg of the trip can be attributed to the experienced leadership of Thomas Fitzpatrick. He was recognized by all as an intelligent and reliable guide. Father Nicholas Point, one of De Smet's Jesuit missionaries, remembered him as "a courageous Irishman, known to most of the Indian tribes as *Tête Blanche* (White Head). He spent fully two-thirds of his life crossing the plains."[4] However, the Reverend Joseph Williams, a sixty-four-year-old Methodist minister from Virginia, had a different point of view. "Our leader, Fitzpatrick," he wrote, "is a wicked, worldly man, and is much opposed to missionaries going among the Indians."[5] For his part, Rev. Williams proved to be a bur under the saddle of the party. He kept up a running feud with the others because they refused to stop traveling on the Sabbath and did not allow the preacher to conduct Sunday services when they did stop. "I tried to preach twice to these people, but with little effect.... Our company is mostly composed of Universalists and deists ... several of the wicked class," wrote Williams. By the end of July, the reverend had given up. "On Sabbath we have nothing but swearing, fishing, etc. Have given myself up to God, ... such swearing I have never heard in my life before. God will surely punish these swearers."[6]

Fortunately for the California-bound contingent, Williams decided at Soda Springs to head for Oregon, thereby sparing them from his constant complaining during the final two months of the trip. While Williams' contribution to the success of the journey was minimal, he did perform the first emigrant marriage[7] on the plains and he presided over the burial of George Shotwell, the only member of the party to die during the journey to Soda Springs.[8] The ironically named Shotwell was killed when he accidentally shot himself in the chest while trying to retrieve a rifle from his wagon. His death occurred on June 13, while the emigrants were making their way up the Platte River in Nebraska. There, remembered Bidwell, "he was buried in the most decent manner our circumstances would admit...."[9]

Despite the tragic death of Shotwell, the long procession to Soda Springs went smoothly for the emigrants considering the inherent difficulties of the endeavor and the dangers involved. While it is often pre-

---

[4]Father Nicholas Point, "Historical Notes," cited in Nunis, p. 227.
[5]Joseph Williams, "Narrative of a Tour of Indiana to the Oregon Territory in the Years 1841–42," cited in Nunis, p. 240.
[6]Ibid., pp. 243, 245.
[7]John Bidwell, *Journey to California* (San Francisco: John H. Nash, 1937), p. 4. A "Miss Williams," the daughter of Richard Williams whose family was in the Bidwell-Bartleson Party, was married by Rev. Williams (no relation) to Isaac Kelsey on 1 June 1841.
[8]Ibid., p. 7.   [9]Ibid.

sumed that hostile Indians posed the greatest threat to overland travelers, such was not the case with the Bidwell-Bartleson party. Guide Fitzpatrick had spent years on the frontier and was well known to the Plains Indians. He officiated over most of the contacts between the Native Americans and his party to ensure that problems did not arise. While some members of the party became terrified at the sight of Indians and expressed their contempt for the "savages," for the most part Indian encounters remained congenial.

Unfortunately, the relative ease of the journey ended abruptly after Soda Springs. Bidwell recalled that when his inexperienced companions lost the services of Fitzpatrick, "We were . . . thrown entirely upon our own resources. All the country beyond was to us a veritable *terra incognita*, and we only knew that California lay to the west."[10] No established trail yet existed between Idaho and California and the emigrants received only vague directions on how best to reach their goal. Fur trappers from Fort Hall suggested that they continue to follow the Bear River as it bent south to the Great Salt Lake, and from there make their way west across the Great Basin until they reached the Mary's (Humboldt) River, which would take them to the base of the Sierra Nevada mountains. The trappers also warned them to keep their compass directions straight: "If you go too far south you will get into a desert country and your animals will perish; there will be no water or grass. . . . You must not go too far north; if you do you will get into difficult can[y]ons that lead towards the Columbia River, where you will become bewildered and wander about and perish."[11] With these dire warnings echoing in their heads, the Bidwell-Bartleson emigrants set out to cross the wilds of northern Utah and Nevada.

Heading southwest, the party skirted the northern shoreline of the

---

[10]Bidwell, "First Emigrant Train," p. 120. Bidwell did not exaggerate. No emigrant wagon train had ever crossed the Great Basin and the Humboldt River route remained largely unknown and completely unmarked, despite having been traversed by Peter Skene Ogden in 1828–1829, Joseph Reddeford Walker in 1833–1834, and Christopher "Kit" Carson in 1834. Ogden, a trapper for the British Hudson's Bay Company, was the first white to trace the entire course of the Humboldt River (so-named in 1843 by John C. Fremont). Walker, an American fur trader working for Benjamin Bonneville, made the first journey to California via the Humboldt and his expedition became famous for the discoveries of Yosemite Valley, the Calaveras Big Trees, and Walker Pass. Carson, on one of his early fur trapping expeditions out of Fort Hall, also travelled the entire length of the Humboldt before turning back to Idaho. See Ted J. Warner, "Peter Skene Ogden" in Hafen and Carter, eds., *Mountain Men and Fur Traders of the Far West*, pp. 132–134; Ardis M. Walker, "Joseph R. Walker," in ibid., pp. 296–300; and William Richter, *The ABC-Clio Companion to Transportation in America* (Santa Barbara, Ca: ABC-Clio, 1995).

[11]Bidwell, "First Emigrant Train," p. 125.

Great Salt Lake and continued toward the headwaters of the Humboldt River, which they located by sending scouts ahead of the main body.[12] The rough travel, averaging fifteen miles a day, took its toll on the oxen. Shortages of feed and water, and the burden of pulling heavy wagons across a trackless country left the oxen exhausted and finally unable to move any further. On September 16, the party was forced to abandon its wagons about seventy-five miles short of the Humboldt. Packing their goods onto the oxen proved to be a nightmare. As Bidwell later explained, "Packing is an art, and something that only an experienced mountaineer can do well. . . . We were unaccustomed to it, and the difficulties we had at first were simply indescribable. It is much more difficult to fasten a pack on an ox than on a mule or horse. The troubles began the very first day. But we started—most of us on foot, for nearly all the animals, including several oxen, had to carry packs. It was but a few minutes before the packs began to turn; horses became scared, mules kicked, oxen jumped and bellowed, and articles were scattered in all directions."[13]

After eight exhausting days the foot-weary emigrants reached the Humboldt River and, for the next three weeks, followed its sluggish course across the deserts of northern Nevada to where it finally disappeared into the Humboldt Sink. From there they continued in a southwesterly direction until they eventually struck the West Fork of the Walker River. The party then followed the Walker upstream into Mason Valley and through Wilson's Gap in the Singaste Range, which opened into the adjoining Smith Valley. Still following the West Fork, they traversed Smith Valley to where the stream spilled out of a narrow and winding passage today known as Hoye Canyon. After making camp at the mouth of this canyon on the evening of October 13, Bidwell and company entered Antelope Valley, through which they found a straight path to the Sierra Nevada.[14] On the evening of October 14, the Bidwell-Bartleson Party camped at the foot of the mountains along Slinkard Creek.[15]

The pioneering journey from Soda Springs to the base of the Sierra had proven to be a severe test of physical strength and mental toughness. Suffering periodic shortages of food and water, fighting unruly oxen and

---

[12]In 1991 the Oregon-California Trails Association honored Bidwell by naming for him the gap through which the party traversed the southern flank of Pilot Peak in eastern Nevada. Today Bidwell Pass is located just west of Wendover, Utah.
[13]Bidwell, "First Emigrant Train," p. 123.
[14]This is the present-day location of Wellington, Nevada.
[15]This is the present-day location of the intersection of California highways 395 and 89.

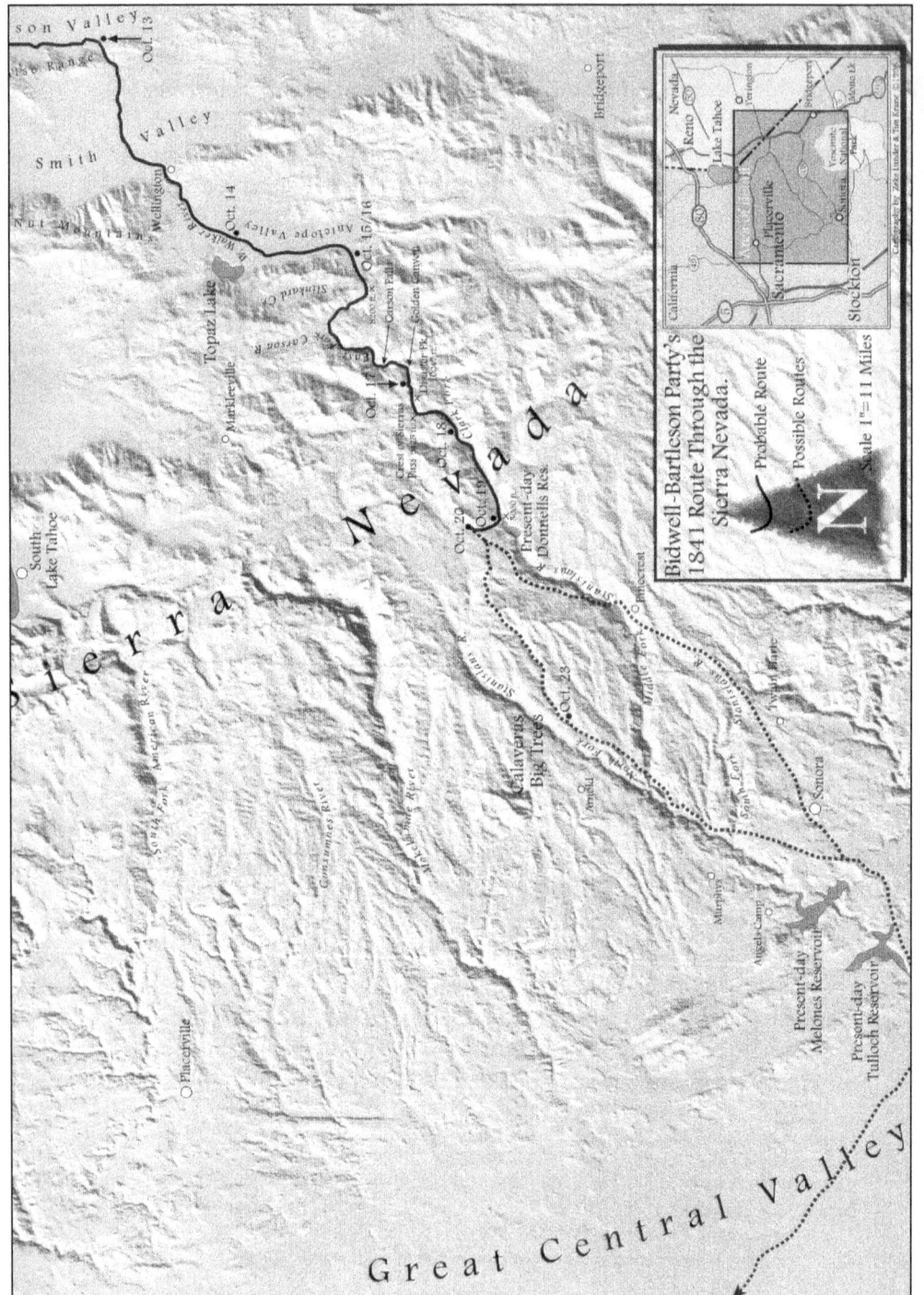

horses, traveling under the watchful eyes of local Indians and often unsure of the route, the party had pressed on, despite increasing dissension in the ranks. As Bidwell frequently recalled, the difficulty of overland travel took its toll on people and often brought out the worst, as well as the best, in them. Captain John Bartleson revealed himself an impatient, unreliable, and miserable sort of character, and soon was Captain in name only. Twice, he and his original comrades dashed off ahead of the rest of the company, complaining of the party's slow rate of travel, only to be discovered days later, lost, hungry, and unrepentant. Bartleson's erratic and impulsive behavior made him a liability to the party and endangered its solidarity.

Perhaps the most remarkable member of the expedition was Nancy A. Kelsey, the wife of Benjamin Kelsey and the only adult female in the party. Born of pioneer stock in Barren County, Kentucky, in 1823, she carried her infant daughter, Ann, all the way to California and, at the age of eighteen, was the first white woman to reach California by overland trail. Bidwell recalled the following incident which typified the hardships and frustrations with which she had to deal. "We had traveled all day and everybody was tired. It was hard work to get a fire built, but she managed to and was frying some bacon and tried to make some coffee. She had I think five children. They were all standing about, crying at the top of their voices for something to eat. Just at that time the coffee upset and it went into the bacon and put out the fire. She threw up her hands and hollered out loud enough for the whole camp to hear: 'I wish to the Lord I had never got married!'"[16]

Nancy Kelsey's regrets undoubtedly grew as the emigrants began the most formidable portion of the entire overland journey, the trans-Sierra crossing. After five months of hard traveling, Kelsey and her companions now faced a labyrinth of mile-deep canyons and snow-capped mountains. Traveling without the benefit of an Indian guide, maps, or even a general notion of how to cross the mountains, they followed Antelope Valley almost to its southern terminus and then, following a drainage, turned southwest into Little Antelope Valley. There, on October 15, the party made camp because, according to Bidwell, it became "impossible to progress further without scaling the mts."[17] Here, for the first time, the party recognized the magnitude of the challenge ahead. They had reached the eastern escarpment of the Sierra Nevada and there was no obvious route for them to enter the mountains. Unsure of how to proceed, the party decided to camp in Little Antelope Valley for two nights while scouts searched for a way through.[18]

---

[16]JB-91, p. 10.   [17]*Journey*, p. 24.   [18]Ibid.

On the morning of October 17 the trek through the Sierra resumed in earnest. They began by ascending a narrow, winding creek that climbed steeply into the mountains just west of their camp in Little Antelope Valley. They followed the creek up to a high flat on a ridge now called Rodriguez Flat.[19] Rather than attempting a direct route which would require numerous mountain ascents, they decided instead to follow river drainages which would weave them around, and hopefully through, the mountains. They departed Rodriguez Flat heading northwest and descended into the canyon drainage of Snodgrass Creek and Silver King Creek. After a four-and-a-half-mile descent they arrived in Silver King Meadows. Heading west across this flat, grassy expanse they intersected the East Fork of the Carson River and began ascending it in a southwesterly direction. The trail up the East Fork proved to be relatively flat for the first several miles with some grassy areas available for grazing. However, the further up the canyon they went the more narrow and steep it became until it was no longer passable on horseback. Unable to continue any further, they explored several adjoining gorges before finally selecting Golden Canyon, which held a small tributary creek and climbed due west. They traveled approximately two miles up Golden Canyon before making camp on the night of October 17.

The next morning they continued the steep climb up Golden Canyon. After ascending about a half mile they reached the head of the canyon and crested the Sierra at an elevation of 9,425 feet. In only four days, thanks to good weather, good luck and some savvy scouting, the Bidwell-Bartleson Party had arrived at the west side of the Sierra. One of the most daunting portions of their trip now lay behind them. Unfortunately, their joy at having successfully located a pass over the summit was quickly tempered by the sobering panorama that now lay before them. Everywhere they looked, Bidwell remembered, "a frightful prospect opened before us —naked mountains."[20]

From their lofty vantage point, the only possible route down led through a steep mountainside drainage created by Disaster Creek and Paradise Valley which, after six miles of trail and a 3,000 foot drop in elevation, eventually empties into Clark's Fork of the Stanislaus River. After completing this deep descent, Bidwell and the others made camp about two

---

[19]Rodriquez Flat is home to the Little Antelope Valley Pack Station, elevation 8,214 feet.
[20]*Journey*, pp. 24–25.

miles west and beyond the confluence of Clark's Fork and Disaster Creek.[21] The next day, October 19, they followed Clark's Fork downstream for ten miles to its junction with the Middle Fork of the Stanislaus.

Like most of the mountainous terrain they had already encountered in the Sierra, the Middle Fork canyon was steep, rocky and heavily forested. Fearful of descending too deeply into the ever-narrowing canyon, the party chose instead to remain high on its north side. Passing just south of the Dardenelles Cones, they pushed westward over a ridge and dropped down into the adjacent defile of the Stanislaus' North Fork. Somewhere in this area, Bidwell became separated from the rest of the party while hunting for game. Although he acquired some acorn mush in trade from an Indian boy he encountered, Bidwell remained desperately hungry and temporarily lost. When darkness fell Bidwell took refuge under the trunk of a fallen tree. He later wrote, "Of course sleep was impossible, for I had neither blanket nor coat, and burned or froze alternately as I turned from one side to the other before the small fire which I had built."[22] With the arrival of daylight, Bidwell realized he had stumbled upon one of the most unique forests in the west—he had spent the previous night of October 23 in a grove of giant sequoias.[23] That day, Bidwell located the rest of his party but they too were lost and unable to find a suitable trail down the canyon. Disoriented, exhausted, and hungry, Bidwell's company spent the next week groping for a passable route, moving all the while slowly westward and paralleling the south bank of the North Fork.

In their desperation, the emigrants initiated the first and only violent

---

[21] Field research conducted by Michael Gillis in July 1997 confirmed speculation regarding the trans-Sierra route traveled by the Bidwell-Bartleson Party first presented by William Guy Paden, "Bidwell's Route Through the Sierras, a Field Study" (MA Thesis, University of California, Berkeley, 1940). Just west of the unnamed pass are the headwaters of Disaster Creek. This steep slope still retained a broad and deep snowfield when explored by Gillis in mid-July, 1997. See Michael J. Gillis, "The 1841 Trans-Sierra Route of the Bidwell-Bartleson Party," *Overland Journal*, 16 (Winter 1999), pp. 21–29.

[22] Bidwell, "First Emigrant Train," p. 129.

[23] Ibid. Bidwell's long night in the cold became the basis of his mistaken belief that he was the first white man to see the giant sequoias of the Calaveras Big Trees (see his 20 April 1896 letter to John Muir excerpted below). In 1834, however, Joseph R. Walker and two of his party had unexpectedly come upon both the giant sequoias and Yosemite Valley, making them the first whites to see these natural wonders. See Ardis Walker, "Joseph R. Walker," in Leroy R. Hafen, editor, *The Mountain Men and the Fur Trade of the Far West*, Volume 5 (Glendale, California: Arthur H. Clark Company, 1965), pp. 361–380; Francis P. Farquhar, *History of the Sierra Nevada* (Berkeley: University of California Press, 1965), pp. 37, 42.

encounter they would have with Native Americans. Shortly after cresting the Sierra, the party had hired an elderly Indian to guide their descent down the rugged western slope. Soon, however, it appeared as though their Indian pilot was deliberately confusing and misdirecting them. Suspicion mounted as the travelers became aware that their vacated campsites were being ransacked each morning by Indians looking for abandoned valuables. When the Indian pilot at last deserted them, the emigrants became convinced that he had been plotting their demise all along.

Furious, one of the emigrants vowed to take revenge. As Bidwell and the others broke camp on October 27, Grove Cook remained behind in hiding to observe their Indian camp followers. When, as expected, the erstwhile pilot appeared in their company, Cook shot him and then fled. In his 1841 journal, Bidwell reported that Cook's shot was fatal. Later, however, he claimed that "we never knew whether the Indian was killed or not."[24]

In any event, it was very fortunate for the emigrants that the shooting took place so late in their trans-Sierra ordeal, and that they were able to escape the mountains before the Indians had sufficient time to organize a retaliatory strike. On October 30, just three days after the incident, the weary members of the Bidwell-Bartleson Party stumbled their way at last into the San Joaquin Valley. Five days later, on November 4, they reached John Marsh's rancho, located fifteen miles inland from San Francisco Bay at the foot of Mt. Diablo. Their arduous but historic six-month journey to California had finally come to an end.

It should be clarified here that, despite the name Bidwell-Bartleson Party, neither Bidwell nor Bartleson was ever really in charge of the pioneering expedition. As noted earlier, Bartleson was an unpredictable character who could not be trusted and who rapidly lost the confidence of the group. For his part, the twenty-two-year-old Bidwell was too young and inexperienced to be the party's leader, and still prone to youthful mistakes. At one point during the trek, for example, Bidwell and companion Jimmy John made a foolish decision to climb what they thought was a nearby mountain in order to surprise their fellow travelers with a gift of snow.[25] The summit was further away than they thought and they ended up spending the night on its slope. Fearing the two men had fallen victim to local Blackfeet Indians, the disappearance of Bidwell and John threw

---

[24]Bidwell, "Journey to California," p. 27; JB–77.

the emigrants into a near panic. A search party was formed and the missing men soon found. Nicholas "Cheyenne" Dawson long remembered his exasperation with Bidwell: "I was riding along, looking for Indian signs and gory corpses, when I saw two men running down the mountain. When they came nearer I saw that it was the supposed dead. As soon as Bidwell was within hearing, he triumphantly held up a handkerchief full of something and shouted, 'Snow!' Then I spoke forcibly. 'Snow! —! —! We thought you were dead.'"[26] Though Bidwell later demonstrated leadership qualities while crossing the Sierra, he never became head of the party. Rather, it was Benjamin Kelsey who emerged as the acknowledged, though unofficial, leader of the emigrants, thanks to his pathfinding skills.[27]

When questioned years later about his motives for going to California, Bidwell provided many different answers. He offered his wife Annie the implausible explanation that he went to California to help liberate it from Mexico and bring it under the flag of the United States.[28] He gave others the equally unlikely answer that his life was molded by circumstances beyond his control and that "my coming to California was a mere accident."[29] Perhaps "Cheyenne" Dawson explained Bidwell's motives best when he wrote of the 1841 emigrants, "There were many adventurous youths like myself, and John Bidwell, who wanted nothing but to see and experience."[30]

## *Recollections of the California Trail*

### Antoine Robidoux tells Bidwell of California

In November or December of 1840, while still teaching school in Platte County, I came across a Frenchman named Roubideaux, who said he had been to California. He had been a trader in New Mexico, and had followed the road traveled by traders from the frontier of Missouri to Santa Fe. He had probably gone through what is now New Mexico and Arizona into California by the Gila River trail used

---

[25]The snow-covered mountain referred to in this episode is Sedgwick Peak located in Idaho's Portneuf Range. See Roy D. Tea and Peter H. DeLafosse, "The First Wagons Across Utah, The Bidwell-Bartleson Party of 1841," *Overland Journal*, 12 (Winter 1994), pp. 19–31.
[26]Nunis, p. 149.       [27]Bidwell, "California 1841," in Nunis, p. 90.
[28]John Bidwell to Annie Bidwell, 5 July 1867, John Bidwell Collection, box 45, fl 21, CSL.
[29]JB-91, p. 9.
[30]Nicholas Dawson, "Narrative of Nicholas 'Cheyenne' Dawson: Overland to California in 1841," in Nunis, p. 146.

by the Mexicans. His description of California was in the superlative degree favorable, so much so that I resolved if possible to see this wonderful land....

Roubideaux described it as one of perennial spring and boundless fertility, and laid stress on the countless thousands of wild horses and cattle. He told about oranges, and hence must have been at Los Angeles, or the mission of San Gabriel, a few miles from it. Every conceivable question that we could ask him was answered favorably. Generally the first question which a Missourian asked about a country was whether there was any fever and ague. I remember his answer distinctly. He said there was but one man in California that had ever had a chill there, and it was a matter of so much wonderment to the people of Monterey that they went eighteen miles into the country to see him shake. Nothing could have been more satisfactory on the score of health. He said that the Spanish authorities were most friendly, and that the people were the most hospitable on the globe; that you could travel all over California and it would cost you nothing for horses or food. Even the Indians were friendly. His description of the country made it seem like Paradise.[1]

### Western Emigration Society formed

The result was that we appointed a corresponding secretary, and a committee to report a plan of organization. A pledge was drawn up in which every signer agreed to purchase a suitable outfit, and to rendezvous at Sapling Grove in what is now the State of Kansas, on the 9th of the following May, armed and equipped to cross the Rocky Mountains to California. We called ourselves the Western Emigration Society, and as soon as the pledge was drawn up every one who agreed to come signed his name to it, and it took like wildfire.[2]

### Western Emigration Society collapses

During that winter I made two trips to Jackson County to see parties who had promised to join our company as well as to gather information respecting California and the route leading to it.

But the skies began to be overcast. The exertions of our enemies began to have its effect. The first great excitement had somewhat cooled down. Just at this time, and it overthrew our project completely, was published the letters of [Thomas J.] Farnham in the New York papers and republished in all the papers of the frontier, at the instigation of the Weston merchants and others.

Our company soon fell to pieces notwithstanding our pledge was as binding as language could make it. Well do I remember the concluding clause, which was to the effect, if not in the exact same language, 'That we pledge to each other our lives, our fortunes, and our sacred honor.'

---

[1]John Bidwell, "The First Emigrant Train to California," *Century Magazine*, 41 (November 1890), p. 109.
[2]JB-77, pp. 7–8.

When May came, I was the only man that [was] ready to go of all who signed the pledge. In Weston, however, there was a man who had never signed the pledge but who had said from the beginning that he would go to California when May came. This was Robert H. Thomes, a wagon maker at that time. As the time approached, I became very anxious about the expedition but supposed a few would go with me. Finally I could not find a single member of the company who was sure to go. I went forward with my preparations, however, and to the extent I could, I purchased an outfit which consisted of a wagon and some provisions, a rifle, and ammunition.

At almost the last moment, every one abandoned the idea of crossing the plains. I cast about, however, and found in Platte County a man by the name of [George] Henshaw who was willing to go. He was old, quite an invalid, and nearly helpless. He had a fine black horse that he allowed me to dispose of. I sold him for a yoke of young cattle and a one-eyed mule for Henshaw to ride. With that much of an out fit we drove to Weston. . . .The people of Weston, notwithstanding their failure to make their pledge and in spite of the breaking up of the company, evinced their good feeling toward us by following us out in great numbers and bidding us goodbye two miles from town. Some even went four and the last six miles ere they said goodbye and turned back.[3]

### FORMATION OF BIDWELL-BARTLESON PARTY AT SAPLING GROVE

To reach Sapling Grove in Kansas Territory we had to travel down the Missouri River some fifty miles and then cross at the place known as Independence Landing. Then to go west about ten miles to the Missouri line and across into Indian Territory. On reaching Sapling Grove no one was there but we saw fresh wagon tracks and followed them to the Kansas River. They belonged to the parties who had come, some from Arkansas, and some from different parts of Missouri to cross the plains. We camped here and waited to see if others would come. Every day for a week or more, wagons arrived with the same object in view. At last we took steps to see how many had arrived and found our numbers to be sixty-nine. Among these were about fifteen women and children. All were anxious for a start. We effected an organization and elected "Col." John Bartleson Captain of the company.

No one of the party knew anything about mountaineering and scarcely any one had ever been into the Indian Territory, yet a large majority felt that we were fully competent to go anywhere no matter what the difficulties might be and how numerous and warlike the Indians. We heard before starting, however, that a party of Catholic missionaries from St. Louis going to the Flathead Indians under the auspices of Father De Smet were soon expected and that they had for their guide the experienced Captain Fitzpatrick.[4]

---

[3]JB-77, pp. 10–12.   [4]JB-77, pp. 12–14.

## Composition of Party

Every one furnished his own supplies. The party consisted of sixty-nine, including men, women, and children. Our teams were of oxen, mules, and horses. We had no cows, as the later emigrants usually had, and the lack of milk was a great deprivation to the children.[5]

## Bidwell on Bartleson

We organized by electing as captain of the company a man named Bartleson from Jackson County, Missouri. He was not the best man for the position, but we were given to understand that if he was not elected captain he would not go; and as he had seven or eight men with him, and we did not want the party to be diminished, he was chosen.[6]

## Fear of Indians

The men in our company were on an average as brave as any of any other country under similar circumstances, but yet when we got out into the Indian country, there were many instances of how easily man can become excited.[7]

## Journey into the Unknown

Our ignorance of the route was complete. We knew that California lay west, and that was the extent of our knowledge. Some of the maps consulted, supposed of course to be correct, showed a lake in the vicinity of where Salt Lake now is; it was represented as a long lake, three or four hundred miles in extent, narrow and with two outlets, both running into the Pacific Ocean, either apparently larger than the Mississippi River.[8]

## Joined by De Smet and Fitzpatrick

At first we were independent, and thought we could not afford to wait for a slow missionary party. But when we found that no one knew which way to go, we sobered down and waited for them to come up; and it was well we did, for otherwise probably not one of us would ever have reached California, because of our inexperience.[9]

The name of the guide was Captain Fitzpatrick; he had been at the head of trapping parties in the Rocky Mountains for many years. He and the missionary party went with us as far as Soda Springs, now in Idaho Territory, whence they turned north to the Flathead nation.[10]

Fitzpatrick knew all about the Indian tribes, and when there was any danger

---

[5]Bidwell, "The First Emigrant Train," p. 113.    [6]Ibid.
[7]JB-91, p. 9.
[8]Bidwell, "The First Emigrant Train," p. 111.
[9]Ibid., p. 113.    [10]Ibid., pp. 113–14.

we kept in a more compact body, to protect one another. At other times we would be scattered along, sometimes for a half a mile or more. We were generally together, because there was often work to be done to avoid delay. We had to make the road, frequently digging down steep banks, filling gulches, removing stones, etc. In such cases everybody would take a spade or do something to help make the road passable. When we camped at night we usually drew the wagons and carts together in a hollow square and picketed our animals inside the corral. The wagons were common ones and of no special pattern, and some of them were covered. The tongue of one would be fastened to the back of another. To lessen the danger from Indians, we usually had no fires at night and did our cooking in the daytime.[11]

Father De Smet had been to the Flathead nation before. He had gone out with a trapping party, and on his return had traveled with only a guide by another route, farther to the north and through hostile tribes. He was genial, of fine presence, and one of the saintliest men I have ever known, and I cannot wonder that the Indians were made to believe him divinely protected. He was a man of great kindness and great affability under all circumstances; nothing seemed to disturb his temper. The Canadians had mules and Red River carts, instead of wagons and horses,—two mules to each cart, five or six of them,—and in case of steep hills they would hitch three or four of the animals to one cart, always working them in tandem. Sometimes a cart would go over, breaking everything to pieces; and at such times Father De Smet would just be the same—beaming with good humor.[12]

### COMPANY ADOPTS OVERLAND RULES, 18 MAY 1841

Having awaited at this place (2 miles W. of Kanzas river) 2 days, and all the Company being arrived ... the Company was convened for the purpose of electing a Captain and adopting Rules for the Government of the Company; when T[albot] H. Green was chosen President—and J. Bidwell Secretary.

After the rules were read and adopted, J[ohn] Bartleson was elected Captain; it will be understood that Fitzpatrick was Capt. of the Missionary Company and Pilot of the whole—Orders were given for the company to start in the morning, and the meeting broke up.[13]

### THE JOURNEY BEGINS, 19 MAY 1841—FIRST INDIAN ENCOUNTER

This morning, the wagons started off in single file; first the 4 carts and 1 small wagon of the Missionaries, next 8 wagons drawn by Mules and horses and lastly, 5 wagons drawn by 17 yoke of oxen....

This afternoon we had a heavy shower of rain and hail. Several Kanzas Indi-

---

[11]Ibid., pp. 115–16.
[12]Ibid., p. 114.     [13]*Journey*, p. 2.

ans came to our camp; they were well armed with bows and arrows, and some had guns, they were daily expecting an attack by the Pawnees, whom they but a short time ago had made inroads upon, and had massacred at one of their villages a large number of old men, women and children, while the warriors were off hunting buffalo.[14]

### First Grumblings on Trail, 23 May 1841

All the oxen were gone this morning excepting nine, there was considerable complaint among the company, some saying at this slow rate of traveling we would have to winter among the Black Hills, and eat our mules &c. We however made a start about 9 in the morning, proceeded about 9 miles and stopped to wait for Chiles' waggon which overtook us about 5 P.M.; 14 Pawnees were seen by the wagon, well armed with spears &c. It was supposed they were on an expedition against the Kanzas.[15]

### Preacher Williams Joins Party, 26 May 1841

Two waggons were broke today; about a dozen Pawnees came to our camp, stopped to repair waggons, having come about 15 miles. A deer was brought in by C[harles] Hopper. A man by the name of [Joseph] Williams, a methodist preacher overtook the company this evening on his way to visit Oregon Territory: he had not arrived in time to start with the company from the settlements, and had travelled entirely alone, without any gun or other weapon for defense, depending wholy on Providence for protection and support.[16]

### Camped on Big Blue, 28 May 1841

Started, about sunrise, travelled about 5 miles and stopped to take breakfast. The heat was oppressive and we were compelled to go 20 miles farther before we came to either wood or water. The stream on which we encamped is a fork of the Kanzas and is well known to all mountaineers, by the name of Big Blue, an Antelope was killed.[17]

### Party Encounters Rocky Mountain Fur Traders, 31 May 1841

This morning about 10 o'clock we met six waggons with 18 men, with Fur and Robes on their way from Ft. Larimie, to St. Louis.... The waggons were drawn by oxen and mules—the former looked as though they received a thousand lashes every day of their existence! the rusty mountaineers looked as though they never had seen, razor, water, soap, or brush. It was very warm, and we travelled till dark before we were able to reach water, and then it was not fit to drink, and then we could not procure any wood, grass scarce.[18]

---

[14]Ibid.
[15]Ibid., p. 3.
[16]Ibid.
[17]Ibid.
[18]Ibid., p. 4.

Some had been trappers in the Rocky Mountains who had not seen civilization for a quarter of a century ... men who would let their beards grow down to their knees, and wear buckskin garments made and fringed like those of the Indians, and who considered it a compliment to be told "I took ye for an Injin." Another class of men from the Rocky Mountains were in the habit of making their way by the Mohave Desert south of the Sierra Nevada into California to steal horses, sometimes driving off four or five hundred at a time.[19]

ARRIVAL AT THE PLATTE RIVER AND A MARRIAGE ON THE TRAIL, 1 JUNE 1841

This morning we hastened to leave our miserable encampment and proceeding directly north, we reached Big Platte river about 12 o'clock. The heat was uncommonly oppressive.... This afternoon we had a soaking shower, which was succeeded by a heavy hail storm. Wonderful! this evening a new family was created! Isaac Kelsey was married to Miss Williams, daughter of R[ichard] Williams. The marriage ceremony was performed by the Rev. Pr. Williams, so we now have five families if we include a widow and child.[20]

MORE GRUMBLINGS ON THE TRAIL, 2 JUNE 1841

This morning the company was convened for the purpose of taking a vote upon the question, whether the companies should continue to travel together? that some were complaining that the Missionaries went too fast; but the very thought of leaving Mr. Fitzpatrick who was so well acquainted with the Indians &c.&c. met, as it ought to have done, the disapprobation of all. We now proceeded directly up the river, making this day about twelve miles.[21]

NICHOLAS DAWSON EARNS THE NAME 'CHEYENNE' (TWO VERSIONS),
4 JUNE 1841

Half past six this morning saw us on the march, the valley of the river was here about 4 miles wide, antelope were seen in abundance—a young man (Dawson) was out hunting, when suddenly a band of Chienne [Cheyenne] Indians about 40 in number came upon him; they were pleased to strip him of his mule, gun and pistol, and let him go. He had no sooner reached the camp and related the news than the whole band, came in sight; We hastened to form a Carral (Yard) with our waggons, but it was done in great haste. To show how it affected the *green ones*, I will give the answer, I received from a stout, young man and he perhaps was but one of 30 in the same situation, when I asked him, how many Indians there were? he answered in a trembling voice, half scared out of his wits, there were lots, gaubs, fields and swarms of them!!! I do really believe he thought there were some thousands, lo! there were but 40, perfectly friendly, delivered up every article taken, but the Pistol.[22]

---

[19] Bidwell, "The First Emigrant Train," p. 111.
[21] Ibid., p. 4.
[20] *Journey*, p. 4.
[22] Ibid., pp. 4–5.

He [Cheyenne Dawson] came in almost frightened to death. In his run he had lost his pistol. He cried "Indians! Indians!" said they were close upon us. I asked him where they were. "Don't you see them?" he exclaimed "the Plains are alive with them, there are thousands of them." He attempted to seize a gun but broke the stock. Then commenced a general stampede for the Platte River distant about three miles. The women and children were crying and screaming. Oxen and mules were put to the gallop and away we all went pell-mell for the river. In this race for life, as we thought, no heed was taken for the hindmost, it was each for himself.

Capt. Fitzpatrick did all that he could to stop the party. He [said] we were cowards, that if the Indians were hostile and should see us running they would be sure to kill us. They ought to, he said, if we were such fools to run.... In the course of half an hour the Indians came in sight. They proved to be a friendly party of Cheyenne Indians and readily gave up the gun and horse they had taken from Dawson. The man went by the name of "Cheyenne" Dawson on the remainder of the trip. These Indians were all mounted on horseback and gaily dressed in their beaded buckskin costume, fancifully painted with vermilion and all, except one squaw or medicine woman, as Captain Fitzpatrick said she was, had guns.[23]

### Cyclone (two versions), 5 June 1841

Started early to get clear of our red visitors—descried a large herd of Buffalo on the opposite side of the river—saw several Boats descending the river, laden with fur, robes &c, they belonged to the American Fur Company—one of our company E[lisha] Stone returned with them.

The latter part of the day was very inclement, high winds, dark clouds rushed in wild confusion around and above us, soon with amazement we saw a lofty waterspout, towering like a huge Column to support the arch of the sky; and while we were moving with all haste lest it should pass over us and dash our wagons to pieces, it moved off with a swiftness of the wind and was soon lost among the Clouds—Rain & hail succeeded, the largest hail stones I ever saw, several were found, an hour after the sun came out bright & warm, larger than a turkey egg—9 of the Indians that left us this morning, returned this evening.[24]

On the Platte River, on the afternoon of one of the hottest days we experienced on the plains, we had a taste of a cyclone: first came a terrific shower, followed by a fall of hail to the depth of four inches, some of the stones being as large as turkeys' eggs; and the next day a waterspout—an angry, huge, whirling cloud column, which seemed to draw its water from the Platte River—passed within a quarter of a mile behind us. We stopped and braced ourselves against our wagons to keep them from being overturned. Had it struck us it doubtless would have demolished us.[25]

---

[23]JB-77, pp. 15–16.   [24]*Journey*, p. 5.   [25]Bidwell, "The First Emigrant Train," p. 118.

## First Emigrants on the California Trail

### Buffalo at the Forks of Platte River, 8 June 1841

There were 8 or 10 Buffalo killed today, but not one tenth of the meat was used, the rest was left to waste upon the Prairie. In the afternoon we passed the confluence of the N. & S. Forks of Platte River & encamped, having come 18 miles, many hundred of Buffalo's were seen at this place. The scenery of the Country on the Platte is rather dull and monotonous, but there are some objects which must ever attract the attention of the observant traveler; I mean the immense quantity of Buffalo bones, which are every where strewed with great profusion, so that the Valley, throughout its whole length and breadth, is nothing but one complete slaughter yard; where the noble animals used to graze, ruminate and multiply in uncounted thousands—but they are fast diminishing. If they continue to decrease in the same ratio, that they have for the past 15 or 20 years, they will ere long become totally extinct. It has been but a few years since they left the frontiers of Missouri, and are now fast retreating towards the Rocky Mountains. The Indians are anxious to preserve them, and it is said of them, that they never kill as long as they have any meat remaining, but behold with indignation the shameful and outrageous prodigality of the whites, who slaughter thousands merely for their robes and leave the meat, which is far more delicious than that of tame Cattle, to waste, or be eaten by Wolves & vultures.[26]

### Buffalo

Before reaching the Platte we had seen an abundance of antelope and elk, prairie wolves and villages of prairie dogs, but only an occasional buffalo. We now began to kill buffaloes for food, and at the suggestion of John Gray, and following the practice of Rocky Mountain white hunters, our people began to kill them just to get the tongues and the marrow bones, leaving all the rest of the meat on the plains for the wolves to eat. But the Cheyennes, who traveled ahead of us for two or three days, set us a better example. At their camps we noticed that when they killed buffaloes they took all the meat, everything but the bones. Indians were never wasteful of the buffalo except in the winter for the sake of the robes, and then only in order to get the whiskey which traders offered them in exchange. It was an easy matter to kill buffaloes after we got to where they were numerous, by keeping out of sight and to the leeward of them. I think I can truly say that I saw in that region in one day more buffaloes than I have seen of cattle in all my life.[27]

We experienced a great danger at this point from the innumerable herds of buffalo. All the plains were literally black with them crowding to the river for water. The ground literally thundered with the vast herds that came rush[ing]

---
[26] *Journey*, p. 5.
[27] Bidwell, "The First Emigrant Train," p. 117.

down to the river. We sat up all night shooting at them to keep them from running us over. The numbers on the south side, however, were vastly greater than on the north side. For a whole day, I think even for two days as we ascended the S[outh] Fork after we crossed over, there was no time when there was not countless thousands of buffalo in sight.[28]

### Crossing the South Platte River, 9 and 10 June 1841

Spent the day in crossing the S. fork of Platte—a Buffalo was killed from a herd that came within 300 yards of the Camp. We crossed the river by fording the water being sufficiently shallow—width of River here about $2/3$ of a mile—its waters are muddy like those of the Missouri.[29]

This morning most of the Oxen were again at large, owing to the neglect of the Owners to the great danger of losing them by the Indians and by their mingling with Buffalo, or by their straying so far that it would be impossible to track them on account of the innumerable tracks of the Buffalo—making therefore, rather a late start, we continued to ascend the river on the N. side. We traveled about 14 miles and encamped on the river, Buffalo were seen in countless thousands on the opposite side of the river; from the time we began to journey this morning till we ceased travel at night; the whole south side of the stream was completely clouded by these huge animals, grazing in the valley and on the hills—ruminating upon the margin of the river, or crowding down its banks for water.[30]

### A False Alarm, 11 June 1841

The Oxen had wandered about ½ mile from the camp this morning, when a man was sent to bring them in; he soon came running back in great haste, crying "the Indians are driving the Oxen off"!! In less than half an hour the oxen were at camp and not an Indian seen—all this is easily accounted for, when we consider how timidity and fear will make every bush, or stone, or stump an Indian, and 40 Indians, thousands.—Vast herds of Buffalo continued to be seen on the opposite side of the river—Distance today about 20 miles.[31]

### A Fatal Accident, 13 June 1841

A mournful accident occurred in Camp this morning—a young man by the name of [George] Shotwell while in the act of taking a gun out of the wagon, drew it, with the muzzle towards him in such a manner that it went off and shot him near the heart—he lived about an hour and died in full possession of his senses. His good behavior had secured him the respect and good will of all of

---

[28]JB-77, p. 18.
[29]*Journey*, p. 6.
[30]Ibid.
[31]Ibid.

the company . . . he was buried in the most decent manner our circumstances would admit of after which a funeral sermon was preached by Mr. Williams.[32]

### CHIMNEY ROCK, 18 JUNE 1841

About 12 o'clock today we passed another object, still more singular and interesting—it is called by the Mountaineers, the Chimney, from its resemblance to that object; and is composed of clay and sand so completely compact, as to possess the hardness of a rock. It stands near the high Bluffs that bound the Valley on the South, and has been formed from a high isolated mound which, being washed on every side by the rains and snows of the ages, has been worn down till nothing is left but the centre which stands upon an obtuse cone, and is seen towering like a huge column at the distance of 30 miles. The column is 150 feet above the top of the cone and the whole, 250 feet above the level of the plain.[33]

### SCOTT'S BLUFF, 19 JUNE 1841

We gradually receded from the river in order to pass through a gap in a range of high hills, called Scot[t]'s Bluff's, as we advanced towards these hills, the scenery of the surrounding Country became beautifully grand and picturesque—they were worn in such a manner by the storms of unnumbered seasons, that they really counterfeited the lofty spires, towering edifices, spacious domes and in fine all the beautiful mansions of Cities. We encamped among these envious objects having come about 20 miles.[34]

### FORT LARAMIE, 22 JUNE 1841

Eight miles this morning took us to Fort Larimie, which is on Larimie's fork of [the] Platte about 800 miles from the frontiers of Missouri, it is owned by the American Fur Company. There is another fort, within a mile and a half of this Place, belonging to an individual by the name of Lupton, the Black Hills were now in view, a very noted Peak, called Black Hill Mountain was seen like a dark cloud in the Western horizon, (Remark.) The Country along Platte River is far from being fertile and is uncommonly destitute of timber, the Earth continues to ascend, to become more strongly impregnated with glauber Salts.[35]

### FORT LARAMIE TO THE GREEN RIVER, 24 JUNE 1841

Left the Fort this morning and soon began to wind among the Black Hills, two of our men stopped at the Fort, ([George] Simpson and [William] Mast) but, two other men with an Indian and his family joined us to travel to Green River—Encamped having made about seventeen miles—hills are sandy—many

---

[32]Ibid., pp. 6–7.
[33]Ibid., p. 7.
[34]Ibid., p. 8.
[35]Ibid.

wild Pears likewise an abundance of Peas, wild—though the bush was dissimilar to ours; yet the pods bore an exact similarity, taste, the same.[36]

### Crossing North Fork of Green River, 1 July 1841

Spent the day in passing over the river to the North side of it; the water ran very rapidly, and it was with considerable difficulty that we forded it. One mule was drowned, and one waggon upset in the river, the water in the N. Fork is not so muddy as the South fork.[37]

### A Bewildering Landscape, 2 July 1841

A man (Mr. [Josiah] Belden) was hunting a short distance from the company, and left his horse tied while he crept in pursuit of a Buffalo, but he was not able to find the same place again and consequently lost his horse. Though the country is perfectly free from timber, excepting near the river, yet there is so great a similarity in the hills that experienced hunters are frequently bewildered in a clear day, when attempting to find a certain place a second time.[38]

### Independence Rock, 5 July 1841

The hills continued to increase in height, after traveling 16 miles we encamped at a noted place called Independence Rock, this is a huge isolated rock covering an Area, perhaps of half a square mile, and rising in shape of an irregular obtuse mound, to the height of 100 feet. It took its name from the celebration of the 4th of July at this place by Capt. Wm. Sublette, and it now bears many names of the early travelers to these regions. Immediately at the base of these rocks, flows a small stream called Sweet Water and is a branch of the N. fork, six Buffalo killed today.[39]

### Bidwell-Bartleson Party at Independence Rock, 6 July 1841

This morning John Gray and [W. G.] Romaine were sent on to Green river to see if there were any Trappers at the rendezvous, and then return to the company with the intelligence, all hands were anxious to have their names inscribed on this memorable landmark, so that we did not start until near noon, went up stream about 8 miles and encamped on Sweet Water.[40]

### Stocking up on Buffalo Meat, 8 and 13 July 1841

This morning we came in sight of Wind River mountains, their snow enveloped summits were dimly seen through the misty clouds that obscured the Western horizon, made about 15 miles today and encamped on Sweet Water, in full view of thousands of buffalo, 20 were killed, we now began to lay in meat to last us over the mountains to California.[41]

---

[36]Ibid.
[37]Ibid., p. 9.
[38]Ibid.
[39]Ibid.
[40]Ibid.
[41]Ibid., p. 10.

Left our hunting encampment and met John Gray and Romaine returning from Green river, they found no person at the rendezvous on Green river, nor any game ahead, it was therefore thought best to lay in more meat, while we were in the vicinity of the Buffalo. We therefore came to a halt having traveled about 15 miles.[42]

### Looking for the Trappers, 15 July 1841

As many of the company had articles of traffic which they wished to dispose of at Green river, a subscription was raised to recompense any who would go and find the trappers. John Gray started in pursuit of them, while the company marched on slowly waiting his return. Travelled about 6 miles today.[43]

### Across the Continental Divide, 18 July 1841

Left Sweet Water this morning, course S.W. crossed the divide which separates the water of the Atlantic and Pacific oceans, and after a travel of 20 miles reached Little Sandy, a branch of Green river—1 Buffalo was killed.[44]

### Gray Almost Dies in Search for Trappers Located on the Green River, 22 July 1841

Descended Big Sandy about 12 miles and stopped where we found plenty of grass—this was very acceptable as our teams were already much jaded for the want of grass. The oxen however stood travel &c. as well as the horses and mules. Gray returned this evening having found Trapp's company, which consisted of about 20 men. They had returned to meet our Company though on their way to hunt buffalo, and were now encamped on Green river about 8 miles distant. Gray had suffered much in overtaking the Trappers, his mule gave out, there being no water for a great distance, and he, himself was so much reduced by hunger and thirst that he was unable to walk, he was therefore compelled to crawl upon his hands and feet, and at last came up with the Company in the most forlorn situation imaginable—if they had been another half mile further, he never could have reached them.[45]

### A Rendezvous on the Green River, 23 and 24 July 1841

Went to Green river—distance 8 miles—spent the remainder of the day trading with the hunters. Remained at this encampment and continued our traffic with the hunters. Chiles sold his oxen 2 yoke, and wagon, another was also left.[46]

### Six Members Leave Party to Return to the United States—Prices of Trade Goods at Green River, Wyoming, 25 July 1841

Left the rendezvous this morning, 6 of the company viz. John Gray, [Henry] Peyton, [Amos E.] Frye, [Edward] Rogers, [Thomas] Jones and Romaine, started

---

[42]Ibid.      [43]Ibid.
[44]Ibid., p. 11.      [45]Ibid.
[46]Ibid.

to return to the United States. [James] Baker stopped in Mountains to trap, crossed Green River and descended it about 8 miles, Trapp and his company likewise left in pursuit of Buffalo.

(Remark) I will not omit to state the prices of several kinds of mountain goods, Powder which is sold by the cupful (pint) is worth $1 per cup. Lead $1.50 per pound, good Mackanaw Blankets 8 to 15 dollars, sugar $1 per cupful, Pepper $1 also, Cotton and Calico shirts from 3 to 5$, Rifles from 30 to 60; in return, you will receive dressed deer-skins at $3, Pants made of deer skins $10, Beaver skins $10, Moccasins $1; flour is sold in the Mts. at 50 cents per cupful, Tobacco at $2 per lb. Butcher knives from 1 to 3$, a good gun is worth as much as a horse, a cap lock is preferred, caps worth $1 per box, We crossed Green river, went about 8 miles downstream and encamped.[47]

### Another Marriage on the Trail, 30 July 1841

Traveled about 5 miles and encamped. Guess what took place; another family was created! Widow Gray, who was sister to Mrs. Kelsey, was married to a man who joined our Company at Fort Larimie, his right name I forget; but his every where name, in the Mountains, was Cocrum [Richard Phelan]. He had but one eye—marriage ceremony performed by Father De Smet.[48]

### Entering the Bear River and Indian Country, 31 July 1841

Left Ham's Fork this morning. A distance of 14 miles, over an uncommonly hilly road, took us to Black's fork of the Green river, on which we encamped.... In the afternoon we descried a large smoke rising from beyond the intervening chain of hills, from this and other signs, we were assured, that there were plenty of Indians in the country. It was necessary therefore to keep a vigilant look-out, lest the Black Feet should leave us minus a few horses.[49]

### On to the Bear River, 3 August 1841

Ascended a high divide and passed down by a most difficult route into the valley of Bear River, the course of this stream was marked out as it wound its way through the vale by the willows that skirted its banks. Reached the river, where we found an abundance of grass, having come about 20 miles.[50]

### Soda Springs, Idaho—Departure of De Smet, 10 August 1841

The day was fine and pleasant; a soft and cheerful breeze and the sky bedimmed by smoke brought to mind the tranquil season of Autumn. A distance of 10 miles took us to the Soda Fountain, where we stopped the remainder of the day. This is a noted place in the mountains and is considered a great curiosity—within the circumference of 3 or 4 miles there are included no less than 100

---

[47] Ibid., pp. 11–12.
[49] Ibid.
[48] Ibid., p. 12.
[50] Ibid.

springs, some bursting out on top of the ground, others along the banks of the river which are very low at this place, and some, even in the bottom of the river. The water is strongly impregnated with Soda, and wherever it gushes out of the ground, a sediment is deposited, of a redish color, which petrifies and forms around the springs large mounds of porous rock; some of which are no less than fifty feet high.... Father De Smet, with 2 or 3 flat head Indians, started about dark this evening to go to Fort Hall which was about 50 miles distant.[51]

### The Party Splits at Soda Springs (Two Versions), 11 August 1841

Having traveled about 6 miles this morning the Company came to a halt—the Oregon Company were now going to leave Bear river for Ft. Hall which is situated on Lewis [Snake] River, a branch of the Columbia—many, who purposed in setting out, to go immediately through to the California, here, concluded to go into Oregon so the California company now consisted of only 32 men and one woman and child, there being but one family. The two companies, after bidding each other a parting farewell, started and were soon out of sight, several of our company however went to Ft Hall to procure provision, and to hire if possible a pilot to conduct us to the Gap in the California Mountains, or at least, to the head of Mary's [Humboldt] river, we were therefore to move on slowly, 'till their return. Encamped on Bear river, having come about 12 miles.[52]

As I have said, at Soda Springs—at the northern most bend of Bear River—our party separated.... Here the missionary party were to turn north and go into the Flathead nation. Fort Hall, about forty miles distant on Snake River, lay on their route. There was no road; but something like a trail, doubtless used by the trappers, led in that direction.... The rest of us—also thirty-two in number, including Benjamin Kelsey, his wife and little daughter—remained firm, refusing to be diverted from our original purpose of going direct to California. After getting all the information we could from Captain Fitzpatrick, we regretfully bade good-by to our fellow emigrants and to Father De Smet and his party.

We were now thrown entirely upon our own resources. All the country beyond was to us a veritable *terra incognita*, and we only knew that California lay to the west.[53]

### Shoshone Indians, 17 August 1841

Traveled about 16 miles; saw a large smoke rising out of the mountains before us. It had probably been raised by the Indians, as a telegraph, to warn the tribe, that their land was visited by strangers. We were unable to procure any fuel this evening, we therefore slept without fire. The Indians, found in this region, are Shoshonees [Shoshones], they are friendly.[54]

---

[51]Ibid., pp. 13–14
[53]Bidwell, "The First Emigrant Train," p. 120.
[52]Ibid.
[54]*Journey*, p. 15.

### Fooled by a Mirage, 19 August 1841

Started early, hoping soon to find fresh water, when we could refresh ourselves and animals, but alas! The sun beamed heavy on our heads as the day advanced, and we could see nothing before us but extensive arid plains, glimmering with heat and salt, at length the plains became so impregnated with salt, that vegetation entirely ceased; the ground was in many places white as snow with salt & perfectly smooth—the mid-day sun, beaming with uncommon splendor upon these shining plains, made us fancy we could see timber upon the plains, and wherever timber is found there is water always. We marched forward with unremitted pace till we discovered it was an illusion, and lest our teams should give out we returned from S. to E, and hastened to the river which we reached in about 5 miles.[55]

### Passing near Great Salt Lake, 20 August 1841

Company remained here while two men went to explore the country, they returned bringing the intelligence that we were within ten miles of where the river disembogued itself into the great salt lake. This was the fruit of having no pilot—we had passed through cash valley, where we intended to have stopped and did not know it.[56]

### Traveling in Triangles, 21 August 1841

Marched off in a N.W. direction, and intersected our trail of Thursday last, having made a complete triangle in the plain. At this intersection of the trails, we left a paper elevated by a pole, that the men, returning from Fort Hall, might shun the tedious rounds we had taken. Found grass and water which answered our purpose very well, though both were salt. Distance 10 miles.[57]

### Great Basin Indian game trap at Great Salt Lake, 23 August 1841

Started, bearing our course west, in order to pass the Salt Lake—passed many salt plains and springs in the forenoon, the day was hot—the hills, and land bordering on the plains, were covered with wild sage. In passing the declivity of a hill, we observed this sage had been plucked up, and arranged in long minows, extending near a mile in length. It had been done by the Indians, but for what purpose we could not imagine, unless it was to decoy game. At evening we arrived in full view of the Salt Lake, water was very scarce. Cedar grows here both on the hills and in the valleys, distance 20 miles.[58]

### Trading with Indians, 28 August 1841

A Shoshonee Indian came to our camp, from him we learned, that there were

---

[55]Ibid., p. 16.
[56]Ibid.
[57]Ibid.
[58]Ibid., p. 17.

more Indians not far off, who had horses; Several men and myself went in search of them: having gone about 5 miles, up hills and down hills covered with thick groves of Cedar (red), we unexpectedly came to an Indian, who was in the act of taking care of some meat—venison—which he had just killed; about half of which, we readily purchased for 12 Cartridges of Powder & ball. With him, as a pilot we went in pursuit of other Indians; he led us far up in the Mountains by a difficult path, where we found two or three families, hid as it were from all the world, by the roughness of nature. The only provision, which they seemed to have, was a few elder berries and a few seeds; under a temporary covert of bushes, I observed the aged Patriarch, whose head looked, as though it had been whitened by the frosts of at least 90 Winters. The Scars, on his arms and legs, were almost countless—a higher forehead I never saw upon [a] man's head. But here in the solitude of the mountains and with the utmost contentment, he was willing to spend the last days of his life among the hoary rocks and craggy cliffs, where perhaps, he, in his youthful gayety, used to sport along crystal streams which run purling from the mountains—not succeeding in finding horses, we returned to the Camp.[59]

### Searching for the Mary's [Humboldt] River, 29 August and 9 September 1841

Capt. Bartleson and C[harles] Hopper started to explore the route to the head of Mary's river, expecting to be absent about 8 or 9 days—the Company to await here his return.[60]

Capt. Bartleson & Hopper returned, bringing Intelligence that they had found the head of Mary's river—distant about 5 days travel, distance traveled today about 12 miles S.W. direction. The Indians stole a horse—day cool.[61]

### Trading with Indians, 3 and 4 September 1841

4 or 5 Indians came to camp—bought three horses of them. Bought a few service berries of the Indians.[62]

### Wagons abandoned in eastern Nevada, 12 and 15 September 1841

Mr. Kelsey left his wagons and took his family and goods on pack horses, his oxen not being able to keep up: distance today about 12 miles.[63]

Started very early, day was exceedingly warm, passed through a gap in a ridge of mountains, came into a high dry plain, traveled some distance into it, saw the form of a high mountain through the smoky atmosphere—reached it, having

---

[59] Ibid., pp. 17–18.
[61] Ibid.
[63] Ibid., p. 19.
[60] Ibid., p. 18.
[62] Ibid.

come about 15 miles—found plenty of water—our animals were nearly given out. We were obliged to go so much further, in order to get along with the wagons: We concluded to leave them, and pack as many things as we could.[64]

### DIFFICULTIES OF PACKING

Packing is an art, and something that only an experienced mountaineer can do so well so as to save his animal and keep his pack from falling off. We were unaccustomed to it, and the difficulties we had at first were simply indescribable. It is much more difficult to fasten a pack on an ox than on a mule or a horse. The trouble began the very first day. But we started—most of us on foot, for nearly all the animals, including several of the oxen, had to carry packs. It was but a few minutes before the packs began to turn; horses became scared, mules kicked, oxen jumped and bellowed, and articles were scattered in all directions. We took more pains, fixed things, made a new start, and did better, though packs continued occasionally to fall off and delay us.[65]

### HUNGER AND HARDSHIP

When you travel all day without water, etc. you are hungry, and perhaps have to go half a mile for something to make a fire with and when we could not find anything else, we had to pick up Buffalo chips. If there is anything bad in a man's character, he will show it then. They used to say that even a preacher could not cross the plains without swearing.[66]

### INDIAN COMES TO COLLECT ABANDONED ITEMS, 16 SEPTEMBER 1841

All hands were busy making Pack saddles and getting ready to pack. While thus engaged, an Indian, well advanced in years, came down out of the Mountains to our camp. He told us by signs, that the Great Spirit had spoken to him, to go down upon the plains in the morning, and on the E side of the mts. he would find some strange people, who would give him a great many things, accordingly he had come. We gave him all such things that we had intended to throw away; whenever he received any thing which he thought useful to him, he paused and looking steadfastly at the sun, addressed him in a loud voice, marking out his course in the sky, as he advanced in his invocation, which took him about 2 minutes to perform—as he received quite a number of articles, it took him a considerable part of the day to repeat his blessings. No Persian, in appearance, could be more sincere.[67]

### SEARCHING FOR OXEN, 18 SEPTEMBER 1841

Morning found us on the East side of a mountain not far from its base but

---

[64]Ibid.
[65]Bidwell, "The First Emigrant Train," p. 123.
[66]JB-91, pp. 9–10.
[67]*Journey*, p. 19.

there were no signs of water; the lost oxen not having come up, I, in company with another young man, went in search of them, while the company went on, promising to stop as soon as they found water. I went back about 10 miles, but found nothing of their trail—the sun was in a melting mood—the young man became discouraged and in spite of all my entreaties returned to the company. About an hour after I found the trail of the oxen which bore directly north—(the Com. were traveling S.W.) after pursuing it some distance, I discovered fresh Mocasin tracks upon the trail, and there began to be high grass which made me mistrust the Indians had got the oxen. But my horse was good and my Rifle ready, and I knew the Indians in these parts to be very timid, for they were generally seen in the attitude of flight. But what made me most anxious to find the oxen, was the prospect of our wanting them for beef. We had already killed 4 oxen and there were but 13 remaining including the lost ones, the Co. was now killing an ox every two or three days. Having followed the trail about 10 miles directly north to my great delight I found the oxen. I was soon in motion for the company, but not being able to overtake them, was obliged to stop about dark. I passed the night rather uncomfortably, having neither fire nor blanket. I knew the Indians to be plenty from numerous signs, and even where I slept, the ground had been dug up that very day for roots, the plains here were almost barren, the hills were covered with cedar.[68]

COOKING ANTELOPE IN A HOT SPRINGS (RUBY MOUNTAINS, NEVADA), 21 SEPTEMBER 1841

Hunters returned: many antelope were seen and 2 or 3 killed. About 10 o'clock A.M. as we were coasting along the mountain in a W. direction we came to some hot Springs, which were to me a great curiosity. Within the circumference of a mile there were perhaps 20 Springs: the most of which were extremely beautiful, the water being so transparent, we could see the smallest thing 20 or 30 feet deep. The rocks which walled the Springs, and the beautifully white sediment lodged among them, reflected the sun's rays in such a manner, as to exhibit the most splendid combination of colors, blue, green, red, &c., I ever witnessed. The water in most of them was boiling hot. There was one, however, more beautiful than the rest; it really appeared more like the work of art than of nature. It was about 4 feet in diameter, round as a circle, and deeper than we could see—the cavity looked like a well cut in a solid rock, its walls being smooth and perpendicular. Just as I was viewing this curiosity, some hunters came up with some meat, we all partook, putting it into the spring, where it cooked perfectly done in 10 minutes—this is no fish story![69]

---

[68]Ibid., pp. 19–20.
[69]Ibid., pp. 20–21.

### Bartleson 'Perfectly Ignorant of Indian Customs,'
### 22 September 1841

This morning 80 or 90 Indians were seen coming full speed from the W many had horses—one was sent about half a mile in advance of the rest—so we ought also to have done, but Capt. B[artleson], was perfectly ignorant of Indian customs, and the whole band of savages were suffered to come directly up to us, and almost surround our Camp, when Mr. B[enjamin] Kelsey showed by forcible gestures, they would be allowed to proceed no further. The Indians were well armed with guns and bows and arrows. The only words, I recollect of hearing Capt. Bartleson say, were "let them gratify their curiosity!!" The Indians were Sheshonees, but like other savages always take advantage where they can. Besides, they were not a little acquainted with warfare, for they undoubtedly visited the Buffalo Country (having many robes) which requires much bravery to contend with the Blackfeet and Chiennes, who continually guard the Buffalo in the region of the Rocky mountains, they traveled as near us as they were allowed, till about noon, when they began to drop off, one by one, and at night there were but 8 or 10 remaining—distance about 12 miles.[70]

### Unsure of Position, 29 September 1841

Traveled about 20 miles, course of the stream was W.N.W. According to the map Mary's river ran W.S.W. Strong doubts were entertained about this being Mary's river. The men who got the directions at Fort Hall were cautioned, that if we got too far South, we would get into the Great Sandy Desert—if too far North, we would wander and starve to death on the waters of the Columbia, there being no possibility of getting through that way. We had now been 6 days on this stream, and our course had averaged considerably North of West.[71]

### Indian encounters along the Humboldt River, 2 October 1841

Having traveled about 5 miles, we all beheld with delight the course of the river change to SW,—here was excellent grass—it was 3 or 4 feet high, and stood thick like a meadow, it was a kind of Bluegrass. The whole valley seemed to be swarming with Indians, but they were very timid. Their sable heads were seen in groups of 15 or 20, just above the tops of the grass to catch a view of us passing by. Whenever we approached their huts, they beckoned us to go on—they were extremely filthy in their habits. Game was scarce, tho' the Indians looked fat and fine. They were Shashonees.[72]

During the forenoon an Indian overtook us. He struck himself and said,

---

[70]*Journey*, p. 21.   [71]Ibid., p. 22.   [72]Ibid.

"Shoshonie! Shoshonie!" We knew these Indians to be friendly. He at the same time held out in his hand the piece of tobacco, which he must have found after we left camp, for no Indians were around at that time. [William] Belty was so unreasonable that he said the Indian was a thief and ought to be shot. I have no doubt he would have shot the Indian if I had not been with him.[73]

### Indians at Humboldt Sink and Their Food

We saw many Indians on the Humboldt, especially towards the Sink. There were many tule marshes. The tule is a rush, large, but here not very tall. It was generally completely covered with honeydew, and this in turn was wholly covered with a pediculous-looking insect which fed upon it. The Indians gathered quantities of the honey and pressed it into balls about the size of one's fist, having the appearance of wet bran. At first we greatly relished this Indian food, but when we saw what it was made of—that the insects pressed into the mass were the main ingredient—we lost our appetites and bought no more of it.[74]

### Problems with Bartleson, 5 October 1841

Today was very warm, and the oxen were not able to keep up with the horses. Traveled about 30 miles and stopped on the river about dark—grass plenty, willows—this going so fast was the fault of Capt. B., nothing kept him from going as fast as his mules could possibly travel. But his dependence was on the oxen for Beef,—for it was now all we had to live upon.[75]

### Indian Pilot Hired, 6 October 1841

Company was out of meat and remained till the oxen came up; several Indians came to Camp, one of whom was hired to pilot us on.[76]

### Conflict with Bartleson (Two Accounts), 7 October 1841

Capt. Bartleson, having got enough meat yesterday to last him a day or two, and supposing he would be able to reach the mountains of California in 2 or 3 days, rushed forward with his own mess, consisting of 8 persons at a rate entirely too fast for the oxen,—leaving the rest to keep up if they could, and if they could not it was all the same to him. The day was very warm. The Indian Pilot remained with us—the river spread into a high, wide swamp, covered with high cane grass—Indians were numerous. Encamped by the swamp about dark, having come about 25 miles—water bad—no fuel, excepting weeds and dry cane grass which the Indians cut in large heaps, to procure sugar from the honey dew with which it was covered.[77]

---

[73]JB-77, p. 48.
[75]*Journey*, pp. 22–23.
[77]Ibid.

[74]Bidwell, "The First Emigrant Train," p. 126.
[76]Ibid., p. 23.

Finally, one day when it was my turn to drive the oxen, the captain led the company on so fast that I could not keep up, and at night I was about nine miles behind the company. The next morning it was no easy task for me alone to get the oxen out of the brush, put the packs on and start on my way. The company, however, having nothing to eat, were obliged to wait till I overtook them, so that an ox could be killed for breakfast. I considered that I had been badly treated, and did not hesitate to tell the captain, and the men whom I thought to blame, what I thought. Curiously enough, they made no response.

An ox was killed and the company breakfasted about noon. About one o'clock we were packed and ready to travel. The captain and his mess came to us and said, "Let us have a double share of meat. Our animals are stronger and can carry it better, and we will kill the next ox and pay you back." We very willingly consented, but as soon as all was ready to start the captain made known his purpose and said, "I have been found fault with and am not going to stand it any longer. I am going to California, and if you can keep up with me it is all right, and if you can't you may go to hell." So he and the seven started off as fast as they could go, and were soon out of sight.[78]

### Bartleson spotted, 14 October 1841

This morning we saw at a distance Capt. B. with his 7 men, coming in a direction towards us, but we made no halt, ascended the stream about 20 miles; the Mountains, continued to increase in height.[79]

### Camping on the east side of the Sierra Nevada Mountains, 15 October 1841

Advanced upstream [West Fork of the Walker River] about 12 miles, and arrived at the base of very high mountains [Little Antelope Valley], the creek had become a small spring branch, and took its rise at no great distance in the mountains. But we saw plainly, that it was impossible to progress farther without scaling the Mts., and our Indian Guides said, they knew no further.[80]

### A chastened Bartleson returns (three accounts), 16 October 1841

This morning 4 or 5 men started to ascend several of the high peaks, to ascertain if it was possible to pass the mountains. Just as they were going to start Capt. B. came up, he was in rather a hungry condition, and had been traveling several days without provision, excepting a few nuts which they had purchased from the Indians and which they had eaten on a very small allowance. We killed yester-

---

[78]Bidwell, "Early California Reminiscences," (Jan. 1904), p. 78.

[79]*Journey*, p. 24. For a more detailed account of this section of the trail see Gillis, "The 1841 Trans-Sierra Route of the Bidwell-Bartleson Party," *Overland Journal*, 16 (Winter 1998–99): 21–29.

[80]Ibid.

day the best ox we had. This we shared freely with them. There were now but 3 oxen left and they were very poor. But there was no time to lose. The explorers returned & reported that they thought it, almost an impracticability to scale the mountains, which continued to increase in height as far as they could see. This evening the Company was convened for the purpose of deciding by vote, whether we should go back to the Lake and take a path we saw leading to the N.W., or, undertake to climb the mountains. We had no more provisions that would last us to the Lake,—nearly all were unanimous against turning back. I should have mentioned that our Indian Pilots last night absconded. This stream I shall call Balm river; there being many Balm Gilead trees upon it.[81]

To make a long story short, it was the eight men that had left us nine days before. They had gone farther south than we and had come to a lake, probably Carson Lake, and there had found Indians who supplied them plentifully with fish and pine nuts. Fish caught in such water are not fit to eat at any time, much less in the fall of the year. The men had all eaten heartily of fish and pine nuts, and had got something akin to cholera morbus. We were glad to see them although they had deserted us. We ran out to meet them and shook hands, and put our frying-pans on and gave them the best supper we could.[82]

Having obtained from the Indians quantities of pine nuts and fresh fish, they had started west for the mountains. Fresh fish had given them all the dysentery, and they were so weak they could hardly stand. I well remember Captain Bartleson's exclamation as he sat eating what we had cooked him. 'Boys! If I ever get back to Missouri, I will never leave there again. Why I would be glad to eat from the same trough with my dogs there.'[83]

## Crossing the Sierra, 17–22 October 1841

This morning we set forth into the rolling mountains, in many places it was so steep, that all were obliged to take it on foot. Part of the day we travelled through vallies between Peaks where the way was quite level—passed down and up thro' forests of pine, fir, cedar, &c., many of the pines were 12 ft. in diameter, and no less than 200 ft. high—encamped on the side of the mountain [Golden Canyon], so elevated that the ice remained all day in the stream—but we had not yet arrived at the summit. Killed another ox this evening—made 12 miles.

The rivulet descended with great rapidity and it was the opinion of all, that we were at least 1 mile perpendicular below the place where we began to descend. The steam had widened into a small valley. Cedars of uncommon size, pines, the most thrifty, clothed the Mountains. (One pine, as it was near our camp, was

---
[81]Ibid.
[82]Bidwell, "The First Emigrant Train," pp. 127–28.
[83]JB-77, pp. 54–55.

measured, though it was far from being the tallest—it was 206 ft. high.) All were pleased to think that we were crossing the mountains so fast.[84]

Having ascended about half a mile, a frightful prospect opened before us:— naked mountains whose summits still retained the snows perhaps of a thousand years.... The winds roared—but in the deep dark Gulfs which yawned on every side, profound solitude seemed to reign. We wound along among the peaks in such a manner, so as to avoid most of the mountains which we had expected to climb—struck a small stream [Clark's Fork of the Stanislaus River]descending towards the W., on which we encamped having come 15 miles.[85]

Descending along the stream, we found several oak shrubs which confirmed us in the hope, that we were on the waters of the Pacific: But the route became exceedingly difficult—the stream had swelled to a river [Middle Fork of the Stanislaus River]—could not approach it—could only hear it roaring among the rocks. Having come about 12 miles a horrid precipice bid us stop—we obeyed, and encamped. Those who went to explore the route had not time to come to any conclusion where we could pass. We had descended rapidly all day, the mts. were still mantled with forests of towering pines. The roaring winds, and the hollow murmuring of the dashing waters, conveyed in the darkness of the night, the most solemn and impressive ideas of solitude. To a person fond of a retired life, this, thought I, would be a perfect terrestrial Paradise, but it was not so to us, when we knew that Winter was at hand, and that Capt. [Joseph] Walker (the Mountaineer) had been lost in these very mountains 22 days before he could extricate himself.[86]

Men went in different directions to see if there was any possibility of extracting ourselves from this place without going back. They returned and reported, it was utterly impossible to go down the creek. One young man [James John] was so confident that he could pass along the Creek with his horse, that he started alone, in spite of many persuasions to the contrary. Capt. B also being tired of waiting for the explorers to return, started down the stream, which so jaded his animals that he was obliged to wait all day to rest them, before he was able to retrace his steps. In the meantime the rest of the Company suffering for water, were obliged to travel. We proceeded directly N. up the mountains, about 4 miles, found a little grass and water—here we killed one of the 2 oxen.[87]

Our route today was much better than expected, though in any other place

---

[84]*Journey*, p. 24.
[86]Ibid., p. 25.
[85]Ibid., pp. 24–25.
[87]Ibid.

than the mountains, it would be considered horrible. Capt. B. with his 7 or 8 overtook us but we heard nothing of J[ames] John's. Distance about 10 miles, could see no prospect of a termination to the mts. mts. mountains![88]

Descended towards the river about 15 miles—had a tolerable road—arrived within a mile of the River—could not approach nearer. Here was considerable Oak, some of which was evergreen, and thought to be live oak. 3 Indians to camp, killed the last ox—let this speak for our situation and future prospects![89]

BIDWELL SCOUTS AHEAD FOR GAME AND BECOMES SEPARATED FROM PARTY; STUMBLES UPON THE CALAVERAS BIG TREES, 23 OCTOBER 1841

Having no more meat than would last us 3 days, it was necessary to use all possible exertions to kill game which was exceedingly scarce. For this purpose I started alone, very early in the morning, to keep some distance before the Company, who had concluded to continue as near as possible to the creek on the N. side. I went about 4 miles—met the Indian who came to us last night—obtained a little provisions made of acorns—got an Indian boy to pilot me to his house. He took me down the most rugged path in all nature—arrived on the banks of the river at least ¾ of a mile perpendicular from where I started with him—found no more provision, continued down the river—oak, in abundance, buckeye, and a kind of maple. The mountains, which walled in the stream, were so steep that it was with great difficulty I scaled them,—having in one place, come within an inch of falling from a craggy cliff down a precipice nearly a fourth of a mile perpendicular. 4 long hours I labored before I reached the summit—proceeded directly to intersect the trail of the Company, Mts. covered with the largest and tallest pines, firs, &c., thick copses of hazel &c.—travelled till dark over hills, dales, crags, rocks, &c. found no trail—lay down and slept.[90]

As the darkness came on I was obliged to look down and feel with my feet lest I should pass over the trail of the party without seeing it. Just at dark I came to an enormous fallen tree and tried to go around the top, but the place was too brushy, so I went around the butt, which seemed to me to be about twenty or twenty-five feet above my head. This I suppose to have been one of the fallen trees in the Calaveras Grove of *Sequoia gigantea* or mammoth trees, as I have since been there, and to my own satisfaction identified the lay of the land and the tree. Hence I concluded that I must have been the first white man who ever saw the *Sequoia gigantea*, of which I told Fremont when he came to California in 1844. Of course sleep was impossible, for I had neither blanket nor coat, and burned or froze alternately as I turned from one side to the other before the small

---
[88]Ibid., p. 26.   [89]Ibid.
[90]*Journey*, p. 26.

fire which I had built, until morning, when I started eastward to intersect the trail, thinking the company had turned north.[91]

### 24 OCTOBER 1841

Concluded the Co. had gone North. I traveled E. found no trail—traveled S.—came to the place where I left the Company, yesterday morning, having made a long quadrangle in the mts., 8 by 10 miles—took the trail of the Company, they had with great difficulty descended the river, saw where they staid last night. Distance about 6 miles, ascended on the S. side of the creek a high precipice, I overtook them, they had traveled today 10 miles. They had hired an Indian pilot who had led them into the worst place he could find and absconded. 5 horses and mules had given out, they were left. I learned likewise that two hunters (A[ndrew] Kelsey & [Thomas] Jones) started shortly after I did, and had not returned, part of a horse was saved to eat.[92]

### 25 OCTOBER 1841

Went about 6 miles & found it impossible to proceed. Went back about two miles and encamped,—dug holes in the ground to deposite such things as we could dispense with—did not do it, discovering the Indians were watching us, among them was the old, rascally Pilot. White oak in abundance.[93]

### 26 OCTOBER 1841

Went S. about 3 miles and encamped in a deep ravine, it was urged by some that we should kill our horses and mules—dry what meat we could carry and start on foot to find the way out of the mountains.[94]

### REVENGE TAKEN ON UNFAITHFUL INDIAN PILOT (TWO VERSIONS), 27 OCTOBER 1841

It commenced raining about one o'clock this morning and continued till noon—threw away all our old clothes to lighten our packs, fearing the rain would make the mts. so slippery as to render it impossible to travel. I have since learned that the Indians in the mountains, here, prefer the meat of horses to cattle, and here in these gloomy corners of the mts. they had been accustomed to bring stolen horses and eat them. Here and there were strewed the bones of horses,—so the design, of the veteran, Indian Pilot, is apparent in leading us into this rugged part of Creation.

As we left this place one of the men, G[rove C.] Cook, remained concealed to see if the old Pilot was among the Indians, who always rushed in as soon we left our encampments to pick up such things as were left. The old gentleman

---

[91] Bidwell, "The First Emigrant Train," p. 129.
[92] *Journey*, p. 26.
[93] Ibid., pp. 26–27.
[94] Ibid., p. 27.

was at the head of this band, and as HE HAD UNDOUBTEDLY LED US INTO THIS PLACE TO PERISH, his crime merited death—A RIFLE BALL LAID HIM DEAD IN HIS TRACKS. We proceeded S. about 6 miles. As we ascended out of the ravine, we discovered the high mountains, we had passed, were covered with new snow for more than half a mile down their summits.[95]

One Indian had been to our camp a number of times and had received presents of clothing; he had promised to show us the way out of the mountains. He had acted very oddly and had failed to return as promised, and it was believed by many that he intended to lead us in the wrong direction or in some way betray us. The man who remained was Grove Cook. We had gone only a half mile when we heard his gun. Overtaking us, he said that the same Indian came, and as he was picking up the things we had left, for we had thrown something away at every camp, he shot him. We never knew whether the Indian was killed or not.[96]

### STILL CROSSING THE SIERRA NEVADA MOUNTAINS, 28 AND 29 OCTOBER 1841

Surely no horses nor mules, with less experience than ours could have descended the difficult steeps, and defiles which we encountered in this day's journey. Even as it was, several horses and mules fell from the mountain's side and rolling like huge stones, landed at the foot of the precipices. The mountains began to grow obtuse, but we could see no prospect of their termination. We eat the last of our beef this evening and killed a mule to finish our supper—distance 6 miles.[97]

Last night, the Indians stole a couple of our horses. About noon we passed along by several huts, but they were deserted as soon as we came in sight, the Indians running in great consternation into the woods. At one place the bones of a horse were roasting on a fire, they were undoubtedly the bones of the horses we had lost. Traveled no less than 9 miles today, the night was very cool, and had a heavy frost. Although our road was tolerably level today, yet we could see no termination to the mountains—and one much higher than the others, terminated our view. Mr. [Charles] Hopper, our best and most experienced hunter, observed, that "If California lies beyond those mountains we shall never be able to reach it." Most of the Company were on foot, in consequence of the horses giving out, and being stolen by Indians: but many were much fatigued and weak for the want of sufficient provision, others however stood it very well. Some had appetites so craving, that they eat the meat of most of the mule raw, as soon as it was killed, some eat it half roasted dripping with blood.[98]

---

[95] Ibid.
[96] JB-77, pp. 66–67.
[97] *Journey*, p. 27.
[98] Ibid., pp. 27–28.

### THE SAN JOAQUIN VALLEY IS FINALLY SIGHTED, 30 OCTOBER 1841

We had gone about 3 miles this morning, when lo! to our great delight, we beheld a wide valley! This, we had entirely overlooked between us and the high mountain which terminated our view yesterday. Rivers evidently meandered through it, for timber was seen in long extended lines as far as the eye could reach. But we were unable to reach it today, and encamped in the plains. Here grew a few white oaks. Travelled today about 20 miles. Saw many tracks of Elk. The valley was wonderfully parched with heat, and had been stripped of its vegetation by fire. Wild fowls, Geese etc., were flying in multitudes.[99]

We were now on the edge of the San Joaquin Valley, but we did not even know that we were in California. We could see a range of mountains lying to the west,—the Coast Range,—but we could see no valley. The evening of the day we started down into the valley we were very tired, and when night came our party was strung along for three or four miles, and every man slept where darkness overtook him. He would take off his saddle for a pillow and turn his horse or mule loose, if he had one. His animal would be too poor to walk away, and in the morning he would find him, usually within fifty feet. The jaded horses nearly perished with hunger and fatigue. When we overtook the foremost of the party the next morning we found they had come to a pond of water, and one of them had killed a fat coyote; when I came up it was all eaten except the lights and the windpipe, on which I made my breakfast.[100]

### 31 OCTOBER 1841

Bore off in a N.W. direction to the nearest timber, day was warm, plain dry and dusty, reached timber which was white oak (very low & shrubby) and finally, the river which we had left in the Mts., joyful sight to us poor famished wretches!!! hundreds of antelope in view! Elk tracks thousands! killed two antelopes and some wild fowls, the valley of the river, was very fertile and the young tender grass covered it, like a field of wheat in May. Not a weed to be seen, and the land was as mellow, and free from weeds, as land could be made by plowing 20 times in the U.S. Distance today 20 miles.[101]

### 1 NOVEMBER 1841

The Company tarried to kill game; an abundance of wild fowl and 13 deer and antelopes were bro't in. My breakfast, this morning, formed a striking contrast with that of yesterday which was the lights of a wolf.[102]

---

[99]Ibid., p. 28.
[100]Bidwell, "The First Emigrant Train," p. 129.
[101]*Journey*, p. 28.
[102]Ibid.

### 2 November 1841

Capt. B with his 7 men remained to take care of the meat he had killed—while the rest of the Company went on. We passed some beautiful grapes, sweet and pleasant. The land decreased in fertility as we descended the stream. Behold! This morning, [Thomas] Jones, who left the camp to hunt on the 23d came to the camp. They (he and Kelsey) had arrived in the plains several days before us, and found an Indian, who conducted them to Marsh's house, but he brought bad news, he said there had been no rain in California for 18 months, and that the consequence was, there was little bread stuff in the country. Beef however was abundant and of the best quality—traveled today 16 miles.[103]

### 3 November 1841

We waited till Capt. B came up, and all started for Marsh's about noon; arrived at the St. Joaquin [River] and crossed it—distance 13 miles—found an abundance of grass here. The timber was white oak, several kinds of evergreen oaks, and willow—the river about 100 yards in width.[104]

### Arrival at Marsh's Rancho, 4 November 1841

Left the river in good season and departing gradually from its timber—came into large marshes of Bulrushes. We saw large herds of elk and wild Horses, grazing upon the plain. The earth was in many places strongly impregnated with salt—came into the hills. Here were a few scattered oaks—land appeared various, in some places black, some light clay color, and in other mulatto (between black and white) sometimes inclining to a red soil, but it was all parched with heat, finally we arrived at Marsh's house, which is built of unburnt bricks, small and has no fireplace—wanting a floor and covered with bulrushes. In fact it was not what I expected to find, a hog was killed for the company. We had nothing else but beef, the latter was used as bread the former as meat. Therefore I will say we had bread and meat for dinner. Several of our company were old acquaintances of Marsh in Missouri, and therefore much time was passed in talking about old times, the incidents of our late Journey, and our future prospects. All encamped about the house—tolerably well pleased with the appearance of Dr. Marsh, but much disappointed in his situation, for among all his shrubby white oaks, there was not one tall enough to make a rail-cut. No other timber in sight, excepting a few cotton woods and willows.[105]

...we found ourselves two days later at Dr. Marsh's ranch, and there we learned

---
[103]Ibid.
[104]Ibid., p. 29.
[105]Ibid.

that we were really in California and our journey at an end. After six months we had now arrived at the first settlement in California, November 4, 1841.[106]

### 5 November 1841

Company remained at Marsh's getting information respecting the Country.[107]

### 6 November 1841

Fifteen of the Company started for a Spanish Town, called the Pueblo of St. Joseph [San Jose], (which is situated about 4 miles from Marsh's) to seek employment.[108]

### Letters to John Muir recalling the Sierra crossing and the 'discovery' of the Calaveras Big Trees

Chico, Ca., April 20, 1896

John Muir Esq., Martinez, Cal.
My Dear Sir,

Your esteemed favor to hand—came during my late absence at San Jose. Glad to hear from you.

In the enclosed statement I have tried to comply with your request.

So you are going to Alaska again! Lookout, for the glaciers there are full of crevasses. (Please pardon my poor pencil writing, my nervous hand being too unsteady to use the pen.)

Mrs. Bidwell joins in her best wishes and kindest remembrances. Come and see us when you can.

Yours always,
John Bidwell

### Statement

In 1841, before Fremont had seen or named Great Salt Lake, Humboldt, Carson or Walker's rivers, or so far as I know before any white man had ever crossed the Sierra Nevada mountains, I crossed the plains to California and saw them all. The party I came with consisted of thirty two men, one woman and child. We struck a stream and ascended it to the eastern base of said mountains. This proved to be what is now known as Walker's river, which was named by Fremont in 1845, after a noted Rocky Mountain trapper, Jo Walker. There we scaled the now famous Sierra Nevada, we first struck waters flowing west. The stream we descended was the Stanislaus river, a tributary of the San Joaquin, both names to us being then unknown. Our party was now entirely out of provisions. One of the last two oxen had been killed before we began the climb, the other when

---

[106] Bidwell, "The First Emigrant Train," p. 130.
[107] *Journey*, p. 29.   [108] Ibid.

in mid journey down the western slope. The oxen became so poor that the bones contained no marrow. Fires had desolated the mountains and it seemed impossible to find or kill any game.

It took about three weeks to get over the great chain, and during that time no game was killed except one wildcat and one crow. The last ox gone, mules and horses could not be spared, except when some became too poor to travel or crippled by falling down precipitous places, and so were our only resource for food. For a large part of the way down the mountain our course lay along the divide, on the north side of the precipitous cañon of the Stanislaus, and was generally west. We knew that California lie to the west, and that was the direction we aimed to travel. With this understanding one morning, (about the 20th of Oct., 1841, I think it was) I started ahead of the party to try to kill some game, and became separated for 36 hours or more. Near night I was hastening <u>north</u> to intersect the trail of the party going west. It was almost too dark to see a trail, when I came to an enormous fallen tree. I tried to go around to the top but it was too brushy. So I passed by the but[t], which seemed to tower some twenty or more feet above my head, I was obliged to hasten on and find a secluded place to spend the night, for Indian fires were seen and tracks fresh and plentiful.

I had come to the conclusion that the party had gone north (and not west), so at daylight I struck out east with all haste, but I found no trail. Then I bore south till I found the camping ground where I left party the day before. But the party had changed direction, followed an Indian path down into the deep canon, and scaled the canon wall on the south side of the Stanislaus. As I climbed along their rugged trail I found several horses and mules had given out (too weak to go farther) and been left to the mercy of the Indians—who were cutting them to pieces even when standing and alive unable to run or kick. My rifle I carried cocked in my hand; but, though alone and several hours after the party had passed, the Indians made no attempt to molest me.

But to return to the big tree which I had seen. The conditions under which I saw it—the darkness that was coming on—the haste to leave as soon as I could see in the morning &c must be my excuse for the meager report I am able to give.

This tree was, beyond a doubt, that huge wonder of the Calaveras grove of Sequoias known as the Father of the Forest. Though I entered the grove and found a hiding place for the night near the east side I saw no standing Sequoias. We had for several days been meandering among (to me) wonderful conifers, of which many must have been that monarch of all pines, the Sugar pine. Besides, tho to me every thing was new and wonderful, there was at the moment no time to consider. And yet the impression that tree made upon my mind could not be forgotten. Ever after when the mention of big trees happened to be made, I never failed to tell my big tree story.

In March, 1844, when [John] Fremont first came to California, I told him in the presence of Capt. [John] Sutter, P.B. Reading, Col. Jos. B. Chiles and others, (at the breakfast table one morning at Sutter's Fort) of the big tree I had seen.

Col. [Joseph] Chiles was of our party. He had seen the Redwoods of the coast, and thought the big tree I had seen was Redwood, and declared he saw Redwood when we were in the Sierra Nevada &c. But of course he was in this mistaken. And certainly too he was never within ten miles of my big tree when we were coming to California. Finally, after the Calaveras grove of Sequoias had been rediscovered in the early fifties I went there and recognized the tree that I saw and the lay of the ground.

John Bidwell

[Included in above letter to John Muir was this letter from Annie Bidwell to John Muir.]

April 20, 1896

Dear Mr. Muir,

When Genl. & my sister & I visited Calaveras grove, Genl. recognized many features of the locality, saying, "Yes, I was here," and when we reached the hotel he so described "The Father of the Forest," to the guide that he later replied "You have been here," tears filled my husband's eyes and he turned away but in a few moments said to me, "Let us slip off alone to that tree" & without any wavering he led us to it. We were all much moved, he as the memories surging in upon him. We in sympathy with those memories.

Sincerely Yours,<br>A.E.B. [Annie E. Bidwell][109]

---

[109] John Muir Collection, microfilm roll #9, University of the Pacific.

# 2

# Mexican California and the American Conquest, 1841–1848

When John Bidwell first arrived in California, he found a sparsely settled Mexican territory inhabited by only 7,000 non-Indian residents, almost all of whom lived along the coast in a narrow band of settlement stretching from San Diego to Sonoma. With the exception of the lonely Russian outpost at Fort Ross, and the handful of isolated rancheros who claimed large tracts of land in the Sacramento and San Joaquin valleys, the rest of California remained completely dominated by the territory's 200,000 Native Americans. Divided as they were into over one hundred tribelets speaking some eighty different languages, the Indians had nevertheless managed to keep the small Hispanic populations of Spanish and Mexican California at bay between 1769 and 1841. They would not, however, be able to mount an effective resistance to the imminent tide of American settlers heralded by the Bidwell-Bartleson party. Neither, of course, would Mexico.

The Republic of Mexico was a troubled young nation in 1841. Its first twenty years of independence from Spain had been marred by civil war, religious strife, chronic political instability, and the loss of Texas in 1836. Mexico's internal difficulties were compounded by constant diplomatic tension and rumors of war with the United States, its more powerful and aggressive neighbor to the north. Anxious to secure its thinly populated northern frontier, Mexico had adopted the risky strategy of encouraging immigration from foreign lands, including the United States. Gambling that generosity could make loyal Mexican citizens out of any foreigners, even American ones, Mexican authorities in 1824 and 1828 permitted immigrants to obtain huge rancho grants of up to eleven square leagues. To qualify, however, they had to reside in Mexico for two years, become naturalized citizens, and convert to Roman Catholicism. The promise of free land, coupled with the fact that the rules for obtaining it were poorly enforced by Mexican officials, proved a powerful lure to American settlers like John Bidwell.[1]

Despite official Mexican generosity, the Bidwell-Bartleson Party did not receive a cordial welcome in California. Though he initially greeted his fellow American expatriates with an openhanded hospitality, John Marsh quickly began grumbling about the expense of hosting so many unexpected guests. The reaction of local California authorities was even less enthusiastic. When fourteen members of the party arrived at Mission San Jose to apply for passports, a suspicious General Mariano Vallejo promptly arrested and jailed them. They were released only after Marsh was summoned several days later to vouch for them.

Bidwell, who had remained behind, then proceeded to the mission on his own to obtain a passport but he too ended up in the *calabozo*. Confined for three days without food, Bidwell at last obtained release through the kindly intervention of Thomas Bowen, an American resident of the nearby pueblo of San Jose. Granted a passport by Vallejo, Bidwell left the mission and returned to Marsh's rancho. Remaining just long enough to collect his personal effects, Bidwell and three companions set out for New Helvetia, a new settlement being developed by frontier promoter John Sutter. Riding on horseback through eight days of pouring rain, the four men arrived at Sutter's rancho near the confluence of the American and Sacramento rivers on November 30, 1841. As Bidwell later recalled, "Sutter received us with open arms and in a princely fashion," thus inaugurating an association that would dominate Bidwell's life for the next eight years.[2]

A German-Swiss immigrant who deserted his family and fled from Europe to avoid his creditors, Johann Augustus Sutter came to the United States in 1834 and settled in St. Louis. Failing in business there and in Santa Fe, Sutter journeyed to the Oregon country and then to Hawaii before arriving in California in 1839. Obtaining a sprawling land grant in the largely unexplored Sacramento Valley, Sutter established his New Helvetia "colony" with a small following of Americans, Hawaiians, and Indi-

---

[1] Hunt, pp. 440–441; David Hornbeck, "Land Tenure and Rancho Expansion in Alta California, 1784–1846," *Journal of Historical Geography*, 4 (1978), pp. 377–383; David Weber, *The Mexican Frontier, 1841–1846: The American Southwest Under Mexico* (Albuquerque: University of New Mexico Press, 1982), pp. 162, 180–181, 339; Christian Fritz, *Federal Justice in California: The Court of Ogden Hoffman, 1851–1891* (Lincoln: University of Nebraska Press, 1991), pp. 140–155.
[2] John Bidwell, "Life in California Before the Gold Discovery," *The Century Magazine*, 41 (Dec. 1890), pp. 164–166.

ans. California governor Juan Alvarado supported Sutter's project as a means of developing the interior and protecting the coast against Indian raids, and consequently invested Sutter with extensive military, judicial, and administrative authority. As a result, Sutter reigned over New Helvetia like a feudal lord.

Planting the seeds of what he hoped would grow into a flourishing settlement and commercial empire, Sutter quickly laid plans for his famous fort, which served as the gateway to California for American emigrants traveling overland between 1843 and 1849. Actual construction was still several months away when Bidwell and his companions arrived on the scene in the closing days of November 1841.[3]

Always in desperate need of reliable and skilled workers, Sutter quickly recognized in young Bidwell "the man who was the answer to [his] prayers," the man who became his "strong right arm."[4] Spending five weeks learning Spanish under Sutter's tutelage, Bidwell departed in January 1842 on his first major assignment in the Swiss entrepreneur's employ: the dismantling of Fort Ross. Sutter had purchased the outpost from the Russian American Company in 1841 and had dispatched Robert Ridley to begin transferring all its moveable assets, including the garrison's muskets and cannons, to New Helvetia. Bidwell arrived to relieve Ridley and, for the next fourteen months, remained at Fort Ross and Bodega Bay, helping to bring down the curtain on imperial Russia's colonial venture in California.[5]

In February 1843, Bidwell returned to New Helvetia where construction had finally begun on Sutter's Fort. Over the next four years, drawing a monthly salary of $25, Bidwell filled a variety of essential roles for Sutter, including those of bookkeeper and manager. He also served as the chief agent in Sutter's effort to locate new settlers in the Sacramento Valley and to assist them in obtaining rancho grants. Beginning with his journey up the valley with Peter Lassen in March 1843, Bidwell regularly scouted out desirable sites for hopeful claimants and sketched the *diseños* required by Mexican law for all rancho applications. By the spring of 1846, about twenty-one settlers had been placed on Sacramento ranchos, many of them located by Bidwell who, as a result, had explored and mapped

---

[3]Ibid. pp. 166–168.
[4]James Peter Zollinger, *Sutter: The Man and His Empire* (New York: Oxford University Press, 1939), p. 103; Richard Dillon, *Fool's Gold: The Decline and Fall of Captain John Sutter of California* (Santa Cruz, Ca.: Western Tanager Press, 1967), p. 133.
[5]Bidwell, "Life in California," pp. 167–169.

most of the valley. Bidwell's travels left a permanent legacy of place names throughout the region. On his trip with Lassen, for example, Bidwell named Deer, Mill, Pine, and Antelope creeks in present-day Tehama County. It was on this trip as well that Bidwell first saw Chico Creek and the site of his future home.

Other important duties also brought Bidwell north from New Helvetia. In 1843, Sutter sent Bidwell to supervise Hock Farm, his estate on the Feather River forty-five miles above the fort, where he had relocated his livestock the year before. Bidwell managed Sutter's large herd of 4,500 cattle for two seasons before returning to New Helvetia in the spring of 1845.

In the meantime, Bidwell started to acquire his own land. Having become a naturalized Mexican citizen (without having become a Catholic), Bidwell received title in 1844 to Rancho Ulpinos in the Sacramento delta region near present-day Rio Vista. He never settled on the property, however, and instead received a second grant the following year. Like Rancho Ulpinos, the five-square-league Colusa grant was never developed by Bidwell, who later sold it for $2,000.[6]

As a landowner, citizen, and employee of the controversial Sutter, Bidwell was inevitably drawn into the complex intrigues of Mexican California politics. In 1845, disgruntled *Californios* led by Juan Bautista Alvarado, Jose Castro, and Pio Pico launched an armed rebellion against General Manuel Micheltorena, the territorial governor and a protégé of President and General Antonio Lopez de Santa Anna. Sutter, who had befriended Micheltorena shortly after the governor took office in 1842, quickly assembled a mostly Indian force of 225 men, the largest ever seen in California, and marched south on January 1, 1845, to help stamp out the revolt. Riding with him was Bidwell, one of ninety American settlers in Sutter's force that included such notable California pioneers as Jasper O'Farrell, John Gantt, Caleb Greenwood, Isaac Graham, Peter Lassen, Ezekiel Merritt, and Kit Carson's brother Moses. Linking up with Micheltorena near Monterey, the combined government forces continued on toward Los Angeles where the rebels had concentrated. On February 20, the opposing armies clashed south of Mission San Fernando in the nearly bloodless yet decisive battle of Cahuenga. The engagement, a complete triumph for the rebels, resulted in the capture of Bidwell and Sutter, and the surrender of Micheltorena. Shortly afterward, the deposed governor returned to Mexico City while the

---

[6]Hunt, pp. 115–118.

defeated Bidwell and Sutter were pardoned and allowed to go home. Following a grueling two-week journey over Tejon Pass and up the length of the San Joaquin Valley, they arrived back at Sutter's Fort on April 1, 1845.[7]

The peace that followed the "Micheltorena War" proved short-lived, however. On December 10, 1845, Captain John C. Fremont of the U.S. Army Corps of Topographical Engineers, accompanied by his guide Kit Carson, suddenly appeared at New Helvetia where Bidwell was presiding for an absent Sutter. Bidwell, who had met the Great Pathmarker two years before during his first expedition to California, tried unsuccessfully to satisfy Fremont's abrupt requests for the provisions and fresh mounts required by his force of sixty well-armed men.

Ostensibly on a journey of exploration, Fremont and his men spent the winter in the San Joaquin Valley before pushing on to Monterey. There, in March 1846, Fremont provoked the ire of local Mexican officials in the famous Gavilan Peak incident. Ordered by Governor Jose Castro to steer clear of California's settled regions, Fremont garrisoned his troops atop Gavilan Peak and raised the American flag in an arrogant show of defiance. For five days, Fremont thumbed his nose at Castro before quietly departing for Oregon.[8]

Whether intended to or not, Fremont's actions emboldened American settlers in the Sacramento and Napa valleys who dreamed of doing in California what Sam Houston and Davy Crockett had done in Texas ten years earlier. When Fremont returned to California in May, his camp at the Sutter Buttes became a rallying point for these discontented elements who, under the command of Ezekiel Merritt, precipitated the Bear Flag Revolt on June 10 by capturing a small squad of Mexican soldiers on the Consumnes River and confiscating their herd of 200 horses.

After delivering the horses to Fremont's camp, Merritt, William Ide, and about twenty of the rebels set out for Sonoma where, on June 14, they captured General Mariano Vallejo, raised their quickly improvised Bear Flag, and declared California an independent republic. The extent to which the Bears acted independently of Fremont has remained a mystery debated by historians ever since.[9] John Bidwell, however, maintained to the end of his life that Fremont had masterminded the entire affair.[10]

As for Bidwell himself, his involvement in the Bear Flag Revolt began

---

[7]Dillon, pp. 19–21, 163–197.
[8]Neal Harlow, *California Conquered: War and Peace on the Pacific, 1846–1850* (Berkeley: University of California Press, 1982), pp. 61–73.   [9]Ibid., pp. 74–103.

on June 16 when Fremont brought the captured Vallejo to confinement at Sutter's Fort. Cold-shouldering Sutter aside, Fremont placed the fort under the command of Lt. Edward Kern and directed Bidwell to assume personal responsibility for guarding Vallejo, Jacob Leese, Victor Proudhon, and Salvador Vallejo, all of whom had been taken prisoner at Sonoma and brought to Fremont's new camp on the American River. Perceived by Kern as too friendly to his charges, Bidwell was excused from his duties several days later and set off for Sonoma to join up with the Bears. He arrived to find Fremont taking over direct command of the rebellion on the fourth of July. At Fremont's request, the Bears regrouped under a one-sentence declaration penned by Bidwell: "The undersigned hereby agree to organize for the purpose of gaining and maintaining the independence of California."[11] Forming into three new companies headed by elected captains, the Bears placed themselves under Fremont's orders and marched off with him to Sutter's Fort and, on July 12, to Monterey. While en route, they finally learned that the United States had been at war with Mexico for nearly two months and that Commodore John D. Sloat had already captured Monterey on July 7.

At that point the Bear Flag Revolt dissolved and, immediately upon their arrival at the capital, the Bears were officially merged with Fremont's regular command to form the California Battalion. On July 23, Commodore Robert F. Stockton, who had just arrived to succeed Sloat as the supreme American commander in the field, promoted Fremont to the rank of major and placed him in charge of the Battalion. Bidwell received a commission as a second lieutenant.[12]

Moving swiftly to complete the conquest of California, Stockton ordered Fremont aboard the USS *Cyane,* commanded by Capt. Samuel F. DuPont. DuPont transported the 165-man Battalion south to capture San Diego on July 29 after a three-day journey.[13] From San Diego, Fremont and the California Battalion then marched north to support Stockton's advance on Los Angeles, which fell to the Americans on August 13. With all of California now occupied, the Americans turned to the business of governing the conquered territory. From Los Angeles, Fremont promoted Bidwell to Captain and dispatched him to preside as *alcalde* at Mission San Luis Rey. Taking charge on August 28, Bidwell spent

---

[10]John Bidwell, "Fremont in the Conquest of California," *The Century Magazine*, 41 (Feb. 1891), pp. 519, 522. John Bidwell, "Early California Reminiscences," part 6, *Out West*, 20 (July 1904), pp. 79–80.
[11]John Bidwell, "Fremont in the Conquest," p. 522.
[12]Harlow, pp. 137–140.

exactly one month as chief magistrate for most of what is now Orange and northern San Diego counties.[14]

Bidwell's service was suddenly cut short at the end of September, when local *Californios* launched a spectacular revolt that erupted in Los Angeles. Spreading west to Santa Barbara and south to San Diego, the rebellion succeeded in completely evicting all American land forces from southern California. Staying just one step ahead of the rebels, Bidwell fled to San Diego where, with Ezekiel Merritt and several other members of the California Battalion, he took refuge aboard the American whaler *Stonington* anchored in the harbor. Then, in a daring bid for reinforcements, Bidwell and another volunteer took one of the *Stonington's* small whale boats and embarked upon a dangerous round-trip journey by sea to San Pedro, where Stockton's squadron was stationed. Shortly after his safe return, Bidwell helped recapture San Diego in a pair of sharp engagements fought in mid-October.[15]

With San Diego back in control, Stockton and Fremont prepared to reconquer rebellious southern California. Raising a brand new force of about 400 men, Fremont marched south from San Juan Bautista on November 29. Precisely one month later, with the aid of General Stephen Watts Kearny's recently arrived Army of the West, Stockton advanced northward from San Diego toward Los Angeles. Serving as "Quartermaster with the rank of Major" in the combined 600-man force, Bidwell witnessed the small but decisive battles of San Gabriel and the Mesa on the eighth and ninth of January, and participated in the reoccupation of Los Angeles the following day.[16]

Meanwhile, having retaken Santa Barbara and Ventura, Fremont arrived at Mission San Fernando just in time to intercept the retreating *Californio* forces under Andres Pico. On January 13, 1847, Fremont received their surrender at Cahuenga Pass, the place where Bidwell and Sutter had been taken prisoner less than two years before.[17] Though the Treaty of Guadalupe Hidalgo would not be signed until February 1848, the Mexican War was over in California, and John Bidwell, along with the rest of the volunteers of the California Battalion, was discharged from

---
[13]Ibid., pp. 144–45.
[14]John Bidwell, Notes on Bear Flag Revolt and Mexican War, in John Bidwell Papers, Part 1, carton 1, Bancroft Library, University of California, Berkeley; JB-77, pp. 181–89.
[15]Bidwell, Notes on Bear Flag Revolt and Mexican War; JB-77, pp. 189–98; Harlow, pp. 162–172.
[16]Harlow, pp. 203–223; Hunt, p. 123; Benjamin, p. 16; Dwight L. Clarke, *Stephen Watts Kearny: Soldier of the West* (Norman: University of Oklahoma Press, 1961), pp. 233–255.

military service. In March 1847, Bidwell once again found himself returning home from war in southern California.

Back at New Helvetia, Sutter put Bidwell to work on a number of important projects. Bidwell resumed laying out the proposed town of Sutterville on the Sacramento River and surveyed a road between Sutter's Fort and Sutter's new flour mill at Natomas. In December, Bidwell and Sutter collaborated on a major undertaking assigned to them by military governor Richard Mason: the first census of California Indians. As Indian sub-agent for the Central Valley, Sutter was instructed by Mason's secretary of state, Henry W. Halleck, to conduct the census for the interior portions of the territory. Sutter assigned Bidwell to the upper Sacramento Valley above the Buttes. Bidwell meticulously reported a count of eighty-two whites and nineteen "tame" Indians, and estimated a total of 19,500 "wild" Indians.[18]

In the meantime, Bidwell had helped Sutter launch yet another project. In August 1847, Bidwell drew up a contract between Sutter and carpenter James Marshall for the construction of a sawmill in the Sierra foothills near the Maidu village of Coloma, on the south fork of the American River. On January 24, 1848, just nine days before the United States officially annexed California with the Treaty of Guadalupe Hidalgo, Marshall discovered gold while inspecting the recently dug tailrace of the sawmill. Though he and Sutter attempted to keep the discovery a secret, the news leaked out. By May, the California Gold Rush had begun, with momentous consequences for Marshall, Sutter, and John Bidwell.

Though he was among the first to learn of the gold strike and had begun prospecting in earnest as early as April, Bidwell did not desert Sutter and remained in his employ for another year. In May 1849, Bidwell completed one last task for Sutter: the construction of a spacious two-story wood-frame house. Located at Hock Farm, the new dwelling became Sutter's primary residence after his long deserted family arrived from Switzerland with the horde of argonauts who drove the Lord of New Helvetia from his fort. Sutter and his family lived at Hock Farm until June 1865, when an arsonist burned down the house that Bidwell had built.[19]

The construction of the Hock Farm residence proved to be the final collaboration between Bidwell and his early California benefactor. By the time he politely declined the proffered hand of Sutter's daughter Anna Eliza in April 1851, John Bidwell was a wealthy bachelor who had struck it rich in the Gold Rush and had gone on to establish a private empire of his own at Rancho del Arroyo Chico.[20]

---

[17]Harlow, pp. 231–32.   [18]Dillon, p. 275.   [19]Ibid., pp. 309, 341–342.   [20]Ibid., p. 329.

## Remarks on Mexican California, the Bear Flag Revolt, and the Mexican War

### Comments on John Marsh

Dr. Marsh had come into California four or five years before by way of New Mexico. He was in some respects a remarkable man. In command of the English language I have scarcely ever seen his equal. He had never studied medicine, I believe, but he was a great reader: sometimes he would lie in bed all day reading, and he had a memory that stereotyped all he read, and in those days in California such a man could easily assume the role of doctor and practise medicine. In fact, with the exception of Dr. Marsh there was no physician of any kind anywhere in California. We were overjoyed to find an American, and yet when we became acquainted with him we found him one of the most selfish of all mortals.[1]

To my friends and others I must speak candidly of Dr. Marsh here. What he was in Missouri I can't say—I speak for the emigrant, that he may be on his guard, and not be gulled, as some have been on coming to this country, by him. He is perhaps the meanest man in California. After the Company had encamped near his house about 2 days, and here had been killed for them a small hog and bullock, he began to complain of his poverty, saying "the Company had already been more than $100 expense to him—God knew whether he would ever get a rial [real] of it or not." But poor as the Company was, he had already got from them 5 times the value of his pig and bullock in different kinds of articles—powder, lead, knives &c. He charged the Company $3 apiece to go and get their passports . . . a good price for his services. There is not an individual in California who does not dislike the man. He is seldom admitted into a house to sleep. If rightly informed, he had to sleep under his cart in a Spanish town to which he had taken some hides. No other foreigner would be obliged to do so. He came to this country pretending to be a Physician. He has, however, gained by it—he has charged and received $25 for 2 doses of salts—he has refused his assistance to a female in labour and not expected to live, without immediate relief, unless the husband promised him for his pay 50 cows. When he first came to this country, he hired in the family of an obliging American, during which time he laid out 50 cents for some fresh fish: after having a whole year clear of charges, he dunned the man for his 50 cts. I might write 50 pages detailing similar incidents, but it is unnecessary to mention but one more, a child being afflicted with the head ache, Dr. Marsh was called, administered 2 or 3 doses of medicine—made a charge of 50 cows. The family was a poor one, not having more than 150 and in order to reduce the price, charged the Dr. 25 cows for washing a couple of shirts, so he went off grumbling with 25. Enough of him.[2]

---
[1] Bidwell, "Life in California Before the Gold Discovery," *Century Magazine,* 41 (December 1890), p. 163.
[2] *Journey,* p. 47.

I was going to say that when I first reached California there were no doctors here, but there was one, Dr. Marsh. He was not supposed to be a regular doctor, but I have since learned from good authority that he had gone through some medical college or institution before coming to this coast. They used to accuse him of charging very high fees—two or three hundred head of cattle when he had to go thirty or forty miles to make a visit.[3]

### Frontier Conditions in Mexican California

There was no money in California at that time. But still it was true that, practically, there was no doctor in California. There was no drug store in California. There was no post-office in California—there was not a mail route in California. There was no road in California that had ever been worked that I know of, unless it was the drive or Alameda between San Jose and Santa Clara.[4]

I have said that there was no regular physician in California. Later, in 1843, in a company that came from Oregon, was one Joe Meeks, a noted character in the Rocky Mountains. On the way he said, "Boys, when I get down to California among the Greasers I am going to palm myself off as a doctor"; and from that time they dubbed him Dr. Meeks. He could neither read nor write. As soon as the Californians heard of his arrival at Monterey they began to come to him with their different ailments. His first professional service was to a boy who had a toe cut off. Meeks, happening to be near, stuck the toe on, binding it in a poultice of mud, and it grew on again. The new governor, Micheltorena, employed him as surgeon. Meeks had a way of looking and acting very wise, and of being reticent when people talked about things which he did not understand.[5]

There was not to my knowledge in all California a lawyer or law book, post-office or mail route, printing office or newspaper; nor was there a fort or fortification that deserved the name, or any military force to speak of.[6]

There were no roads, merely paths, trodden only by Indians and wild game. ... There was not a hotel in San Francisco, or Monterey, or anywhere in California, till 1846, when the Americans took the country. The priests at the Missions were glad to entertain strangers without charge. They would give you a room in which to sleep, and perhaps a bedstand with a hide stretched across it, and over that you would spread your blankets.[7]

When I came to California in 1841 there were very few foreigners here. By foreigners I mean Americans, English, Scotch, Irish, etc. In other words, all not Californian or Mexican born, the people here are called foreigners.... The Mex-

---
[3] *Pioneers*, p. 16.    [4] Ibid., pp. 16–17.
[5] Bidwell, "Life in California Before the Gold Discovery," p. 175.
[6] JB to Professor Rockwell Hunt, 3 April 1895, BFP.
[7] Bidwell, "Life in California Before the Gold Discovery," pp. 166, 171.

icans in California were mostly native-born. Their occupation was pastoral. There were practically no mechanics among them. Occasionally you would find one who was something of a tinker, not a blacksmith, and he might make a pair of spurs or a bridle bit. That was about all. I think I never saw a native Californian who was a carpenter.[8]

There was one feature in those early times that I remember. We were scattered all over California: certain events would transpire, and would be told all over the country, and I never knew of any exaggeration. We had no printing presses, and yet those events never became distorted or exaggerated, and that gives me more confidence in "legendary history" than I would otherwise have. Papers were very scarce. We used to read papers twelve months old.[9]

### California Cart

The California cart—I do not know whether you have ever seen one. The wheels were made out of the largest oak trees that could be found, not sawed crosswise but hewed down to a great slab, about the size of an ordinary wagon fore-wheel, eight to ten inches thick on the periphery of the wheel and a little thicker in the center where the axle went through. The hole for the axle would, at the beginning, perhaps be large enough for a man to put his head through, but after the cart had been used for a while a small man might quite easily crawl through. They had no such thing as oil to grease the wheels, but used instead soapsuds as thick as well could be. Then a boy would run along beside the cart and put in with a paddle the soapsuds to lubricate the huge axle, but in spite of that you would generally hear a California cart coming a half-mile, it would squeak so. They used these carts to travel in. They would have sort of a rude frame on them, some uprights around, and stretch some calico over them to make a shade, and sometimes the families, that is, the richer families, would go off on journeys and travel thirty or forty miles in a day.[10]

### Hide and Tallow Trade

At that time the only trade, foreign or domestic, was in hides, tallow, and furs; but mostly hides. With few exceptions the vessels that visited the coast were from Boston, fitted out by Hooper to go there and trade for hides. Occasionally vessels would put in for water or in distress. San Francisco was the principal harbor; the next was Monterey. There was an anchorage off San Luis Obispo; the next was Santa Barbara, the next San Buenaventura, then San Pedro, and lastly San Diego. The hides were generally collected and brought to San Diego and there salted, staked out to dry, and folded so that they would lie compactly in the ship, and thence were shipped to Boston. Goods were principally sold on board the vessels: there were very few stores on land; that of Thomas O. Larkin

---

[8] *Pioneers*, p. 9.   [9] *JB-91*, p. 63.   [10] *Pioneers*, pp. 10–11.

at Monterey was the principal one. The entrance of a vessel into harbor or roadstead was a signal to all the ranchers to come in their little boats and launches laden with hides to trade for goods. Thus vessels went from port to port, remaining few or many days according to the amount of trade. When the people stopped bringing hides, a vessel would leave.[11]

### JOHN GILROY AND OTHERS WERE RUNAWAY SAILORS

The early foreign residents of California were largely runaway sailors. Many if not most would change their names. For instance, Gilroy's ranch, where the town of Gilroy is now located, was owned by an old resident under the assumed appellation of Gilroy. Of course vessels touching upon the coast were liable, as they were everywhere, to lose men by desertion, especially if the men were maltreated. Such things have been so common that it is not difficult to believe that those who left their vessels in early days on this then distant coast had cause for doing so. To be known as a runaway sailor was no stain upon a man's character. It was no uncommon thing, after my arrival here, for sailors to be skulking and hiding about from ranch to ranch till the vessel they had left should leave the coast.[12]

### *VAQUEROS Y CABRESTAS*

A large and well-trained ox, called the *cabresta*, was turned loose from the corral or little field where he was constantly kept and he immediately started for the band of cattle feeding upon the open plain, perhaps a mile away. A couple of *vaqueros* would ride leisurely behind him and when the band of cattle was reached a fat steer was selected and the lariats thrown upon him, one holding his head and another his hind feet. The *cabresta* then approached and held his broad horns down alongside of those of the wild steer. One of the *vaqueros* ran up and quickly strapped the horns of the two animals firmly together, the wild steer was released from the lariats. He would dash here and there trying to pull the big ox beside him, but the *cabresta* would slowly but surely lead him in spite of his utmost exertions to the corral or to the tree where he was to be slaughtered. When the spot was reached, one of the *vaqueros* would shoot the steer in the head killing him instantly. As he fell the *cabresta* would drop his own head and bend down his neck and wait patiently until the straps were removed when he would at once repair to the place where he was in the habit of being kept. Without the aid of this trained ox it was difficult to get a steer into the corral unless the whole band was driven up, and if the animal was caught with the lariat he could only be held, not led or driven for he would fight like any wild beast. With the aid of the *cabresta* the task of getting a fat animal to the slaughter yard was not difficult. These trained animals were highly esteemed and when sold brought a large price.[13]

---

[11]Bidwell, "Life in California Before the Gold Discovery," p. 174.
[12]Ibid., pp. 173–74.
[13]Rockwell D. Hunt, *John Bidwell, Prince of California Pioneers* (Caldwell, Idaho: Caxton Printers, 1942), pp. 82–83.

### Wealth determined by animals owned

I know a few Spaniards who are industrious and enterprising. They have become immensely rich, this likewise is the case with the foreigners, who have used the least industry. Wealth here principally consists in Horses, Cattle, and mules.[14]

### Rancho horses and cattle

If you wanted a horse it was no crime to catch one and ride him, provided you turned him out at the next ranch. Then you could get another, and if you turned him out thirty or forty miles away at the next place, it was all right. If you became hungry and killed a bullock, that was no crime, provided you hung the hide upon a tree so the owner could see and get it. Nothing was said. That was not stealing.[15]

### Ranchos unfenced; open range system

When asked if there were fences in the Sacramento Valley, Bidwell replied, "Not in 1841. There was not a fence in the valley then.... What was a fence in those days was an Indian camped on each corner of the field and you were obliged to keep awake all night and holler all night."[16]

### Horticulture at the Missions and Fort Ross

The date of my arrival in California was 1841. At that date all the fruit, with few exceptions, was grown at the missions, or at points that had been occupied and improved by the missions. The most important exceptions were:

The orchard at Fort Ross, planted by the Russians some time during their thirty odd years' occupation, and prior to 1841. This orchard consisted of apples and peaches, all seedlings, I think, and covered possibly half an acre.

Edward McIntosh, near Bodega, had a few grape vines, the eighth of an inch perhaps, not in bearing at the date (1842) when I first saw them.

At that date there was a small vineyard between Bodega and Fort Ross, half an acre in extent. This had been planted and owned by a Russian gentleman of leisure, by the name of "Don Jorge." These grapes were said to be of a better variety than those cultivated at the missions; but though they had borne fruit, yet the pruning and little attention I was able to give were not such as to restore them. The place was too shaded by the redwood forest, the soil too wet, grass too luxuriant, deer, hare, and cattle too plenty, fences too poor, etc.

General Vallejo had at that date a few grape vines where he resided at or near the old mission of San Solano (the place now known as Sonoma). He had also a few fruit trees, but I did not see them in bearing and cannot recall the kinds, whether apples or pears. There were, I think, other instances on the north side of the bay, where a few vines were seen; but of this I am certain, namely, the only fruit I saw in 1842 was found at the missions and at Fort Ross.

---

[14]*Journey*, p. 38.  [15]*Pioneers*, p. 12.
[16]*Edwards Woodruff v. North Bloomfield*, Vol. 24, pp. 9833–834.

The mission of San Rafael had the best grapes,—the "mission" grape, but better than anywhere else; it had also apples and pears.

The mission of San Jose had an orchard and vineyard, five or six acres perhaps. The principal trees were olives and pears. The best early pear was called "Pera de San Juan." This mission I first saw in 1841. The trees were mostly seedlings, I think, at least the fruit was mostly inferior.

The largest orchard as well as the largest trees, mostly pear trees, were at Santa Clara and San Jose (now the city of San Jose). These, however, I did not see till 1844. There were also grape vines. All, both trees and vines, had belonged to the mission, and were of the kinds found at the other missions.

The mission of San Juan Bautista, near Pajaro valley, had also an old orchard, at least a few trees.

In January and February, 1845, I saw more or less of attempts to raise vines and fruit trees at other points, namely, missions of San Miguel, San Luis Obispo, and Santa Ynez. The trees, like the missions, were in a condition of neglect and ruin.

Santa Barbara was better cared for; but the state of all the missions that I saw was to a greater or less extent that of neglect and decay, including San Buenaventura, San Fernando, and San Gabriel. In 1845 Los Angeles had the largest vineyards that I had seen, and the vines were the most thrifty, even as thrifty as those of San Rafael. Wine was also abundant,—even the Angelica. Los Angeles had orchards also, mostly of oranges. The largest orange orchards at that time (Feb., 1845) were those of [William] Wolfskill, [Lemuel] Carpenter, and Louis Vigne (known as "Don Aliso," from the large sycamore tree standing by his house).

About the last days of February or first of March, I visited the mission of San Gabriel, and found old vineyards and orange orchards, but all in a neglected condition. The orange trees had evidently been injured by frost, but not perhaps wholly killed.

In returning to the Sacramento valley we entered the mountains about thirty miles this side of Los Angeles, and reached the San Joaquin valley by the Tejon pass. Captain Sutter had procured a few olive and orange shoots, cut off at or a little below the ground, without roots, but with a little of the root bark; also a few grape vines. The padre at the mission of San Fernando assured us that the shoots would grow, so we carried them on our pack animals to Sutter's Fort, and there they were planted. We even watered them with buckets. The vines lived, but not the olives nor the oranges.

The next year, 1846, the Mexican war occurred. That year I again saw Los Angeles. I saw oranges growing at [Isaac] Williams' ranch (about 30 miles from Los Angeles), also a vineyard and trees at [Francisco] Ocampo's ranch. Ocampo had wine and brandy which he had made. I also saw a fine vineyard at Santa Margarita, owned by Pio Pico, the last governor of California under Mexican rule.

At the mission of San Luis Rey there were orchards and vineyards, but everything in neglected condition,—magnificent ruins, I might say. There were the remains of olive orchards even then gone to utter ruin, hundreds of acres in extent. Pala and Temecula were dependencies of that gem of a mission.

The old mission of San Diego had the finest of olives and pomegranates.... it was in 1848 that I went to San Rafael to get pear trees and grape vines. I obtained them from Don Timoteo Murphy, who for many years under Mexican rule had been the *Administrador* of the mission. This was the first week in March, 1848, and I carried with me the news of the discovery of gold by Marshall at Coloma the last week in January. At least, no one whom I met on the way or at San Francisco (for I went over to that place on my trip), had heard of the discovery till I told him.[17]

## FLORA AND FAUNA OF THE CENTRAL VALLEY

In the latter part of '41 two men and myself started from Marsh's to go to Sutter's establishment. It was in winter and the country was considerably inundated. The streams were swollen and traveling very difficult and even dangerous, for we had to swim across the streams—across the San Joaquin, the Mokelumne, and the Consumne rivers. Our provisions were getting low and I was detailed to go ahead and kill an antelope. The antelope could be seen in those days by the thousands. When frightened they would gather into immense herds, preparatory to taking flight. I tried to approach them, but in crawling over the ground my gun became thoroughly wet as I thought, and not in a condition to fire. I put in some dry powder, intending to get the load out, wipe it out and put in a fresh one. I held the gun up and fired at random way off where the antelope were, never thinking that I had accomplished anything. Went away hoping that sometime before night I would find an opportunity of approaching the antelope. Going along the plains about a mile I saw an antelope lying down, saw he was rather fresh, felt of him and found he was still warm. I turned him over and found that my ball had struck him exactly in the eye! Another one of my accidents. I never was a very good shot, and yet I have always been lucky in an emergency.[18]

The valley abounded in elk, deer, antelope, geese and ducks, cranes, beaver and otter. Grizzly bears were almost an hourly sight. In the vicinity of the streams, it was not uncommon to see from thirty to forty in a day.[19]

Of horses, there were thousands in the San Joaquin Valley. I have seen herds twenty miles long on the west side.[20]

---

[17]JB to Edward J. Wickson, 16 November 1887, in Wickson, "California Mission Fruits," *Overland Monthly*, 11 (May 1888): 503–504.   [18]JB-91, pp. 10–11.
[19]Bidwell, "Early California Reminiscences," *Out West* (February 1904), p. 182.
[20]Ibid., p. 185.

[In July 1844] I ascended the valley on the west side of the Sacramento River as far as the present town of Colusa, having with me only one man, and he an Indian, who had been civilized at the Mission San Francisco de Solano, in Sonoma Valley. My first encampment hereabouts was on a slough some miles west of Colusa. Before reaching camp I had killed a large grizzly bear, and carried with me the only part fit to eat—the foot. The next day we went directly west across a large plain. It was a hot, terrifically hot day, and we found no water in our march, except toward night, and this was so salty that neither ourselves nor our animals could drink it, so we were obliged to sleep without water. We observed many deserted Indian villages, which had been abandoned because the springs had dried up. I should here mention the fact that the summer of 1844 was an exceptionally dry one, because the previous winter had been almost rainless. We were in the saddle by daylight, making our way toward the high mountains that lay to the southwest, feeling sure of finding water there. About ten or eleven o'clock in the morning, from the top of a ridge we beheld the grateful sight of a large, clear, flowing stream. We reached it as soon as possible, and our nearly famished horses soon plunged into the middle of it. At the same time we observed large numbers of Indians, men, women, and children, in a state of flight, running and screaming. Unsaddling our horses under a wide-spreading oak, they began eating the wild oats which grew in abundance around them, and were here obliged to give them rest. In less than an hour the Indians whom we had seen fleeing from us, that is, the men, were discovered coming toward us from many directions. The Indian who accompanied me became greatly alarmed. I had a gun with me, but he had none. By certain signs we gave them to understand that they must not approach us, but still large numbers came closer and very near. We saddled our horses, jaded as they were, so as to be ready if obliged to retreat. Four or five of the Indians, chiefs or head men, I have no doubt, came nearer than the others. We tried to converse in Spanish, but they understood not a word of it. My Indian, who came originally from the country between Sonoma and Clear Lake, was able to understand a few words spoken by a very old Indian. They asked what I came for. They said they had never seen a white man before. Here I felt obliged to show them what I could do, by exhibiting to them what I had done, so I pointed to the bear's foot which I had with me, and told them I wanted to kill grizzly bears—the grizzly being regarded by the valley Indians, and I thought by those of the Coast Range, with superstitious awe. They regarded these animals as people, but very bad people, and I have known Indians to claim that some of their old men could go out in the night and talk with the bears. I told them I did not want to kill Indians, because I considered them good people, but bears I regarded as very bad people.[21]

---

[21]Justus H. Rogers, *Colusa County* (Orland, CA: n.p., 1891), pp. 48–50.

### Trees, Grasses, and Crops Observed in 1841

Oak—here are many kinds of oak, but the only kind which I remember to have seen in the U.S. resembling the oak of this, is the White oak; this grows on almost every stream, frequently among the mountains, sometimes in the middle of the plains, the other kinds of oak, are principally evergreen, as they retain their leaves all the year, I have been told by many, that it answers every purpose that the oak does in the U.S. excepting for rails and building, it being generally too shrubby. It grows very large in places, I have seen trees 10 or 12 feet in diameter.

Black Walnut—I am not aware that this grows in any other place than on the Sacramento river, even here, confined to a few miles, grows shrubby.

Red Wood—This is abundant in almost every mountain, it is a kind of hemlock or cedar, found on both sides of the St. Francisco Bay, sometimes grows in valleys, it is the most important timber in California, generally 150 feet high; but I have seen many 200 feet high and not less than 15 feet in diameter, it splits the easiest of any timber I ever saw, it is very durable, houses, doors, &c. are made of it.

Sicamore—Grows in plenty along the Sacramento river, principally used for canoes, not hollow, as in the U.S.

Madrone—Grows as abundant as the oak, it is one of the most beautiful trees I have ever seen—is an evergreen, retaining a bright green foliage, but that which renders it so pleasing, is the color of the bark of all its branches, it is smooth like a Sicamore, and of a lively scarlet color, is a most excellent fire wood, and I have been informed by creditable gentlemen, that it is an elegant substitute for Mahogany.

Grass—The grass is not like that of the Prairies of the United States, it is of a finer and better quality, it ceases to grow about the first of July in consequence of the heat, and dries, the cattle however eat it, and become remarkably fat, it begins to grow again in October or November, when the rainy season sets in and continues to grow all winter. When I went to Ross the Russian Establishment, the grass all along the Pacific (on the 3rd Feb), was at least a foot high; green and growing finely.

Mustard grows in abundance.

Here on this side of the Bay, is an abundance of Red and White clover growing with the grass.

Here are also innumerable quantities of wild oats, which I am told, grow nearly all over California, and grow as thick as they can stand, producing oats of an excellent quality; but as neither cattle nor horses are ever fed here, they are never harvested.

Wheat—On the South side of the Bay of San Francisco, the soil, climate &c. are as well adapted to raising wheat as in any part of the World. I have been credibly informed, that it yields from 70 to 115 fold—wheat will always come up the second year and produce more than half as much as it did the first. This is because of its scattering on the ground while harvesting. Wheat is sown in December, Jan. and February, harvested in June and first of July. North side of the Bay, will not yield more than 15 or 20 fold.

Potatoes—Irish Potatoes grow well and are of good quality—should be planted in April.

Sweet Potatoes have never been tried.

Beans are produced abundantly, likewise peas; peas are planted in gardens about the 10th of March and are ripe about the last of May.

Barley yields well, and is sown at the time of wheat.

Onions, Cabbages, Parsnips, Beets, Turnips grow well.[22]

Tule Marshes. Tule is a name given by Spaniards, to a kind of Bulrush. They grow very large, sometimes an inch in diameter, and occupy large portions of the valley of the Sacramento; they are called marshes, because they grow on the lowest ground and are covered in the rainy season with water, which continues till evaporated by heat of summer, these are haunts of incalculable thousands of wild geese, ducks, brants, cranes, pelicans etc.etc.[23]

### Fish, Wildlife and Other Observations in 1841

Fish. There is a great abundance of salmon in every stream, particularly, in the Spring of the year, when they are very fat, the Sacramento and its branches contain an abundance.

Whales likewise I see almost daily spouting along the coast. There are other fish which come up from the ocean.

There are few snakes here, the Rattlesnake and Coral the others are common.

Bears are plenty—they are of the Grizzly kind, but are not so tenacious of life as those of the Rocky Mountains; they are very large.

The animals along the coast are the sea Lion, sea Elephant, Seals etc. There are an abundance of Prairie Wolves, Wolves of another kind also, very large. An animal is found here, called by the Spaniards the Lion, but I think it is the real Panther, it frequently kills horses, it latterly killed two on the place I have charge of.

Crows.—Buzzards and Vultures are large and numerous.

Musquitoes are not troublesome, excepting on the Bay of St. Francisco, and in the neighborhood of Marshes, Horseflies are not numerous or bad.

Here grows a Root in great abundance which answers every purpose of soap to wash with.[24]

### Travel and Hospitality of the Californios

It is true that the inhabitants and native Californians were the most hospitable

---

[22] *Journey*, pp. 31–34.     [23] Ibid., p. 39.     [24] Ibid., p. 42.

people in the world, that is, that I have ever seen or heard of. It cost you nothing in those days to travel all over California. They never pretended to charge you anything. You had to carry your own bedding to sleep on. They might give you a dry bullock hide to sleep on, but you had to have your own blankets. At the Mission they would give you a bedstead, or kind of rough frame with a bullock hide stretched over it, but no blankets, and you were always glad to get it. You had to carry your own knife with you, for they had no knives for guests. I will not say that the richer people did not have knives or forks. I think they did, but the common people did not have any, did not pretend to have any. And I very seldom saw a chair in the houses, sometimes a bench, but seldom a chair. But everybody expected to entertain strangers wherever night overtook them. And please remember that there were no hotels in those days. Not a hotel in all California, from San Diego to the Oregon line. The Missions, to an extent, took the place of hotels and always entertained people, but made no charge.[25]

The kindness and hospitality of the native Californians have not been overstated. Up to the time the Mexican regime ceased in California they had the custom of never charging for anything; that is to say, for entertainment—food, use of horses, etc. You were supposed, even if invited to visit a friend, to bring your blankets with you, and one would be very thoughtless if he traveled and did not take a knife with him to cut his meat. When you had eaten, the invariable custom was to rise, deliver to the women or hostess the plate on which you had eaten the meat and beans—for that was about all they had—and say, "*Muchas gracias, Senora*" ("Many thanks, madame"); and the hostess as invariably replied, "*Buen provecho*" ("May it do you much good").[26]

### DISTRUST OF AMERICANS

The native Californians seemed to have an inborn distrust of Americans. While nothing openly hostile to Americans occurred, yet their coming here met with no cordial welcome. In fact, it was quite natural that Americans should be unpopular on account of the war that had been raging for so many years in Texas.[27]

### MEXICAN CALIFORNIA'S MOST PREVALENT "DISEASE"

This country is surely a healthy one—I have known but one person to die, and it was the opinion generally the cause of his death was intemperance and want of exercise. I asked a respectable Physician, what disease prevailed most in California, he answered "the knife" having reference to the treacherous Spaniards. I have not seen one without a knife since I have been here, but I cannot say that I fear them—I too carry a knife and pistol.[28]

---

[25]*Pioneers*, pp. 11–12.
[26]Bidwell, "Life in California Before the Gold Discovery," pp. 170–71.
[27]*Pioneers*, p. 22.         [28]*Journey*, pp. 46–47.

### Ranchero Horsemanship

It is a proverb here (and I find a pretty true one) that a Spaniard will not do anything which he cannot do on horseback—he does not work perhaps on an average, one month in the year—he labors about a week, when he sows his wheat, and another week, when he harvests it, the rest of the time is spent riding about.[29]

The dexterity with which the Spaniards use the latso [lasso] is surprising, in fact, I doubt if their horsemanship is surpassed by the Cossacks of Tartary. It is a common thing for them to take up things from the ground going upon a full run with their horses, they will pick up a dollar in this way; they frequently encounter the Bear on the Plain in this way with their losas, and two holding him in opposite directions with ropes fastened to the Pomels of their saddles. I was informed that two young boys encountered a large buck Elk in the plains, & having no saddles fastened the ropes round the horses necks, and actually dragged the huge animal into the settlements alive.[30]

The California horses were good, for the purposes they used them, and they used them a great deal for they did almost everything on horseback. If a man had a pile of bullock hides and wished to remove them, no matter how short the distance, he would get on horseback, catch his lasso onto one of the hides, pull it to the place, then disengage his lasso, return for another, and so on, till he had taken all the hides away—without once dismounting his horse.[31]

You can ride a Mexican horse anywhere if you spur him.[32]

### Hunting Mountain Lion with Russian Muskets at Fort Ross

[Sutter's] purchase [of Fort Ross] included about two thousand head of cattle and horses, one little vessel of about twenty-five tons burden, forty or fifty old rusty cannon, and one or two hundred old flint-lock muskets, some of which Capt. Sutter recognized as French muskets, probably lost by Napoleon in 1812 on his way to Moscow. By the way, I once shot off one of those old muskets. On one occasion when out with two Indians our dogs treed a California lion. The lion stood one hundred and fifty feet above on two limbs looking down at us, till I sent for one of the old muskets and shot him. The recoil of that weapon nearly knocked me down, bruised my face, lamed my shoulder, and still lingers unfaded on the page of my memory.[33]

### Dismantling Fort Ross

My first occupation in California was at Bodega and Fort Ross, taking charge with Robert T. Ridley, who preceded me there, of the Russian property still remaining at those points, and removing the same as fast as practicable to Sutter's settle-

---

[29]Ibid., p. 38.   [30]Ibid., p. 43.   [31]*Pioneers*, p. 10.
[32]Bidwell, "Early California Reminiscences" (February 1904), p. 186.
[33]*Pioneers*, p. 20.

ment at Sacramento, whither everything was eventually transferred. (All the Indians on the coast at that time in the vicinity of the Fort, spoke the Russian language, the Spanish gradually superseding it.) There I remained about fourteen months. During that time my occupation consisted in demolishing the houses at Fort Ross, and shipping the lumber up the Sacramento River, and sending also everything in the shape of personal property. Russian plows, yokes, carts, house furniture, and every transportable that could be made useful at Sacramento were sent. The Russians had carried on farming and gardening to a limited extent, sowing some wheat, corn, potatoes, melons, and other things. There was an orchard and small vineyard belonging to a Russian nobleman called here "Don Jorge."

Sutter also had lumber sawed by hand in the redwoods near Bodega, and sent by sea in his schooner and up to Sacramento.[34]

### BIDWELL'S FIRST VISIT TO COLUSA AND CHICO AREAS: CHASING GRIZZLY BEARS

I might say that my first visit in 1843 to Colusa County and beyond was the result of a fortuitous circumstance. I had lost some animals at a place now known as Washington [Broderick], opposite Sacramento, when I was returning from Bodega to Sutter's Fort. I spent much time in endeavoring to recover them. I had scoured the Sacramento Valley for them, but could hear nothing of them, but heard of something which led to their discovery, viz., that a company had started for Oregon.

I was advised to overtake it. The leaving of a company for Oregon was an event, as I was advised, of sufficient importance to make people look out carefully for their horses. Sutter furnished an Indian to go with me. The company had been gone over a week. Peter Lassen, whose name now attaches to Lassen Peak and Lassen County, happened to be at this time at Sutter's Fort in search of a place to locate a ranch. He joined me to come up the valley for that purpose. At Hock Farm, on Feather River, forty miles from the fort, we took fresh horses, traveling as rapidly as possible. At a place now called Nicholas, on Feather River, a German named Joe Bruheim also joined us. We were on no trail, but simply pushed through the center of the valley. Approaching Butte Creek, we camped for the first time since leaving Hock Farm. Here we had an episode with grizzly bears, which will afford some idea of that region in its natural state.

In the spring of the year the bears chiefly lived on clover, which grew luxuriantly on the plains, especially in the little depressions [vernal pools] on the plains. We first saw one, which made for the timber two or three miles away; soon another, then more, all bounding away to the creek. At one time there were sixteen in the drove. Of course we chased, but had no desire to overtake them; there were too many of them. As we advanced, one, the largest of them all, diverged to the left.

---
[34]Bidwell, "Early California Reminiscences" (February 1904), p. 184.

I pursued him alone. He was the largest bear I have ever seen; his hair was long and shaggy, and I had the keenest desire to shoot him. I rode almost up to him, but every time I raised the gun to shoot, the horse would commence bucking. My desire to fire into him became so great that it overcame my prudence. I charged as near as I dare and dismounted, intending to give him a shot and mount again before he would get me, but the moment I alighted on the ground, it was all I could do to hold the horse, who jumped and plunged and sawed my hands with the rope. When I could look toward the bear, I found that he had stopped, reared on his hind legs, and was looking toward me and the horse. My hair, I think, stood straight up, and I was delighted when the bear turned and ran.

The Indian with us killed a large one, and skinned him, leaving all the fat on him, but the fat was always useful to us in frying our bread, taking the place of lard. Horses and mules are always frightened at bears or with the smell of bears. It was difficult to control the horses; they snorted and tried to get away all night. The next morning I took another lesson in the pastime of chasing a bear, a very large and swift one. When you chase a bear, you must run by his side and not immediately behind, for if he turns he can catch you more easily if you are directly behind than if you are at his side. I was chasing directly behind, and before I could turn, the bear turned, and was so close that his claws struck my horse's tail. Coming to better ground, I widened the distance between us. As soon as he began turning from me, I made after him, when I heard him plunge into the stream and swim across it. Stationing myself where I could see him when he got across, I waited and saw him as he gained the bank, standing on his hind legs. I shot, and the blood flew out of his nostrils two or three feet high, when he bounded off a hundred yards and fell dead. These scenes were a common occurrence, in fact, almost of hourly occurrence.

Hastening up the valley, we at last struck the trail of the Oregon company, on what is now known as the Rancho Chico, and to me the loveliest of places. The plains were dotted with scattering groves of spreading oak, while the clover and wild grasses, three or four feet high, were most luxuriant. The fertility of the soil was beyond question. The water of Chico Creek was cold, clear, and sparkling; the mountains, flower-covered and lovely. In my chase for stolen horses I had come across a country that was to me a revelation. And as I proceeded up the valley, through what was later Colusa County, and beyond it, I was struck with wonder and delight at this almost interminable land of promise.[35]

BIDWELL SEES CHICO AREA FOR THE FIRST TIME (A SECOND VERSION)

Hastening on up the valley we struck the trail of the Oregon company on what is now known as Chico Creek, Rancho Chico, and to me one of the loveliest of places. The plains were covered with scattered groves of spreading oaks; there

---
[35]Rogers, *Colusa County*, pp. 43–45.

were wild grasses and clover, two, three and four feet high, and most luxuriant. The fertility of the soil was beyond question, and the waters of Chico Creek were clear, cold, and sparkling; the mountains were lovely and flower-covered, a beautiful scene. In a word, this chase was the means of locating me for life. I never was permanently located till I located here, which was early in March, 1843.

It is not easy to conceive and understand the change in the condition of the country caused by the extensive pasture of horses and cattle in these plains. We seldom or never were out of sight of game, deer, elk, antelope, and grizzly bear. The snow-capped mountains on each side of the valley seen through the clear atmosphere of spring, the plains brilliant with flowers, the luxuriant herbage, all truly combined to lend enchantment to the view. In fact this valley, with two or three unimportant exceptions, was as new as when Columbus discovered America.[36]

## Remarks on John Sutter

Though I always esteemed Sutter for his many good traits, yet there was one peculiarity about him which I must mention. He never could keep a secret. Of course, Americans and others desired a change—something to take the place of the uncertain Mexican Government. Well, Hastings told his plans to Capt. Sutter as a great secret. Sutter took me aside and told me in the most solemn manner all that Hastings intended to do. "Now," said he, "my life is in your hands; tell this to no one for it would cost me my life." I promised that I would not, but it was not a week till I found Sutter had told everyone the same thing.[37]

Sutter was a man who treated everybody well, especially strangers. He had unbounded confidence in other men—in fact, too much, at times. Everyone was welcome at his table, and at his fort. I had more direct relations with him than many men. There was a man there, named Chas. W. Flugge, a German, who seemed to be an intimate friend of Sutter's. I was not as intimate with Sutter perhaps as Flugge, but he treated me with great consideration, gave me employment by sending me to Bodega, the Russian settlement, to take charge of his business there. It was quite a charge, considering that I was a very young man and an entire stranger. I never left his employ, but that he wanted me to return. He was a peculiar man, however. He would seem to have more confidence in strangers than in those more intimate with him. For instance: a fellow named Kinney came across the plains—a ruffian always fully armed, and continually threatening to shoot people, so that no one dared to cross him. Sutter employed him and put him in charge of his farm. The first thing the rascal did was to take 75 mares belonging to Sutter and brand them with his own name. Sutter declared that he must give the mares up, but could not get anyone to go up and deal with the fellow. I told him I would, and did. I had to go pretty well armed,

---

[36]Bidwell, "Early California Reminiscences" (February 1904), p. 187.
[37]*Pioneers*, p. 15.

but went quietly. I told him that he had to bring every one of those mares down and rebrand them. I stayed there until it was done. It was quite an undertaking, as I had no assistance.

Well, Kinney concluded that he would leave the country but he must have some cows, and other provisions, and offered to pay Sutter by selling him a "fine rifle." Rifles were little better than gold at the time. Knowing the fellow was a rascal, I was rather suspicious, asked him to let me try the gun. He was willing but wanted to load it himself. I took the gun, however, loaded it myself, shot it off and then brought it over to the blacksmith and had it taken apart. He did so, and I found that it was cracked inside, utterly worthless. I told Sutter that the gun had been burst and was worthless. "Well" he said, "I did say I would take it but I will not now." The next morning he came in the office, looking somewhat different than usual, and said "Give Mr. Kinney credit for $100." "Capt. Sutter what is it for?" "Well, I have taken the rifle; he said it was a good gun." I left his employ immediately. I did not know where to go to. Walked perhaps ten miles, revolving in my mind as to how I could get out of California. I had stood by Sutter many times when his life was in danger, and could not understand why he should believe a stranger's word before mine. I returned that night and Sutter begged me to remain.[38]

## Sutter's Death

Rancho Chico                                             June 28, 1880
My Dear Wife,

...Am glad you gave so much attention to Gen. Sutter, I was afraid, his remains might be sent away before you found out he was dead. It is a wonder Mrs. Reading was not at the funeral service. I suppose General Sutter was utterly destitute. It is too sad to think about!...

I would presume nothing would suit Mrs. Gen. Sutter as well as money, for she must be in need. She is no doubt a very kind lady, and was devoted to her husband. But she never seemed to me to be like him in any respect. That is to say, she was never attractive—could speak no language but German—had none of the courtly and pleasing refinement of her husband—was very tall, and not prepossessing &c. But she is entitled to unfeigned sympathy and cheerful aid. It will be a shame if she be allowed to suffer....

    y.a.h. [your affectionate husband]
        John Bidwell[39]

My Dear Wife,

...I have felt very sad about Gen. Sutter's death; and yet I forgot to raise the flag at half mast today.[40]

---

[38]JB-91, pp. 11–12.    [39]JB-CSL, b. 55, f. 17.    [40]Ibid., b. 55, f. 12.

### BIDWELL'S ESTIMATE OF SUTTER

... It seems almost a mockery to starve the noble pioneer to death, and starve his broken hearted wife to death also, and then immediately proceed to do grand things to perpetuate his memory. The State of California can never efface the stain of ingratitude for withdrawing the pittance of aid once extended him. No pioneer ever did so much for this State as Sutter. More, I verily believe no pioneer ever did so much for the United States, and that few men in modern times have done so much for the world at large, as General Sutter. He suffered almost every hardship incident to pioneer life. Dangers on every side. Obstacles almost innumerable confronted him. But ever trying, persevering, struggling, never discouraged, the fruit of all his labors emerged in the discovery of gold at his saw mill in February 1848, which made our country rich, benefited all countries, and ushered in an era of prosperity such as the world has never seen....

Sutter was a man of hospitality in the largest sense. There were no hotels in those days. All who came staid at his fort and ate at his table free of charge, no matter how short or long the stay might be.

Considering his limited means, he was a man of great—I may say boundless—enterprise. He had a faculty of inaugurating many kinds of business, and, though often failing by reason of dry seasons and other reverses, he never faltered or became discouraged, but went forward without taking into consideration, seemingly, the possibility of failure in the future. In the light of what he accomplished Sutter had large business capacity. But his hope in the future always led him to undertake too much....

Sutter was a man of fine presence and agreeable deportment. When I first saw him in 1841 he surpassed in many respects any man I have ever known. He spoke several languages [such] as German, French, Spanish, English, etc. and all of them most politely. As a conversationalist he was entertaining, and at home in refined and intelligent company. There was nothing of the egotist about him. Courteous and princely in manner himself, he listened respectfully to others, and made everyone his friend. His politeness was ingrained—he was the same to all, the high and lowly, poor and rich—the Governor, the workman in his shop, the wild Indian, each felt equally at ease in his presence.

And this pleasing address was largely his capital, and gained him confidence and credit. His promises were made in good faith, and no man ever strove harder to meet them, though he often failed to do so at maturity....

While we cannot recall the past and remedy the wrongs the great pioneer suffered in his lifetime, we can and ought to do honor to his memory....[41]

---

[41]JB to Capt. W. F. Swasey, 12 March 1881, in Jane Grabhorn, ed., *Pioneers of the Sacramento: A Group of Letters by and about Johann Augustus Sutter, James W. Marshall, and John Bidwell* (San Francisco: Book Club of California, 1953), pp. 26–33.

Sutter ought to have been the richest man in California, but he died poor—almost literally starved to death at Washington, the capital of the nation.[42]

### Remarks on Robert Livermore

... I started off traveling south, and came to what is now called Livermore Valley, then known as Livermore's Ranch, belonging to Robert Livermore, a native of England. He had left a vessel when a mere boy, and had married and lived like the native Californians, and, like them, was very expert with the lasso. Livermore's was the frontier ranch, and more exposed than any other to the ravages of the Horse-thief Indians of the Sierra Nevada. That valley was full of wild cattle,—thousands of them—and they were more dangerous to one on foot, as I was, than grizzly bears.[43]

The people I found at Sutter's belonged to various nationalities. Robert Livermore had charge of the stock, cattle, and horses, of which Sutter had about two thousand head. This same Livermore had a farm in Livermore Valley (now in Alameda County), and gave his name to it. He was a runaway English sailor and had grown up in this country, was familiar with the customs of the people, and spoke the Spanish language fluently.

Without imputing dishonesty to the people—cattle and horses were so plentiful that the loss of one was scarcely noticed. Herds of them roamed at will; they got mixed up, and unlawful appropriation was not uncommon, and sometimes designedly. Livermore was, as I have said, a stockman, and there was quite a competition between him and a neighbor in the pride of owning the largest herd or securing the greatest number of hides. One day, so the story ran at the time, a friend of Livermore's hurried breathlessly, telling Livermore that his competing neighbor had just killed one of his, Livermore's, bullocks, and if he would be quick about it he would catch him in the act of skinning it. Livermore coolly replied, "No, I'm too busy just now skinning one of his bullocks myself."[44]

### Locating the Larkin Grant

Thomas O. Larkin was a prominent American in California when I arrived in 1841. He lived in Monterey and had a store there, probably the largest in California. His children were Americans, the father and mother both Americans (the wife being the only American woman in California, except Mrs. Kelsey, who came in our party). He wished to obtain for them from the Mexican Government a grant of land of ten or twelve square leagues. For this purpose I engaged to find him a tract, and began explorations about July, 1844. I ascended the valley on the west side of the Sacramento River as far as Colusa, having with me

---

[42]JB to Johnson, 7 September 1890, The Robert Underwood Johnson Papers, BANC.
[43]Bidwell, "Life in California Before the Gold Discovery," p. 164.
[44]Rogers, *Colusa County*, pp. 38–39.

one man only, and he an Indian who had been civilized in Mission San Solano, in Sonoma Valley.... Finding no considerable extent of level land in the mountains, I mapped out the Larkin grant on the Sacramento River above Colusa in Colusa County.[45]

### BIDWELL OBTAINS COLUSA AND ULPINOS GRANTS

In 1844 I went to Monterey and made application for a grant of land at the mouth of the Sacramento river, the Ul Pinos ranch, and in due time the Governor issued a title to me. In the fall of the same year I began a settlement on it. It was just below those immense tule marshes. I found the mosquitos so bad that after living there for some time, I was so sick from the loss of blood that I could scarcely walk. I went with Sutter to Monterey, leaving an Indian and his wife in charge of the place. I did not settle there again, but finding the mosquitos so bad, the next year I made application for two leagues of land, where Colusa now is. That was granted to me by Gov. Pio Pico, so that I had two grants made to me. At the time I saw the land where I now am, I was looking after some horses which had been stolen by a company on its way to Oregon, but my former companion, Mr. Dickey had been up there, and wanted a grant of the land. In those days we never interfered with one another. I was asked by the Governor if there was a tract of land I liked better than that in Colusa; I told him there was, but that Mr. Dickey had confided to me his application for it, and of course, I would not take it, so I got a title for him. Later I bought him out. Never settled on the Colusa grant, and afterwards sold it for $2,000. It must be worth now about a million dollars. When the secretary asked me to take any other land, I asked for five leagues, he told me to take ten, but I thought five was all I could handle; yet I could have had ten if I wanted. I have never bought land at any time that I did not want for my own use, yet I am ranked among the land monopolists. I am really opposed to land monopoly.[46]

### BIDWELL ADVISES JOHN TOWNSEND ON SECURING A LAND GRANT

John Townsend                                New Helvetia, Nov. 27, 1845
Dear Sir,

Your very friendly and interesting letter (not signed) duly came to hand. I approve of your prudence in thus communicating, and must return my sincere thanks for the interest which you take in our safety and welfare.

The storm however, I hope has partially past, but we cannot, in the face of such threats even from the Supreme Gov't, be [unreadable] and unconcerned. Our interests are identical and we must be united.

I now send you the map of this land adjoining Capt. Sutter and have obtained

---
[45]Bidwell, "Early California Reminiscences" (April 1904), pp. 377, 379.
[46]JB-91, pp. 58–59.

the favorable information of Capt. Sutter,—I have dated it 1846, and left the <u>day</u> and <u>month</u> blank,—as this paper is not to be presented until after you become a citizen—where the day of the month is to be inserted I have put in pencil mark 1, and the month 2, which you can get done by some one in whom you have confidence. You will also have to make out another petition to the Governor to accompany this one, but this is all to be done after you get your citizenship. I would write you a petition for citizenship; but, it will cost you not much to get it done in Monterey. I could do a number of things for you, were you present.

Please [do] not show this paper to any one, except when you get your citizenship, and then to a person whom you can trust, to fill out the dates in Spanish, for it would not do to expose Capt. Sutter's name in an official document with <u>blank dates</u>.

You must excuse me for not sending the other plan of the land on the San Joaquin—you have no idea how much engaged I have been since the arrival of the company from the U.S. But in a short time I will forward it. Capt. Sutter now leaves for the Yerba Buena, to return in a few days.

If you can obtain a grant of land on the San Joaquin, say of 18, 25, 30 or even of 50, leagues on such conditions that if you put on the said land, certain number of families, within one or two years, and then if you should not in that time fulfill the requisition, to have your obligations—null, leaving you free from all responsibility, I would heartily approve of the measure.

It should be stated in the title to the grant, that the number of leagues, should be selected from the vacant land lying between the Calaveras, and the head of the San Joaquin, I mean on the E. side of the river to where it comes out of the mountains. There might be a hundred leagues of good land selected in this extent, if the gov't would be willing to grant so much.

We received Castro with a salute of 7 guns, and as much friendship as we were able to show. I hope you have received your wagon safe by this time.

My respects to Mrs. Townsend & Mr. Shallanberger,

I remain Dear Sir, Yours most truly,<br>John Bidwell

P.S. Perhaps they may try to persuade you that it is necessary to become a Catholic in order to the getting of a citizenship; but do not believe them for I particularly asked the Mexican commissioner, on this subject.[47]

### Traveling with Peter Lassen

Peter was a singular man, very industrious, very ingenious, and very fond of pioneering—in fact, of the latter stubbornly so. He had great confidence in his own power as a woodsman, but, strangely enough, he always got lost. As we passed

---

[47] Grace Nelson Papers, b. 1, f. 36. HUNT.

Butte Mountain going south, our route of course lay between the Sacramento and Feather Rivers. The point we wished to reach that night was Sutter's Hock Farm, on Feather River. Night had overtaken us when some fifteen miles from it. Peter Lassen insisted on keeping the lead. Our Indian vaquero, however, who knew the country well in that vicinity, pointed to the eastward as the way we should go. Lassen, however, could not be persuaded to diverge to the east, and finally at midnight we concluded to tell him he must go to the east or we would leave him. But this had no effect on Lassen; he kept on to the south, while we, following the Indian, came to the farm.

The only place Lassen could reach was the intervening tule marsh. Now if you have any curiosity to observe a man's humor after being in a tule swamp full of mosquitoes all night, you ought to have seen Peter Lassen. The next morning, when he came to camp at Hock Farm, he was so mad he would not speak to any of us; would not travel the same path, but kept a hundred yards to either side of us all day. I think he never forgot nor forgave us. Still he was a man possessed of many good qualities. He was always obliging in camp. He was a good cook and would do any and everything necessary to the comfort of the camp, even to the making of coffee, provided those traveling with him would pretend to assist. If they did not offer to aid him, they became the target for the best style of grumbling that any man born in Denmark was capable of inventing. Of course, everyone would offer to assist him, and that is all one had to do, for then Lassen was sure to drive him away, and do everything himself, even to staking the tent.[48]

### FREMONT CONFRONTS AND INSULTS SUTTER

... Sutter and Fremont met, face to face, for the first time since Fremont, a month before, had passed on his way towards Oregon. I do not know what words passed between them; I was near, but did not hear. This, however, I know, that Sutter had become elated, as all Americans were, with the idea that what Fremont was doing meant California for the United States. But in a few minutes Sutter came to me greatly agitated, with tears in his eyes, and said that Fremont had told him he was a Mexican, and that if he did not like what he (Fremont) was doing he could set himself across the San Joaquin River and he could go and join the Mexicans. But, this flurry over, Sutter was soon himself again, and resumed his normal attitude of friendship towards Fremont, because he thought him to be acting in accordance with instructions from Washington.[49]

### BIDWELL CLAIMS FREMONT STARTED BEAR FLAG REVOLT
### TO TRIGGER WAR WITH MEXICO

Fremont's hasty departure for Oregon and [Lt. Archibald] Gillespie's pursuit of him had been the occasion of many surmises. Fremont's sudden return excited

---
[48]Rogers, *Colusa County*, pp. 47–48.
[49]Bidwell, "Fremont in the Conquest of California" (February 1891), p. 520.

increased curiosity. People flocked to his camp: some were settlers, some were hunters; some were good men, and some about as rough specimens of humanity as it would be possible to find anywhere. Fremont, hearing that the horses were passing, sent a party of these promiscuous people and captured them. This of course was done before he had orders or any positive news that war had been declared. When Gillespie left the United States, as the bearer of a dispatch to Larkin and Fremont and of letters to the latter, war had not been declared. The letters included one from Senator Benton, who had the confidence and knew the purposes of the Administration. As Gillespie had to make his way through Mexico, he committed the dispatch and his orders to memory, destroyed them, and rewrote them on the vessel which took him, *via* the Sandwich Islands, to the coast of California. There had been no later arrival, and therefore no later dispatches to Fremont were possible. Though Fremont was reticent, whatever he did was supposed to be done with the sanction of the United States. Thus, without giving the least notice even to Sutter, the great friend of Americans, or to Americans in general, scattered and exposed as they were all over California, he precipitated the war.[50]

Fremont reached Butte Mountains, now in Sutter county, and encamped. Hunters and settlers in the valley immediately flocked to his camp to see what was up. It so happened at that time a band of horses, belonging, in part, to the Mexican forces, had been collected on the north of the Bay of San Francisco, and, in charge of Lieut. Arce, of the Mexican service, was on the way to Castro, going from Sonoma by way of Sacramento to the Santa Clara Valley. Here was an opportunity for Fremont to have revenge on Castro. He sent and seized these horses, which was an act of war and precipitated at once hostilities upon this coast. Fremont, it is presumed, did this upon the strength of his dispatches, the purport of which, so far as we have been able to learn, was that war was imminent between the United States and Mexico. Before Fremont knew this, however, his first act had actually precipitated the war, which he was obliged to follow up by sending and capturing Sonoma, and taking the leading men, viz: General Vallejo, Jacob P. Leese, and Victor Prudon, prisoners, and bringing them to Sacramento and Sutter's Fort, and raiding generally all the settlers on the north of the Bay of San Francisco, with all the forces at his command. It was more than a month after the first blow was struck before Fremont, or any one on the coast, actually knew that war existed between the United States and Mexico.[51]

Previously, however, to the coming of the intelligence, and while I was still at Sonoma, the war which Fremont waged was, as Fremont well knew, premature and without authority, but as it had begun, to carry it on was a necessity, and to find an excuse for it was an obligation. Hence, we were all called together by Fremont at Sonoma, on the 4th or 5th of July, 1846, to consider what, under

---

[50]Ibid., p. 519.   [51]Bidwell, "Early California Reminiscences" (July 1904), p. 79.

the circumstances, was to be done. We all felt that we could not go back. Fremont was willing to help all he could, provided it could be done under the pretext of defending American residents here in California against pretended threats of expulsion by the Mexican authorities.[52]

In past years rumors of threats against Americans in California had been rather frequent, several times causing them and other foreigners to hasten in the night from all places within one or two hundred miles to Sutter's Fort, sometimes remaining a week or two, drilling and preparing to resist attack. The first scare of this kind occurred in 1841, when Sutter became somewhat alarmed; the last, in 1845. But in every case such rumors had proved to be groundless, so that Americans had ceased to have apprehensions, especially in the presence of such an accessible refuge as Sutter's Fort. And now, in 1846, after so many accessions by immigration, we felt entirely secure, even without the presence of a United States officer and his exploring force of sixty men, until we found ourselves suddenly plunged into a war. But hostilities having been begun, bringing danger where none before existed, it now became imperative to organize. It was in everyone's mouth (and I think must have come from Fremont) that the war was begun in defense of American settlers! This was simply a pretense to justify the premature beginning of the war, which henceforth was to be carried on in the name of the United States.[53]

### The "Bear Flag"

Another man left at Sonoma was William L. Todd, who painted, on a piece of brown cotton, a yard and a half or so in length, with old red or brown paint that he happened to find, what he intended to be a representation of a grizzly bear. This was raised to the top of the staff, some seventy feet from the ground. Native Californians looking up at it were heard to say "*Coche*," the common name among them for a pig or shoat.[54]

So much has been said and written about the "Bear Flag" that some may conclude it was something of importance. It was not so regarded at the time: it was never adopted at any meeting or by any agreement; it was, I think, never even noticed, perhaps never seen, by Fremont when it was flying. The naked old Mexican flagstaff at Sonoma suggested that something should be put on it. Todd had painted it, and others had helped put it up, for mere pastime. It had no importance to begin with, none whatever when the Stars and Stripes went up, and never would have been thought of again had not an officer of the navy seen it in Sonoma and written a letter about it.[55]

---

[52]Ibid., p. 80.
[53]Bidwell, "Fremont in the Conquest of California" (February 1891), p. 522.
[54]Ibid., p. 520.    [55]Ibid., p. 522, note 1.

## First Phase of Mexican War in California

The first conquest of California, in 1846, by the Americans, with the exception of the skirmish at Petaluma and another towards Monterey, was achieved without a battle. We simply marched all over California from Sonoma to San Diego and raised the American flag without opposition or protest. We tried to find an enemy, but could not. So Kit Carson and Ned Beale were sent East, bearing dispatches from Commodore Stockton announcing the entire conquest of California by the United States.[56]

## Mexican War unjust

If there ever was an unjust war in this world, it was that war. It was an unjustifiable war.[57]

## An unflattering portrait of Ezekiel Merritt

Merritt, the quartermaster, could neither read nor write. He was an old mountaineer, and trapper, lived with an Indian squaw, went clad in buckskin fringed after the style of the Rocky Mountain Indians. He chewed tobacco to a disgusting excess, and stammered badly. He had a reputation for bravery because of his continual boasting of his prowess in killing Indians. The handle of the tomahawk he carried had nearly a hundred notches to record the number of his Indian scalps. He drank deeply whenever he could get liquor. Stockton said to him: "Major Merritt" (for he was now major), "make out a requisition for some money, say two thousand dollars. You will need about that amount at the start." . . . Major Reading wrote the requisition and Merritt got the money, two thousand Mexican silver dollars. That afternoon I met him in Monterey, nearly as drunk as he could be. He said, "Bidwell I am rich; I have lots of money"; and putting both hands into the deep pockets of his buckskin breeches he brought out two handfuls of Mexican dollars, saying, "Here, take this, and if you can find anything to buy, buy it, and when you want more money come to me, for I have got lots of it."

Merritt was never removed from his office or rank, but simply fell into disuse, and was detailed, like subordinate officers and men, to perform other duties, generally at the head of small scouting parties. Merritt's friends—for he must have had friends to recommend him for quartermaster—in some way managed to fix up the accounts relating to the early administration of his office. In fact, I tried to help them myself, but I believe that all of us together were never able to find, within a thousand dollars, what Merritt had done with the money. How he ever came to be recommended for quartermaster was to every one a mystery. Perhaps some of the current theories that subsequently prevailed might have had in them just a shade of truth, namely, that somebody entertained the idea that quartermaster meant the ability and duty to quarter the beef![58]

---

[56] Ibid., p. 523.   [57] Hunt, p. 131.
[58] Bidwell, "Fremont in the Conquest of California" (February 1891), p. 523.

### Raising the American Flag

As soon as it was known that the American flag had been raised in Monterey it superseded the Bear Flag and was raised at Sacramento and all places in possession of the Americans. Commodore Stockton had already arrived at Monterey.... Commodore Sloat was still there but Stockton having come to supersede him, soon left on his return to the United States. Commodore Stockton took full charge, advised and authorized the organization of the California Battalion, commissioning Fremont as Major, Gillespie as Capt. and appointing and commissioning other officers.... Within three days Commodore Sloat had left and we were all on board the United States sloop of war *Cyanne* en route for San Diego. ... Fremont and the Battalion reached San Diego about the last of July and met with no opposition in landing and immediately raised the flag of the U.S.

In a few days we were on the march for Los Angeles, our route lay through the Mission of San Luis Rey, San Juan Capistrano and Santa Anita. No hostile demonstrations were observed anywhere on that march. When we arrived at Los Angeles, we found Com. Stockton already there. He had proceeded with the frigate *Congress*, his flagship, to San Pedro, landed a force of sailors and marines and marched to Los Angeles without meeting the enemy.[59]

### Premature Claims of Conquering California

It was rumored and believed that Pio Pico the Gov. had fled to Mexico and that [General Jose] Castro was somewhere in the region of Los Angeles planning resistance, but where no one could tell. Other reports said that both Pio Pico and Castro had fled to Sonora. The native Cal. were everywhere friendly and in a word the country was considered conquered.

For greater certainty, however, Fremont returned by another route to wit: via Rancho Chino, and Temecula to San Diego. Stockton and his force in due time returned on board their ships but not without providing military occupancy of Los Angeles. On Fremont's return to Los A[ngeles] later in August, Stockton, considering the country conquered, determined to appoint him—Fremont—Gov. of Ca.... During Fremont's trip to the north, Capt. Gillespie with a small force was left in command of Los Angeles. Lieut. [Theodore] Talbot with a few men was stationed at Santa Barbara. Dispatches had already gone from Stockton and I think from Fremont too by special courier overland via New Mexico to wit: Kit Carson to the effect that Cal. was conquered and the American flag floating at every principal point.

Carson met Gen. Kearny with five hundred men on his way to aid in the conquest of California. Learning that the country was already conquered, Kearny with one hundred men as an escort went in advance, bringing back Carson as a guide and forwarding Stockton's dispatches by other means, and leaving the

---
[59]JB-77, pp. 176–79.

remainder of his force to follow him more slowly to California, under Colonel [Philip St. George] Cook.

Scarcely three weeks had elapsed after Fremont's departure for the north when the whole country south of Monterey rose in revolt. Castro and Pio Pico had certainly ere this fled but other leaders were not wanting. [Jose Maria] Flores and Andres Pico were just the men to lead in such a revolt. Gillespie at Los Angeles was besieged and had to capitulate and retire on board a vessel.

One of the conditions I remember was that he should leave his cannon at the place of embarkation, San Pedro. He did so but spiked them first. Talbot at Santa Barbara also retreated.

A skirmish took place at Rancho Chino when the detachment of Americans surrendered after the killing of a sergeant. The sergeant was on the side of the Californians.[60]

### BIDWELL PLACED IN CHARGE OF MISSION SAN LUIS REY

[In August 1846] I was appointed by him [Fremont] as magistrate of the district of San Louis Rey and directed to take possession of the Mission and to make an inventory of the property, caring for the same, examining into the title to the property, protecting the Indians and so on.... During all this time my situation at San Louis Rey, without any force to protect me, was by no means comfortable. Wild rumors came to me daily in regard to the rise and progress of the [Californio] revolt. No neighbor among the California population could be depended on for information or assistance.

The Indians, however, were faithful. It was not long after I went to San Louis Rey before owners of ranches came to reclaim Indians, asking me to command them to return to their service, generally on the ground of indebtedness and of their right to make the demand, because of the laws and customs of the country which obtained under Mexican rule. These applications were invariably refused by me and highly appreciated by the Indians. In a word, the Indians, by this course, had become my friends and they were friendly to the American cause. They were willing to take up arms and fight against the Californians, upon whom they looked as oppressors. But I had nothing with which to arm them. I succeeded however in placing in the hands of a few three or four bayonets and several long spikes fastened on long poles to answer as spears and some furnished themselves with bows and arrows. With these faithful recruits I was able to keep faithful guard and send out as far as they could be induced to go, to learn of the events transpiring in the direction of Los Angeles and elsewhere.

I take this occasion to bear testimony to the fact that the information thus received was truthful beyond my expectation and almost invariably verified. In this way I had learned of Gillespie's capitulation at Los Angeles, of the surren-

---

[60]Ibid., pp. 179–83.

der at Rancho Chino, and later of the approach of danger. I wish to bear testimony also to the friendship and timely warning received at the hands of Don Juan Forster of San Juan Capistrano which were greatly appreciated.

The Indians at the Mission of San Louis Rey were by no means wild and untutored. They had lived, many, if not most of them, at the Mission from infancy, and had been taught to do all kinds of work by Padre Antonio Peyri, the founder of the Mission. Him they had loved with a friendship truly wonderful.

When the achievement of her independence by Mexico brought about a new order of things in California, it required but little sagacity to see the downfall of all the missions, and that in the no distant future. This priest, so loved by the Indians, rather than wait and see the beautiful Mission which he had erected, destroyed, resolved to leave California forever and return to Europe. But the Indians would not suffer him to go and watched him for weeks to prevent his leaving. In a dark night at last Peyri succeeded in eluding the friendly vigilance of the Indians and embarking at San Diego on board the vessel which was to bear him from the coast. From one who aided him in his escape, it was told that on gaining the high hill in front of the Mission he looked back, knelt down and made a prayer blessing the Mission.

I found these Indians very intelligent; most could speak the Spanish tongue fluently. Some could read. One, a chief named Samuel, was not only fluent but eloquent, and no Mexican to my knowledge had so fine a command of the Spanish language.

In addition to the other preparations for defense I had a small three pound iron cannon, old and rusty. This I mounted on wheels as best I could, loaded it with rifle powder and pieces of iron in place of balls and kept inside of the front door of the main building. In another room of the mission building I kept a horse saddled nights as well as by day. At last when from reliable information I knew Flores with one hundred and fifty men to be at Santa Margarita—the ranch of Governor Pio Pico—only two leagues distant on his march southward, I made my escape in the night to San Diego. Just before starting, however, I called Samuel and told him I was going to San Diego and that the Indians must disperse for awhile till the Americans should put down the revolt as they surely would. Samuel helped me to take the little cannon from its carriage and drop it in the black mud just below the spring about one hundred yards distant from the mission building. No one saw us and I charged him not to tell the Californians where it was, or even the other Indians. I had scarcely gone as I afterwards learned when Flores and his forces arrived. They inquired for the cannon and when they could not learn where it was, Flores threatened to shoot Samuel and another Indian chief named Andres who were the principal men. They were tied, told they had only so many minutes to live unless they would tell where the cannon was. Guns were raised and pointed at their breasts. They remained faithful to the last. Flores however thought it best not to shoot them and they were set free.[61]

### BESIEGED IN SAN DIEGO AND SAILING TO SAN PEDRO FOR HELP

Flores near approach [to San Diego] caused us to go on board of the little whale ship *Stonington* which happened to be in the harbor whither it had put in almost in distress by want of bread and other supplies. Entering that port for such a purpose was strange, nothing could have been wider of the mark for San Diego had absolutely nothing.

Flores without resistance soon occupied the town. Some of the native Californians at San Diego had been from the time of Fremont's first arrival in California friendly to the American cause. Some of these left San Diego for their ranches in the country and some took refuge with us on board the whale ship. Among these were notably Don Miguel de Pedro Rena [Pedrorena] and Don Santiago Arguello.

Several brass cannon spiked during some Mexican revolution years before were found near the entrance of the harbor. Two of these were brought on board the whale ship and the work of drilling out the spikes and mounting them began.

But having brought on board nothing in the shape of provisions we were rapidly exhausting the little remnant belonging to the ship. An effort must be made to go for aid, I volunteered to go up the coast in a whale boat which was furnished by the ship with a crew of four men. A Mr. Russell of San Diego volunteered to go with me. We reached the harbor of San Pedro with a fair wind in about thirty hours without any incidents worthy of note, except in passing San Juan Capistrano we attempted to land and were fired at by a detachment of soldiers left there by Flores.

In the harbor of San Pedro our eyes were gladdened by the unexpected sight of several vessels. Stockton with the frigate *Congress* and *Savannah* had arrived and one or more merchants vessels. Stockton with all the available force at his command consisting of Gillespie and his forces who had so recently capitulated and embarked on a vessel, and all the sailors and marines which he could spare from his ships, were in plain view on the march to retake Los Angeles. The California forces were apparently in front and on both flanks and the cannon of both sides were cannonading each other.

Captain [William] Mervine had as I then learned attempted a few days previously to march to Los Angeles but the Californians had succeeded in compelling him to retreat or retire on board the ships.

Having acquainted the officers in command of the vessels at San Pedro with our condition at San Diego, that relief might be sent as soon as possible and having laden a whale boat with such supplies as it could carry, I set out after a

---

[61]Ibid., pp. 181–89.

stay of only two hours to return to San Diego. Previous to leaving San Diego I provided myself with the means of leaving a message at San Pedro acquainting any vessel of our destitute condition at San Diego. This was in the form of a written statement sealed in a bottle and placed in a keg which was to be anchored in the harbor in case I should find no vessel there and have to proceed on up the coast to Monterey or further for relief.

Soon after setting out from San Pedro a most fearful storm arose from the south-west. Finding it impossible to come under the lee of Santa Catalina all our energies were taxed to keep off the iron-bound coast between San Pedro and San Juan Capistrano. Many times our boat filled almost to the brim, everything was thrown overboard to lighten it, including all our bread and water and other provisions. With a heavy wind before daylight came rain. The fatigue of that night exhausted our strength, the darkness was terrific, our only light the breaking waves.

Day dawned, the wind lulled, but the waves continued high while our condition was perilous, and our progress very slow. At sundown, however, San Diego was reached. All were glad to hear of the movements at San Pedro and that relief would soon be sent to us.

The storm had been so heavy that all were hoping that we were in some secure place—or harbor. The Capt. of the whale ship was surprised to learn that we had weathered it and had said before our arrival that unless we were in some harbor we were surely lost.

Among other things thrown overboard was the communication in the keg. The finding of vessels at San Pedro doing away with the necessity of leaving it anchored in the harbor. Subsequently we learned that an Indian found the keg upon the shore. Carrying it by the old mission of San Juan Capistrano where some of Flores men were stationed, it was taken from him, opened and the communication read. Believing that he was secretly carrying messages for the enemy, he was shot by the Californians as a spy.[62]

### Retaking San Diego

The cannon were taken ashore the next day and twenty-five men including some of the sailors of the whale ship began the march to retake the town of San Diego three miles distant.

The way lay all the way through soft sand, the dragging of the cannon, was very difficult, requiring most of the way all the men to move a single piece. When about half way our movements were discovered. Flores came out with his men in line of battle, all were mounted.

But our march continued without the slightest hesitation, one of the brass pieces being hauled a hundred yards or so was left in charge of three or four men.

---

[62]Ibid., pp. 189–95.

While they were aiming and firing, the rest went back to bring up the other and so on alternately, loading and firing till Flores fled with all his force and we entered and took possession of the town, raising the flag where it has floated from that day to this.

At that time all the country between San Diego and Monterey was in a state of revolt. Stockton also had failed to repossess Los Angeles and the flag floated at no place south of Monterey except at San Diego.[63]

### A FINAL SKIRMISH IN SAN DIEGO

In a word the country had to be reconquered or rather I should say conquered, for all operations or nearly so, worthy of the name war were yet to come. Fremont was directed to raise a force in the north and march to the south while Stockton with all his vessels, sailors and marines was to come to San Diego for the purpose of filling out an expedition to march to retake Los Angeles.

The day before the arrival of the *Magnolia* some men of Flores appeared on the hill overlooking the old town of San Diego with a small cannon about the size of the one I had sunk in the mud at San Luis Rey, and with it annoyed us by firing first point blank into the enclosure of adobe walls, which we had made our headquarters.

Twelve of us started for the hill, the remainder holding possession of our post. The little piece of artillery on the hill was loaded and fired three times as we ascended the hill upon the run, as well as many shots from smaller arms.

But the missiles every time passed over our heads and when we reached the top of the hill the cannon of the Californians was loaded and primed for another shot and was only abandoned when we were within fifty feet from it.

The Californians retreated pell-mell down the hill to the north and then our cannon was instantly reversed and fired at them, killing a horse. The next day on the arrival of Gillespie, some of the Californians were still in sight but on the more distant hills.[64]

### THE BATTLE OF SAN PASCUAL

In the meantime, Gen. Kearny with his escorts arrived at Aqua Caliente. Mr. Stokes living in the vicinity brought a letter from Kearny to Stockton, announcing his arrival. Stockton immediately sent Capt. Gillespie with about forty men to meet, welcome, and escort him to San Diego.

Camping for the night together they heard of a small force under Andres Pico at San Pascual. Kit Carson had led Gen. Kearny to believe the country already conquered and even if it were not so, a hundred men would be ample to overcome any force the Californians would bring into the field against them. Kearny had supplied a portion of his escort with such fresh animals as he had been able

---

[63]Ibid., pp. 195–96.     [64]Ibid., pp. 197–98.

to procure, most still had to use the jaded animals which they had brought with them.

It was proposed to start next morning a little before day, attack the Californians under Andres Pico while sleeping and signalize the march by an easy and brilliant victory. Unfortunately, the Californians were early risers and rose even earlier than the Americans. In the mist and darkness of the early morning they went to attack the alert and dashing cavalry of Andres Pico.

Kearny ordered a charge. His men who had fresh horses out-ran the others and thus his forces became scattered and an easy prey to the horsemen of the Californians.

The result was the battle of San Pascual in which twenty-two of Kearny's men lay dead upon the field including two Captains and a Lieut. and Kearny himself was severely wounded.[65]

### Conflicts between Kearny and Stockton

The relations of Stockton and Gen. Kearny at first were very cordial, so much so, that when the subject as to who should be in chief command was first breached at a complimentary dinner given by Commodore Stockton to Gen. Kearny both said in a complimentary way that the other should have the leadership.... there is no doubt Gen. Kearny believed himself entitled to the command provided he should recover so as to be able to go on the march. And this in virtue of his rank and duty as an army officer, on land as well as in accordance with his more recent instructions and the object of his coming to this coast.

And that Stockton believed himself entitled to command either by virtue of his having been longer on the coast and once conquered the country as well as his having a larger part of the forces composed of sailors and marines, or by the deference expressed by Kearny at the dinner table, or for all these reasons: from that time on all of Stockton's orders showed that he considered himself in command.

Gen. Kearny too manifested his disposition to command and both soon knew the disposition of the other.

The day we left San Diego on the march towards Los Angeles, I as the Quarter Master of the forces received orders from both and as far as I could I obeyed both. Sometimes when I desired to report to Com. Stockton, Purser Speiden always near and generally the medium of communication with Stockton, would tell me to see and report to Gen. Kearny saying that the Commodore was engaged, or asleep, or very nervous. But Stockton would have his own way and was determined to command and did command.

To the observant, a conflict was growing between them from the beginning

---
[65]Ibid., pp. 199–201.

of the march. Sometimes I thought I could see Gen. Kearny bite his lips with rage.

At a time when we were on the march and about half way to Los Angeles a white flag was seen. Stockton and his staff were in advance and went out to meet it. Gen. Kearny had observed their action and as soon as Stockton dropped back near Kearny I heard the latter say: "Commodore, what flag was that?" Stockton answered in effect that Flores had sent a message, making a certain proposition (which I did not distinctly hear) and added, "I told him I would agree to no such thing and that if I caught him I would hang him."

Gen. Kearny suppressed his rage but looked offended and exasperated and made no further reply.[66]

## The Battle of San Gabriel

Further on the march to wit: at the San Gabriel River when the enemy had captured all the horses of one of our companies and at least six hundred strong were in the attitude of disputing our passage. Gen. Kearny ordered some of the guns to be unlimbered to protect our crossing. But Stockton immediately countermanded the order and directed baggage and cannon to ford the stream.

There is no doubt that Kearny's order was right and strictly in accordance with military usage, for had the Californians availed themselves of that moment to attack us while fording the river they could certainly have almost accomplished our defeat, as it was however, our forces rushed across, Stockton at the head—and gained the bluff on the opposite bank firing all the time as opportunity would permit, in time to see the whole force of Californians in full retreat. Two of our men were killed and several wounded.

All were much elated over our victory. The Californians had lost their best opportunity for attacking us. That ford with its quick-sand dangers and with our heavily laden Mexican carts afforded the enemy to strike us at a disadvantage.

Stockton's dash and the successful result were considered by his devoted friends as something brilliant. Stockton himself was brave, resolute, and impetuous and the men caught his spirit and charged across the river feeling confident of success.[67]

## Final victory

The next day our march from the north bank of the San Gabriel where we encamped began. It was not long before the enemy came in sight. They had undoubtedly received reinforcements and numbered from eight hundred to one thousand men.

They had also several cannon stationed on the declivity to the eastward and

---
[66]Ibid., pp. 204–08.   [67]Ibid., pp. 208–09.

for a time sent ball and shot in a lively manner, but their range was too long as they kept a mile or two distant.

In most cases the range of their balls by their striking the ground could be determined with precision in time to dodge them. Several times during the day their whole force charged toward us in the wildest and most threatening manner and when within a hundred yards or so they would invariably wheel and fly. In these charges they would sometimes lose a few horses but they always managed to take with them their wounded comrades and even the saddles from the horses shot.

Unable to break our ranks, the Californians gave up the contest and fled to meet Fremont and we entered the City of Los Angeles in triumph.

At this time Fremont was nearing that city and within perhaps fifty miles. A day or two after when he had reached the Mission of San Fernando the Californians met and surrendered to him in preference doubtless to Stockton who had so promptly refused to treaty as before stated.

Fremont's making and concluding a treaty with the enemy within so short a distance of his superior officers without consulting them was at the time considered by some as a stretch of authority and his right to make the conditions would perhaps have been questioned but Stockton and he were fast friends and whatever there might be of irregularity or assumption of authority was overlooked. This was in January 1847. The country was believed as it really proved to be, reconquered. The Mexican War in Cal[ifornia] was ended.[68]

### Going Home and Swimming Horses Across the Carquinez Straits

The war being over, nearly all the volunteers were discharged from the service in February and March, 1847, at Los Angeles and San Diego. Most of us made our way up the coast by land to our homes. I had eleven horses, which I swam, one at a time, across the straits of Carquinez at Benicia, which J. M. Hudspeth, the surveyor, was at the time laying out for Dr. Robert Semple, and which was then called "Francisca," after Mrs. Vallejo, whose maiden name was Francisca Benicia Carrillo.[69]

### Swimming Horses Across the Carquinez, an Earlier Instance

It so happened that Castro had sent Lieutenant Arce to the north side of the bay of San Francisco to collect scattered Government horses. Arce had secured about one hundred and fifty and was taking them to the south side of the bay *via* Sutter's Fort and the San Joaquin Valley. This was the only way to transfer

---
[68]Ibid., pp. 209–11.
[69]Bidwell, "Fremont in the Conquest of California" (February 1891), p. 525.

cattle or horses from one side of the bay to the other, except at the Straits of Carquinez by the slow process of swimming one at a time, or of taking one or two, tied by all four feet, in a small boat or launch.[70]

### BIDWELL DECLINES THE HAND OF ELIZA SUTTER

... to crown all your acts of attention and esteem you [have] made me an offer—and I know it must have been from the fullness of an affectionate heart and a sincere desire for my happiness,—of the hand of an only daughter. Capt. Sutter I am not ungrateful, but I often want either means or ability to display my gratitude.... I hope you will believe me sincere when I tell you, that in spite of all the changes of time, my grateful affection and friendship, which began with my first interview with you and have grown up and become a part of myself and nature, can never be obliterated. I shall ever cherish the warmest regards for you and your family. During my recent calls at your farm on business, your family have shown me the politest attentions. I felt bad because they tried so much to make me comfortable—for I was afraid they would discommode themselves.

Eliza speaks English very well and I was pleased with her accomplishments. I regretted much that I could not converse with Mrs. Sutter, but her attentions were unceasing and kind. Now Capt. Sutter I am at a loss to know what to say. My determination is made. I desire to prove to you on all occasions my gratitude. In matters of *business* you have only to say what you want done and it shall be done, so far as I can do. Whatever assistance I can render yourself or family in all time to come, I shall consider it a first duty.... I desire to see you frequently, and to live, so long as we both may live, on terms of intimacy and friendship. I shall be happy to visit you frequently—have you do the same to me when convenient, and try and make life as pleasant as possible. But I cannot persuade myself to marry. [*crossed out*: I shall keep this offer a profound secret.] I hate the very name of old bachelor, and yet I do not know that I shall ever marry. Let this be a secret between you and me.[71]

---

[70]Ibid., p. 519.
[71]JB to John Sutter, 2 April 1851, in Grabhorn, *Pioneers of the Sacramento*, pp. 7–9.

# 3
# Bidwell and California Gold

Late in the summer of 1847 John Sutter ordered his trusted clerk, John Bidwell, to prepare a contract for the construction of a lumber mill to be built by James W. Marshall. Marshall had proposed building a sawmill on the South Fork of the American River about forty-five miles east of Sutter's Fort. The site he chose for the mill was a place the local Nisenan Indians called Culloomah [Coloma].[1] Sutter wanted to use the mill to provide lumber for his growing empire at New Helvetia. He also intended to sell milled wood to newly arrived immigrants, but Bidwell was skeptical of the plan. Unlike the broad, slow moving rivers of the eastern United States, the streams on the west slope of the Sierra Nevada were often steep, narrow and filled with boulders. The idea of floating timber down the American River to Sutter's Fort seemed foolhardy to Bidwell, but he drew up the contract for Sutter and Marshall nonetheless.

On January 24, 1848, in the midst of constructing the sawmill, Marshall found "some kind of mettle . . . that looks like goald" while inspecting the tailrace.[2] Marshall carried a sample of the gleaming stones to Sutter's Fort for examination. Upon his arrival, Marshall and Sutter withdrew to a private room and began to test the sample. After it was bitten, boiled in lye, and pounded with a hammer, both men declared it to be gold. Later that day, Sutter called Bidwell into the room and asked his opinion. Bidwell too thought it was gold.[3] Marshall became so excited that he rode back to Coloma that night in a driving rainstorm to protect his discovery. Bidwell, under orders from Sutter, went to San Francisco

---

[1] Walton Bean, *California, An Interpretive History* (New York: McGraw-Hill, 1973), p. 109. The Nisenan are often referred to as the Southern Maidu.
[2] Rodman W. Paul, *California Gold: The Beginning of Mining in the Far West* (Lincoln: University of Nebraska Press, 1947), p. 17.
[3] John Bidwell, "Recollections, 1897," Annie E.K. Bidwell Papers, California State Library.

to have the gold tested again in order to get an expert opinion. Keeping Marshall's discovery secret proved to be an impossible task. By the end of the year, word of the gold strike spread across the continent and around the world. The famous California Gold Rush had begun.[4]

Unlike the ill-fated Marshall and Sutter, John Bidwell profited immensely from the Gold Rush. He made his own gold strike in July 1848 while prospecting on the Middle Fork of the Feather River at a place that soon became known as Bidwell's Bar.[5] He was fortunate in that he was able to work the area thoroughly with a couple of white partners and a team of Indian laborers before news of his discovery spread. During his two seasons of mining on the Feather River, Bidwell also opened up a store in cooperation with his friend George McKinstry, who kept it supplied from his base at Sutter's Fort. Their store at Bidwell's Bar, a boomtown by 1849 with a population of over six hundred people, provided miners with all the essentials: gold pans, picks, shovels, work clothes, boots, and whiskey.[6] Precisely how much money Bidwell made mining gold and operating his store is unknown, but one contemporary observer estimated his profits at over $100,000.[7] Whatever the exact amount, it was substantial enough to allow him to purchase and outfit Rancho Chico. The restless son of poor New York state dirt farmers had finally struck it rich in California and he was determined to hold on to his good fortune.

For a brief while, Bidwell's Bar flourished with its namesake. A typical gold rush boomtown, Bidwell's Bar was filled with barking dogs and young footloose men seeking quick wealth. Saloons, gambling halls, and stores competed for the gold dust that served as currency. The streets were

---

[4]Ibid.; Bean, *California, An Interpretive History*, pp. 109–10.

[5]Bidwell first discovered some particles of light, "scale" gold in April 1848 while camping along the Feather River at what soon became the town of Hamilton. His big strike, however, occurred at Bidwell's Bar. George C. Mansfield, *History of Butte County* (Los Angeles: Historical Record Company, Los Angeles, 1918), pp. 254, 257.

[6]Ibid., p. 67. Bidwell's mining partners in 1848 included John Potter, John Williams, William Northgraves, and William Dickey, the original grantee of Rancho Chico. With McKinstry, Bidwell also struck a lucrative deal with T. H. Rolfe and Edward C. Kemble, to whom he leased a primitive but effective gold washing device. Kemble, a pioneer California newspaper editor who first worked for Sam Brannan's *California Star*, went on to found the San Francisco *Alta California* and the San Francisco *Chronicle*. See Hunt, pp. 152–153; Lois McDonald, "Decade of Decision: John Bidwell's First Ten Years in California," in *Ripples Along Chico Creek: Perspectives on People and Times* (Chico, Ca.: Butte County Branch, National League of American Pen Women, 1992), pp. 25–27; Bean, pp. 91, 150, 159; Chico *Enterprise*, 12 February 1886.

[7]Paul C. Phillips, ed., *Forty Years on the Frontier as Seen in Journals and Reminiscences of Granville Stuart* (Glendale, Ca.: Arthur Clark Co., 1957), p. 54.

choked with dust in the summer and clogged with foot-deep mud during the rainy season. In the early years, there were few wooden structures in the town. Instead the hotels, saloons and supply stores were made of canvas stretched across wooden frames.[8] Bidwell's Bar served as the county seat of Butte in 1850 and again from 1853 to 1856, when its gold fields at last played out and the local boom turned to bust. Shortly thereafter, fires swept through the almost deserted town destroying what was left of the once prosperous community. Bidwell's Bar became just another gold country ghost town.[9]

California gold mining methods and labor systems changed quickly following Bidwell's departure from the diggings after 1849. What began with self-employed placer miners using gold pans and rockers changed by 1850 into associative groups of miners working elaborate sluice boxes. By 1852, corporate owned mines manned by wage earning employees appeared in the gold fields.[10] The rapid shift to large-scale, capital intensive industrial mining was accelerated by the development of hydraulic mining after 1852. California's first and most damaging contribution to mining technology, hydraulic mining required an extensive network of canals, ditches, flumes, and pipes to deliver water under high pressure to large cast-iron nozzles called "monitors" that directed water jets against the hillsides. As the topsoil gave way, the water and earthen debris combined to form a muck called "slickens." The slickens were then directed into sluice boxes, some over thousands of feet long, where the gold was washed from the rock and soil.

Hydraulic mining was an inefficient technology that lost a quarter to one-half of the potential gold yield.[11] Hydraulic miners tried to compensate for this deficiency by operating round the clock, washing away hillsides while flushing more and more slickens into local waterways. Tons of mud, sand, and gravel eventually filled the riverbeds of the Sacramento, Feather, Yuba, and Bear destroying navigation and fish habitat. By 1878,

---

[8]Mansfield, *Butte County*, p. 67.
[9]In 1964 the California Department of Water Resources completed construction of Oroville Dam and began filling Lake Oroville. The upstream site of Bidwell's Bar was inundated and now lies under fifty feet of water.
[10]W. H. Hutchinson, *California, Two Centuries of Man, Land, and Growth in the Golden State* (Palo Alto, Ca.: American West Publishing, 1969), p. 137.
[11]North San Juan *Hydraulic Press*, 25 June 1859; "Editor's Table," *Hutchings' Illustrated California Magazine*, III (1858–59), p. 432, cited in Rodman W. Paul, *California Gold* (Lincoln: Univ. of Nebraska Press, 1947), p. 159.

the bed of the Yuba River had been raised thirty feet by hydraulic debris, leaving the levee-protected city of Marysville below river level. For farmers downstream, the annual rains meant floods and the loss of valuable farmland as the debris-filled rivers overran their banks.

Ironically, the initial source of John Bidwell's fortune, gold mining, quickly became the subject of his sharp criticism now that he had become a farmer. As early as 1865, Bidwell warned the members of the State Agricultural Society about the evils of hydraulic mining and, by the early 1880s, the damage brought on by the practice was apparent to almost everyone.[12] Still, the mining corporations had plenty of political clout and were able to stymie legislative attempts to regulate their operations. In 1882, Bidwell addressed the California Anti-Debris Convention in Sacramento and called for legislative action to stop "... the wide ruin already begun and the greater impending ruin" caused by hydraulic mining.[13] His appeal for action was cheered at the convention hall, but taking on the powerful mining companies proved to be much more difficult in the halls of the state legislature.

The farmers of the Sacramento Valley thus remained at the mercy of hydraulic miners upstream until the case of *Woodruff v. North Bloomfield* was decided in U.S. Circuit Court in 1884. Edwards Woodruff, a farm owner on the Feather River near Marysville, sued the North Bloomfield Mining Company and others for the damage done to his property by debris and flooding. Woodruff asked the court for a permanent injunction against the miners and, backed by Bidwell and other northern California growers, presented a strong case. In January 1884, Judge Lorenzo Sawyer ruled in favor of Woodruff and held that the mines were a public nuisance. His ruling, which permanently restrained the miners from discharging or dumping debris into the waterways, was a major victory for the farmers of the Sacramento Valley and struck a mortal blow to the hydraulic mining industry in California.[14]

---

[12]CSAS 1865, pp. 211–212; CSAS 1881, pp. 28–29; JBD, 23 June 1881, 22 Sept. 1882, 10 June 1892. See also Gillis, "John Bidwell, Gentleman Farmer or Iconoclast?" Butte County Historical Society *Diggin's*, 36 (Summer 1992), pp. 31–41.

[13]Bidwell, Speech before the Anti-Debris Convention, Sacramento, 1882, cited in C.C. Royce, *John Bidwell, Pioneer, Statesman, Philanthropist* (Chico, Ca.: 1906).

[14]For details of the Woodruff case, see Duane A. Smith, *Mining America, The Industry and the Environment, 1800–1980* (Lawrence: University Press of Kansas, 1987), pp. 67–72; and Robert L. Kelley, *Gold vs. Grain: The Hydraulic Mining Controversy in California's Sacramento Valley* (Glendale, Ca.: Arthur Clark, 1959).

Besides the ravages of hydraulic mining, John Bidwell worried about other environmentally destructive practices associated with the gold mining industry. He knew that unrestricted logging and clear cutting of the Mother Lode pine forests to support mining and water projects would lead to soil erosion and damage the watersheds on the western slope of the central Sierra Nevada. Great stands of sugar pine and yellow pine were cut to build flumes for the hydraulic industry and to brace the shafts of hard rock mines in California and neighboring Nevada. It has been estimated that 600 million board feet of mostly California timber and about 2 million cords of wood were cut to supply Nevada's Comstock silver mines.[15] In addition, free running forest fires intentionally set to clear land and burn lumbering slash destroyed valuable timber and silted streams. Meanwhile, large herds of cattle and sheep brought in to feed the hungry miners overgrazed the grasslands of the Gold Country and the Sacramento Valley. This resulted in the loss of bunch grasses and other native vegetation which gave way to invasive annual grasses with little nutritional value for livestock. The damage done to the farmland, rivers, grasslands, and forests all combined to make John Bidwell one of the mining industry's harshest critics.

## *Remarks on Gold Rush & Gold Mining*

### BIDWELL RECALLS JAMES MARSHALL

James W. Marshall went across the plains to Oregon in 1844, and thence came to California, the next year. He was a wheelwright by trade, but, being very ingenious, he could turn his hand to almost anything. So he acted as carpenter for Sutter, and did many other things, among which I may mention making wheels for spinning wool, and looms, reeds, and shuttles for weaving yarn into coarse blankets for the Indians, who did the carding, spinning, weaving, and all other labor.... Besides his ingenuity as a mechanic, he had most singular traits. Almost everyone pronounced him half crazy or hare-brained. He was certainly eccentric, and perhaps somewhat flighty. His insanity, however, if he had any, was of the harmless kind; he was neither vicious nor quarrelsome. He had great, almost overweening confidence in his ability to do anything as a mechanic. I wrote the contract between Sutter and him to build the mill. Sutter was to furnish the means; Marshall was to build and run the mill, and have a share of the lumber for his compensation. His idea was to haul the lumber part way and raft it down the

---

[15] Smith, p. 13.

American River to Sacramento, and thence, his part of it, down the Sacramento River, and through Suisun and San Pablo bays to San Francisco for a market. Marshall's mind, in some respects at least, must have been unbalanced. It is hard to conceive how any sane man could have been so wide of the mark, or how any one could have selected such a site for a sawmill under the circumstances. Surely no other man than Marshall ever entertained so wild a scheme as that of rafting sawed lumber down the canyons of the American River, and no other man than Sutter would have been so confiding and credulous as to patronize him.[1]

### CLAIMS TO BE FIRST TO DELIVER NEWS OF GOLD DISCOVERY TO SAN FRANCISCO

I crossed over to San Francisco and reported the discovery of gold. I believe I was the first man to tell the news in S.F. The discovery by Marshall was perhaps made on Jan. 24th. I am guided in this belief by Sutter's old diary, which fell into my hands and which I presented to the Pioneer Society. When gold was discovered, everything else was neglected.[2]

### BIDWELL DISCOVERS GOLD ON THE FEATHER RIVER; MINES WITH PARTNERS AND INDIAN WORKERS

Marshall discovered gold on a branch of the American river. I went up, as others did, to see the place, and made arrangements to hold mining claims there. Marshall built a little cabin on my claim so that I could hold it. The next night, on my way home [to Little Butte Creek], I camped one night by the [American] river. Next morning I traveled to the east of the Feather river. We always carried provisions with us, and camped wherever night overtook us. While my horse was off feeding, I took a tin cup and went down to the river; washed the sands as well as I could, and every cupful took out small particles of gold. I returned to my place and made arrangements to go to the mines. Meantime the mines were becoming known. Soon a party joined me to prospect for gold, but before we had gone far, they all became discouraged with the exception of one man. We came to a place which is now about six miles from Oroville. We struck a pick into a shelving rock near the water's edge, and found it all brilliant with gold. It was almost pure gold and black sand. We washed a panful and got about an ounce of gold. My companion said "cover it up, don't say anthing about it." Said I, "all right." I went to camp and told the boys there was plenty of gold along the river, which they could surely find if they would look for it.

We showed them our gold, but could not get them to make any effort to prospect. We had to return to the valley because we had only prepared for three

---

[1]Bidwell, "Life in California Before the Gold Discovery," *Century Magazine*, 41 (December 1890), p. 181.
[2]JB-91, p. 58.

or four days' absence. We then prepared to work together on the American river. The first night we found little gold. The next day we were searching around in the crevices and found plenty. I had brought up five or six Indians with me. They did not know anything about gold, didn't seem to recognize it as anything they had ever seen. Most of the gold we found in the crevices of the rocks way up over our heads. It had been there perhaps for hundreds of years: every great rain and flood carrying some dirt away from it. The Indians very soon learned that there was value in the gold. While I was gone to wash a panful of earth I left an Indian to wash another panful. When I went back I spoke to him but received no reply. When he was compelled to speak, I found he had his mouth filled with gold. My Indian boy reported he had seen some of [the] other Indians with gold. Mr. [William] Dickey was for shooting them right away. I said "No, I'll settle that." I asked the Indians if they had any gold; they brought some in. I gave them a handful of sugar and they gave me their gold. They liked the exchange and gave up cheerfully all the gold they had for sugar. At the end of the day we had about $90. We moved to another place, and there we washed it out with our hands several days and succeeding in getting about $1500 a day.[3]

### Another account of Bidwell's gold discovery

On my return to Chico I stopped over night at Hamilton, on the west branch of the Feather River. On trying some of the sand in the river, I found light particles of gold, and reckoned that if light gold could be found that far down the river, the heavier particles would remain near the hills. On reaching Chico, an expedition was organized, but it took some time to get everything ready. We had to send up twice to Peter Lassen's mill to obtain flour; meat had to be dried; and we had to send to Sacramento for tools. Our party was Mr. Dicky, [John] Potter, John Williams, William Northgraves, and myself. We passed near Cherokee and up the North Fork. In nearly all the places we prospected, we found the color. One evening while I camped at White Rocks, Dicky and I in a short time panned out about an ounce of fine gold. The others refused to prospect any, and said that the gold we had obtained was so light that it would not weigh anything. At this time we were all unfamiliar with the weight of gold dust, but I am satisfied what we had would weigh an ounce. At length we came home, and some of the men went to American River to mine. Dicky, Northgraves, and I went to what is now Bidwell Bar, and there found gold and went to mining.[4]

### Mining at Bidwell's Bar, 1848–1849

I found what was called Bidwell's Bar, but . . . our diggings though rich at

---

[3]Ibid., pp. 54–56.
[4]George C. Mansfield, *History of Butte County, California* (Los Angeles: Historical Record Company, 1918), p. 42.

first were very limited. A man came along and couldn't find any place to dig. I had a crevice where I was working, and told him if he could not find any place, he could work on that. He went to work, and it was so rich that when I came near, he would throw his blanket over it, so I should not see it. This was in 1848. At that time we were working under very great disadvantages. It was impossible to get the proper tools. A common iron crowbar was worth $100. A pick was worth about $20. We made various things. For instance, we had a little sluice way, putting the earth in above we worked it through a riddle we made ourselves. We collected the gold through that but I believe we lost three fourths of it. We could see the bright particles floating away almost every instant. We took out that summer over $30,000 over our expenses which I think were fully half that amount. We had to saw our own lumber with a whip-saw. One man standing on the log pulling the saw down and the other up.[5]

I mined two seasons on the Feather river, that is in 1848–49. I have never been in the mines since, except on one occasion when I was persuaded to take an interest in a rich copper mine. I was promised a discover[er]'s share which is double the share of another man. I remained with the company until I lost two or three thousand dollars. The mine gave out.[6]

### Stocking Bidwell's Bar before prices rise

Dear Mac [George McKinstry],            New Helvetia, 21 May 1848

I foresee the great struggles which are going to be in the mining regions which impresses me with the importance of finding if possible, a more retired place above.

To this end in your absence I shall make every endeavor: We ought to make early arrangements for cattle for beef, because every thing in the provision line is about to command an exorbitant price, and unless we guard in time against it we shall lose a great deal.

Yours etc.,<br>J. Bidwell[7]

Feather River below first camp, Saturday 24th June 1848

Dear Mac,

Last week we did tolerably well washing along the river—we made something not far from $1000. This week we have done but little.... We are not making over $50 per day with all the Indians.... I am entirely out of coffee; I would like a few more shirts having sold nearly all these which I brought up. I see plainly that we cannot keep goods in camp to supply miners unless we can find a place

---

[5]JB-91, pp. 56–57.             [6]Ibid., p. 58.
[7]JB to George McKinstry, 21 May 1848, McKinstry Papers, b. 232, f. 5, CSL.

where we can establish ourselves permanently for some time or are better provided with means of transportation.

Yours etc.<br>
J. Bidwell[8]

Dear Mac,                                      Feather River, 10 July 1848

... Let the cargo consist in a considerable quantity of Liquors, in Bbls & cases both. 1,000 lb. Sugar, 50 Picks ... you can get Nicolas boat to bring these, if you do it immediately, before the river falls so much that his boat cannot come up this far. ...

Yours etc.<br>
J. Bidwell[9]

### INDIAN MINERS "TREATED LIKE SLAVES"
### BY COLUSA COUNTY PIONEER GRANVILLE SWIFT

Three men named [Granville] Swift, Gibson and Marr went across the Sacramento valley and brought in some 30 or 40 Indians [from Stony Creek] to help them dig gold [on the Feather River]. They compelled them to come. If the Indians did not bring a sufficient amount of gold to suit them, they were whipped. The Indians would often try to escape but were always brought back by these men, and treated like slaves. Swift was one of the best prospectors I ever knew. It seemed as if he could almost smell the gold. He made an immense amount of money. When these three men had worked all winter and fall I believe they must have had some $100,000 apiece and maybe more. Swift took up the business of stock and sheep raising. ... about 20 miles west of Colusa [on Stony Creek].[10]

### BIDWELL ACCUSED OF MURDERING HIS INDIAN MINERS

Camp, 30th Sept. 1848

Dear Mac,

... I was back in camp early Sunday morning after I left you on Friday at Charle's—the 5 new Indians had run away on Friday night and I have not been able since to prevail upon them to return. The Paegnes, however have submitted since I paid them a visit and made them some presents, and I have 11 of them at work also some of the Yunos. Last week we had 20; this 33 hands. A great many people have crowded upon this stream since you left. About 300 people have arrived from Oregon expressly for Gold digging.

... I have been told by a great many persons that there is a report all through the country, that I have killed most barbarously two Indians who were at work

---

[8] JB to George McKinstry, 24 June 1848, Ibid., b. 232, f. 7.
[9] JB to George McKinstry, 10 July 1848, Ibid., b. 232, f. 11.
[10] JB-91, p. 57.

for me—and that it came from [Michael] Nye,[*] and was told and repeated by him without any reserve all down the river the day he left our camp.... One Indian was said to be cruelly beaten by my vaquero —and that he fell and dashed his brains out against a rock—the other, it was said, I had stabbed with my knife in the act of stealing meat, and thrown him in the river....

It must be on account of the sway which we hold over the Indians in these regions, which prevents his success on this river. However, the Indians come constantly to work here from the plains but almost invariably complain of Nye's Alcalde interfering with them. The Toto Indians came this morning with complaints that Pumul (Nye's Alcalde) was at their rancheria and had taken all their things from them. I sent one of the men to find out certain before I do farther.

Yours truly,
J. Bidwell[11]

*Michael Nye had accompanied Bidwell on the overland trek of 1841.

### VIOLENT AND MISERABLE CONDITIONS OF THE GOLD FIELDS

Sutter'sville, 5 April 1849

My Dear Friend [Dr. John Townsend],

Your kind letter of 15th Dec. last was received only ten days since. I have come down to this place from our camp on Feather River, and now embrace the first opportunity to reply.

When I wrote to you before my intention was to carry on a considerable trade connected with the mining business.... Time has passed, and brought some changes with it.... I have not given up the idea of making my home in California. My great desire is to close my business in this valley. I must close it for two reasons—first it is too sickly here—I am subject to the ague and fevers. I mean to say that my constitution is such that it is not calculated to endure these hot summers. Some point over the [unreadable] would suit me better. I have spent a very disagreeable time in the mountains this winter. I was quite unwell about a month since, from pains in the breast and side. I had also a considerable cough —to a hard cold which I had taken....

So many changes have been wrought within the last year, that—I feel myself almost a stranger here, where I was formerly wont to be at home. Every where, in the plains and in the mountains—I meet a heterogeneous mass of strangers. I am sure I should not fear the change more sensibly if I were placed in the wilds of Siberia. Among such a population as is bound to enter here we may expect, from what has already passed, the greatest confusion, resulting in the perpetuation of the most horrid outrages and crimes, etc. etc. etc. etc....

Yours Sincerely,
J. Bidwell[12]

---

[11]JB to George McKinstry, 30 September 1848, McKinstry Papers, b. 232, f. 8, CSL.

## SOME EXTREMES OF GOLD CAMP SOCIETY

In this whirl of the political and social elements the prospect of acquiring sudden and almost fabulous wealth seemed to control every other consideration, and produced a state of things wholly anomalous. Here were brought into striking contrast scenes of order, good will, and the noblest acts of friendship, against anarchy, outrage, and crime. Men were good without compulsion, and took no advantage of the absence of law to defraud each other, and malefactors received sentence and execution on the same day, or perhaps within the same hour, or escaped the penalty due to their crimes altogether.[13]

## LATER, AND MORE POSITIVE, REFLECTIONS ON GOLD RUSH SOCIETY

It will be sufficient to say, that during all the wild excitement of those early days, that liberty-loving, law-abiding sentiment, and that peculiar adaptability to self-government so characteristic of the American people, were in the ascendant and naturally tended to organization. And in due time order was brought out of chaos; a State government was created and put in motion and California added a new star to the bright galaxy of the Confederation.[14]

...as a general rule no more enterprising people ever existed than those who have come to California since the discovery of gold. They have explored every nook and corner of the Pacific slope. No danger has been sufficient to check their explorations. They have brought to light hidden treasures that have astonished and almost revolutionized the commerce of the world. Their herculean efforts are literally moving mountains towards the sea. They have built cities, towns, and villages innumerable and been pioneers of civilization all over the Pacific coast, from Arizona to Cariboo. They have carved States and Territories from the regions of former savage desolation, and made the deserts to bud and blossom as the rose. I have an abiding faith in the Anglo-Saxon race. I believe they can do and perform wonders, and even withstand the allurements to idleness of this or any other climate. I speak of them as a class, of course, and believe a noble destiny awaits them in the future.[15]

...the gold discovery literally awoke to life the sleeping commerce of the world, and sent hither people from every land by swarms and thousands. The so-called military authorities—Stockton, Kearny, Mason and Riley—each discharged his duties with commendable fidelity, if not signal ability. The maintenance of order was the paramount consideration. During the military period, resort to lashings and lynchings in aggravated cases was not unknown, but it was very infrequent even in the mines and distant places beyond the reach of law. As a rule people fresh

---

[12]JB to Dr. John Townsend, b. 126, f. 48, JB-CSL.
[13]CSAS 1860, pp. 326–27.
[14]Ibid., p. 327.   [15]CSAS 1865, p. 209.

from the east seemed to bring with them good habits and behavior. Hence riots were almost unheard of. As far as I can now recall those early scenes there was not much complaint or cause of complaint here under military administration.[16]

In the midst of the whirl of events in 1848 and 1849 when the rush for golden fortunes was at its zenith—when uncounted thousands from all lands thronged to the mountains, the newborn cities, and towns, mines, camps and thoroughfares—when there was scarcely the resemblance of law, or officers to enforce law had it existed—it is a matter of wonder to note how few were the acts of lawlessness violence and crime in comparison with [what] would be naturally expected.

My solution is this: The law abiding element predominated. The most enterprising men were the ruling spirits. They lived and dealt according to law—the law they carried in their hearts.[17]

### Protests against Hydraulic Mining

There was not a muddy stream in California before the discovery of gold.[18]

The rivers of this portion of the State are becoming so rapidly filled up as to threaten the total destruction of navigation. The raising of the beds of rivers by continual deposition from the mines, while it destroys navigation and increases the danger from floods, diminishes the labor of transferring the waters into artificial channels. Preservation from this danger of inundation should impress upon us the necessity of giving this subject early consideration.[19]

I wish hydraulic mining could continue, and the whole country prosper. At the same time, I admit that it is not to me a pleasing scene to see havoc made of hills, and mountains, and stately forests, and a once lovely prospect changed to a desolation.[20]

Mining is a legitimate industry, and all other industries must of necessity be friendly to it. But that class known as hydraulic has grown to be intolerable, and its stoppage has become inevitable.... Hydraulic mining is a landmark never to be obliterated in the history of this State, both because of its good and bad results. The bad results are seen and known by all. They caused vast expenditures, ruin, terror and desolation. To effect even partial restoration to lands, streams and navigation will require vast sums in the future.[21]

### California Gold saves Union and wins Civil War

It is a question whether the United States could have stood the shock of the

---

[16]JB to Rockwell Hunt, 3 April 1895, BFP.
[17]Ibid., 14 August 1895.
[18]*Woodruff v. North Bloomfield*, vol. 24, p. 9802.
[19]CSAS 1865, pp. 211–12.
[20]CSAS 1881, pp. 28–29.
[21]Sacramento *Record-Union*, 22 January 1884.

great rebellion of 1861 had the California gold discovery not been made. Bankers and business men of New York in 1864 did not hesitate to admit that but for the gold of California, which monthly poured its five or six millions into that financial center, the bottom would have dropped out of everything. These timely arrivals so strengthened the nerves of trade and stimulated business as to enable the Government to sell its bonds at a time when its credit was its life-blood and the main reliance by which to feed, clothe, and maintain its armies. Once our bonds went down to thirty-eight cents on the dollar. California gold averted a total collapse, and enabled a preserved Union to come forth from the great conflict with only four billions of debt instead of hundreds of billions. The hand of Providence so plainly seen in the discovery of gold is no less manifest in the time chosen for its accomplishment.[22]

When I was in New York in 1864, about the gloomiest time of the rebellion, the people told me in the banks and business houses that but for the five or six millions of gold that came from California every month, the bottom would drop out of everything.[23]

### Sutter deserves chief credit for Gold Rush

While there is no question of Marshall's discovery, the real credit of evolving the world-renowned event which so revolutionized the world belongs to Sutter. It was his money, it was his enterprise which set in motion Marshall himself and all the conspiring conditions which converged in and unfolded that great discovery, under the eye of a guiding Providence.[24]

### Sutter and Marshall "turned the world upside down"

This discovery gave impetus to trade, commerce, immigration, and almost everything else throughout the world, and was brought about by two men of most peculiar characteristics—Sutter, so confiding as to believe Marshall's report of the feasibility of making a saw-mill where I feel sure no sane man would advise, in light of a profitable lumber enterprise; and Marshall, so wild and erratic in judgment about such matters as to select a site most difficult, impracticable, and unprofitable. Yet the two together by this means turned the world upside down. Of course, I believe the matter was providential.[25]

---

[22]Bidwell, "Life in California," pp. 182–83.
[23]*Pioneers*, p. 28.
[24]Ibid., p. 25.
[25]Bidwell, "Early California Reminiscences," *Out West*, 20 (August 1904), p. 195.

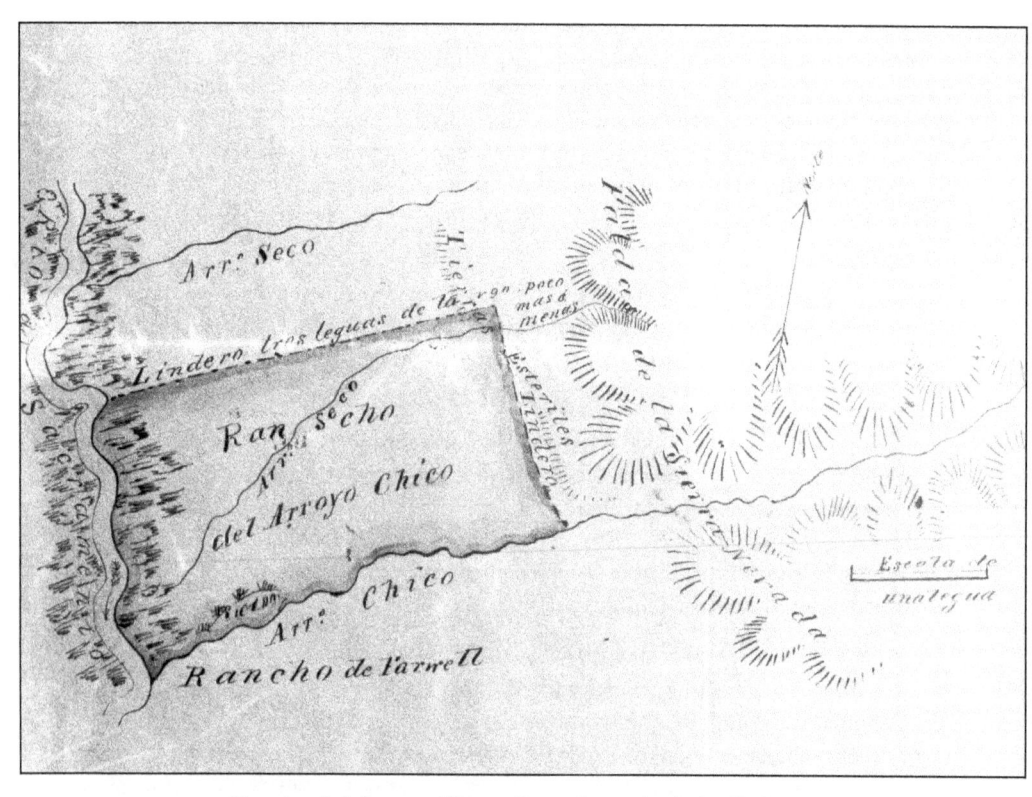

Rancho del Arroyo Chico *diseño* drawn by John Bidwell.
Reprinted with permission by Special Collections, Meriam Library,
California State University, Chico.

# 4
# Rancho Chico and the Development of California Agriculture

Of John Bidwell's many contributions to California's history and development, his pioneering achievements in agriculture rank as the most important. Bidwell was first and foremost a farmer, and the agricultural empire he established at Rancho Chico served as a model farm for the rest of the state. Between 1849 and 1900, Bidwell helped set the pace for a series of revolutionary changes that eventually established California as America's leading farm state and its most diverse agricultural producer.

Despite his success at Bidwell's Bar, Bidwell never intended to make a career out of mining. Rather, the search for gold provided the means to an end he had already begun pursuing before Marshall's great discovery at Coloma. In April 1845, determined to strike out on his own and eventually leave Sutter's employ, Bidwell obtained a part interest in Edward Farwell's rancho New Salem. Located in the upper Sacramento Valley ninety miles north of New Helvetia, the Farwell grant contained five square leagues that ran along the south bank of Chico Creek and the east side of the Sacramento River. Transecting the property was Little Butte Creek, where Bidwell built a small cabin and began residing in 1847. Registering his brand with local justice of the peace John Sinclair on May 6, 1848, Bidwell assembled a herd of cattle on the property before heading to the foothills to hunt for gold along the nearby Feather River. During the next two mining seasons, Bidwell amassed the fortune which enabled him to acquire Rancho del Arroyo Chico. In July 1849, Bidwell purchased an undivided one-half interest in the property from George McKinstry, his former partner in the Bidwell's Bar trading post. Two years later, he bought out the remaining half-share and became Rancho Chico's sole proprietor.[1]

---
[1]Hunt, pp. 150, 245, 248; Lois McDonald, "Decade of Decision: John Bidwell's First Ten Years in California," in *Ripples Along Chico Creek: Perspectives on People and Times* (Chico, Ca.: Butte County Branch, National League of American Pen Women, 1992), pp. 17, 22.

Bridge over Chico Creek. John Bidwell's adobe and store.
Reprinted with permission courtesy of the John Nopel Collection.

Like the neighboring Farwell grant, Rancho Chico encompassed five square leagues. Three to four miles wide, and with Chico Creek forming its southern boundary, the huge estate sprawled fourteen miles eastward from the Sacramento River into the Sierra foothills. Bidwell moved onto the property immediately after his initial purchase and, in 1852, built a large two-story adobe home that would serve as his permanent residence until the completion of the more elegant Bidwell Mansion in 1868.[2] Together with his portions of the Farwell grant, Rancho Chico's 22,214 acres gave Bidwell a total of 33,000 contiguous acres in what became northwestern Butte County. While he retained most of Rancho Chico for the rest of his life, Bidwell sold or gave away almost all of the Farwell properties after he laid out and founded the city of Chico in 1860.[3]

First, however, Bidwell had to secure title to his vast holdings. Under the Treaty of Guadalupe Hidalgo and the California Land Act of 1851, Bidwell, like every other holder of a Mexican or Spanish land grant, was

---
[2]Hunt, p. 249; McDonald, p. 27.
[3]San Francisco *Chronicle*, 14 July 1875.

required to confirm his title by obtaining a patent from the United States government. Securing a patent, however, proved difficult for most rancho owners.

The Mexican government had kept few land records, and the grants themselves were poorly defined. None of them had ever been surveyed, and the hand-sketched *diseños* acceptable under Mexican law provided only a vague approximation of their actual boundaries. Such lax and informal documentation worked well enough as long as California's population remained small, but the sudden influx of land-hungry settlers during the Gold Rush created intense competition for prime agricultural land. Property disputes became common and were aggravated by the American tradition of preemption or "squatters' rights" that allowed settlers to stake out farmsteads on unsurveyed federal land. With their boundaries unclear and contested, many *rancheros* found their estates overrun by trespassing squatters who refused to budge. This tense situation quickly led to a violent climax in August 1850. When the sheriff of Sacramento County attempted to evict squatters occupying portions of John Sutter's New Helvetia grant, a riot erupted that lasted for two days and resulted in the deaths of eight people, including the sheriff.

The Sacramento squatters' riot forced Congress to establish the California Land Commission, a three-man board appointed by the President to adjudicate all rancho grant disputes and award patents to legitimate owners. From 1852 to 1856, the commission met in San Francisco and heard over 800 cases. Though the commission worked with considerable efficiency, its decisions were not final and could be appealed all the way up the federal judiciary to the United States Supreme Court. As a result, few cases were settled swiftly and the average length of time required to secure a patent was seventeen years! This protracted legal process effectively bankrupted many *rancheros* who, despite holding valid claims, nevertheless lost their property as they struggled to meet the mounting demands of their lawyers, surveyors, and other creditors.

Bidwell survived the ordeal but not without incurring considerable costs. In May 1852, he had to secure a quitclaim from William Dickey, his former mining partner and Rancho Chico's original grantee. He also had to contend with numerous squatters, some of whom he evicted, but others had to be bought out. At last, in December 1857, Bidwell's claim to Rancho Chico was upheld by the United States Supreme Court and, on April 4, 1860, he received his coveted patent signed by President James

Buchanan.⁴ In the meantime, his involvement in the land grant cases had extended far beyond the defense of his own claims. As the original locator of most of the Sacramento Valley ranchos, Bidwell was frequently called upon to testify as an expert witness before the land commission. Bidwell's highly-prized testimony carried considerable weight thanks to his longtime residence in California, coupled with his reputation for honesty. Federal justice Ogden Hoffman, who heard a majority of the California land cases before the U.S. District Court in San Francisco, considered Bidwell among the few witnesses "upon whose veracity" he felt he could rely.⁵

In the meanwhile, Bidwell did not allow his legal difficulties to interfere with his big plans for Rancho Chico. As California's non-Indian population soared from about 15,000 to over 380,000 between 1845 and 1860, the Gold Rush created a lucrative domestic market for farm produce in the Bay Area and the mining towns. Moving to meet the urgent demand for beef, flour, and other foodstuffs, Bidwell rapidly transformed his estate into a flourishing agricultural empire that soon exceeded the dreams of his old mentor at New Helvetia.

Like most California rancheros, Bidwell began by focusing his efforts on stock raising. By 1860 his cattle numbered over 1,300 head, a figure that remained relatively constant until the mid 1870s, when Bidwell began to gradually reduce the size of his herds. Meanwhile, inspired by the high wool prices of the Civil War era, Bidwell began investing heavily in sheep, buying high quality specimens of the Merino and Cotswold breeds. Between 1860 and 1880, the flocks pasturing on Rancho Chico's foothill ranges grew from 180

---
⁴Ogden Hoffman, *Reports of Land Cases Determined in the United States District Court* (San Francisco: Numa Hubert, 1862), Appendix, p. 20; D. F. Crowder, "The Eventful Yesterdays: The Story of Early Chico," Chico *Enterprise*, 2 January 1918; "Epitome of Title to Rancho del Arroyo Chico" in Royce, *In Memoriam*, p. 248-A; Hunt, p. 248. The Farwell grant was upheld by the U.S. District Court in June 1858 and finally patented in July 1863. Bidwell had also purchased a large part of a third grant, the Aguas Nieves rancho, in 1853. Located on the east side of the Farwell property and south of Chico Creek, Aguas Nieves had originally been granted to Samuel Hensley in 1844. Bidwell gave Hensley $6,000 in exchange for several hundred acres that he quickly subdivided and resold. After being confirmed by the Land Commission in 1853 and the U.S. District Court in 1855, the Hensley grant was ruled invalid by the U.S. Supreme Court in 1863! See Hoffman, Appendix, pp. 28, 89; Mansfield, pp. 173, 179. For summaries of Bidwell's extensive real estate transactions and title disputes between 1848 and 1870, see McDonald, "Decade of Decision," pp. 19–31; Margaret E. Trussell, "Land Choice by Pioneer Farmers: Western Butte County Through 1877," (Ph.D. Dissertation, University of Oregon, 1969), pp. 63–80, 235–241.

⁵Christian Fritz, *Federal Justice in California: The Court of Ogden Hoffman, 1851–1891* (Lincoln: University of Nebraska Press, 1991), p. 173.

to 4,500 head, and the annual wool clip rose accordingly. In 1870, Bidwell's shearers gathered 5,600 pounds of wool. Twenty-one years later, in 1891, the Rancho Chico wool clip came in at over 45,000 pounds (see Table 1).[6]

Bidwell's substantial flocks and herds did not lead him to defend California's open range cattle system against mounting criticism from farmers after 1855. Convinced that California's future lay with farming, Bidwell enthusiastically joined with grain growers who demanded repeal of the state's fence laws, which favored the cattle industry. Under the open range system sanctioned by the laws, stock raisers were under no obligation to confine their livestock. Consequently, farmers wishing to protect their crops against roving bands of foraging cattle had to bear the expense of building fences. As more and more farmers settled in California, however, the political tide began to turn their way. At last, in 1872 and 1874, the state legislature shifted the onerous burden of fencing upon the unwilling shoulders of the stockmen. The days of the open range were over.[7]

Bidwell's decision to side with the grain growers clearly reflected the priority of Rancho Chico. While wool, beef, and other livestock products comprised an essential part of Rancho Chico's economy, the foundation of Bidwell's prosperous and diverse enterprise was, and always remained, winter wheat. Sown in the fall and harvested in the summer, winter wheat was admirably suited to the natural water cycle of California's Mediterranean climate, which normally featured wet winters followed by virtually rainless summers. Winter wheat thrived so well that California growers began producing surpluses as early as 1856 and, by 1867, commenced regular exports to Great Britain. Industrial England's insatiable demand for imported grain sparked a second boom for California agriculture and gave rise to the so-called Bonanza Wheat Era of 1867–1902. During this period, California became one of America's leading wheat producers, harvesting an average of over thirty million bushels each year. Typically, two-thirds of the state's enormous crop ended up in Great Britain after traveling 14,000 nautical miles around Cape Horn from San Francisco to Liverpool, one of the longest commercial connections in the world.[8]

---

[6]Chico *Enterprise*, 16 June 1876; Hunt, p. 271; JB-91, p.63.
[7]Hazel A. Pulling, "California's Fence Laws and the Range-Cattle Industry," *Historian*, 8 (Spring 1946), pp. 140-55; JB to AB, 18 and 30 January 1872, CSL, b. 50, f. 36 and b. 126, f. 82.
[8]Rodman Paul, "The Wheat Trade Between California and the United Kingdom," *Mississippi Valley Historical Review*, 45 (December 1958), pp. 391–412; Lawrence Jelinek, *Harvest Empire: A History of California Agriculture* (San Francisco: Boyd and Fraser, 1979), pp. 39–46.

Table 1: Rancho Chico Field Crops, Livestock, and Produce

| Field Crops | 1860 | 1870 | 1880 |
|---|---|---|---|
| Barley (bushels) | 3,500 | 20,000 | 36,000 |
| Corn (bushels) | 1,000 | 1,000 | 1,000 |
| Hay (tons) | 150 | 250 | 1,400 |
| Oats (bushels) | 650 | 1,500 | 1,900 |
| Potatoes (pounds) | | 600 | 574 |
| Rye (bushels) | | | 230 |
| Wheat (bushels) | 13,000 | 37,000 | 33,000 |
| Livestock | | | |
| Cattle | 1,331 | 1,300 | 675 |
| Chickens | | | 1,200 |
| Hogs | 400 | 1,500 | 350 |
| Horses | 441 | 150 | 150 |
| Milch Cows | 60 | 100 | 75 |
| Mules | 40 | 35 | 20 |
| Oxen | 10 | | |
| Sheep | 180 | 1,800 | 4,500 |
| Produce | | | |
| Butter (pounds) | | 2,000 | 5,675 |
| Cheese (pounds) | | 1,000 | |
| Honey (pounds) | | | 1,611 |
| Wool (pounds) | | 5,600 | 10,664 |

Note: Production figures are for the twelve months preceding June 1 of census year.

Sources: U.S., Census Office, *Eighth Census of the United States, 1860*, Partial Schedules for California, vol. 2, Productions of Agriculture; U.S. Department of the Interior, Bureau of the Census, *Ninth Census of the United States, 1870*, California Schedules, vol. 1, Schedule 3, Productions of Agriculture; U.S. Department of the Interior, Bureau of the Census, *Tenth Census of the United States, 1880*, California Schedules, vol 1, Schedule 2, Productions of Agriculture.

Though many small family farmers participated in the grain trade, California's Bonanza Wheat industry was dominated by large-scale entrepreneurs who laid the foundation of modern corporate "agribusiness." Chief among them was John Bidwell's neighbor to the west, Dr. Hugh J. Glenn, who owned a 60,000 acre estate fronting the Sacramento River in northern Colusa County. California's largest single wheat producer, the Glenn Ranch harvested a record crop of over one million bushels in 1880. Such massive production required a substantial investment in heavy machinery, and California became home to a flourishing manufacturing industry specializing in heavy farm equipment. Centered in Stockton and San Leandro, California factory owners like Benjamin Holt and Daniel Best pioneered in the production of innovative machinery designed for California conditions. Gang plows, headers, and combines, pulled by large teams of horses and mules, were among their most important products. They also helped lead the way in developing steam-powered equipment, beginning with mammoth stationary threshers in the 1870s followed by gigantic self-propelled combines a decade later.[9]

Though not as extensive as the Glenn Ranch, Rancho Chico was also characterized by large acreage and heavy mechanization. Throughout the Gold Rush and Bonanza Wheat eras, John Bidwell constantly enlarged and improved his grain business. Always investing in the latest technology, Bidwell owned $5,000 worth of farm machinery by 1870 which included twenty-five gang plows, three headers, nine header wagons, and a ten-horsepower steam separator that could thresh 1,200 bushels per day. These machines, along with the fifty horses and mules required to pull them, enabled Bidwell to steadily expand his granaries. Between 1857 and 1879, Bidwell's wheat fields grew from 225 to 1,650 acres yielding 33,000 bushels. By 1895, they had grown to 6,500 acres bearing an average of thirty-seven bushels each. The proportion of Rancho Chico devoted to barley increased at a similar rate, growing from less than fifty acres in 1857 to over one thousand in 1895 (see Table 1). Ever eager to test new crops, visitors to Rancho Chico in 1858 found Bidwell raising three different varieties of wheat: white flint, club, and Sonora. Twenty-five years later, an Australian guest touring Bidwell's special experimental plots counted "some forty different kinds of cereals grown under various conditions of agriculture." Such constant experimentation usually paid well. In 1862, Bidwell's grain farm was declared the best in California by the state agricultural society and, in 1878, his wheat earned a gold medal at the Paris International Exhibition after being judged the finest in the world.[10]

---

[9]Bean, pp. 271–272; Jelinek, p. 41.
[10]John Tubbesing, "Economics of the Bidwell Ranch, 1870–1875" (M.A. thesis, CSUC, 1978), p. 8; Edmonson, p. 49; CSAS 1857, p.20; CSAS 1858, pp. 221–222; *Pacific Rural Press*, 26 July 1873; S. G. Wilson, "The Heart of the Sacramento Valley," *Overland Monthly*, 27 (Feb. 1896), p. 201; Hunt, p. 257; Benjamin, pp. 29–30; U.S., Department of the Interior, Bureau of the Census, *Tenth Census of the United States, 1880*, California, vol. 1, Schedule 2, Productions of Agriculture; Thomas K. Dow, *A Tour in America* (Melbourne: *Australasian* Office, 1884): 43.

Bidwell raised much of his grain for export and shipped it to the Bay Area on steamboats and barges plying the Sacramento River or, starting in 1870, by rail. His highest grade wheat was saved, however, for milling into flour. Capitalizing early on the domestic market for food products, Bidwell erected a water-powered grist mill on Chico Creek in 1853. Located just east of his home, the two-stone mill ground one hundred bushels of grain per day in 1857. Two years later, Bidwell replaced the mill and built his three-story Chico Roller Flouring Mill which boasted three run of stone and a daily capacity of eighty to one hundred barrels of flour. By 1885, Bidwell had expanded the mill and installed steam driven machinery which enabled him to operate at full capacity during the summer when Chico Creek ran low. Steam power also helped boost the plant's potential output to a range of 200 to 250 barrels per twenty-four-hour run. For nearly forty years, the mill provided Bidwell with his largest single source of income until he finally sold it, for $50,000, to representatives of the Sperry Flour conglomerate in 1892.[11]

While flour and wheat provided Bidwell's primary sources of income, he did not, like Hugh Glenn and the other wheat kings of California, base his fortune exclusively upon a single crop. Instead, Bidwell emerged as an early champion of diversified commercial farming and became a firm believer in specialty crops as the future source of California's greatness as an agricultural producer. Long before the disadvantages of Bonanza Wheat became apparent, Bidwell was staking Rancho Chico's future growth and prosperity on exotic specialties rather than familiar and reliable staples. Bidwell thus anticipated, and then helped lead, the great transformation of California agriculture that saw specialty crops arise to overtake and finally replace wheat between 1870 and 1910.[12]

Bidwell launched his first major venture into specialty crops shortly after moving onto the Farwell grant in 1848. Given his subsequent conversions to temperance and prohibition, it is ironic that Bidwell nearly usurped Agoston Haraszthy's place in history as the father of California's modern wine industry. Well before Haraszthy purchased his famous Buena Vista vineyard in Sonoma County in 1857, Bidwell had begun his own experiments

---

[11] *California Farmer*, 29 May 1857; Harry Wells and W. L. Chambers, *History of Butte County, California* (San Francisco: Harry L. Wells, 1882), p. 228; John Bidwell, "Testimony," *Edwards Woodruff v. North Bloomfield, et al.*, transcript of testimony, August 1883, vol. 24, p. 9813; Butte *Record*, 29 November 1884, 6 December 1884; Chico *Enterprise*, 28 July 1885 and 31 December 1886; Chico *Chronicle-Record*, 20 September 1892; Chico *Record*, 12 July 1899.

[12] Jelinek, pp. 47–60.

in viticulture. Impressed by the mission vineyards he had seen during the Bear Flag Revolt and the Mexican War, Bidwell made two return visits to San Rafael and San Luis Rey shortly before the Gold Rush began. There, he selected choice cuttings which he used to start his own eight-acre vineyard in Butte County. By 1857, Bidwell had 15,000 vines growing on his property and began making his own wine and brandy, producing 650 gallons in 1860.[13] When he went to serve in Congress five years later, Bidwell used his position as chairman of the House Agriculture committee to protect California's fledgling wine industry from federal taxation.

Congressman Bidwell's enthusiasm for viticulture quickly cooled, however, when he met and began courting Annie Kennedy, a devout Presbyterian and staunch prohibitionist. In the year preceding their marriage on April 16, 1868, Bidwell had returned home to Chico already a changed man. He promptly uprooted his wine grapes and pioneered a new crop for California in his vineyard: raisins. In October 1868, Bidwell harvested and marketed the Golden State's first commercial raisin crop. Raisins became an important money-maker for Rancho Chico and, at its height, Bidwell's born-again vineyard covered 300 acres planted to Muscat, Malaga, and Tokay grapes. Toward the end of the 1880s, however, Rancho Chico's raisins began to face stiff competition from growers in Fresno County whose soil enabled them to raise a superior product. Once again Bidwell was forced to start digging up his vines, only this time he replaced them with fruit trees to expand his more profitable orchards. By 1891, the vineyard had shrunk to 150 acres. Still, even with his acreage reduced by half, Bidwell harvested over 385,000 pounds of raisins that year, along with 86,000 pounds of table grapes.[14]

Such bounty was typical on Rancho Chico. With the notable exception of lemons, Bidwell's remarkable estate produced nearly every major specialty crop associated with California agriculture's great transition during the late nineteenth century (see Table 2). Its magnificent orchards covered 1,200 acres in 1891 and contained over 72,000 fruit and nut trees. Of these, more than 29,000 were in bearing and yielded large harvests of figs, olives, walnuts, quince, nectarines, apples, cherries, pears, prunes, almonds, plums, and, especially, peaches. The latter, the pro-

---

[13]Hunt, pp. 151, 246, 258; CSAS 1857, p. 20; U.S., Census Office, *Eighth Census of the United States, 1860*, partial schedules for California, vol. 2, Productions of Agriculture.

[14]Hunt, pp. 258–259, 270–271, 325–328; George M. Gray, "Reminiscences of the Life of General John Bidwell," (Chico) *Sandy Gulch News*, 23 March 1939; San Francisco *Occident*, August 1892; Benjamin, p. 26.

Chico Roller Flouring Mills.
Reprinted with permission by Special Collections, Meriam Library,
California State University, Chico and Bidwell Mansion.

duce of 12,000 bearing trees of differing varieties, was the most important of the numerous orchard crops raised on the ranch.[15]

Whether canned, dried, or shipped fresh to their markets in San Francisco, Chicago, or New York, California's specialty crops each fetched a more attractive price than wheat. Competing in a vast and volatile international market, the price of the golden staple steadily declined after 1870 and growers like Bidwell were fortunate to receive more than seventy cents per sixty-pound bushel during the final fifteen years of the century. By contrast, cherries brought Bidwell ten cents a pound in 1888. And, with each of his 1,100 bearing trees yielding at least a half ton of fruit, Bidwell could gross roughly $150,000 annually from his cherry orchard.[16] Similarly, Bidwell's peach trees, yielding an average of over 240 pounds each, earned anywhere from twenty to forty dollars

---

[15]Hunt, pp. 260–271.
[16]C.C.Parry, "Rancho Chico," *Overland Monthly*, 11 (June 1888), p. 568; S. G. Wilson, p. 188.

per ton in the depression year of 1893, when California wheat was selling at a record low of sixty cents per bushel.[17]

Despite the obvious advantages they enjoyed over wheat in terms of per-acre yield and income, specialty crops imposed costly demands upon growers because they required more labor, more careful management, and, in some cases, irrigation. At Rancho Chico, these increased costs were compounded by the sheer size and diversity of Bidwell's operation. Bidwell, of course, was more than just a farmer, and Rancho Chico was more than just a farm. Similar to his involvement in the wheat industry where he became a prominent miller as well as grower, Bidwell's innovative ventures into specialty crop production led him to take on the role of pioneer food processor as well as orchardist. Here, however, the usually successful Bidwell suffered his greatest reversals as an agricultural experimenter and patron of new technology. In 1877, Bidwell invested $13,000 in a two-story fruit dryer designed to replace the older and slower method of simply setting cut fruit out on trays to dry in the sun. The newly patented evaporator utilized blowers driven by a steam engine and contained 228 trays with a combined drying surface of 3,700 square feet. When operating at maximum capacity it could dry one railroad carload of fruit per day. Unfortunately, costly mechanical malfunctions rendered the dryer unprofitable and Bidwell closed it down after just four seasons.[18]

The building then sat idle for a year or two until Bidwell decided to enter the canning business. In 1882, he leased the vacant structure to local merchant Amos F. Blood, who converted it into a factory for the manufacture of tin cans and the canning of fruit. Blood managed the operation for two years before turning it over entirely to Bidwell in time for the 1884 season. With a daily capacity of 2,500 two-pound cans and a seasonal workforce that varied from 50 to 200 employees each year, the cannery put out 65,000 containers of fruit during its first run. Five years later, in 1887, Bidwell expanded the plant and built an adjoining warehouse to handle a spectacular output of 370,000 cans. Then, in 1889, the cannery fell victim to the great bane of early California orchardists: a glutted eastern market. Prior to the development of efficient marketing cooperatives that did not emerge until after 1900, California growers engaged in uncoordinated and self-destructive salesmanship that often resulted in over-

---

[17]CSAS 1893, pp. 164–177.
[18]Gray, "Reminiscences," 23 March 1939; Chico *Record*, 5 April 1936; Wells and Chambers, p. 208; Edmonson, p. 53.

| Table 2: Growth of Rancho Chico's Orchards* | | | | | | | |
|---|---|---|---|---|---|---|---|
| Crop | 1855 | 1856 | 1880 | 1883 | 1891 | 1894 | 1900 |
| Almond | | 25 | 2,800 | 2,800 | 10,344 | 13,800 | 10,900 |
| Apple | 100 | 100 | 1,825 | 1,955 | 4,040 | 2,550 | 2,819 |
| Apricot | | | 940 | 3,990 | 7,140 | 6,300 | 7,500 |
| Blackberry | | | | 8 acres | | | |
| Cherry | | | 1,675 | 1,675 | 2,199 | 2,250 | 2,900 |
| Chestnut | | | | | 100 | 150 | 125 |
| Fig | 100 | 50 | 50 | 50 | 250 | 225 | |
| French Prune | | | | | 11,300 | 10,850 | 26,160 ** |
| Grape | 2,000 | | 50,000 | 62,000 | 75,745 | | |
| Nectarine | | | | | | 487 | 336 |
| Nursery | | | 5 acres | | | | |
| Olive | | | | | 2,650 | 2,100 | 2,750 |
| Orange | | | | | 300 | 150 | 200 |
| Peach | 250 | 300 | 6,200 | 12,500 | 23,800 | 39,700 | 56,000 |
| Pear | 100 | 200 | 1,130 | 1,735 | 5,700 | 5,600 | 5,650 |
| Pecan | | | | | | 125 | |
| Plum | | | 2,440 | 5,465 | 3,500 | 4,100 | |
| Quince | 25 | 50 | 60 | 60 | 112 | | 200 |
| Walnut | | 10 | | | 275 | 250 | 250 |

*Total number of trees or grape vines (bearing and non-bearing).
**Includes plum trees.

Sources: Mansfield, *History of Butte County*, p. 168; Chico *Enterprise*, 22 June 1883; Hunt, p. 270; Oroville *Register*, 10 May 1894; Benjamin, *John Bidwell, Pioneer*, p. 26.

stocked urban markets and drastically reduced prices. Such a surplus in 1889, coupled with a very poor fruit yield on Rancho Chico itself, brought Bidwell's eight-year stint in the cannery trade to a quick end.[19] In 1890, Bidwell announced his withdrawal from the trade, but threw his support behind a group of local investors willing to take up the slack. With Bidwell's encouragement, the Chico Canning Company was incorporated in April 1892. The new cannery enjoyed only moderate success before it too fell prey to a glutted market in 1896.[20]

The failures of the Chico canneries and Bidwell's dryer illustrate the fact that California's transition to specialty crops was anything but auto-

---

[19] Chico *Enterprise*, 13 October 1882, 11 July 1884, 30 July 1886, 15 July 1887, and 8 March 1890; Chico *Record*, 5 April 1936; C. C. Parry, p. 569; Edmonson, p. 55. JBD, 21 June 1886.

[20] Butte County, *Articles of Incorporation*, 25 April 1892; Butte County, *Index to Leases*, Book C, p. 457; Chico *Enterprise*, 8 March 1890, 7 September 1894, 3 May 1895; Chico *Chronicle-Record*, 3 August 1895; Chico *Record*, 19 April 1936.

Annie Ellicott Kennedy Bidwell,
ca. 1868.
Reprinted with permission by
Special Collections Meriam Library,
California State University, Chico.

matic or risk free. Great and costly obstacles lay in the way that often defied even the best efforts of a well run outfit like Rancho Chico. By and large, however, Bidwell was remarkably successful in his prolific attempts to gain entry into nearly every aspect of California's increasingly complex agricultural sector. With each passing year, the number of different commercial activities based on Rancho Chico continued to grow so that Bidwell's estate became a virtual microcosm of the state's farm industry. To successfully manage his increasingly disparate affairs, Bidwell divided Rancho Chico into specialized farming and "industrial" units, each supervised by its own resident foreman.[21] There were fourteen such divisions in 1870–75, and twenty by 1895. In addition to the orchards, grain fields, and vineyard, Rancho Chico's divisions included the well tended

---

[21]Most prominent among Bidwell's ranch foremen were Abram Bidwell, a nephew who served as general superintendent from 1872 through 1883, and George M. Gray, the nephew of renowned Harvard University botanist Asa Gray, a close friend of the Bidwells. Hired in October 1879, Gray supervised Rancho Chico's orchards for over ten years. See San Francisco *Alta California*, 10 November 1879; McDonald, "The Bidwell Family" in *Ripples Along Chico Creek*, pp. 182–183; Hunt, pp. 267–268, 284.

John and Annie Bidwell on mansion grounds in Chico.
Reprinted with permission by Special Collections, Meriam Library,
California State University, Chico.

Drying fruit on Rancho Chico.
Reprinted with permission courtesy of the John Nopel Collection.

Rancho Chico and the Development of California Agriculture   143

Rancho Chico cannery.
Reprinted with permission courtesy of the John Nopel Collection.

John Bidwell's office, above store on 1st St. and Broadway, ca. 1895.
Reprinted with permission by Special Collections, Meriam Library,
California State University, Chico and Bidwell Mansion.

mansion grounds, flour mill, dairy, cattle ranch, sheep ranch, apiary, meat market, and commercial nursery. Among its sixty or more buildings, Rancho Chico also boasted its own olive oil and vinegar factories, three packinghouses, three drying houses, and at least ten barns, along with the "neat two-story houses" occupied by the division foremen and their families. Most impressive of all, besides the mansion, was Bidwell's water tower and observatory that stood one hundred feet high and supplied running water to his residence and several other structures. Like the mercantile store and the hotel Bidwell operated nearby in the town of Chico, many of these buildings and ranch divisions comprised full-fledged businesses unto themselves. The dairy, for example, with its herd of 150 milch cows, grossed $12,000 each year. Sales from Bidwell's nursery, which offered shade and ornamental trees as well as commercial orchard stock, exceeded $25,000 in 1891.[22]

Remarkably, this beehive of agricultural industry and productivity had yet another vital, but often overlooked function. Long before making their famous plans to donate the scenic property that became Bidwell Park, John and Annie Bidwell generously opened Rancho Chico to the public. Though protected by seventy miles of well-maintained fences, the attractive grounds and oak groves of Rancho Chico remained accessible to picnickers and excursionists. Local townspeople were encouraged to take advantage of Rancho Chico's forty-five miles of picturesque drives and to visit Bidwell's ornamental gardens and four-acre deer park stocked with eighteen deer.[23]

Rancho Chico's important role as *de facto* public park helped showcase Bidwell's influential views on environmentalism. Although he and Annie were close friends of Sierra Club founder John Muir, Bidwell was not primarily an advocate of wilderness preservation. Instead, Bidwell championed a now-forgotten late nineteenth century brand of conservation that historian Ian Tyrrell has labeled "environmental reform" or "environmental renovation."[24] Convinced that nature could be improved

---

[22]Wells and Chambers, p. 208; Tubbesing, pp. 8, 28; Parry, pp. 568–69; SG Wilson, p. 201; Dow, p. 45; Hunt, pp. 269, 272; Benjamin, p. 26; Edmonson, pp. 57–58. Bidwell established the nursery in January 1872 (see Tubbesing, p. 35); Rancho Chico produced 10,000 gallons of vinegar in 1882 (see Chico *Enterprise*, 22 June 1883).

[23]Wells and Chambers, p. 208; "Butte County," *Resources of California* (April 1888), pp. 3–4; Chico *Enterprise*, 16 June 1876. Bidwell's manager in 1906 said that over ninety varieties of trees and shrubs could be seen from the portico of the mansion. See Edmonson, p. 53.

[24]Ian Tyrrell, *True Gardens of the Gods: Californian-Australian Environmental Reform, 1860–1930* (Berkeley: University of California Press, 1999): 12–13.

by human intervention, Bidwell joined forces with like-minded visionaries who dreamed of transforming arid California's wheat fields and rangelands into a lush, man-made Garden of Eden that would be both profitable and beautiful. This they proposed to accomplish through their enthusiastic promotion of irrigation, horticulture, and aggressive afforestation. Consequently, the liberal planting of exotic eucalyptus and other decorative trees, shrubs, and flowers became almost as important to Bidwell as the nurturing of his many commercial crops.

Indeed, as Tyrrell argues, Bidwell soon emerged as a leading "apostle of the garden" who had, at great personal expense, deliberately transformed his estate into an "ambitious project to create a garden landscape in the midst of the wheat fields of the Sacramento Valley." By 1880, Rancho Chico stood as "a model of environmental philanthropy that inspired many visitors."[25]

Among Bidwell's inspired guests was Australian journalist Thomas K. Dow, who toured Rancho Chico in 1883 and proclaimed it "the most interesting and best-conducted farm in California." Dow praised Bidwell as a "lover of trees and natural beauty" who "values some things in the world more highly than money." On Rancho Chico, "not even the all-powerful American dollar would be able to bring about the destruction of a favorite oak, an avenue, or a bit of charming scenery. Not only have the natural beauties of the country been preserved, but heaps of gold derived from its productiveness have been expended upon developing and increasing the pleasing appearance of the estate. The property of 25,000 acres is like a group of delightful parks, and one drives for hours in every direction along charming avenues . . . without ever losing the sense of rural beauty."[26]

The aesthetic appeal of Rancho Chico drew a steady stream of locals onto the property. Dow noted that "the whole of the estate, . . . (even the orchards and grounds around the mansion) are open to the public, and in the afternoons the avenues are busy with townspeople riding and driving in every direction" along Bidwell's "winding roads, which have been all laid out under his personal direction."[27]

Inevitably, a few serpents managed to enter Bidwell's Eden, visitors who did not fully share his environmental vision or appreciate his philanthropy. Over time, Bidwell's generosity came to be taken for granted

---

[25]Ibid., pp. 3, 42, 105.   [26]Dow, pp. 42–44.
[27]Ibid., pp. 44–45.

and some tended to forget that Rancho Chico was, after all, still private property. Thefts from the orchards caused Bidwell to close the grounds to "unworthy persons" in the summer of 1876, though "persons of respectability and taste" remained welcome. Nine years later, excessive weekend frolicking forced an exasperated Bidwell to impose restrictions on Sunday recreation in order to preserve the dignity of the Sabbath. Like religion, politics could also pull the welcome mat from Rancho Chico's doorstep. During the anti-Chinese boycott of rancho products in 1886, Bidwell publicly declared boycott supporters *persona non grata*, henceforth they had to picnic somewhere else.[28]

Despite such occasional and temporary changes in policy, Bidwell's estate always remained a place of public enjoyment, and keeping the grounds attractive for visitors added greatly to Bidwell's heavy labor demands. Rancho Chico required a large workforce that grew dramatically as Bidwell extended his various enterprises. In 1857, the California agricultural society reported that Bidwell "has twenty-five Indians constantly employed on his place, and not infrequently from fifteen to twenty white men."[29] By 1891, Bidwell kept eighty to one hundred people employed year round. The core of this expanded and mostly male workforce comprised three groups: white American citizens, Chinese immigrants, and the resident Mechoopda Indians. The whites and Chinese worked for regular wages, while the Mechoopda drew both cash and in-kind compensation. During the busy spring and summer harvest seasons, Bidwell supplemented his labor supply by hiring large numbers of seasonal workers, many of whom were white women and children. At the height of the fruit season each July and August, the total number of people on Bidwell's payroll usually exceeded 500. During the last two decades of the nineteenth century, Bidwell paid out as much as $100,000 in wages and grossed $750,000 in sales each year.[30]

Such a large and complex operation placed constant demands on Bidwell's skills and patience as a manager. As early as the mid-1850s, Rancho Chico's development had reached the point where Bidwell could never afford to be absent for very long. His business suffered terribly during the two

---

[28]Chico *Enterprise*, 16 June 1876 and 12 March 1886; Butte *Record*, 30 March 1885.

[29]CSAS 1857, p. 20. In 1860, twenty-eight white employees, all males, resided on Rancho Chico. These included ranch superintendent Oliver Sproule, chief clerk George Wood, and master millers John Size and L. Brown. Rounding out Bidwell's white workforce were three clerks, a millwright, a master wagon maker, two master blacksmiths, two teamsters, two gardeners, and thirteen farm laborers. See *Eighth Census, 1860*, partial schedules of population for California, vol. 2.

[30]Parry, p. 569; S. G. Wilson, p. 201; Hunt, p. 271; Benjamin, p. 29.

years he spent in Congress, and the financial losses he incurred while serving his country were among the main reasons he declined to seek reelection in 1866. For the next sixteen years following his return home, Bidwell personally supervised each one of Rancho Chico's department foremen, who reported directly to him.[31] Then, in the fall of 1882, mounting debts and responsibilities finally forced an overextended Bidwell to begin delegating greater authority to his subordinates. Summoning his foremen to his mansion office, Bidwell announced that he was creating from their ranks a board of directors to assist him for the next five years. Hoping they might also provide him with greater fiscal discipline, Bidwell decreed that henceforth, all expenditures, even those proposed by the General himself, had to secure a majority vote of approval from the six-man board, which was to meet each Monday afternoon.[32] Bidwell surrendered even more authority four years later when he took another major departure from his previous management practices. Following the harvest of 1886, he decided to give up direct supervision of his grain fields and adopted the leasing system long employed by other large growers like Hugh Glenn. Splitting his 6,600 acres of wheat and barley into nine separate units, Bidwell began renting the subdivided tracts to sharecroppers on one-year renewable leases.[33]

These changes set the stage for an even greater delegation of duties in 1888. As he approached his seventieth birthday, a weary Bidwell gladly turned most of his remaining responsibilities over to Colonel Charles C. Royce, whom he had befriended at an annual encampment of the Grand Army of the Republic in San Francisco two years before. A Union navy veteran and noted anthropologist who had published several books on the Indians of North America, Royce had spent twelve years with the Smithsonian Institution's department of ethnology before moving west to take the reins at Rancho Chico. An extremely able administrator, Royce presided success-

---

[31]S. G. Wilson, pp. 199–200.
[32]Bidwell declared himself president of the board which included grain ranch foreman William King (vice president), head bookkeeper Henry H. Camper (secretary), chief miller J. C. Hunt, stock and dairy foreman William Seagraves, and orchard foreman George M. Gray. See Chico *Enterprise*, 1 November 1882; Gray, "Reminiscences," *Sandy Gulch News*, 30 June 1938, 28 July 1938, 4 August 1938.
[33]Chico *Enterprise*, 3 and 17 September 1886. Despite the *Enterprise's* description of the leases as "share" arrangements, some might actually have been cash rentals. See, for example, Bidwell's 1899 contract with Jacob Ladenberger and John Seaver in Butte County, *Chattel Mortgages*, Book J, p. 163. There is some evidence that Bidwell experimented with short-term lease agreements during the economic slump of the mid 1870s. He apparently did so in order to share some of the costs and risks of the wheat trade, as well as to bring new lands under grain cultivation. See Chico *Northern Enterprise*, 14 November and 12 December 1873, and 16 June 1876.

fully over the controversial leasing of Bidwell's fruit orchards to Chinese tenants after 1894 (see Chapter 7) and remained superintendent at Rancho Chico for twenty-six years until submitting his resignation in 1914.[34]

Though Royce now attended to all the daily details, Bidwell remained very much in command at Rancho Chico and still worked actively to maintain its reputation as one of the finest showplaces of California agriculture, a model farm that continuously explored and tested the potentials and capabilities of the state's rich soils and climate. Among his many pioneering innovations Bidwell proudly listed the successful introduction of the casaba melon to California and the excavation of the Sacramento Valley's first irrigation ditch in 1847. As one admirer noted of Rancho Chico, "It is quite probable ... that none of the Government's [agricultural] experimental stations has given to the public more useful information than have these valuable grounds."[35]

Bidwell no doubt enjoyed the compliment but would have been quick to challenge the hint of criticism directed at the state and federal farm experiment stations. Bidwell was an ardent advocate of government aid to agriculture, especially in the fields of viticulture and horticulture. While chairing the farm committee of the House of Representatives in 1865–1867, he fought hard to strengthen the newly created United States Department of Agriculture as well as the famous Morrill Land Grant College Act of 1862, which provided federal funds for the establishment of state agricultural colleges. His support of publicly funded research was such that in 1888 he donated thirty-seven acres of his ranch to the California State Forestry Commission for use as an experimental forestry station. Located on the south bank of Chico Creek, the site was transferred to the University of California in 1893 and operated as a tree nursery until 1921, when it became part of today's Bidwell Park.[36]

Recognizing early on that California's dry Mediterranean climate would pose unique challenges to American farmers accustomed to more humid conditions back East, Bidwell had joined the California State Agricultural Society in 1858. Designed to collect and disseminate useful information about crops, soils, and farming techniques, the CSAS became a branch of the state government in 1880 and eventually evolved

---

[34]Royce was a national officer in the GAR and a former head of the land division of the United States Office of Indian Affairs where he worked from 1866 to 1876. See Chico *Record*, 5 October 1920; Hunt, pp. 274–275, 396, 416.

[35]S.G. Wilson, p. 199.

[36]Hunt, pp. 374–376.

into the modern California Department of Agriculture. To better educate and inform California growers, the CSAS issued reports and sponsored state and local district fairs each fall after harvest. The fairs, subsidized by state funds filtered through the CSAS, were organized by local CSAS county and district boards composed of enterprising and progressive farmers. Naturally, the Upper Sacramento Valley Agricultural Society counted John Bidwell among its most important leaders and, after serving as the first president of the Butte County association in 1867, Bidwell was elected president of the Valley district society in 1869 and again in 1872.[37]

Until he broke with the society in 1873 over his opposition to fairground horse racing, Bidwell used his prominent position as a bully pulpit from which he delivered ringing sermons on behalf of his visionary dreams for California agriculture. Most prophetic were his calls for an elaborate statewide system of irrigation canals, reservoirs, dams, and levees; a remarkable plan that anticipated by more than a half century the enormous Central Valley and California State Water projects.[38] Bidwell also took up the cause of Sacramento farmers battling the hydraulic gold mining industry of the Sierra foothills. Commencing in 1853 and escalating constantly thereafter, hydraulic miners washed tons of mud, sand, gravel, and other debris called "slickens" down the eastern tributaries of the Sacramento River. The resulting damage caused to downstream cities and farms was enormous. Mining debris clogged the streams, destroyed navigation, caused massive flooding, and buried thousands of acres of productive farmland under barren sediments. Angry farmers responded by forming the Anti-Debris Association which challenged the miners in court and before the state legislature. Bidwell assumed a leading role in the struggle and his outspokenness on behalf of agriculture led to his election as chairman of the 1882 Anti-Debris convention in Sacramento. Two years later, in 1884, the farmers triumphed in United States Circuit Court where they secured a favorable decision in the case of *Woodruff vs. North Bloomfield Mining Company*. Judge Lorenzo Sawyer's landmark ruling effectively shut down the worst of the hydraulic mining operations.[39]

---

[37]Gerald Prescott, "Farm Gentry vs. The Grangers: Conflict in Rural America," *California Historical Society Quarterly*, 56 (Winter 1977–1978), pp. 328–345; Wells and Chambers, p. 207; Hunt, p. 306; Edmonson, pp. 44–45.
[38]Edmonson, p. 52; Hunt, pp. 201–204; CSAS 1865, p. 211; CSAS 1867, pp. 422–426; CSAS 1881, pp. 38–39, JB-91, p. 66.
[39]Hunt, pp. 226–229; Kelley, *Gold vs. Grain*, pp. 195, 226.

Bidwell contributed directly to the victory by testifying as an expert witness who recalled the pristine clarity of northern California's streams prior to the advent of hydraulic mining. In retrospect, Bidwell's participation in the trial seems especially fitting, since *Woodruff vs. North Bloomfield* is frequently regarded as a signal event that marked the end of gold mining's glory days and heralded the ascendancy of agriculture as California's premier industry. No other man or woman had done more to effect that great transformation than the pioneer proprietor of Rancho Chico.[40]

Sadly, Rancho Chico did not long survive the death of its founder. Despite its achievements and productivity, Bidwell's elaborate enterprise failed to lift him out of the red after 1870. Poor management during his absence in Washington, compounded by the cost of building his $60,000 mansion, placed Bidwell in tremendous debt between 1865 and 1868. The subsequent and sustained decline of wheat prices, coupled with the lengthy depression that followed the Panic of 1873, plunged Bidwell below the point where he could reasonably expect to pay off his accumulating debts. Still, his credit remained sound because he was able to meet his annual operating expenses and interest payments. Consequently, he maintained his ability to secure the loans he needed to finance new projects and expansions. Nevertheless, Bidwell was walking an increasingly fine line. The great Panic of 1893, which occurred in the midst of a prolonged drought, pushed Bidwell's total indebtedness to a staggering $400,000.[41] Three years later, Bidwell privately confessed to his good friend John Muir that "financially we are literally crushed, fruit practically all killed, grain brings scarcely cost."[42]

To relieve his growing financial burdens, Bidwell had already begun to sell off portions of Rancho Chico beginning in 1887, when he laid out the subdivision of Chico Vecino immediately north of the mansion. Still, Bidwell bequeathed a mortgaged indebtedness of $350,000 to his widow when he died in 1900. On the advice of her attorney, Annie Bidwell expedited the breakup and sale of Rancho Chico prior to her death in 1918 and, by the

---

[40] Bidwell had also testified two years earlier in a similar suit tried before Judge Jackson Temple of the Sacramento County Superior Court. Judge Temple, whom Bidwell had defeated for Congress in 1864, sided with the farmers and set the stage for their final victory in the Woodruff case. See Chico *Enterprise*, 24 January and 16 June 1882; Kelley, *Gold vs. Grain*, pp. 196–219.

[41] Hunt, pp. 415–418; Edmonson, pp. 47–48. Bidwell had been forced to borrow $90,000 in 1874 from a San Francisco bank which assumed a mortgage on Rancho Chico. In 1884, Bidwell mortgaged his property once again, this time to secure a $235,000 loan from the German Savings Bank. See Edmonson, pp. 52, 54–55.

[42] John Bidwell to John Muir, 20 April 1896, John Muir Papers, Holt-Atherton Center for Western Studies, University of the Pacific, Stockton, Ca.

time the terms of her elaborate will were finally completed in 1936, only the mansion and surrounding grounds remained.[43] The rest had all been subdivided and sold, with the noteworthy exceptions of the Mechoopda rancheria, a small children's playground deeded to the city of Chico in 1913, and the spectacular Bidwell Park. Encompassing 2,300 acres donated to the city in 1905 and 1909, Bidwell Park stretches eastward from downtown Chico to the upper canyon reaches of Chico Creek nearly eight miles away. Among the nation's largest municipal recreation areas, the park preserves intact a sizable portion of the original Mexican land grant that John Bidwell developed into one of nineteenth century California's most important farms.[44]

## Bidwell on California Agriculture

### THE PRIMACY OF AGRICULTURE

... in every well regulated State, agriculture must ever be deemed the paramount interest, because it furnishes the necessaries of life, food and raiment, on which all depend, and without which no government, or society, can exist. It is a safeguard against the contingencies of war and famine, and should ever be the pride of the people and receive the fostering care of the government.[1]

... where would be the manufacturing interests which are deemed of vital importance to every independent nation, without agriculture as a basis for their very existence and growth? Where would be your commerce whose sails are beginning to whiten almost every sea? ... Blot out this paramount interest and hardly a nation would survive. Organized society and labor would cease, there would be no division of labor, no manufactures, no commerce, none of the arts of peace and civilization. Every civilized country must of necessity derive its principal means of subsistence from the soil; everything else is merely auxiliary. Keep the agricultural interest in a prosperous condition, and the future of our own country will be grand beyond the power of human conception.[2]

... we cannot ignore the fact, that agriculture is the foundation, and, there-

---

[43]In a letter to Annie dated March 14, 1904, her attorney Franklin C. Lusk informed her that Rancho Chico had not made a profit in over fifteen years, and that he was "fully satisfied that nobody can take it in the condition that it now is and run it at a profit, and am certainly convinced that you cannot...." Lusk suggested that Annie "sell just as rapidly as possible, taking advantage of the present boom, all the real estate that you have, except the park that you desire to give to the city and your own residence grounds." In BFP.
[44]Edmonson, pp. 59, 62; Valerie Mathes, "Annie E. K. Bidwell: Chico's Benefactress," *California History,* 68 (Spring/Summer 1989), pp. 16–17, 23, 25.
[1]CSAS 1860, p. 328.
[2]*Congressional Globe,* 39th Congress, 1st Session, p. 1574.

fore, the most important of all other pursuits. Without increasing production by cultivating the soil, no civilized nation could exist—blot out this paramount pursuit, and but few of the present population of the globe would be able to survive. But while agriculture is by common consent placed first in the scale, do not understand me to lightly estimate the value of other branches of industry. They are as important in developing agriculture as agriculture is important to the existence of man. Without the aid of mechanic arts, and of science, and of all useful professions and occupations, the intelligent agriculturist of to-day would have advanced but a short distance upon the wide space which now separates him from barbarism. There is, then, Mr. President, a harmony or co-ordination of interest between agriculture and all other useful pursuits. One cannot flourish without the other. . . . Advance agriculture, and you advance all other branches of human industry.[3]

Agriculture is the first and most important occupation of man, and embraces, in the general and practical idea of rural employment, both the cultivation of the soil and the rearing of useful animals. It is as old as sacred history, and may be said to date from the creation of man. "And the Lord God planted a garden eastward in Eden." Thus the Creator himself set the first example for man to imitate—a decree which in all ages he has been forced to obey or suffer the penalty. Man must plant or he cannot reap—he must earn his food or suffer the pains of hunger.[4]

### AGRICULTURE MORE IMPORTANT THAN HYDRAULIC GOLD MINING

Mining is a legitimate industry, and all other industries must of necessity be friendly to it. But that class known as hydraulic has grown to be intolerable, and its stoppage has become inevitable. . . . Hydraulic mining is a landmark never to be obliterated in the history of this State, both because of its good and bad results. The bad results are seen and known by all. They caused vast expenditures, ruin, terror and desolation. To effect even partial restoration to lands, streams and navigation will require vast sums in the future. But I believe, and all whom I have conversed seem convinced, and we fondly hope that, with the stoppage of hydraulic mining, a new and important era in the near future will dawn upon California, and witness at least the beginning of restoration—the once crystal waters to purity, the streams to navigation, etc. . . .

Irrigation is the natural successor to hydraulic mining, and important beyond computation. Without it we can never know or have any conception of California's productive capacity. By showing that waters can be conducted almost everywhere, hydraulic mining has unwittingly solved a most important feature in the problem of irrigation. . . .

---

[3]CSAS 1865, pp. 206–07.
[4]CSAS 1867, p. 419.

The water already flowing in the artificial channels ... has made the transition from mining to cultivation not only possible, but easy and inviting.[5]

I wish hydraulic mining could continue, and the whole country prosper. At the same time, I admit that it is not to me a pleasing scene to see havoc made of hills, and mountains, and stately forests, and a once lovely prospect changed to a desolation.

There can be no question that agriculture is the only enduring interest, and that an immediate and adequate remedy is demanded, not wholly repair the injury done, for that may be impossible, but to avert greater impending peril. And, without attempting to discuss remedies, I must confess my inability to see how the continual and widespread destruction is to cease without stopping the cause. The miners have a rule or common law which governs among themselves, and it is just, namely: that miners working claims above, on the same stream, must not dump their tailings on claims below them. Let them apply this rule to their brother farmers, and the trouble is at once settled. It is justice, pure and simple. . . . [6]

### CALIFORNIA AGRICULTURE AND ITS PROSPECTS, 1841

Wheat—On the South side of the Bay of St. Francisco, the soil, climate &c. are as well adapted to raising wheat as in any part of the World. I have been credibly informed, that it yields 70 to 115 fold—wheat will always come up the second year and produce more than half as much as it did the first. This is because of its scattering on the ground while harvesting. Wheat is sown in December, Jan. and February, harvested in June and the first of July. North side of the Bay, will not yield more than 15 or 20 fold.

Corn does not grow well in any part of California, it however thrives far better on the North side of the Bay than on the South, it will not yield more than 15 or 20 bushels to the acre—when you read my description of the Climate you will not wonder, the corn is of a small kind planted in April and May.

Potatoes—Irish Potatoes grow well and are of good quality—should be planted in April.

Sweet Potatoes have never been tried.

Beans are produced abundantly, likewise peas: peas are planted in gardens about the 10th of March and are ripe about the last of May.

Barley yields well, and is sown at the time of the wheat.

Onions, Cabbages, Parsnips, Beets, Turnips grow well.[7]

The cool nights, together with the dryness of the summer, are undoubtedly the reason why corn, and many other things, do not come to so great perfection here as in many other parts of the world. Water melons and pumpkins are pro-

---

[5]Letter to Sacramento *Record-Union*, 22 January 1884.
[6]CSAS 1881, pp. 28–29.
[7]*Journey*, pp. 33–34.

duced here in abundance, though I fear not so well as in Missouri, they are said not to be so sweet as in the U. States but they last longer, frequently to December, up in June. Strawberries are found in many places in abundance large and delicious, and are ripe about the middle of April.[8]

All concur in pronouncing the country, good for fruit; apples &c. I presume it is so; I went to [Fort] Ross (this is the most northern settlement in California) on the 25th of January. I saw here a small but thrifty orchard, consisting of Apple, Peach, Pear, Cherry and Quince trees—the Peach trees had not shed their leaves and several were in blossom, the Quince and more than half the apple trees were green as in summer. There were roses, marigolds and several kinds of garden flowers in full bloom....

Pear trees I am informed come to great perfection, Fig trees likewise are found in almost every orchard and grow well.

The Wine Grape is cultivated and grows to great perfection.[9]

The Sacramento [Valley] spreads into a wide valley or plain, through which run most of its tributaries, the St. Joaquin etc.—these plains are now the Province of thousands of Elk, Antelope, Deer, wild horses etc. they might easily be changed to raising of thousands of fine cattle.[10]

Sheep—In some places there are a great many: on the farm of [Robert] Livermore, I saw 6,000, Capt. Sutter has 1,000, they are small and the wool rather coarse.

Hogs—There are few hogs here, but they can be raised here, as well as in the U.S. the few I have seen looked fine. A hog weighing 200 lbs. is worth four or five dollars.

Cattle—Of all the places in the world, it appears to me, that none can be better adapted to the raising of cattle than California. The cattle here are very large, and a person who has not a thousand is scarcely noticed as regards stock.

R. Livermore and the Spaniard adjoining, have about 9,000 head; I Reed [an Irishman] has 2,000; Vallea [Vallejo] is the most wealthy Spaniard in the country, and has 12,000 head! Capt. Sutter has 2,000 head. There is no regular price for cattle, but it is about $4 dollars per head. I have been assured any quantity might be bought for $2 per head—yet, such opportunities, I do not think common—a few years ago, cattle could be bought for $1 per head, times have changed. Hides are worth anywhere on the coast $2—tallow $6 per hundred lbs.—many persons own from 1,000 to 6,000 but it is unnecessary to insert names here.

Horses—These are next in number to cattle, they are not in general large, but they answer every purpose, the price is various. I have known good horses to sell from 8 to 30$—mares are never worked or rode, they are worth 3 to 5$.

---

[8]*Journey*, p. 37.     [9]*Journey*, p. 37.     [10]*Journey*, pp. 38–39.

Capt. Sutter has about 600 head of horses, Valleo has from 2,000 to 3,000—a hundred persons might be mentioned, who have from 300 to 800. Horses here are not subject to diseases.

Mules—These are large and fine, and are worth before they can be rode about $10 per head, after being broke to the saddle $15. Jacks worth from 100 to 200$.

Oxen—The Spaniards work oxen by lashing a straight stick to the horns, good tame working oxen worth about $25. It is actually more work to haul, the clumsy, awkward, large, unhandy Carts of the Spaniards, than an American wagon with a cord of wood.[11]

Butter and Cheese—But little butter and cheese made in this country; pains not being taken to milk the cows; butter is worth 50 cents per lb.: what a chance there is in this line of business for industrious Americans. No doubt sale for any quantity could be made to Ships, but the price would become somewhat less.[12]

Honey Bee—I have been informed that there is kind of a Honey Bee in this country that makes honey; but they are not like the honey bee of the States, and are neither plenty nor common, if bees were brought to this country I think they would do well.[13]

### California Plow, 1840s

I think I never saw a native Californian who was a carpenter. And yet everyone, even Indians, could make a California plow, which consisted of a crooked stick, a limb coming up for a handle, and on the point of the stick that went into the ground a little piece of flat iron about the size of a man's hand. That was the only plow Californians had. They had no such thing as a harrow, but instead they used a brush after plowing in that fashion to cover the ground and smooth the ground.[14]

### California Ox Cart, 1840s

California oxen were yoked together—they always used oxen to draw these carts, and if one ox happened to be twice as large as the other it made no difference, the little one kept up with the other by force of necessity, for if they did not keep even, the yoke was so made that it would twist their heads off. And strange to say, they worked better and traveled faster than American oxen.[15]

## *Growing and Marketing "Bonanza Wheat"*

### Gold Rush Stimulates Wheat Production

Farming necessarily followed mining, because the mining created a demand for

---

[11] *Journey*, pp. 39–40.
[12] *Journey*, p. 40
[13] *Journey*, p. 41.
[14] *Pioneers*, p. 9.
[15] *Pioneers*, p. 11.

farm products. We immediately began raising more and more wheat, more cattle and horses. The mines at first were our only market, but they furnished a very good market. I was almost the first to build a grist-mill on the Sacramento valley. Sutter had started one, but when gold was discovered, the work was stopped, and was never finished. I built the mill in 1853. I furnished flour to the mines, and the valley generally. When we began cultivating grain we did it after the manner of the Mexicans, having no agricultural machinery different from the Mexicans. All our grain was cut with sickles by hand. We had not even cradles. It was gathered and laid in great heaps in the shape of a mound, in the center of a round corral made high and strong. It was threshed by turning into the corral bands of wild horses, and sending in Indians almost as wild to pursue them. The faster the horses ran, the faster the grain was threshed. The grain was then several feet thick, and in order to press it down, the Indians would suddenly run in front of the horses, and the horses would stop so quickly that their feet would stir it to the bottom. In that way we would thresh 2,000 bushels of grain in an hour. Then we had to separate the straw with forks and rakes. After we had done this, we would have to wait for the wind to blow the light stuff to one side. We brushed the light chaff to one side with a broom. What we could thresh in an hour, it would take us a month or five weeks to clean up. While one part was very rapid, the other was correspondingly slow. If you had seen the process of threshing, it would have been a wild scene for you. We some times put in 250 wild horses. It was not long before we had cradles and reapers, and other farming implements, until now I think we have the most improved and efficient harvesting machinery in the world.[16]

### Cost of Wheat Production, 1860

I have made some figures in reference to the cost of raising wheat and the result shows 75 cents the bushel. In this calculation I have estimated the general yield at 25 bushels to the acre. As follows, for plowing, sowing, harrowing, brushing, rolling and seed $12.50 [per acre] or 50 cents per bushel;

| | |
|---|---|
| for reaping & binding &c | 7 [cents per bushel] |
| " " hauling, threshing, &c | 18 [cents per bushel] |
| Total | 75 |

This result would be diminished by a larger yield. My grain has generally averaged about 40 bushels to the acre. Had it not been injured this year it would have yielded beyond a doubt 50 to 60 bushels....[17]

### Typical Weather Anxieties, December 1876

... Of course it [beautiful December weather] is bad for farmers, but then we must hope for rain a little later. Some parts of the country can not be plowed—

---

[16]JB-91, pp. 59–60.
[17]JB to Warren, 19 June 1860, James L. L. Warren Papers, b. 1, BANC.

ground too dry. Our farm is generally in perfect condition for plowing, and I think there is yet no cause of alarm. A few showers in January and February, and a wet March, would save the country. The season, however, bears a striking resemblance to the dry one just 33 years ago, when there was almost no rain, and as a consequence, nothing was raised![18]

### Hoping for rain, February 1864

In reference to the grain crop, the prospect is not good—it is bad. Unless a very considerable amount of rain come—more than what has already fallen—the failure in crops will be general. Rain, rain is the only thing that will save them. There is yet time for this to come, and I live in hope. But I have seen one year (1844) dryer than this; what has been may be again—it is only a question of time.[19]

### Preparing for harvest, 1880

...Harvest however is evidently nearing, for the green of the wheat and barley fields are fading into yellow. The last wheat sown—which was in March—looks fine—it may be the best of all! While it looks so well, there is danger of hot weather shrinking it. I intended it only for hay, but may save it, or part of it, for hay and cut the rest for wheat![20]

### Anticipating a good crop, 1880

Barring the wild oats and weeds that have rendered the wheat in some fields undesirable for grain, and so has to be cut for hay, the wheat crop is going to be good, I think.[21]

### Sultry harvests

...here in California labor is performed even in the most sultry valleys during all hours of the day and at all seasons of the year. On my farm in Chico, in this valley, where we claim to have a reasonable degree of heat, especially in time of harvest, I can scarcely remember an instance of a hand becoming sick in the harvest field. Perhaps some will say we don't kill ourselves with work at Chico. In reply, I will answer that we do not; and what is more, we do not intend to do so.[22]

### Wheat harvest, 1868

...We may be said now to be fairly at harvesting,—and average about a thousand bushels per day of wheat—I have just made a sale of 200 tons of wheat 6,666 $^2/_3$ bushels, at 90 cents per bushel—amounting to $6,000—one half to be deliv-

---

[18] JB to AB, 24 December 1876, JB-CSL, b. 53, f. 17.
[19] JB to Warren, 26 February 1864, James L. L. Warren Papers, b. 1, BANC.
[20] JB to AB, 20 June 1880, JB-CSL, b. 55, f. 10.
[21] JB to AB, 28 June 1880, JB-CSL, b. 55, f. 13.
[22] CSAS 1865, p. 211.

ered this, and the other half next week. There is so much wheat in this State this year that we fear low prices—hence I prefer to accept offers at this price named rather than run the risk of inferior rates as soon as the grain is harvested....[23]

### WHEAT HARVEST, 1869

... We find the grain rather green and tough to thresh well. Wherefore the reapers have been ordered to operate for a day or two, binding the grain in bundles—a thing now rarely done in California, since the introduction and general use of headers.[24]

... Our harvesting is progressing very well—averaging about 1,000 bushels of wheat per day....[25]

### COMBINE HARVESTER, 1870

... It is my purpose to go as far as Davisville tonight so as to have a few hours to spend in seeing a harvesting machine work on the farm of Gen. Ridington—a new invention and said to be a success. It cuts, threshes, cleans the grain, and sacks &c. Please tell Mr. Cochran that I expect another machine (the one he has heard me speak of) to go up next week to make a trial on our place—it is the machine the Mrs. Rev. Wm. Taylor of Alameda wrote me about, and I want Mr. Cochran to give it a fair trial, and have all the farmers of the country see it work.[26]

### GRAIN YIELDS, 1865

It will be sufficient for this occasion to say that the soil, climate, and many other features of California, are unsurpassed. It is a region of wonderful variety and production. The cereals are here produced of superior quality, and in larger quantity per acre than in any other part of the United States. It would be a poor farm indeed, and badly cultivated at that, if it failed to yield twenty-five bushels of wheat, and thirty of barley or oats per acre. Fifty bushels of wheat are no uncommon crop, and other grains in proportion. In some localities, generally in rich alluvial bottoms like those of the Yuba [River], Indian corn flourishes in a manner to compare favorably with the famous Valley of the Mississippi.[27]

### WHEAT YIELDS, 1873

Look at the cereal capacity of your State. Take for instance wheat—bread, the staff of life. If a premium were offered for the smallest yield of wheat in this State—on any land timely and properly managed—it would be difficult, in my

---

[23] JB to Joseph C. G. Kennedy, 7 July 1868, BFP, b. 1.
[24] JB to AB, 23 June 1869, JB-CSL, b. 47, f. 28.
[25] JB to AB, 6 July 1869, JB-CSL, b. 47, f. 40.
[26] JB to AB, 1 July 1870, JB-CSL, b. 49, f. 6.
[27] CSAS 1865, p. 207.

opinion, to establish a smaller showing than ten bushels per acre, in any ordinary or average season, from land chosen by any sane man, up to this date. On the other hand, sixty to seventy bushels per acre are not uncommon....[28]

### DRAWING IMPORTANT LESSONS FROM CROP FAILURE

... The report of my grain crop being injured by the *blight* is, I regret to say, but too true, and with all pains which it will be proper to use, can I expect more than one fourth of a crop. I estimate my loss at 15,000 bushels of wheat. The barley was slightly affected. Being absent during the unusually wet and cold spring, I depend on the opinion of my superintendent Mr. Oliver Sproule who is an excellent farmer, for the cause, to wit—the heavy frost in May which came upon the wheat in early bloom. The grain was very rank, and the rain and wind had lodged a considerable portion of it. The weather had been for a long time damp as well as cold, but no marked effect was noticed till the second day after the frost, when the change was so apparent that those who witnessed it think there can be no mistake as to the cause. My own opinion is that the humidity prevailing at the time should not be lost sight of when we attempt to account for such unusual & complete destruction. The excessive moisture alone must have been injurious to rank grain. Late sown grain escaped, and some sown late in March, promises best of all, and that too on land which, if sown later than January in ordinary seasons, would hardly pay for harvesting. As a general rule grain should be sown early. These exceptional seasons cannot be made a criterion & until the clerk of the weather performs his duties more satisfactorily, we cannot expect to be wise enough to turn them to advantage....[29]

### WHEAT, DEBT, AND TAXES, 1876

... The wheat sold will amount to some twenty two (22) thousand dollars. But that will not make the bank account even by seven thousand in Chico and nineteen (19) thousand in San Francisco. The taxes must be paid this month and amount to, state and county tax $11,500 including the school tax—and where is the money coming from?[30]

### WHEAT PRICES, 1876

... I sold wheat at $1.68 per 100 pounds = one dollar and 8 mills per bushel, thus $1.008. Dr. Glenn sold for $1.65, equal to 99 cents per bushel. Therefore I got nearly 2 cents per bushel more than he did, or, to be exact, $1\,^4/_5$ more.... Mrs. Ludwig has written me about Mrs. Reading's wheat. I have advised her to sell at $1.75 which she has been offered because Mrs. Reading wants the money

---

[28] Charles C. Royce, *John Bidwell: Pioneer, Statesman, Philanthropist: A Biographical Sketch* (Chico: n.p., 1906), Speech to Farmers' Union Convention, San Francisco, April 8, 1873.
[29] JB to Warren, 19 June 1860, James L. L. Warren Papers, b. 1, BANC.
[30] JB to AB, 7 December 1876, JB-CSL, b. 53, f. 6.

by New years, she says. Wheat will go higher no doubt, but few people can afford to hold it.[31]

### WHEAT SURPLUS, 1860

It is true we produce a sufficiency, even a surplus, of some things; but we seem prone to extremes and inconsistencies. For instance, we have this year raised twice as much wheat as we know what to do with, and more than can be sold, even at ruinous rates, because there is but limited demand; our home market is not adequate, because we produce too much of one thing and not enough of another; and we have done this, too, when labor was up to thirty, forty, and, in harvest, fifty dollars, per month, and wheat worth at the same time only sixty to ninety cents a bushel. These things will, however, eventually regulate themselves, on the principle of supply and demand, but intelligent foresight could materially abridge the time.[32]

### RANCHO CHICO FLOUR MILL

...The mill is a success and runs to our entire satisfaction. We are now making flour of the new wheat. Sometimes the wheat standing in the field is made into flour in a few hours—sometimes I say—but I should have said it is a daily occurrence on our place. You know how the teams go direct from the machine (threshing) to the mill.[33]

### BUILDING NEW FLOUR MILL, 1885

...Today has been an important business day—for I have let the contract to rebuild the mill—to Mssrs. Nordyke, Marmon co. of Indianapolis, for $30,000. The mill will of course cost more than that, because that is the price over and above the machinery we saved from the old mill and the brickwork and changes in the foundation. The new mill when completed will probably stand up to an actual cost of $40,000. But I expect and believe it will be the best (not the largest) mill in the State.[34]

### WHEAT SACK PRICES AND SHIPPING COSTS, 1873

One of the grievances of the past year complained of by farmers is the enormous price imposed for sacks in which to market or store their wheat. Instead of eleven to thirteen cents, which would have been a fair price, they have had to pay fifteen to nineteen cents, or an aggregate overcharge in the State of half a million of dollars. Instead of $12.50 per ton freight on wheat from San Francisco to Liverpool, which would have been a fair rate, ocean tonnage became monopolized and demoralized, and farmers were made to suffer to the tune of probably $2,500,000 more. That interior freights are too high, all agree, and the overcharge on wheat alone may

---

[31]JB to AB, 12 December 1876, JB-CSL, b. 53, f. 9.
[32]CSAS 1860, p. 329.
[33]JB to AB, 12 July 1869, JB-CSL, b. 47, f. 44.
[34]JB to AB, 20 January 1885, JB-CSL, b. 59, f. 26.

be within the actual limits if placed at half a million more. In how many other ways farmers are and have been unjustly taxed I will not undertake to enumerate.[35]

### FREIGHT AND SACK RINGS

It is true the elements which bear so heavily on your prosperity are not the growth of a day, but they are none the less dangerous, for they have become well-nigh formidable.

But when speculation and reckless adventure organize against you, and demoralize every legitimate business, enhance every risk and increase every expense—in other words, when freight rings, grain rings, sack rings, and all sorts of combinations, regulate their own charges, dictate the prices of your produce, and practically block up every avenue between you and your markets—can you remain insensible, silent, apathetic?[36]

### BIDWELL HURT BY FAILURE OF SAN FRANCISCO GRAIN MERCHANTS, 1887

... Dresbach and Rosenfelt (the grain merchants) have failed—and thereby we shall lose several thousand dollars. Cannot now tell how much, but fear it may go to 3 to 5 thousand dollars. For this reason and others I want you to be as economical as possible. The price of wheat has dropped so low a figure that our own grain will bring but little. . . .[37]

### BANKING ON THE NEXT CROP, DECEMBER 1876

... I answer again, no money here, but a largely overdrawn bank account instead! You are ready to ask 'how then did you get the money to send?' Well, I will tell you: Seeing that you must have means, I put on a bold front and went into the bank and called for a draft and drew a check to pay for it! trusting to the next wheat crop! So you see I am going it on credit![38]

[January 13, 1877] ... The weather continues clear, but it is cool—and today we had a dry N. wind, bringing clouds of dust! This evening however is calm. But it is such a strange winter—two months now and not a drop of rain! Unless it comes soon much grain will be utterly ruined, and if there come no rains at all, or almost none as in 1843 + 44, there will be no harvest.[39]

[January 18] ... A rain has at last come! and done a good deal of good. The surface of the ground is very wet, but the water has not penetrated over two or three inches.[40]

---

[35] Charles C. Royce, *John Bidwell: Pioneer, Statesman, Philanthropist: A Biographical Sketch* (Chico: n.p., 1906), Speech to Farmers' Union Convention, San Francisco, April 8, 1873.
[36] Charles C. Royce, *John Bidwell: Pioneer, Statesman, Philanthropist: A Biographical Sketch* (Chico: n.p., 1906), Speech to Farmers' Union Convention, San Francisco, April 8, 1873.
[37] JB to AB, 27 August 1887, JB-CSL, b. 59, f. 19.
[38] JB to AB, 28 December 1876, JB-CSL, b. 53, f. 19.
[39] JB to AB, 13 January 1877, JB-CSL, b. 52, f. 26.   [40] JB to AB, 18 January 1877, JB-CSL, b. 53, f. 18.

## Wheat, Soil Depletion, and the Need for Crop Rotation and Diversification

Diversify your agriculture. It is written, "man shall not live by bread alone." This was true more than three thousand years ago; may it not be true in California to-day.

That wheat culture exhausts fertility, does not admit of argument. So does everything we raise exhaust, but wheat more than almost anything else. Rest and summer fallow simply mean postponement of exhaustion. If we are to enjoy the benefit of inexhaustible fertility we must make restoration. We cannot, with impunity, continue to violate an inexorable law of nature, which requires the return, in some form, of that which is borrowed from the soil.

... By diversified agriculture I do not mean that we are to cease raising wheat; but to raise many other products which we either need or for which we can find profitable markets at home or elsewhere.[41]

## *Specialty Crops and Diversification*

### California to be 'One Grand Fruit Orchard'

I think this state is to be largely a fruit garden. I don't think it is to be used continuously for the production of grain. Of course we will always produce cereals, but the capabilities of California are in the direction of fruit raising. It is capable of being made one grand fruit orchard. In order to do that, two things have to be done, some portions of the country must be drained and other portions irrigated, but this will have to be done systematically in order to be successful.[42]

### California Imports Too Many Crops It Should Grow on Its Own, 1860

There is no reason why we cannot supply ourselves with the thousands of barrels, boxes, hogsheads, and casks, of dried apples, nuts, raisins, and other fruits which are constantly imported hither. ... On my own farm, in a black alluvial soil, and where during a portion of the day, the sun beams down with almost tropical heat, I have found the Early Harvest, Summer Pearmain, and Rhode Island Greening (apples), to do well, and about thirty other varieties give flattering indications of success. ... We have not less than a million head of cattle, and our plains, pastures, and even highways, are beginning to swarm with porcine life, and yet we export one million dollars annually to pay for butter, and five hundred thousand dollars for lard.[43]

### Still Too Many Imports, 1865

We can and ought to produce all or nearly all of the thousands of barrels, boxes, and cases of dried apples, raisins, and other fruits, which we import,

---

[41]CSAS 1881, pp. 32–33.   [42]JB-91, p. 61.   [43]CSAS 1860, pp. 329–30.

amounting annually to half a million dollars. We could produce nearly all of the brandies, wines, malts and other liquors, if we must have them, which we import, and thereby save, annually, a quarter of a million dollars more. We have the means and should produce all of the butter, cheese, bacon, pork, lard, lard oil, linseed, and in time, even olive oil, which we import, and thereby make a saving of at least half a million of dollars more every year.[44]

### Almonds, Walnuts, and Cranberries

Almonds grow to perfection here, and can be raised almost as easily as peaches and in quantities to supply all the markets on the Pacific Ocean. We can also grow the Persian Walnut, or Madeira Nut, and without a doubt the filbert also. The cranberry can, doubtless, be raised here. It grows in abundance in Oregon, near the mouth of the Columbia River, and is cultivated with success on the marshy lands of the New England States. High in our sierras are to be found similar marshy meadows, as well as similar climate—increased altitude corresponding to higher latitude—so that we can not only produce the cranberry, but possess the conditions of soil and climate adapted to almost every desirable fruit and production known to the civilized world.[45]

### Wines

California is emphatically the land of the vine; and can there be any doubt that we can produce the finest wines? This is an important question, because we are actually importing, in casks, barrels, baskets, and cases, millions of gallons every year. And yet it is admitted that there is not a land beneath the sun better suited to grape culture than California. The name of Los Angeles is as famous for wine and for the grape as that of California for gold. But the grape flourishes well everywhere, and its cultivation is being expanded all over the State.[46]

### Getting Grape Vines from Mission San Jose, 1850

I have just returned from the Mission of San Jose—I have made arrangements to have some grape vines sent up to you. . . . I want one half of the vines for the Chico ranch.[47]

### Bidwell urges Congress not to Tax California Wines, 1866

Understanding well, as I think I do, the condition of the wine-growing interest upon that coast, I can say that the smallest tax that you can impose upon the wine-growing interest in California would be burdensome, for the reason that that interest has not yet attained a self-sustaining position. Those in possession of vineyards most advanced, those who are manufacturing wines upon the greatest scale, are not doing it at a profit upon their investments. The reason is plain. They have to contend there against many expenses which are not encountered in

---
[44]CSAS 1865, p. 210.    [45]CSAS 1860, p. 330.    [46]CSAS 1860, p. 330.
[47]JB to George McKinstry, 25 February 1850, McKinstry Papers, b. 232, f. 15, CSL.

other sections of the country. In the first place, the cost of labor is much higher. All the materials out of which are made the casks in which to keep this wine must be imported from this side of the continent. It will not do to put the wines into old casks, for wines spoil very quickly. When a cask has been used for other liquors, it is almost impossible to purify it sufficiently to make it fit to keep wine in.

Besides, it is impossible to draw the line of distinction between the condition of the grape juice in the form of must and the condition in which you would call it wine. When it is first expressed, it is grape juice or must, after it is perfectly fermented it ceases to be must. But when does that fermentation cease? With some kinds of wine it may cease in two years; with other kinds it may not cease in five years. So long as the wine contains impurities which continue to be fermented and it requires to be racked off and the cask purified, it is liable to spoil in your hands. It is not a wine that you can pronounce a merchantable article, and which should be taxed.

Let me make one further comment. Vineyards in California are even now only in their infancy. When a vineyard is planted, from four to ten years must elapse before it even pays expenses, much less produces any profit. Hence the smallest tax which you may put upon that interest must be onerous. In California last year some seventeen thousand dollars of tax was collected. Now, there are some five or six revenue districts in that State, and the collection of the revenue must require in each district perhaps two persons, each at a salary of not less than $1,000 per annum. Hence the revenue collected scarcely exceeded the cost of collecting it. . . .

I feel persuaded that if the true condition of the wine-producing interest of California could be understood by this House no tax would be imposed upon it, unless it was done with the purpose of crushing that interest. After wine is made in California you then have to transport it seventeen thousand miles around Cape Horn in order to find a market. You have to pass twice through the tropics, during which time the wine is liable to spoil on your hands. You have to pay interest and insurance upon the risks of the ocean, all of which accumulates immensely the expense.

I have already said that even the smallest tax would be a burden. It takes fourteen pounds of grapes to make a gallon of wine. Those grapes at the vineyard where they are raised are worth perhaps a cent a pound. When you have expressed the juice it is worth from twenty to thirty cents a gallon, including all the cost of labor.

But that is not the cost of the wine. The labor upon it, the cask in which you have to put it, the cost of transporting it to San Francisco, a distance of four or five or six hundred miles oftentimes in California, in many cases where there are no railroads; all these things enhance the cost. And taking everything into consideration, labor, transportation, etc, you cannot produce wine in California for less than ninety cents to $1.25 a gallon. Now, if Congress wishes to crush this interest then impose this tax. Five cents a gallon, as low as it appears, is one third of the value, after deducting the cost of labor, etc. I think that we ought rather to encourage this interest in order to do away with strong drinks and substitute for them a beverage pure, healthful, and invigorating. I am not a wine drinker myself, nor am I an advocate for wine drinking. But if you will foster this interest upon the Pacific coast in a short time we will be able to produce all the raisins and all the wine and all the brandy that will be required in the United States or upon the American continent. But put your tax upon it at this time and you will crush it in its infancy just as it is struggling into existence.[48]

### RAISINS AND TABLE GRAPES, 1872

... The grape vines have arrived from Mr. Nickensons—got about 11,000 from him this year, and 5,000 of them are Muscats of Alexandria and 2,500 Flame Tokays.[49]

### PEACHES AND PEARS

Of [California] peaches and pears it would be vain to attempt description that would be credited abroad—to be appreciated they must be seen. No country can equal, much less surpass, them.[50]

### CASABA MELONS

Am very fond of fruit. I was the only one that succeeded in raising the Casaba melon, named after the town of Casaba, in Asia. The Agricultural Department imported some of the seeds, and I procured some of them. They were sent all over the U.S. but I am the only one that succeeded in raising them. They would not grow on the coast very well, but in the warm valleys they do better. The first year that I raised them the editor of the "Springfield Republican" came out to California, I invited him to come up to the ranch and tried to induce him to stay, but no, he could not. He had made arrangements to leave early. We had some of the melons for breakfast and he tasted them. He got over his hurry, and stayed three days with us.[51]

### ORANGE TREES

... I have something new to tell you—the orange tree nearest to the library, out next to the olive trees, has good oranges—I ate one today. They are not very large, but perhaps they would be if irrigated. The orange, like other acid fruits, requires a good deal of water. The fruit of this tree is by no means acid—I call it good, perhaps it would be equal to those on Butte Creek if as ripe. Somebody has already found them out and picked several, as I see by the stems. The rind or peel is tender, as also the pulp. I cannot tell how much gratified I feel at making this discovery....[52]

---

[48] *Congressional Globe,* 39th Congress, 1st Session, pp. 2728–30.
[49] JB to AB, 21 February 1872, JB-CSL, b. 126, f. 86.
[50] CSAS 1860, p. 330.   [51] JB-91, p. 64.
[52] JB to AB, 3 December 1876, JB-CSL, b. 53, f. 3.

### Contemplating an Experiment with Cotton, 1864

I embrace the earliest moment to acknowledge the receipt of your favor of the 23rd as also the package of cotton seed, for which I thank you. The Sea Island Cotton, from the best information I have been able to obtain, will not be suited to this locality. I will not therefore try the experiment without—the important item of seed right—such as those acquainted with the cultivation of cotton can recommend. If I raise any cotton at all, to justify the expense of machinery which would be required, labor, &c. I must plant at least 200 acres. Here the middle of April will be as early as it will do to put the seed in. Should I be able to procure by that time, say 1,000 to 2,000 lbs. of the right kind of seed, I will try the experiment—otherwise not.[53]

### Cannery Running Day and Night, August 1887

...went to the Cannery—a very busy scene to behold—over 200 hands. Last week the Cannery hand's wages amounted to over $800. This week they will perhaps be $900 or more.[54]

You have never seen more stir about Rancho Chico than now—cans coming and going—long lines of wagons loaded with grain for our warehouse—cannery running day and night etc., etc.[55]

### Rancho Chico in 1891, a Model of Diversified Agriculture

Our ranch is between twenty-four and twenty-five thousand acres. I have tried to diversify instead of raising grain only. I have raised stock, cattle, sheep, fruit, corn, cereals, hay; have carried on the milling business; raise all kinds of vegetables. The farm is the largest in the county. We do not now raise much cattle, simply sheep. The raising of horses and cattle is not possible now. The land is too dear.[56]

## *Mechanization*

### Farm Machinery and Production for Local Consumption

... agriculture in California, as in other countries, is vastly indebted to the mechanic arts for the ease and success with which the farmer is now able to perform his rural labors. Witness the plows, the threshers, the engines, and say if California is behind in inventive skill and enterprise. He who, in the face of high labor and many other obstacles, has established and successfully carried on manufacturing branches of industry, for the purpose of supplying home demands, has helped create the country, and is a patriot and useful member of the State, and is deserving of the patronage and the grateful thanks of the people.[57]

---

[53] JB to Warren, 26 February 1864, James L. L. Warren Papers, b. 1, BANC.
[54] JB to AB, 18 August 1887, JB-CSL, b. 59, f. 14.
[55] JB to AB, 18 August 1887, JB-CSL, b. 59, f. 15.     [56] JB-91, pp. 62–63.
[57] CSAS 1860, pp. 334–35.

## Farm Machinery

Agriculture is so intimately related to and dependent upon the arts and sciences, and especially the mechanic arts, as to be inseparable from them. They must all flourish together and exist in harmonious co-operation as the several parts of a great whole. A state of civilization and advancement renders a division of labor absolutely essential, for in order to excel a man must concentrate all his energies on a single object. Without this, there could be no advancement.

Labor-saving machinery in almost all industrial occupations has become necessary—I may say indispensable—and in no one more than that of the farmer. It is demanded by the intelligent laborer—by the employer and the employed—everywhere....

The farmer who has the best machinery, the latest improvements and keeps up with the age, can hire cheaper and his men work more cheerfully and better—other conditions, of course, being equal.[58]

### Steam Plough Experiment, 1869

... The steam Plow at Oroville is not so near a success as I thought it would be. Still by improvement it may yet be victorious. Humanity is so organized that there is always room for improvement. So great an invention as that which is to successfully apply the wonderful power of steam to the pulverization of the soil, cannot be expected to leap, like Minerva, into full panoplied existence. Time will doubtless bring about a revolution in agriculture—through the agency of steam—but it is as yet not an accomplished fact....[59]

### Bidwell Designs a New Subsoil Plow, 1871

... Last night Mr. Matteson [a farm implements manufacturer] called at the Yosemite House [in Stockton], to see my subsoil plow model—he was much pleased with it. This morning I went to his plow factory and saw his partner (a Mr. Williamson). He expressed himself not only pleased, but says it is ingenious, and knows it will work. The drawback is, they are so pressed with work, they can do nothing towards it before January—and I want all my new vineyard land plowed before that time—I want to have all my winter work done early so as to go and see you, and be there as long as possible. The reason I prefer to have Matteson make my plow is, he is a practical farmer as well as mechanic, he is ingenious, inventive, knows the wants of the country, and is, when he undertakes anything, indefatigable. He never gives up—has spent nearly all he was worth inventing & improving agricultural machinery, especially his combined harvester &c. He excited my sympathy when he said: "If I undertake this I will make it succeed, for I never give up. I never stop at cost—have spent all I was

---
[58]CSAS 1867, p. 420.
[59]JB to AB, 24 February 1869, JB-CSL, b. 47, f. 5.

worth and impoverished my family almost in trying experiments with machinery. Oh how my wife would hate to see this", as he pointed to my model. I then told him if he would make my plow precisely as I directed, I [would] pay him for his work, whether it prove a success or not...[60]

... In regard to my subsoil plow, Mr. Davison (who invented a plow intended to accomplish the same thing) thinks I ought to get a patent for my invention—he is highly pleased—and if I can get my model out of the hands of Matteson & Williamson, Stockton, without trouble or hard feelings, I shall have Mr. Davison go right to Chico and make my plow there—perhaps combine my principle with a part of his plow and make it one concern—though I believe mine to be capable of standing the test of any trial on its own merits. I believe it is destined to come into extended, if not general use at an early day, in some form or other. The more I think of it I am filled with surprise that such an invention has never before been made![61]

... In regard to my subsoil plow, you shall be my agent of, after trial, & I shall deem it worthy of a patent. Several have applied, and one man to my knowledge has obtained a patent for precisely what professes to be the thing I want: namely, a subsoil plow connected with a common plow, so as to stir or pulverize to any desired depth the soil by running in the previous furrow behind the horse, but just in advance of the common plow, for the purpose of loosening the ground for vineyards or other purposes, without the labor raising the subsoil to the surface or the leaving of the smooth subsurface made by the common plow.... Farmers have had many ways to stir the soil to a greater depth than the common plow. The necessity is known by all cultivators of the soil. The implement used must not be attached behind the common plow where it can be most easily done because the horse which goes in the furrows would sink and fatigue himself out in the mellowed earth. Now the desideratum is this: To pulverize the soil deeper than can be done economically by the common plow—to leave no such surface as is made underground by the bottom of the common plow (which acts like a large flat iron). The placing of the subsoil plow behind the horse in the previous furrow is simply position ... and I trust that idea or position—is not patentable.... In a word the device by which a desirable object is attained is patentable—and not position and if so then I am all right and will be clearly entitled to a patent.... But I do not profess to know anything about the patent laws....[62]

... My subsoil plow is progressing very well—and I hope to see it on trial within a week. Am not sanguine that it will at first do all I wish to accomplish

---

[60]JB to AB, 11 November 1871, JB-CSL, b. 49, f. 29.
[61]JB to AB, 19 November 1871, JB-CSL, b. 49, f. 34.
[62]JB to AB, 12 December 1871, JB-CSL, b. 50, f. 9.

Combined harvester at work on Rancho Chico, ca. 1890.
Reprinted with permission by Special Collections, Meriam Library,
California State University, Chico and the California State Library.

Wheat sacks ready for shipment from Chico landing.
Reprinted with permission courtesy of the John Nopel Collection.

or that the proportions may be found perfect when it comes to actual trial—but that the principle is correct, and will sooner or later do all that I claim, I have no doubt. It will need improvement and simplification—to bring it within the reach of all and secure it for general adoption.... The world moves—agriculture must move with it....[63]

---

[63]JB to AB, 20 December 1871, JB-CSL, b. 50, f. 13.

## Livestock and Dairy Production

### OVERGRAZING NATIVE GRASSES

It cannot have escaped the observation of those engaged in rearing stock in California that the indigenous grasses, once so abundant as to pasture thousands of animals where only hundreds are able to subsist now, are fast disappearing from the plains. This is attributable no doubt to excessive grazing, especially by sheep and horses, which destroy the seed, and consequently the essential condition of reproduction. Weeds spring up and encumber the ground, and stock disappear. That these grasses can never be restored in their original excellence is, to me extremely problematical . . . it becomes us to be careful of the grazing capabilities of our land; otherwise we destroy what cannot be replaced.[64]

### SUBSTITUTING ALFALFA FOR NATIVE GRASSES

California never had so many cattle, horses, and other stock, as at the present time, and hence the importance of ascertaining and cultivating the best grasses and forage crops adapted to our soil and climate. Alfalfa sown and properly attended to on our ordinary alluvial soils, will remain as green and luxuriant in September as in May, and during the whole year, producing ten times the quantity of forage, in the shape of hay and pasture, as would grow from the native grasses and forage plants without cultivation. The native grasses of California are not generally perennial, and consequently, by being mown and closely pastured, they are fast disappearing from existence. Hence the necessity of substituting something better in their place.[65]

### BERMUDA GRASS AND ALFALFA AS FODDER CROPS

Editors Bee: . . . In the first place I beg to dissent from your expression that I am "an authority on Bermuda grass." At the same time, from my standpoint of limited experiences with that product, I very cheerfully state a few facts. Bermuda has no seed (in this country or anywhere, so far as I know) and has to be propagated by roots. Plant anytime after frosts have disappeared and before dry, warm weather sets in—say last of March, April, and early in May—in shallow furrows, about eighteen inches apart, and cover two to three inches deep. It seems to flourish everywhere that I have seen it tried—in moist places and dry—except in places most shaded. It will require careful attention, and should not be pastured the first year or till it gets a good start, covering all the ground; for stock, especially horses, will eat it into the ground and exterminate it (if it can be exterminated.) Alfalfa will certainly produce more feed, I think,—that is to say, on land adapted to alfalfa—but Bermuda grass will grow in places too dry for alfalfa, and is less liable to injury from gophers. Bermuda grass in fact is not remarkable for quantity, but is very nutritious, and there is nothing that stock eat with greater avidity.

---

[64]CSAS 1865, p. 212.   [65]CSAS 1860, pp. 333–34.

Some traits may become objectionable, and among them are; The grass, while it is green and growing during all our long glowing summer, dies to the ground and looks dead all winter, and will furnish no pasturage in the winter months. It has a habit of spreading into orchards, requiring one or more extra plowings to keep the same well cultivated. It is particularly fond of spreading along the banks of irrigating ditches, but it forms a good sod protection to them.

In conclusion, my advice would be to every one, first give it a fair test on a limited scale, and so prove its adaptability to varied conditions.

In haste and very respectfully,<br>John Bidwell

P.S.—My opinion is that neither alfalfa nor Bermuda grass will be just the thing for land once covered with wild oats. The best grass for such land has probably not been discovered.[66]

### Butter

But a few years ago nearly all the farmers of this [Sacramento] valley, and I among the rest, purchased nearly all the butter they used—butter that had been imported across the Isthmus of Panama, or around Cape Horn. Some of it seemed old enough to have made a voyage around the world. I became ashamed of it, and resolved that if I could not, with thousands of cattle, which I had at the time, make sufficient butter to supply my own family—and my family is large, over fifty, and sometimes a hundred in number—I would do without. And with many other things I have made similar resolves; and I am happy to be able to say that they have resulted in success.[67]

### First cheese produced, 1869

For the first time we have had cheese made on the ranch.... It is I think very good for new cheese—and I like new better than old.[68]

### Sheep inbreeding

...when they were first brought here I have no doubt they were fine Spanish Merinos, but they had been bred in and in, and out and out until they had no wool on them except a little along the back. All the rest was hair, the same as on a deer. And when animals of that kind run out they run to horns. It was very common to see sheep with three horns, and some with five, and some with even seven horns. After two the number was always odd, and the odd horn always grew out in front between those on either side.[69]

### Horses and selective breeding

The horse is the noblest and most beautiful animal that walks the earth. His

---

[66]Chico *Enterprise*, 13 June 1884.
[67]CSAS 1865, p. 210.
[68]JB to AB, 8 August 1869, JB-CSL, b. 126, f. 70.
[69]*Pioneers*, p. 10.

fleetness, strength, and docility, distinguish him above all others. Even the California Horse, the descendant of the Moorish stock in Spain, so well adapted to the purposes of the country in earlier times, possesses these noble qualities in a very high degree. But he, too, must yield to the march of civilization. So, too, with all the animals of the country; they are all fast yielding to superior importations from distant lands.[70]

### Horse Racing Degrades County Fairs

[1867] In regard to our County Fair, let me say, and I say with regret, it is going to be a failure. Do not come, I beg of you. It is true I am the President [of the Butte County Agricultural Society]. But I was chosen against my will, because I saw that it would not be possible, under the circumstances, to make the Fair a success. I think some of the moving spirit in it only meant it for a kind of a horse race any how. But having dignified it with the name of a Fair, and sent forth hand bills and premium lists, I find myself obliged, at a late moment, to take hold and do what I can to elevate the occasion a shade or two, if possible, above a horse race—for horse racing I know nothing about and will have nothing to do with it.... Another year we might, I think, have a fair that would do us some credit—but this year we cannot.[71]

... erase from your premium list, and that of every District Society receiving State aid the speed [horse racing] programme. Concentrate and use the energy, time, and money now wasted in this one useless and demoralizing trait of most of our so-called agricultural Fairs, upon all such other features as are by common consent admitted to be unobjectionable. I say this with no view to censure this Society, or any society, or to offend any individual here or elsewhere, but I submit the question to the good sense and moral convictions of the people of this State, that horse racing (for that in common phrase is what it is) is not an innocent recreation unless gambling is innocent. At these races they sell pools and bet money. This is the programme, and the daily unblushing practice; ... If it is right to have the speed programme, then give it a purse, or purses, from the public money. No one, I believe, has ever yet been bold enough to ask that of this State, yet inadvertently the public money has been used for that very purpose.

And for myself, I have another objection, which is, that these races are unmitigated cruelty to that noble animal, the horse.... I am not the keeper of any man's conscience, and I have no desire to dictate to any one; but I do say that, in my view, a race horse has no place in agriculture.... Banish that "speed programme"....[72]

[1887] The district fair, which was to have come off here Sept. 6th has been

---

[70]CSAS 1860, p. 334.
[71]JB to James Warren, 27 September 1867, James L.L. Warren Papers, b. 1, BANC.
[72]CSAS 1881, pp. 37–39.

postponed till Oct. 11th—because the races have not been filled!!! What a comment!!! admitting their inability to do anything for the benefit of agriculture, the mechanic arts and all the varied industries that go to make up the various sources of wealth and diversity of human occupations! All must depend on the gambling and coarse—even cruel—amusement called a horse race![73]

[1888] ... The district fair is to begin here day after tomorrow. It is, I fear, to be a repetition of former ones—the races and the gamblers to be the principal features. At least I have heard nothing about an opening or an annual address! Sporting men are arriving with their horses, etc.....[74]

[1891] I have generally exhibited at the State Fairs, but of late years, since they have made it a horse-racing affair, I have quit it. But until then I had been quite active. In fact three times, perhaps four times, I delivered the annual address before the [California] State Agricultural Society.... In my address before the Society I spoke very plainly on this business of pool selling and horse races. It is no more than gambling ... [and] these fairs have become largely horse-racing affairs. [Leland] Stanford and [George] Hearst ought to be able to keep up the speed progress without getting the State to pay for it.... I love a horse, but when they put them to the degree of cruelty, I do not like that. I thought sometime the horse is the noblest animal created for the use of man. I love him and I love a mule. At home I drive a span of mules. We have a double wagon, and the nicest fellows you ever saw.[75]

## *Irrigation and Reclamation*

### BIDWELL THE FIRST TO IRRIGATE IN THE SACRAMENTO VALLEY

The very spring that gold was discovered, I was preparing to set out my farm, and had dug the first irrigating ditch in the Sacramento valley. As soon as I got my ditch ready and the ground prepared, I went over to San Rafael and Sonoma to get my trees.[76]

### FERTILIZER AND IRRIGATION

The farmer should drain off stagnant waters; save his fertilizers and spread them upon his fields, ... By judicious cultivation, and the proper use of fertilizers, lands will yield to the cultivator more than a double profit. Such is the case in other countries, and there can be no doubt it would prove to be so in California. Irrigation would, of itself, go far to reclaim extensive tracts now considered almost worthless. That such lands can be made to yield abun-

---

[73]JB to AB, 24 August 1887, JB-CSL, b. 59, f. 18.
[74]JB to AB, 19 August 1888, JB-CSL, b. 127, f. 51.
[75]JB-91, p. 66.   [76]JB-91, p. 58.

dantly, is certain—that they will be at some future period, can hardly admit of a doubt.[77]

### IRRIGATION AND RECLAMATION

Almost innumerable as are the places in this State which will admit of varied culture, the number may be greatly increased. And how? you ask. Can we change the climate? I answer, yes, to an extent. You can clothe the surface with verdure, and thereby modify the heat. You may not, perhaps, practice any known theories of storms, to the extent of calling down, at will, copious showers to cool and fructify the earth, but you can, in numberless places, and over vast regions, substitute irrigation for showers, and almost literally purple the landscape with ripening fruits; but diversity is not to be achieved in a day or a year, it will take time; this society may find it the labor of long years of trial.[78]

### LAND RECLAMATION THROUGH IRRIGATION

In regard to the aridity of certain portions of this State, and the apparent sterility of large tracts of land before referred to, we have the means of their complete reclamation at hand. The great remedy is irrigation. . . .

Some have pretended to believe that irrigation was detrimental, and therefore not to be recommended. So is food, or any other useful and indispensable thing, detrimental if not used in a proper manner, in proper quantities, and at proper times. . . .

In fact, such are the wonderful capabilities of the soil of California, that irrigation, properly conducted and applied to these barren hills, and plains, and mountains, would awake them as if by magic into such fertility, and life, and beauty, and fruitfulness, as to astonish even Californians themselves.[79]

### IRRIGATION AND RECLAMATION

There are millions of acres of dry and apparently sterile land to be found all over the Pacific slope. Is it always to remain in its present condition? There exists no necessity that it should do so. This land possesses in abundance all the elements of fertility. There is but one remedy—irrigation. Some have prejudices against irrigation, that must be overcome, because it will require the united effort of all who have a proper interest in the State to begin and carry out such an enterprise upon a scale worthy of the object in view. Once accomplished, lands that are now absolutely worthless would become most valuable. The same encouragement should, in my judgment, be given to bring water on land which is worthless without it. The dry, as well as swamp, lands alike require reclamation—one will cost relatively as much as the other. Why then should not the [federal] Government be willing, to donate the dry lands to the State as well as the swamp lands?[80]

---

[77]CSAS 1860, pp. 332–33.
[79]CSAS 1865, p. 211.
[78]CSAS 1881, p. 33.
[80]Letter to San Francisco *Alta*, 19 October 1865.

## IRRIGATION AND RECLAMATION

With all the known and acknowledged advantages of California in respect to fertility of soil, serenity and salubrity of climate and beauty of general topography, there still is enough, even here, for man to do. We have swamp lands to drain and fortify against periodical inundations; we have sterile lands to reclaim by irrigation and the application of fertilizers; we have to construct canals, roads and highways for travel and commerce, and many other indispensable improvements—and these are to be brought about only by the one now universally acknowledged source of all true wealth—labor. . . .

That the drainage of the vast tule marshes is important, nay, a necessity, none will deny. That these vast regions, which occupy the central and most accessible part of our great interior valleys, would be the very best lands as regards fertility, and their capacity to yield almost everything required to supply human wants, is an undeniable fact. [81]

Liberal premiums should be paid by the State for the best system of reclamation, and no considerable amount of money ought to be expended till a system has been adopted—a system that shall look to the ultimate and complete reclamation of all these lands. . . . My suggestions are given for what they are worth. I therefore may be permitted to say, generally, that I believe the floods and inundations before named can, in a great measure, if not entirely, be prevented; and, consequently, that the swamp and tule lands can be reclaimed by the use of three co-operative works or measures:

First—The building of reservoirs at all feasible points, to retain the waters in the mountains.

Second—The construction of canals, so made as to occupy the shortest possible distance between their termini, in order to secure the greatest possible amount of fall to a given distance, and thereby the discharge of the largest possible quantity of water by a canal or channel of given dimensions—and also in order to economy.

Third—The raising of suitable levees along the banks of rivers and streams to retain the remaining waters within their proper channels.

If all three of these measures do not suffice, it is certain, that no one or two of them can.[82]

## IRRIGATION AND RECLAMATION

The art of irrigation is as old as the cultivation of the soil. . . . There is probably no civilized or even half civilized people who have not found its use beneficial and often indispensable. . . . In agriculture, as in almost everything else, something useful may be learned from all nations without regard to rank in the scale of civilization. We shall find it profitable now to adopt the practice of irri-

---

[81]CSAS 1867, p. 422.   [82]CSAS 1867, p. 425.

gation in use by the ancient inhabitants of Peru for centuries before the discovery of America.

The Chinese are known to have practiced for many centuries both drainage and irrigation.... Some of their canals are of great length and prodigious dimensions. The one connecting the City of Pekin with the Yangtze-Kiang River is said to be from two hundred feet to one thousand feet in width and over six hundred miles in length. Perhaps the Chinese, should they be permitted to remain in this country and increase in numbers by immigration, may be profitably employed on works of a similar character.

... I am bold to assert it is my belief, founded upon observation, that the development of the agricultural capabilities of this State have hardly begun; and yet California has acquired a reputation for fertility and productiveness that is world-wide. An extensive and judicious system of irrigation is, in my judgment, the only thing that will ever enable the State to attain its highest development.[83]

### Irrigation and Reclamation

I look upon the future of agriculture in California to depend largely upon irrigation. In fact, I do not believe that Americans have learned as yet to properly appreciate irrigation. It is a branch of cultivation that Americans have to learn.... In Fresno and other places they irrigate a good deal, but I am satisfied they do it too much. Too much of anything is not good. I have found great difficulty in making men in my employ conform to my ideas in irrigating my garden. Intelligent gardeners that I have had, would seem to think that when the dry season comes round everything was suffering for water. The Mexicans would irrigate but once or twice in the season. But when they did irrigate, they put in an abundance.[84]

### Irrigation, the Unexpected Offspring of Hydraulic Mining

Irrigation is the natural successor to hydraulic mining, and important beyond computation. Without it we can never know or have any conception of California's productive capacity. By showing that waters can be conducted almost everywhere, hydraulic mining has unwittingly solved a most important feature in the problem of irrigation....

The water already flowing in the artificial channels ... has made the transition from mining to cultivation not only possible, but easy and inviting.[85]

Irrigation is an established fact, because it results from mining. The search for gold stimulated engineering, so that waters have been brought from places so difficult that I think it can be said there is no obstacle that cannot be overcome. In our county in order to work the Cherokee mines, water was taken from

---

[83]CSAS 1867, pp. 426–27.   [84]JB-91, pp. 60–61.
[85]Letter to Sacramento *Record-Union*, 22 January 1884.

one stream and carried across to a place where a certain valley could be converted in[to] a great reservoir. All the streams that run through the valley were also brought into the reservoir. . . .

Mining has unwittingly solved the great problem of irrigation. The people have used the mining ditches for irrigation purposes. It is a wonderful turn, inasmuch as agriculture is considered vastly more important than mining, how mining should have preceded it and resulted to such great advantage to agriculture. Agriculture would not have stood the expense of such a means of development, but mining could stand anything.[86]

I wish hydraulic mining could continue, and the whole country prosper. At the same time, I admit that it is not to me a pleasing scene to see havoc made of hills, and mountains, and stately forests, and a once lovely prospect changed to a desolation.

There can be no question that agriculture is the only enduring interest, and that an immediate and adequate remedy is demanded, not wholly repair the injury done, for that may be impossible, but to avert greater impending peril. And, without attempting to discuss remedies, I must confess my inability to see how the continual and widespread destruction is to cease without stopping the cause. The miners have a rule or common law which governs among themselves, and it is just, namely: that miners working claims above, on the same stream, must not dump their tailings on claims below them. Let them apply this rule to their brother farmers, and the trouble is at once settled. It is justice, pure and simple. . . . [87]

### Reservoirs for Irrigation and Growth

The conclusion is irresistible, therefore, that the waters of all the streams of the State are destined to become very valuable, and it is consequently important that they should, as far as possible, be stored away in the mountains in Winter, to be used when required in Summer. It will cost immense sums of money, of course, to construct the almost numberless reservoirs which will be required throughout all the mountain regions of the State. The General Government will never be able to give its attention to this (to us) most important subject. The State alone can and ought to control it, and enact the requisite regulations.[88]

## *Promoting Scientific Agriculture*

### Need for a California Agricultural Literature

. . . there is something so peculiar in our surpassingly rich soils—in our wet and dry seasons—in our dry and apparently barren lands, but which, when irrigated, astonish us with their productiveness—in the indomitable energy of our

---

[86]JB-91, pp. 61–62.

people—and, in short, in almost everything, as to require for California a new system of agriculture, and, as a matter of course, a new agricultural literature. Every practical farmer must be aware how comparatively inapplicable here are the periodicals and treatises on agriculture published in the Atlantic States and Europe. No farmer can afford to dispense with the agricultural publications; but those published nearest the locality of his farming operations ought to be most valuable and consequently preferred. How would a paper published in Greenland or at Panama suit a California farmer?[89]

### Soil science

... we should invoke the aid of science to analyze soil and its productions, at different periods and under various conditions. We should become thoroughly versed in vegetable chemistry, and the anatomy and physiology of plants. We should bring together, compare and combine our varied experiences, and thus continue to do, till our efforts have been crowned with success.[90]

### Bidwell argues in favor of federal support for agricultural colleges

Agriculture must, to be successful for all time be in the hands of free and intelligent labor. There must be no mudsills, because agriculture will not thrive in the mud; and yet the mud contains within itself all the elements of fertility. Drain it, cultivate it, and bring forth its latent powers, and the reward will be fruits, flowers, and golden grain to gladden the heart and supply the wants of the laborer. And this illustration may not be inapplicable to the laboring classes whom slavery, with haughty pride, denominated as "the mudsills of society." Cultivate these classes, and train them in the way to intelligence, usefulness, and honor, and the choicest fruits of the human intellect and the most gifted minds may crown the labors of this nation. From these classes may spring Presidents, statesmen, poets, orators, and loyal heroes to perpetuate the blessings and the glories of this nation in peace, "for peace hath her victories no less renowned than war," and defend the emblem of our national freedom against all enemies from within or from without.[91]

## *Fences and Fence Laws*

### Fences in Mexican California

I spoke about the gardens. They were fenced sometimes, always by cutting the limbs off the trees and making a sort of brush fence two or three feet high. In the winter that fence was used for firewood, and in the spring it was built up again.[92]

---

[87] CSAS 1881, pp. 28–29.
[88] CSAS 1867, pp. 427–28.
[89] CSAS 1867, p. 428.
[90] CSAS 1860, pp. 331–32.
[91] *Congressional Globe*, 39th Congress, 1st Session, p. 1575.
[92] *Pioneers*, p. 10.

No one in those days ever cut any hay. Not a particle of hay was ever cut in California till after the Mexican War, nor was even a pasture fenced.[93]

Wheat, Corn and Potatoes are seldom surrounded by a fence, they grow out in the plains and are guarded from the Cattle and horses by the Indians, who are stationed in their huts by the fields.

You can employ any number of Indians by giving them a lump of Beef every week, and paying them about one dollar for same time. Cattle are so wild however, as to keep some distance from houses. Since my residence in the country I have become sick of the manner of fencing or protecting grain etc. from cattle as done by the Spaniards. To farm well, you must make fence as in the U. States.[94]

The wheat fields had no fences around them. The way they guarded a field when sown was to put an old Indian at each corner of the field if it happened to be large. Many, in fact most of the fields were very small, say from five to twenty acres, in which case one old Indian and his family would suffice to guard each field. For large fields, which seldom exceeded one hundred acres, an old Indian and his family were expected to keep the cattle away night and day, storm and sunshine, and if they failed to do so they were severely whipped. They were generally given a quarter of beef a week—enough perhaps for them to eat, but that would be about all they had to live on.[95]

### The importance of good fences

Above all, for his reputation as a farmer, and as he values his own peace of mind, the friendship of neighbors, and the preservation of his crops, it should be an object of primary importance to construct good fences. Nothing displays the character, the thrift, the good judgment, or the negligence, unskillfulness, or slothfulness, of a people with more certainty than the condition of their fences. These indicate the prosperity, or decline, of agriculture, and give character and consideration to whole regions of the country. It may be remarked that anything will do for a fence which will turn hogs and cattle, but ditches should not be resorted to if the country abounds in squirrels, for by so doing, they are invited to burrow around the fields, and destroy the crops.[96]

### Sides with farmers against stockmen on fence law issue, 1872

... it is now daylight, and I must send James for some stamps to put on a large bundle of Petitions to the Legislature—sent me by the people living in the South West part of our county (near and west of Biggs station) asking me to cooperate with, and secure for them a law to prevent stock from running at large, just the thing we want here, and every where in the county and State. But there are a few interested men, who have nothing but stock—pay no taxes—drive their

---

[93]*Pioneers*, p. 17.  [94]*Journey*, p. 38.  [95]*Pioneers*, pp. 9–10.
[96]CSAS 1860, pp. 332–33.

animals to the mountains in the summer, but in winter turn them upon the plains and foothills to shrink or starve—or, as is very often the case, trespass upon the grain and pastures of permanent residents—who are very active in circulating petitions to prevent the enacting of such a good and wholesome law. Those who habitually turn their stock into our pastures are bitterly opposed to it.

And strange to say, some very good men have wrong ideas on this question—for instance, Mr. [J. C.] Mandeville. It was not to be wondered at that stockmen, especially that nomadic class of the Southern and Western States, who like a drink of whiskey or brandy and are familiar with the Saloons, should be able to get all the loose floating population which haunts such places, to sign their petitions—and occasionally get good men to do so under a misapprehension of their purport. But I am surprised at Mandeville and some others. Harmen Bay & some others called yesterday, principally on this business.[97]

... Yesterday I was laying out Almond orchard—to do it well takes time—and I have so many letters to write, especially to members of the legislature on the fence law question. All from our county—both in the Senate and Assembly, are wrong on this important question. They have had very plausible petitions circulated and signed by the floating population around the saloons, and the idlers generally, and have, strange to say, got a good many very good men. And now I want to counteract their operations and have a proper trespass law against all kinds of stock, for our county—and if I cannot get that, then I want the law to apply to that part of the county north of Chico creek.[98]

## *Financial Hazards of Farming*

### BIDWELL LOSES MONEY WHILE SERVING IN CONGRESS

I ought to make from my farm 40,000 to 50,000 dollars per year. A neighbor told me the other day that if my place was properly managed I ought to clear $75,000 a year in gold. And still, in my absence I found they had so badly done my business as to find 36,000 dollars of debts.

I don't want to have you think I am embarrassed—for I am not....[99]

### RANCHO CHICO FALLS INTO DEBT

I never was in debt until I went to congress, but in my absence my agent made mistakes. He sold thirteen or fourteen thousand dollars worth of cattle to a supposed good firm, and lost all the money, and I never saw any of it. I had 18 head

---

[97]JB to AB, 18 January 1872, JB-CSL, b. 126, f. 82.
[98]JB to AB, 30 January 1872, JB-CSL, b. 50, f. 36.
[99]JB to AB, 5 July 1867, JB-CSL, b. 45, f. 21.

Indian workers shelling almonds on Rancho Chico.
Reprinted with permission by Special Collections, Meriam Library,
California State University, Chico and Bidwell Mansion.

of fine mares that I kept separate. He put them into stubble field where there was no water and went off three weeks on his own business, and neglected to tell anyone to give the horses water. They all perished. I had about $10,000 worth of hogs, and was offered 9 $^1/_2$ cents for them. He wanted 10. He would not take 9 $^1/_2$, a high price, but kept feeding them for a month and a half, and when prices went down he undertook to make them into bacon, and when the summer came, it spoilt. I got in debt that way and have never gotten out since. I am not discouraged, but I do not think it will do me any good to worry about it. I have learned by experience to be cautious in business matters for the sake of my wife, and others. Although I lost a good deal in that way, I got some thing worth more than I lost. I got my wife by going there [to Congress].[100]

ASSESSED VALUE OF RANCHO CHICO, 1874

... The sum total of our assessment this year is $500,671—over half a million...."[101]

A RUN OF BAD LUCK, FALL 1884

[September 14] At 6:30 (while we were at tea) it rained very hard. Have a

---
[100] JB-91, p. 32.
[101] JB to AB, 25 June 1874, JB-CSL, b. 51, f. 29.

good deal of grain yet unthreshed! And besides the brick granary is nearly full of grain in the sack, and no roof on!! Will calamities never cease![102]

[September 29] Tomorrow I have to go to San Francisco to make arrangements for the interest money ($8,000) due day after tomorrow. Times are so bad that the bank here cannot let me have it.[103]

[October 12] ... Began raining about 9 A.M. ... Nearly all our corn fodder is out and will certainly be ruined! for corn is more easily damaged than hay. I was more anxious to save the corn fodder, because the hay (as you know) was mostly spoiled by the rains last June! The raisins too are mostly exposed—and may be a total ruin—and there is a vast amount of them this year—and they promised to be good. Some of them are on trays in the vineyards; but most are spread on boards at the vineyard house. When I passed there two days ago it seemed to me that there must have been nearly two acres of ground occupied with boards covered with raisins and grapes in all stages of the drying process from green grapes to raisins nearly cured. So located it is not possible to cover them. Besides this rain gave little or no notice. ... A train (an extra) last night killed a good many of our sheep—Gen. Davidson says the R.R. Co. will pay for them. ... Peter says he heard 40 were killed and 40 wounded![104]

[October 14] I failed to write you yesterday—felt too gloomy over the havoc made by the rain, perhaps. ... The band was crossing the track ... about 4 P.M. The engineer neither stopped nor slowed—only whistled—and plunged right along! 40 sheep were killed outright—12 were so badly bruised and mangled that they had to be killed—and 28 were more or less hurt. Of course the R.R. Co. must pay for them. This train came along at an unusual hour, and besides the engineer ought to have seen in time to stop the train.[105]

[October 23] Have just received the news from Reading that Chappell and Houston have failed. They are owing us for flour over $900—a heavy loss! under the circumstances. I blame Mr. Camper for allowing the account to stand without collection or letting me know that they had failed to make remittances after account was overdue.[106]

[November 5] Another great disappointment has recurred—Mr. Hunt (miller) is on another spree! This morning he was found in one of the lowest dives in town at a gambling table. He had evidently been on a debauch all night long. (He will have to go). ... His loss will be irreparable! for there is no doubt that

---

[102] JB to AB, 14 September 1884, JB-CSL, b. 57, f. 8.
[103] JB to AB, 29 September 1884, JB-CSL, b. 57, f. 20.
[104] JB to AB, 12 October 1884, JB-CSL, b. 57, f. 29.
[105] JB to AB, 14 October 1884, JB-CSL, b. 57, f. 30.
[106] JB to AB, 23 October 1884, JB-CSL, b. 57, f. 35.

he is the best miller in the State. What a pity that prohibition could not be now an accomplished fact! Mr. Hunt voted for [Prohibition Party candidates] St. John and Daniels, I think—I know he intended to do so the day before the [presidential] election.[107]

[November 28] . . . I have left to the last the bad news, which is: Our mill burned today! It is not all burned up—All the roof and second and third stories were burned. But what is not burned is so changed and drenched with water [unreadable] that the ruin seems complete.

The loss will probably be about $30,000 and the insurance is about $28,000. Our actual loss therefore will be but trifling, I hope.

The delay we must suffer in building another mill is a serious matter, because we may lose our flour trade. It is not always easy, when trade falls into other channels, to get it back.

The fire occurred at about 3 P.M. today. I was up at Vallombrosa burning brush, and knew nothing of the fire till they sent for me. No one can tell or give any information as to how the fire originated. It was however in the third story. My own idea is that the fire came from the heating of a journal. The fire companies did noble service, or both warehouses would also have gone, and our water tower as well. The weather is lovely.[108]

### BIDWELL IMPOSES RESTRICTIONS AGAINST SUNDAY RECREATION ON RANCHO CHICO, 1885

I do not wish them [Rancho Chico roadways] solely for my own use; but I wish others to feel perfectly free to use them in a proper way and at all proper times. They are not, however, at any time, to be considered open as public highways. All Sunday driving, Sunday fishing or picnic excursions, and Sunday sporting generally, on my premises, I feel it my duty henceforth strictly to prohibit.[109]

---

[107]JB to AB, 5 November 1884, JB-CSL, b. 57, f. 44.
[108]JB to AB, 28 November 1884, JB-CSL, b. 57, f. 56.
[109]Butte *Record*, 30 March 1885.

Portrait of President Millard Fillmore handing John Bidwell a copy of the Official Declaration admitting California to the Union, which Bidwell brought back to California aboard the *S.S. Oregon* in 1850. Painting by Natalie Bixby.

Reprinted with permission by the California State Library, California Section.

# 5
# A Career in California Politics

Though he proudly identified himself as a simple farmer, John Bidwell harbored strong political ambitions. Between 1849 and 1867, Bidwell's wealth and reputation as a California pioneer enabled him to pursue an initially successful political career that nearly carried him into the Governor's mansion. Bidwell's gubernatorial aspirations were never realized, however, and his election to Congress in 1864 proved to be the final campaign victory in a public life that would last another twenty-eight years.

Bidwell's ill-starred career in politics began with great promise in 1849, when he scored two separate triumphs at the polls. In August, Bidwell's neighbors chose him to be a delegate to California's founding state constitutional convention, which met at Monterey from September 1 to October 12. Unfortunately, Bidwell never showed up. Off in the Sierra mining for gold, Bidwell did not learn of his election until after the rest of the Sacramento Valley delegates had departed for Monterey. Luckily, his failure to attend and take part in the deliberations did not deter voters from electing him in November to the California state senate.[1]

With a new state capital temporarily established at San Jose, California's first legislature convened on December 15, 1849. Over the course of a busy four-month session, the legislators successfully laid the statutory and fiscal foundations for California's state and local governments. Bidwell played an active role in the proceedings and served on the committee that named California's original twenty-seven counties.[2]

In the summer of 1850, Bidwell set out for Washington, D.C. where he helped lobby for California's formal admission to the Union.[3] His comfortable and speedy return back East aboard the new oceanic steamers

---
[1] Hunt, pp. 162-163.      [2] Ibid., pp. 163-169.
[3] Bidwell journeyed to Washington as part of a two-man deputation dispatched by Governor Peter Burnett. The official pretext was to deliver a block of gold-bearing quartz to the capital as California's contribution to the new Washington Monument. See Hunt, pp. 169–170; Benjamin, p. 20.

plying the Panama route offered a plush contrast to his arduous overland trek nine years before. It also provided a striking example of the tremendous change and progress that had overtaken California since the Mexican War and the discovery of gold. Bidwell spent three weeks on the east coast and did not leave until September 13, four days after President Millard Fillmore signed the bill that finally granted statehood to California. On October 18, Bidwell arrived in San Francisco aboard the steamship *Oregon*, which delivered the eagerly awaited news to the Pacific Coast.[4]

Though Bidwell did not seek reelection in 1850, he remained politically active and helped organize California's Democratic party. For the next eleven years, the Democrats dominated California politics, losing only in 1855 when the nativist Know-Nothing party swept the field. Unfortunately, 1855 was the year Bidwell chose to run again twice for public office. In April, he suffered the first, and perhaps most embarrassing defeat of his career. Running in the Third District for a seat on Butte County's first board of supervisors, Bidwell lost to rival Robert Moore by a resounding vote of 71 to 47. Then, in the statewide general elections held in September, Bidwell went down to a second defeat with the rest of the Democratic ticket. Campaigning to recapture his old state senate seat, Bidwell carried Butte County with just sixteen votes to spare against his Know-Nothing opponent, Assemblyman John B. McGee. Bidwell's narrow margin in Butte was eclipsed, however, by McGee's majority in neighboring Plumas County, which comprised the second half of the Fourteenth Senate District.[5]

Three years later, the Democratic party split into two warring factions when Kansas applied for statehood with a pro-slavery constitution adopted at the town of Lecompton. In the bitter intraparty struggle that followed, Bidwell aligned himself with the "anti-Lecompton" or "Douglas" Democrats led by Senator Stephen Douglas of Illinois. This put Bidwell in the minority faction of his party, for the California Democracy was dominated by the pro-Southern "Chivalry" forces headed by Senator William Gwin, a native of Tennessee. When Douglas announced his candidacy for the Presidency in 1860, most California Democrats lined up against him. Of the eight delegates sent by the party in April to the Democratic national convention in Charleston, South Carolina, only Bidwell sympathized with Douglas. The rest eagerly supported the reckless efforts of Southern delegates to block Douglas's nomination by preventing the Illinois front-run-

---
[4]Hunt, pp. 169–172.
[5]Harry L. Wells and W. L. Chambers, *History of Butte County, California* (San Francisco: Harry L. Wells, 1882), pp. 138, 166–167; Hunt, p. 174.

ner from securing the required two-thirds vote. After fifty-seven fruitless ballots, Southern obstructionism prevailed and the convention adjourned without selecting a nominee. A frustrated Bidwell assigned his proxy to Samuel Hensley and returned home in disgust. In June, the reconvened but still feuding Democrats went on to nominate two rival tickets, one headed by Douglas and the other by Vice President John C. Breckinridge of Kentucky. Bidwell remained loyal to Douglas but, with Douglas and Breckinridge dividing the Democratic vote, Republican Abraham Lincoln triumphed easily and the southern states seceded from the Union.[6]

The outbreak of the Civil War in 1861 led to another major split in Democratic ranks. Those who opposed secession and supported the war against the Confederacy merged with the Republicans to form the Union party. Left behind were Northern Democrats still sympathetic to the South, whom the Unionists condemned as Copperheads. An ardent Union man, Bidwell left the Democratic party and never returned.[7] In 1863, he was named to the Union party's state executive committee and, on September 3, was appointed a Brigadier General in the state militia by Republican governor Leland Stanford. This was no ceremonial post. Earlier in the year, the legislature had enacted a wartime poll tax to support the formation and provisioning of state militia units. As commander of the Fifth Brigade, Bidwell presided over the raising of fifteen companies throughout his territorial jurisdiction, which covered all of California north of Marysville and east of the Coast Ranges. At any one time, Bidwell had over 500 men under his command, organized into locally based volunteer companies like the Oroville Guards, the Lassen Rangers, and the Chico Light Infantry.[8]

His chief duties were to bolster public support for the Union war effort and, more ominously, to suppress political dissent. Soon after the Civil War had broken out, President Lincoln moved aggressively to silence his Cop-

---

[6]Hunt, pp. 175–177. For details on Bidwell's role at the Charleston convention, see David Williams, "California Democrats of 1860: Division, Disruption, Defeat," *Southern California Quarterly*, 55 (Fall 1973), pp. 239–252.

[7]Bidwell's last hurrah as a Democrat came at the Union Democratic state convention of 1861, where his name was placed in nomination for governor against four other contenders. After fourteen ballots, John Conness finally emerged victorious. Along with the rest of his ill-fated ticket, Conness went on to defeat in the general election at the hands of Leland Stanford, who became California's first Republican governor. See Benjamin, p. 31; Winfield J. Davis, *History of Political Conventions in California, 1849–1892* (Sacramento: California State Library, 1893), p. 178.

[8]California, Adjutant General, *Report of the Adjutant General for the Year 1863* (Sacramento: 1864), pp. 39–40, 112–13; *Report of the Adjutant General from May 1, 1864 to November 30, 1865* (Sacramento: 1866), pp. 652–55. Asa M. Fairfield, *Fairfield's Pioneer History of Lassen County, California* (San Francisco: H.S. Crocker Co., 1916), pp. 355–62.

perhead critics, whom he regarded as disloyal subversives bent on undermining the Union cause. In an unprecedented breach of First, Fifth, and Sixth Amendment rights, Lincoln, with the ultimate backing of Congress, suspended the cherished privilege of the writ of *habeas corpus*, and authorized military and civil authorities to arrest and detain anyone for speaking out against the war or in favor of secession. Meanwhile, in California, Leland Stanford and the Union-dominated legislature followed Lincoln's lead by approving a series of measures in April 1863 that outlawed the display of rebel flags, imposed loyalty oaths on public school teachers, and prohibited any public expression of support for the Confederacy.[9]

As they did throughout the nation, such laws led to a wave of repression as military and civil authorities jailed outspoken "peace" Democrats and shut down bellicose Copperhead newspapers. In northern California, Brigadier General Bidwell played a key role in this muscular enforcement of home front loyalty by monitoring the activities of his Democratic neighbors. Whenever they could, members of the "home guard" units apprehended and harassed suspected Copperheads, usually by compelling them to carry heavy packs of sand or bricks back and forth until they were exhausted enough to submit to a loyalty oath. On election days, the home guards helped man the polling places and did whatever was necessary to ensure a Republican victory. As a member of the Chico Light Infantry, nineteen-year-old Sim Moak cast his first vote for Abraham Lincoln in 1864. Hesitant because he was under age, Moak received encouragement from his comrades who assured him that no one would dare challenge his vote, expecially since his company lieutenant happened to be on the election board.[10]

Meanwhile, Bidwell kept in regular contact with U.S. Army officers stationed in San Francisco and called upon them for help whenever local Copperhead demonstrations proved too much for his own volunteers to control. Indeed, with Bidwell's support, federal troops kept a constant watch on Colusa, where Southern sympathies ran so deep that the county became known as the "South Carolina of California." In Butte County, Bidwell actually played host to the U.S. Army which, at his invitation, set up Camp Bidwell on the grounds of Rancho Chico in August 1863.[11]

---

[9] Robert J. Chandler, "Crushing Dissent: The Pacific Coast Tests Lincoln's Policy of Suppression, 1862," *Civil War History*, 30 (September 1984), pp. 235–54; Chandler, "Democratic Turmoil: California During the Civil War Years," *Dogtown Territorial Quarterly*, 31 (Fall 1997), pp. 32–46.

[10] JB-91, pp. 13–14, 26–28; Mansfield, pp. 226–38; Sim Moak, *The Last of the Mill Creeks and Early Life in Northern California* (Chico: n.p., 1923), pp. 9, 14–15.

[11] Rogers, *Colusa County*, pp. 90–105; Mansfield, pp. 228–29; Norris Bleyhl, "Camp Bidwell," in Bleyhl, *Three Military Posts in Northeastern California, 1849–1863* (Chico: ANCRR, 1984), pp. 1–18.

Like the local militia, the army rode roughshod over the Bill of Rights. Following the murder of Abraham Lincoln, for example, General Irvin McDowell of the U.S. Army's Department of the Pacific issued an order for the arrest of any person "so utterly infamous as to exult over the assassination of the President." Fanning out from Camp Bidwell, soldiers apprehended at least three men in Butte County and fifteen more in Colusa. Among the sixty-eight Californians arrested under McDowell's order, the Camp Bidwell prisoners were immediately transferred to Fort Alcatraz in San Francisco Bay, and put to work at hard labor for two or three months.[12]

Bidwell's unapologetic support for such raw displays of military power during the war generated hard feelings and deep resentments that lingered in the local community for the rest of the century. In the short run, however, Bidwell's steadfast loyalty greatly enhanced his prestige within the Union party. In June 1864, Bidwell traveled to Baltimore as a delegate to the Union party convention that nominated President Lincoln for a second term and gave him a new running mate, Union Democrat Andrew Johnson of Tennessee. Bidwell then returned home and, in August 1864, received the Union nomination for congress in the Third Congressional District. In November, Lincoln carried California while Bidwell swept the third district with fifty-six percent of the vote, trouncing Democrat Jackson Temple.[13]

Due to the unique circumstances of the war, over a year elapsed between the election and seating of the Thirty-Ninth Congress. During the extended interval, the American political scene shifted dramatically. On April 9, 1865, Robert E. Lee surrendered to Ulysses S. Grant at Appomattox and, five days later, John Wilkes Booth murdered Abraham Lincoln. Suddenly elevated to the Presidency, Andrew Johnson moved swiftly to readmit the Confederate states to the Union under the generous terms offered by Lincoln's Reconstruction plan of 1863. The readmitted states, dominated by former rebels, immediately enacted the Black Codes, laws designed to restrict the civil rights of the recently liberated slaves. The so-called Radical Republicans objected to Johnson's policy and were outraged by his willingness to act while Congress remained in recess. Led by Senator Charles Sumner of Massachusetts and Congressman Thaddeus Stevens of Pennsylvania, the radicals insisted that tougher conditions be imposed on the defeated South. They also

---

[12]Rogers, *Colusa County*, pp. 104–05; Moak, *Last of the Mill Creeks*, p. 15; Chandler, "Democratic Turmoil," p. 43; *Union Record* (Oroville), 10 June and 1 July 1865.
[13]Hunt, pp. 177–89; Butte *Record*, 19 and 20 July 1886.

demanded that the freedmen be protected by the federal government and guaranteed full legal equality, complete with voting rights. When Congress finally convened in December 1865, the stage had been set for the intense conflicts over Reconstruction that ultimately led to the impeachment of President Johnson and the breakup of the Union party coalition.

Despite the fact that he, like President Johnson, was a former Democrat, John Bidwell sided squarely with the radicals, supporting each of their major proposals and voting repeatedly to override Johnson's numerous vetoes. Bidwell backed successful legislation to strengthen the Freedmen's Bureau in the South and to grant the right to vote to blacks residing in the District of Columbia. He also voted for the Civil Rights Act of 1866, the Reconstruction Act of 1867 and, most importantly, the Fourteenth Amendment to the United States Constitution.[14]

Bidwell's unwavering commitment to Radical Reconstruction policy led him to break completely with President Johnson. To protect Radicals within the Johnson administration, Bidwell voted for the controversial Tenure of Office Act, which prohibited the president from dismissing members of his own cabinet without Senate approval. And, while it would remain for the Fortieth Congress to actually impeach Johnson and bring him to trial before the Senate in 1868, Bidwell supported early Radical efforts to launch the impeachment process and remove the president from office. These attempts culminated on January 7, 1867, when the House passed an impeachment resolution introduced by Congressman James M. Ashley of Ohio. Bidwell voted in favor of Ashley's resolution, which directed the House Judiciary Committee to investigate the president on five counts of corruption and alleged criminal behavior. Fortunately for Johnson, the action came too late. With time running out on the Thirty-ninth Congress, the judiciary committee was unable to conduct a complete inquiry or bring forth an actual bill of impeachment. The Radicals would have to wait.[15]

As a freshman congressman, Bidwell did not play a starring role in the tumultuous debates over impeachment or Reconstruction. He did, however, take a leading part in other areas. His knowledge of farming helped him secure the chairmanship of the House Committee on Agriculture,

---

[14] *Congressional Globe*, 39th Congress, 1st Session, pp. 311, 688, 1367, 1861, 3149, 3850, 4182; 2nd Session, pp. 344, 1733, 1739. Another important measure that Bidwell helped pass over Johnson's veto was the admission of Nebraska into the Union as the thirty-seventh state. Bidwell also voted to admit Colorado, but that territory did not achieve statehood until 1876. *Congressional Globe*, 39th Congress, 1st Session, p. 2373; 2nd Session, pp. 1121–122.

[15] *Congressional Globe*, 39th Congress, 2nd Session, pp. 319–21, 1754–55.

and he introduced a number of bills dealing with important California issues. One of the most significant of these dealt with the confused condition of land titles in California. As it had with the settlement of Mexican rancho grant claims, the population boom triggered by the gold rush played havoc with the orderly disposal of the public domain in California. Like all new states admitted to the Union, California had received a generous birthright from the federal government in the form of land grants. In California's case, these federal gifts totaled over 8.8 million acres. Intended to provide the state with a source of revenue for essential public services, the proceeds of all sales of these lands were earmarked by state and federal law for the construction of internal improvements, civic buildings, colleges, and public schools.[16]

Before the state could begin disposing any of its inheritance, however, it first had to secure title from the federal government. This was done by making selections from available properties already surveyed by the U.S. Land Office and then filing claims with the federal land commissioner in Washington. Unfortunately, impatient California officials decided to dispense with these essential formalities. Faced with a booming population clamoring for land and government services, the financially strapped state government began to sell land warrants or scrip to private individuals who, in turn, used them to lay claim to the public domain. The result was chaos, as swarms of settlers took up residence on parcels that had never been conveyed to the state by the U.S. Land Office! Though many of the settlers had purchased from the state in good faith, the federal government refused to recognize their titles. Matters grew further complicated as federal officials began to survey these "state lands" and to make them available to rival claimants under the Preemption Act and other federal laws.

To rectify this increasingly intolerable situation, Bidwell, together with Senator John Conness, introduced legislation calling upon Congress to simply accept this *fait accompli* handed to it by California. This was a bitter pill for many in Washington to swallow, particularly George W. Julian of Indiana, the powerful chairman of the House Committee on Public Lands. Julian, an ardent champion of the family farm and a fierce foe of land monopoly, vigorously opposed the Bidwell-Conness proposal. Though he sympathized with the legitimate settlers Bidwell sought to protect, he was incensed by the fact that California had sold lands still

---

[16]Paul W. Gates, *Land and Law in California: Essays on Land Policies* (Ames: Iowa State University Press, 1991), pp. 250–68.

held by the United States and had, in many cases, completely disregarded the homestead ideal by disposing vast acreages to real estate speculators.

Julian especially opposed a provision in the bill that extended the controversial "Suscol principle" throughout California. Originally applied by Congress in 1863 to Mariano Vallejo's Suscol Rancho in Solano County, the Suscol principle was designed to protect *bona fide* settlers who had purchased portions of Mexican rancho grants later ruled invalid. Since, in all such cases, the disputed lands reverted to the federal public domain, the Suscol principle allowed settlers to retain their holdings by filing preemption claims covering the full extent of their improvements. At Suscol, this had resulted in preemption grants of up to 5,000 acres, far in excess of the usual 160-acre maximum. To Julian, this constituted yet another gross violation of the homestead ideal that opened the door to widespread fraud and land monopoly.

Nevertheless, Bidwell and his California colleagues, Donald McRuer of San Francisco and William Higby of Calaveras, prevailed over Julian after a spirited debate on the floor of the House. To his lasting disappointment, however, the California Land Act of 1866 quickly became known as the "Conness bill," and Bidwell never felt he received proper credit for what he believed was his single most important success in Congress.[17]

Disappointment also marred Bidwell's second crowning achievement in Washington, the passage of the California and Oregon Railroad bill. Making the most of his position on the House Pacific Railroads Committee, Bidwell successfully promoted this landmark legislation which he coauthored with Senator James Nesmith, an Oregon Democrat. Modeled after the original transcontinental railroad acts, their bill provided generous public land grants and other federal subsidies to aid construction of a railroad running up the Sacramento Valley from Marysville and terminating at Portland.[18]

Though it represented the most tangible result of his congressional service, the eventual completion of the C&O in 1887 probably left Bidwell with mixed feelings. Within two years of the enactment of his legislation in 1866, the C&O had sold out to the Central Pacific Railroad owned by Leland Stanford and his associates, who comprised the notorious Big Four.

---

[17] *Congressional Globe*, 39th Congress, 1st Session (28 June, 7 July 1866), pp. 3461, 3650–3655; U.S. Congress, *Statutes at Large*, 14 (1866–1867), pp. 218–21; JB- 91, pp. 29–31. In retrospect, Bidwell is rather fortunate that Conness received all the credit. The late Paul Wallace Gates, for years the dean of American land law history, roundly condemned the legislation. Siding with Julian's interpretation, Gates concluded that "The 1866 law was a great victory for the spoilsmen inhabiting California's state and county land offices." See Gates, *Land and Law in California*, pp. 45–46, 221–23, 260.

[18] *Congressional Globe*, 39th Congress, 1st Session, pp. 1574–75, 3269, 3298–3300, 4128; 2nd Session, pp. 1699–1700.

Between 1863 and 1870, while in the midst of constructing the western half of the nation's first transcontinental railroad, the Central Pacific had amassed a virtual monopoly over California's emerging rail network by purchasing one rival company after another. The result was a transportation empire that not only included railroads, but steamship lines as well.

Reorganized in 1884 as the Southern Pacific Company, the holdings of the Big Four became known in common parlance as "the Octopus," a corporate monster that seemed to hold nearly every California farmer, merchant, town, and city in its monopolistic grasp. While often overstated by its critics, the economic strength of the railroad was indeed immense, and its power had a corrupting influence over California politics. Symbolized by the free transit passes they liberally distributed to California legislators, the Big Four's ability to sway public officials by means both legal and illegal enabled them to successfully dodge taxes and to escape effective government regulation for over forty years.[19]

Thus, by the time he delivered the keynote address to the jubilant Fourth of July crowd that welcomed the C&O's completion to Chico in 1870, Bidwell was no longer an ally of Leland Stanford.[20] A staunch Jacksonian with a deep-seated antipathy toward corporate monopolies, Bidwell had grown concerned about the rising power of the Big Four while still serving in Congress. His C&O bill, and his vote in favor of the Atlantic and Pacific Railroad grant in 1866, were both intended to help ensure competitive rail service for California.[21] So too was his support of Senator Conness' proposal to subsidize the construction of the California Pacific Railroad between Vallejo and Marysville by way of Sacramento. Like Bidwell, Conness was a Union Democrat who became Leland Stanford's chief nemesis in California politics between 1859 and 1867. His bill posed a major threat to the Big Four because it would have positioned a rival road in the strategic gap between San Francisco Bay and the Central Pacific's western terminus at Sacramento. After considerable delay, Conness' bill passed the Senate but Bidwell was unable to move it through the House before the Thirty-ninth Congress expired in March 1867.[22]

Bidwell's growing opposition to the Big Four was not simply a matter of ideological principle, it was also a matter of business. Shortly after founding Chico in 1860, Bidwell had moved boldly to ensure the city's future by establishing it as the western terminus of a trans-Sierra toll road

---

[19] Bean, pp. 208–224, 240–241, 298–310.
[20] Chico *Northern Enterprise*, 9 July 1870.
[21] *Congressional Globe*, 39th Congress, 1st Session, p. 4182.
[22] *Congressional Globe*, 39th Congress, 2nd Session, pp. 694–95, 976–77, 1699–1700.

linking the Sacramento Valley to the booming Humboldt mining district of northern Nevada. In April 1863, Bidwell and four associates obtained a twenty-year franchise from the state legislature to build and operate such a road between Chico and Susanville in the Honey Lake Valley of Lassen County. Though competing against two similar projects sponsored by merchants in Oroville and Red Bluff, Bidwell's group successfully raised $40,000 and incorporated as the Chico and Humboldt Wagon Road Company in 1864. By the end of the year, pack trains and stagecoaches were hauling freight and passengers across the Sierra to Susanville and the Humboldt district beyond (see map).[23]

In the meantime, another western mining boom had erupted in the Owyhee and Boise river basins of southwestern Idaho. Hoping to tap into these wealthy new regions, Bidwell joined forces with several Idaho entrepreneurs who proposed to run stage lines from Ruby City to Chico by connecting with the Humboldt road in Nevada's Black Rock Desert. Despite obstacles posed by periodic Indian attacks and long stretches of desert and mountain terrain, substantial traffic over the 450-mile overland route in 1865 and 1866 promised to make Chico the entrepôt for a sprawling interior hinterland blessed with rich deposits of silver and gold.[24]

The Humboldt and Idaho road projects pitted Bidwell against powerful corporate rivals. In the Pacific Northwest, the Oregon Steam Navigation Company maneuvered to attach Idaho to its sphere of influence by exploiting its control of Columbia River commerce. At the same time, the Central Pacific Railroad, still building its way through the rugged Sierra, planned to project its transcontinental line straight through the Humboldt region. It also hoped to draw traffic southward from Idaho by encouraging new stage connections between Humboldt and the Owyhee district.

In the face of such opposition, Bidwell had no qualms about using his influence in Congress to protect his private business interests. In cooperation with Senator Conness, Bidwell attempted to secure $50,000 for the construction of a federal wagon road from Susanville to Boise. The House of Representatives approved the scheme but the Senate let it die in committee.[25] Bidwell did not come away empty handed, however. Over the com-

---

[23] Anita L. Chang, *The Historical Geography of the Humboldt Wagon Road* (Chico: Association for Northern California Records and Research, 1992), pp. 9–20, 35.

[24] Clarence McIntosh, "The Chico and Red Bluff Route: Stage Lines From Southern Idaho to the Sacramento Valley, 1865–1867," *Idaho Yesterdays*, 6 (Fall 1962), pp. 12–19; Alan H. Patera, "The Chico Route to Idaho," *Western Express*, 40 (April 1990), pp. 8–33; Larry Bourdeau, "The Historic Archaeology of Cabo's Tavern, CA-BUT-712," (MA Thesis, CSUC, 1982), pp. 37–41, 123–36.

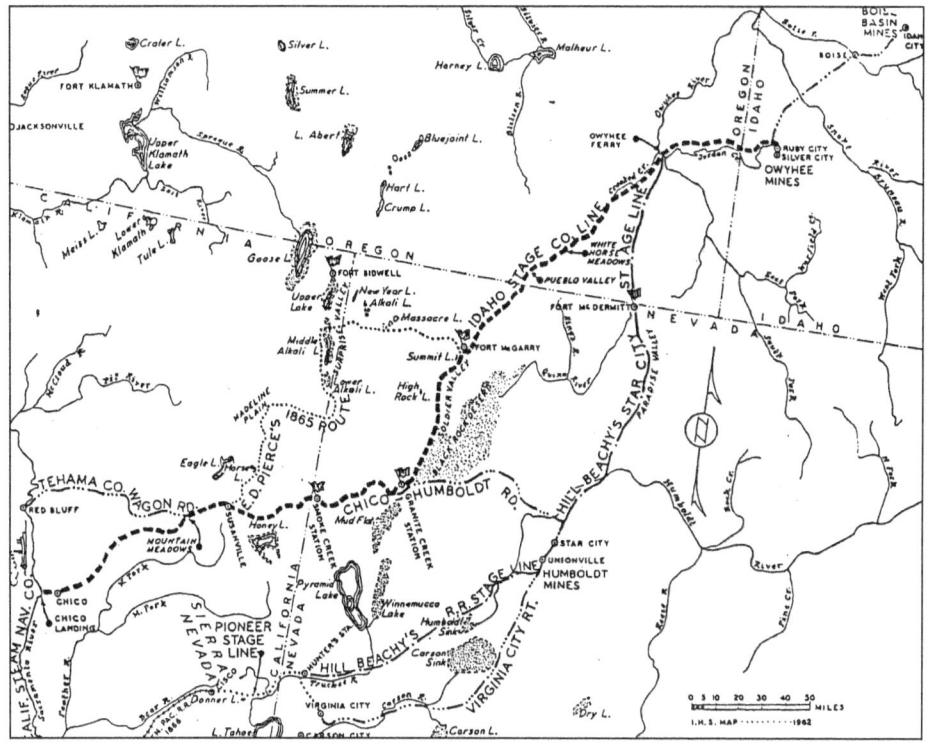

Chico-to-Humboldt Wagon Road and Idaho Stage Routes.
Permission to reprint courtesy of the Idaho State Historical Society and *Idaho Yesterdays*.

bined objections of Oregon Steam and the Big Four, Bidwell helped obtain a federal mail contract for the Boise-Susanville stage route in 1866 and arranged for the establishment of ten new post offices along the way. He also managed to wrest from Oroville the western terminus of the Susanville mail route, which the U.S. Post Office obligingly transferred to Chico.[26] When Indian raids threatened to sever the Idaho line, Bidwell persuaded

---

[25] Chico *Courant*, 2 June 1866; Mansfield, p. 243; Patera, p. 13; Fairfield, *Pioneer History of Lassen County*, pp. 383–86.

[26] McIntosh, p. 18; Patera, pp. 13–14; Mansfield, p. 244. This would not be the last time Bidwell tried to promote Chico's fortunes at Oroville's expense. In 1874 he helped orchestrate an aggressive effort to relocate the Butte County seat to Chico. In a bitter election campaign, Oroville prevailed by a vote of 1,904 to 1,693. After this setback, Bidwell lobbied the state legislature in 1878 on behalf of an unsuccessful scheme to cut Butte County in half. Like previous attempts in 1862 and 1866, this plan would have made Chico the seat of a new "Chico County." In 1892, a similar proposal to create Bidwell County, again with Chico as its seat, failed in the state assembly on a 33-37 vote. See Wells and Chambers, p. 148; Mansfield, pp. 259–260, 284–287, 331.

Chico store and Post Office.
Reprinted with permission courtesy of the John Nopel Collection.

the U.S. Army to deploy troops along the route. In August 1865, General Irvin McDowell established Fort Bidwell in the far northeast corner of California. Named in Bidwell's honor, the remote army post dedicated itself to guarding the investments of its congressional patron and namesake.[27] Unfortunately, these efforts failed to guarantee success. As Edwin B. Crocker of the Central Pacific had predicted in 1866, the completion of the transcontinental railroad across Nevada and the inauguration of a C.P.-backed stage service into Idaho spelled doom for Chico's trans-Sierra dreams. By April 1867, Bidwell's Humboldt Wagon Road was reduced to the status of a strictly local highway.[28]

---

[27]Brigadier General George Wright to Bidwell, 30 April 1864, *The War of the Rebellion: A Compilation of the Official Records of the Union and Confederate Armies,* Series I, Vol. 50, Part II, Serial 106, p. 833; Major General Irvin McDowell to Bidwell, 7 February 1865, ibid., pp. 1129–1130; Bidwell to Wright, 27 March 1865, ibid., pp. 1171–1172; Bidwell to McDowell, 28 April 1865, ibid., p. 1214; Bidwell to Wright, 17 June 1865, ibid., p. 1264; Patera, pp. 14–15; Tim Bousquet, "'Wiping Out the Red-Skins': A Look Back at Chico's Role in the Idaho Indian Wars," *Chico News and Review,* 12 Jan. 1995, pp. 16–19; Robert W. Frazer, *Forts of the West* (Norman: University of Oklahoma Press, 1965), pp. 20–22. Frazer's brief but useful account is marred by his confusion of Fort Bidwell with Camp Bidwell, the earlier post garrisoned by troops stationed on Rancho Chico from 1863 to 1865. See Mansfield, p. 228; and Joseph F. McGie, *History of Butte County, I, 1840–1919* (Oroville: Butte County Board of Education, 1983), p. 104.

Bidwell clashed directly with the Big Four again in 1867 when he decided to forego reelection to Congress and to run instead for Governor.[29] Bidwell's record in Washington made him the favorite choice of the dominant "long hair" faction of the Union party, composed primarily of former Republicans. Most of the old Douglas Democrats who comprised the "short hair" faction, including John Conness, backed George C. Gorham, who also enjoyed the support of the Big Four.[30] At the Union party state convention of June 1867, Gorham defeated Bidwell on the first ballot by a narrow vote of 148 to 132. It was the closest John Bidwell would ever come to the governorship.[31]

Deeply disappointed and convinced that he had been cheated of his prize by railroad bribery, Bidwell came away from the convention with a bitter hatred of both Gorham and the Big Four. For the sake of party unity, Bidwell refused an independent nomination offered to him by renegade long hairs and dutifully backed the Union ticket in the November election. Following Gorham's defeat and the dissolution of the Union party, however, Bidwell never again ran for office on a major party ticket. The politician one newspaper declared "too good a man to be Governor" henceforth put his personal beliefs ahead of all partisan loyalties and compromises. While much admired, Bidwell's principled stance doomed the rest of his political career to failure.[32]

As much as he liked to blame the railroad, Bidwell and his new bride-to-be probably contributed as much to his loss of the governorship as did the Big Four. As fate would have it, the campaign of 1867 occurred in the midst of Bidwell's two-year courtship of Annie Kennedy, the greatest single turning point of his life after 1841. As a pious Presbyterian, the future Mrs. Bidwell entertained high moral expectations of her ardent suitor. Although widely and justly regarded as an honest and upright man, Bidwell was

---

[28]McIntosh, p. 19. Crocker, a railroad executive and California state supreme court justice, was the brother of Charles Crocker, one of the Big Four. See also Patera, pp. 16–18.

[29]Regarding Bidwell's growing disenchantment with Congress, see JB-91, pp. 8, 31–32.

[30]A newspaper editor in Marysville and Sacramento, Gorham also served as a lobbyist for the Big Four. In 1867, he had successfully steered the railroad's controversial "subsidy bill" through both houses of the state legislature, only to see it vetoed by Governor Frederick Low. See Sacramento Union, 16 February 1909; Alexander Saxton, *The Indispensable Enemy: Labor and the Anti-Chinese Movement in California* (Berkeley: University of California Press, 1971), pp. 80–91.

[31]Davis, *History of Political Conventions*, p. 247.

[32]Hunt, pp. 300–306; Royce Delmatier, Clarence McIntosh, and Earl G. Waters, eds., *The Rumble of California Politics, 1848–1970* (New York: John Wiley & Sons, 1970), pp. 56–58; Gerald Stanley, "The Whim and Caprice of a Majority in a Petty State: The 1867 Election in California," *Pacific Historian*, 24 (Winter 1980), pp. 443–455.

still in many respects a worldly frontiersman who did not attend church or consider himself a Christian. However, part of Annie's attraction for him was her ability to awaken the latent spiritual longings that had evidently lain dormant in Bidwell since youth. These, in turn, formed a good deal of his appeal to her. From the beginning, Annie seems to have seen in Bidwell a potential convert as well as a prospective groom. Consequently, Bidwell's lengthy courtship of Annie involved an equally protracted conversion to Christianity.[33]

From the standpoint of his political career, nothing could have been worse or more poorly timed. Bidwell had hoped his religious conversion would come in one great shining moment like St. Paul's on the road to Damascus. Instead, conversion on the road to Sacramento turned out to be an agonizing process of self questioning that caused Bidwell to spend most of the campaign wrestling with his conscience and searching his soul. It is clear from his private correspondence that Bidwell was, at least for the moment, a deeply troubled man and at best a reluctant candidate, torn between his secular ambitions and his desire to achieve worthiness in the eyes of both God and Annie Kennedy. When the seamy demands of politics threatened finally to undermine his hard-won spiritual progress, Bidwell responded by becoming morally inflexible. His opponents, meanwhile, unhindered by religious contemplations or the demands of a blooming love affair, focused tenaciously on the task at hand. They won. As Bidwell confessed to Annie with a mixture of bitterness and pride, his new-found principled purity proved no match for the professional politicians. Nor would it ever. From 1867 forward, Bidwell always ran for office on his own terms as a political outsider, and he always lost.[34]

For the next ten years, however, Bidwell remained a popular figure and a force to be reckoned with in state politics. Indeed, the economic crisis of the 1870s revived Bidwell's gubernatorial hopes and propelled him into a new role as a champion of radical agrarianism.[35] In 1869, California's robust economy suddenly began to falter and, four years later, the nationwide Panic of 1873 plunged the ailing state into a full-scale depression. The hard times

---

[33] Hunt, pp. 291–299, 384–385; Chad L. Hoopes, *What Makes a Man: The Annie E. Kennedy and John Bidwell Letters, 1866–1868* (Fresno, Ca.: Valley Publishers, 1973), pp. 1–25, 29.

[34] Hoopes, pp. 24, 36–55, 63–64. In addition to the demands of his simultaneous courtship and conversion, Bidwell was also distracted during the campaign by the serious illness of his brother Thomas. One of four family members who eventually followed John Bidwell to California between 1854 and 1886, Thomas Bidwell settled in Chico in 1856 and later purchased Bidwell's store. Never in good health, Thomas had fallen gravely ill toward the end of John's term in Congress, and died on September 8, 1867. See JB-91, pp. 8 and 32; McDonald, "The Bidwell Family," pp. 178–80.

of the "Terrible Seventies" resulted in hard feelings. Workingmen blamed immigrant Chinese for rising unemployment and falling wages, while farmers, particularly wheat growers, denounced the Big Four and other corporate middlemen for charging monopolistic rates that consumed agriculture's dwindling profit margins. In 1877, militant labor activists led by Denis Kearney of San Francisco launched the anti-Chinese Workingmen's Party of California to advance their cause. Farmers, meanwhile, banded together in a series of organizations designed to challenge the power of the Big Four and grain brokers like Isaac Friedlander, who controlled the sale of wheat sacks to growers and the overseas export of grain from the Bay Area.[36]

In September 1872, Bidwell attended the founding convention of the California Farmers' Union and was elected president. The Union struggled for a year before merging with the more powerful Patrons of Husbandry, better known as the Grange. A national organization, the Grange, like the Union, demanded government regulation of the railroads and spearheaded the formation of farmer-owned cooperatives to collectively market crops and purchase farm supplies. California growers flocked to the Grange and Bidwell joined the movement in June 1873. By October, the state Grange claimed more than 3,000 members organized in 104 local branches. One year later, the California Patrons boasted 231 local chapters and a total membership of over 13,500.[37]

By then, the Grangers had entered politics by forming the People's Independent Party in 1873. At the party's founding convention, Bidwell was elected to the state central committee. Dubbed by their critics the "Dolly Varden" party, the independents made a spectacular showing in their first campaign, capturing eight seats in the state senate and thirty-four, a plurality, in the assembly.[38] Two years later, setting their sights on

---

[35]Despite his social position as a wealthy gentleman farmer, Bidwell's lifelong commitment to Jeffersonian values made him very sympathetic to the plight of small farmers and therefore something of a "class renegade," particularly during the tumultuous 1870s. See Gerald L. Prescott, "Farm Gentry vs. The Grangers: Conflict in Rural America," *California Historical Quarterly*, 56 (Winter 1977–1978), pp. 332, 344.

[36]Bean, pp. 236–241; Rodman Paul, "The Great California Grain War: The Grangers Challenge the Wheat King," *Pacific Historical Review*, 27 (November 1958), pp. 331–349.

[37]JBD, 14 June 1873; Ezra Carr, *The Patrons of Husbandry on the Pacific Coast* (San Francisco: A. L. Bancroft, 1875), pp. 84–103; Paul, p.345.

[38]Davis, pp. 321–34; Don Allen, *Legislative Sourcebook: The California Legislature and Reapportionment, 1849–1865* (Sacramento: California State Assembly, 1965), p. 272. Dolly Varden was an attractively dressed heroine in Charles Dickens' novel *Barnaby Rudge* whose name was later applied to a popular style of women's apparel featuring bright and varied colors. Political wags used the name as a derisive reference to the Independents' heterogeneous and unwieldy following. See Bean, p. 308; and Delmatier, et al., p. 62.

the governorship, the Dolly Vardens nominated Bidwell to head their ticket.[39] The ensuing gubernatorial election of 1875 was one of the most bitter in California history. Pitted against Democrat William Irwin and Republican Timothy Guy Phelps, Bidwell ran on a strident antimonopoly and anticorporate platform which he helped write. The Independents condemned the practices of the Big Four in no uncertain terms and demanded state regulation of all railroad, steamship, gas, and water companies. Denouncing the major parties for their subservience to corporate power, the Independents promised to end government railroad subsidies, reduce transportation rates, and outlaw the granting of free passes to public officials. In a bid for labor support, the Independents also endorsed the eight-hour day and the exclusion of Chinese immigration. On the potentially vexing issue of prohibition, the Independents remained silent, but Bidwell was forced to take a stand when members of the new Temperance Reform party launched an effort to endorse his candidacy. In a brief public statement, Bidwell tactfully explained that, while he believed firmly in temperance, he would accept no further nominations. "I stand," he declared, "upon the people's independent platform."[40]

Though he chose to conduct a front porch campaign rather than hit the hustings, Bidwell still had to endure a torrent of personal abuse and invective during the ensuing two months. His opponents attempted to smear him as a hypocrite on the monopoly and labor issues by portraying him as a grasping land baron who employed Indian slaves and Chinese coolies. They also accused Bidwell of monopolizing the waters of Chico Creek. Most serious was Senator Aaron Sargent's charge that Bidwell held Rancho Chico illegally. Sargent, a close ally of the Big Four, claimed that Bidwell's title was invalid and insinuated that Bidwell had only managed to obtain a federal patent after paying a $10,000 bribe to his friend, U.S. Attorney General Jeremiah S. Black. Bidwell effectively refuted Sargent's accusations, but to no avail. On election day he finished third with 29,752 votes to Phelps' 31, 322 and Irwin's 61,509.[41] Still, for a third party candidate, Bidwell's twenty-four percent of the statewide vote was a remarkable showing, and he ran especially well in rural areas. Bidwell carried tiny

---

[39]Bidwell's running mate was the incumbent governor Romualdo Pacheco, California's first Hispanic and native-born chief executive since statehood. Pacheco had been elected lieutenant governor in 1871 and had assumed the governorship in February 1875 when his predecessor, Newton Booth, resigned to become a United States Senator. See Benjamin, p. 36; Davis, p. 349; Delmatier, et al., pp. 12–13, 34–35, 64.

[40]Davis, pp. 330–34, 341–49, 354–55.

Alpine, Mono, Lassen, and Sierra counties, and finished ahead of Phelps in twenty-five others, including Butte, Sacramento, Fresno, and Los Angeles. Bidwell also outpolled Phelps in San Francisco, where the Dolly Vardens' denunciation of the Spring Valley Water Company monopoly evidently struck a responsive chord with city voters (see Table 3).[42]

Interestingly, the Dolly Varden insurgency seems to have occurred almost entirely within Republican ranks, and the third party never succeeded in attracting much Democratic support. By nominating Irwin, a state senator who had earned a reputation as a leading proponent of railroad rate regulation, the Democrats managed to deflect the Dolly Varden threat and to keep their party intact. In an electorate that expanded by just 2,400 voters between 1871 and 1875, the Democratic total actually rose by 4,000. Meanwhile, the Republican vote fell by fifty percent. These trends reflected the earlier impact of the Dolly Varden legislative gains in 1873, most of which appeared to come at the expense of the GOP.[43]

Fortunately for the Republicans, Bidwell's defeat doomed the Independent party, which lost all but four of its seats in the assembly. This devastating setback, however, did not end Granger influence in state politics. In 1879, the Patrons teamed up with the Workingmen's party in a successful effort to rewrite California's constitution. Narrowly approved in a statewide referendum, the Constitution of 1879 embodied many of the reforms demanded by farmers. Chief among these was a new railroad commission elected by the voters and endowed with the power to establish maximum transportation rates.[44]

Bidwell, however, opposed the new constitution. Between 1877 and 1879, the rise of the anti-Chinese movement had driven a permanent wedge between Bidwell and organized labor. Because he employed a substan-

---

[41] Hunt, pp. 307–321; Davis, p. 355; Delmatier, et al., pp. 60–66; Hoopes, pp. 22–23. Like Bidwell's *bête noire* George C. Gorham, Sargent was another Bidwell nemesis. Sargent sided with Gorham at the 1867 Union Party convention and, in return, Bidwell had opposed Sargent's election to the United States Senate in 1871. That year, the GOP-dominated state legislature decided to replace incumbent Republican Cornelius Cole with the pro-railroad Sargent, who also received backing from Gorham. In a bitter contest that deeply divided the Republican caucus, Bidwell lobbied strenuously but unsuccessfully on Cole's behalf. See Chico *Northern Enterprise*, 21 October 1871; Cornelius C. Cole, *Memoirs of Cornelius Cole: Ex-Senator of the United States from California* (New York: McLoughlin Brothers, 1908), pp. 349–351.

[42] California, Secretary of State, *California Election Returns*, microfilm reel 7 (1873–78).

[43] *Guide to U.S. Elections* (Washington, D.C.: Congressional Quarterly, 1994), p. 670; Allen, *Legislative Sourcebook*, p. 272; Ward McAfee, "Local Interests and Railroad Regulation in Nineteenth Century California," (Ph.D. diss., Stanford University, 1965), pp. 26–68.

[44] Bean, pp. 238–241.

tial number of Chinese workers on Rancho Chico, Bidwell was branded an enemy of white labor by local union militants who directed a prolonged campaign of violence and intimidation against him. This bitter personal experience, coupled with the alarming outbreaks of violence all across the country during the great railroad strikes of 1877, forever soured Bidwell's attitudes toward trade unionism. Apparently viewing the new constitution as primarily the handiwork of Denis Kearney and other W.P.C. radicals, Bidwell voted against the revised charter and backed victorious Republican George Perkins for Governor in 1879. Perkins, a former Oroville merchant and politician who had served as Bidwell's aide-de-camp during the Civil War, rewarded him in 1880 with an appointment to the University of California Board of Regents.

Bidwell's subsequent involvement with California's expanding system of higher education deepened in 1887, when he helped lead a successful campaign to locate a new state normal school at Chico. By donating eight acres of his cherry orchard as a campus site, Bidwell enabled Chico to outbid several rival towns for the coveted college. Another gubernatorial appointment soon followed, this time from a Democrat, Washington Bartlett, who placed Bidwell on the first board of trustees for the newly established Chico State Normal School. Bidwell served on the board from 1887 until his resignation in 1896, and gave the keynote address when the cornerstone of the first campus building was laid on July 4, 1888. In September of the following year, the first students at what eventually became the California State University, Chico, arrived for the commencement of instruction.[45]

Bidwell's gubernatorial appointments did not signal a return to major party politics. Bidwell remained true to his antimonopoly and agrarian principles, and he expanded them during the 1880s to include female suffrage and the nationalization of railroad companies. Still, it soon became clear that John Bidwell was developing a strong conservative streak in his old age and that two major forces were continuing to propel him in the rightward direction he had begun taking in 1877–1879. First, the growing influence of his wife Annie led Bidwell to drift away from the mainstream of

---

[45]California Legislature, "Report of the Regents of the University of California," *Appendix to the Journals of the Senate and the Assembly, 1881*, 2 (Sacramento: 1881), p. 7; Clarence McIntosh, "Chico Normal, Teachers College, and State College, 1887–1962," Butte County Historical Society *Diggin's*, 6 (Fall 1962), p. 7; McIntosh, "A Brief History of California State University, Chico," *Diggin's*, 31 (Summer 1987), pp. 31, 40; William H. Hutchinson, Clarence McIntosh, and Pam Herman Bush, *A Precious Sense of Place: The Early Years of Chico State* (Chico: Friends of the Meriam Library, 1991), pp. 26–29; Hutchinson, *When Chico Stole the College* (Chico: Butte Savings and Loan Association, 1983).

## Table 3: 1875 California Gubernatorial Election Returns

| County | Phelps (R) | Irwin (D) | Bidwell (PI) | Lovett (Proh.) |
|---|---|---|---|---|
| Alameda | 1,956 | 2,483 | 895 | 45 |
| Alpine | 51 | 80 | 87 | |
| Amador | 638 | 1,150 | 393 | 5 |
| Butte | 318 | 1,375 | 1,146 | |
| Calaveras | 522 | 903 | 402 | |
| Colusa | 68 | 1,275 | 548 | |
| Contra Costa | 765 | 699 | 396 | 9 |
| Del Norte | 48 | 236 | 136 | |
| El Dorado | 740 | 1,238 | 556 | 1 |
| Fresno | 49 | 651 | 197 | |
| Humboldt | 951 | 714 | 272 | 2 |
| Inyo | 179 | 359 | 248 | 5 |
| Kern | 138 | 694 | 376 | 1 |
| Lake | 82 | 663 | 211 | 6 |
| Lassen | 134 | 199 | 200 | |
| Los Angeles | 667 | 2,898 | 1,543 | |
| Marin | 310 | 471 | 298 | |
| Mariposa | 58 | 484 | 412 | |
| Mendocino | 204 | 1,071 | 481 | |
| Merced | 172 | 585 | 397 | |
| Modoc | 7 | 336 | 284 | |
| Mono | 37 | 80 | 133 | 1 |
| Monterey | 736 | 886 | 441 | |
| Napa | 629 | 989 | 248 | |
| Nevada | 1,067 | 1,664 | 990 | 2 |
| Placer | 1,065 | 881 | 606 | 7 |
| Plumas | 230 | 550 | 425 | |
| Sacramento | 1,483 | 2,361 | 1,649 | |
| San Benito | 285 | 643 | 199 | 49 |
| San Bernardino | 204 | 729 | 427 | 1 |
| San Diego | 593 | 755 | 252 | 1 |
| San Francisco | 5,179 | 14,199 | 6,080 | 71 |
| San Joaquin | 1,805 | 1,440 | 449 | 1 |
| San Luis Obispo | 199 | 756 | 596 | 17 |
| San Mateo | 828 | 623 | 141 | 11 |
| Santa Barbara | 409 | 798 | 541 | 3 |
| Santa Clara | 1,695 | 2,634 | 733 | 22 |
| Santa Cruz | 645 | 834 | 578 | 8 |
| Shasta | 288 | 614 | 296 | 4 |
| Sierra | 348 | 470 | 519 | 10 |
| Siskiyou | 490 | 886 | 154 | |
| Solano | 1,391 | 1,480 | 532 | 4 |
| Sonoma | 736 | 2,106 | 737 | 38 |
| Stanislaus | 382 | 788 | 137 | |
| Sutter | 184 | 555 | 490 | |
| Tehama | 404 | 599 | 136 | 1 |
| Trinity | 334 | 400 | 75 | 10 |
| Tulare | 285 | 846 | 434 | |
| Tuolumne | 501 | 931 | 322 | |
| Ventura | 120 | 414 | 413 | 17 |
| Yolo | 136 | 1,169 | 889 | |
| Yuba | 577 | 865 | 652 | 4 |
| | 31,322 | 61,509 | 29,752 | 356 |

Source: California, Secretary of State, *California Election Returns*, MF Reel 7 (1873–1878).

radical agrarianism. Unlike many former Grangers, Bidwell did not join the Farmers' Alliance or the Populist party during the 1890s. Instead, he came to see the outright prohibition of alcohol as the most urgent reform issue of the late nineteenth century. Abandoning his earlier and more mild temperance stances, Bidwell began to advocate total prohibition as the most effective means of ending the evils of vice and poverty in industrial age America. By the mid-1880s, Bidwell had formally joined the Prohibition party and was already prominent enough to serve as a delegate to the party's national convention in 1888.[46]

Meanwhile, Bidwell had begun to yield before the immense anti-Chinese sentiment prevalent in California. Though he had employed Chinese workers ever since the 1860s, political necessity forced Bidwell to support calls for Chinese exclusion beginning in 1875. His slow but steady retreat on the Chinese question, combined with the tremendous influx of southern and eastern Europeans into America after 1880, caused Bidwell to rethink the entire immigration issue. It also seemed to awaken his latent anti-Catholicism, which had already been stirred by the agitations of Denis Kearney and the other Irish immigrants who dominated the Workingmen's party. By 1890, a much more conservative John Bidwell had emerged: the erstwhile agrarian rebel and radical Republican was now a confirmed nativist as well as prohibitionist.

That year, Bidwell received the Prohibition party's gubernatorial nomination and accepted the endorsement of the American party, a small extremist group that advocated tight immigration restrictions and the repeal of *all* naturalization laws! Despite this double-billing, Bidwell finished a distant third with a scant four percent of the vote.[47]

Bidwell's defeat was followed by one last campaign, his celebrated run for the Presidency in 1892. There was, of course, never any serious chance that Bidwell would trade his Chico mansion for the White House, but his 264,133 votes did set a Prohibition party record that stands to this day. In the context of the 1892 election, however, Bidwell's record represented a mere two percent of the total vote and a very distant fourth-place finish. Bidwell never figured prominently in the campaign, and his candidacy was completely overshadowed by those of President Benjamin Harrison and the president's two main challengers, Populist James B.

---

[46] Hunt, pp. 330–331.
[47] Davis, pp. 553–560; Hunt, pp. 331–335, 423; John Higham, "The American Party, 1886–1891," *Pacific Historical Review*, 19 (February 1950), pp. 37–46.

# A Career in California Politics

John Bidwell, ca. 1880.
Reprinted with permission by Special Collections, Meriam Library, California State University, Chico.

Weaver and the victorious Democrat, Grover Cleveland. All in all, Bidwell's presidential campaign provided a very anticlimactic end to a political career that had begun rather brilliantly over forty years before.[48]

## *Bidwell on His Political Beliefs and Career*

### ELECTED TO STATE CONSTITUTIONAL CONVENTION BUT FAILS TO ATTEND

The first time I had anything to do with politics was when I was elected to the constitutional convention in '49. I never went among the people [to campaign], but they elected me.... The other delegates from the Sacramento valley had gone down before I received notice of the election. Had no idea how long it would take to form the constitution, and I was not prepared, and so did not go to the convention. It was not because I did not feel interested in it, for I did.[1]

### SERVING IN THE STATE SENATE

... I was elected State Senator in December 1849.... We had to frame a code of laws, and our constitution was almost a literal copy of the constitution of New York. A few members who had been able to get copies of the statutes of N.Y.

---
[48]Hunt, pp. 336–350.    [1]JB-91, p. 24.

introduced nearly all the bills, and they were almost literal transcripts of the N.Y. laws. A Southerner, named A. P. Crittenden, was foremost in introducing bills. I was head of the committee on corporations, also on the committee of county boundaries. I was chosen for this because I had more knowledge of the counties than perhaps any one else there. I wrote the first charter of the City of San Francisco, for which the newspapers gave me great credit, but I didn't deserve the credit, because I had copied it almost entirely from the charter of St. Louis. There was nothing very remarkable in getting up the code of laws.[2]

### VOTES FOR JOHN C. FREMONT IN CALIFORNIA'S FIRST SENATE ELECTION

While in the legislature we had to elect two U.S. senators. A good many people may suppose I had prejudices against Fremont because of his treatment of Sutter. Still I had none, and when it came to voting for senators, I voted for Fremont, not because he was the best qualified, because I did not think he would be a good public speaker, but because of his influence with his father-in-law, [Missouri Senator Thomas Hart] Benton. And I knew that the people of California could not afford to throw away any points on that. He had been here longer than any of the others, and I voted for him very willingly, and always when I met him, did so in a very friendly manner.[3]

### ON GOVERNOR JOHN BIGLER

I did not approve of Bigler's administration [1852–1856]. Altho' I was democratic, I did not vote for him [in 1851]. I voted for [the Whig candidate, Pierson B.] Reading; my personal friendship for Reading caused me to do so. I did not vote for Bigler when he was nominated the second time because I did not like his first administration. When he became a third time a candidate for renomination, I was out against him; that is, I spoke with firmness against him. I met him once on the streets of Sacramento, and he gave me "Hail Columbia"[4] because I had blamed him for some of his acts; but I stood my ground. And I cannot say that Bigler was a very bitter enemy of mine, but he was a politician of the worst kind. He belonged to that class that thought anything they could do to win would be right.[5]

### 1860 DEMOCRATIC NATIONAL CONVENTION

When I was sent as a delegate to the Charleston convention in '60, everything was under democratic rule, and you might say the phase of the democracy was southern. Breckenridge was with the southern democrats. When I went to that convention and saw that the south meant disunion, I could not agree with

---

[2]JB-91, pp. 24–25.                      [3]Ibid., p. 25.
[4]A popular slang expression derived from the title of the patriotic song composed in 1798 by Joseph Hopkinson, "Hail Columbia" served as a euphemism for "Hell." See J. E. Lighter, ed., *Random House Historical Dictionary of American Slang*, 2 (New York: Random House, 1997), p. 5.
[5]JB-91, p. 25.

them. I differed with all the other delegates from California and Oregon. Senator Gwin was one of them, and [Senator] M[ilton] S. Latham another, and while he was from Ohio, he was under the influence of the southern democracy. Really if he could have been disentangled, he would have stood half way between Douglas democracy and the extreme southern, but he owed his election to the southern element and of course he had to affiliate with them. I returned to Washington, and the convention made no nomination. Afterward one wing held its convention and nominated Breckenridge, and the other wing nominated Douglas. Of course I was with Douglas. After I got back to Washington, on my way home to California, Stephen A. Douglas, before he was nominated for president, sent for me. He wanted to see the man that dared to differ with Gwin and the rest of them from California. They called me the black sheep and everything else, but that did not hurt me. When I got home to California, Gwin and [San Francisco customs collector Benjamin] Frank[lin] Washington called upon me. The latter was the finest political writer on the coast. He was the leader of the southern democracy here. They stayed with me and talked almost to midnight, to try and induce me to vote for Breckenridge. I treated them very politely, took them in my carriage to the county seat, and bid them good-by. I never could be persuaded to yield to the disunion element that was growing up at the time.[6]

CIVIL WAR—"THERE CAN BE NO MIDDLE GROUND"

In the great crisis there can be but one issue—our Government must be sustained or it will go down. There can be no middle ground. He who is not for it is against it.[7]

CONTROLLING AND SPYING ON REBELS IN CHICO

They were very bitter against me during the war. There was a large majority of southerners here. Some went east to join the Confederate army, but not so many as Union men. The time came when we had to prevent the Union men from going east. We had to organize the military here, and that was what held California; otherwise there would have been an attempt to carry the state out of the union. Two things prevented it, the sending of General [Edwin V.] Sumner here to take the place of [Albert Sidney] Johns[t]on, and the organization of the military. We had the Union league well organized, but they organized also what was called the Knights of the Golden Circle. This was a rebel organization; the name was changed afterwards to that of the organization of American Knights. Whenever the Unionists were defeated, they became very bold. I employed a man to join that society; paid his initiation fees, etc. Every night after they had a meeting he reported to me. He reported their signs and pass words. At one time they had under consideration and actually did resolve that every man of them should

---

[6]Ibid., p. 26.     [7]San Francisco *Alta*, 23 June 1861.

kill one republican. Two men were selected to kill me. Things went on in that way until the Union army began to be victorious and until the soldiers came up. Then we arrested every fellow who hurrahed for Jeff Davis and kept him under guard and made him walk with a load of bricks on his back. When they would promise positively we would let them go. Pretty soon those things were over. But we had to be firm in those days in order to be secure. Among the warmest friends I had at that time, I could point to one or two southerners who did not want war, who sympathized with slavery, but really were not in favor of the rebels. Yet they voted the democratic ticket all the time. In emergencies I would consult them, and they promised to advise me of anything that would lead to danger. We had eight military companies. Some came on foot 120 miles to attend the appointment, showing how strong the union sentiment was. Many of us would have been glad to go east to join the Union army, but we could not all go.[8]

I have had men dispute me: for instance during the war where I lived the country was full of rebels. I was on good terms with many of them, but politically were at sword's point. A man came to me and told me that he wanted me to leave home and go away for a few months. He said you don't know what an amount of prejudice is here against you. I want you to go away until the excitement is over; I should [not] be surprised if the men would come up and shoot you down. I replied I intended to stay at home, if they attacked me I expected to kill one man, which one I couldn't say, but intended to stay at home unless business called me away. Sometimes thirty or forty men would go by hurrahing for Jeff Davis. Finally I got sick of it. Gen. [George] Wright sent two companies of infantry and a company of artillery up, and they remained with us until the close of the war.[9]

### ATTENDS GOP NATIONAL CONVENTION IN BALTIMORE AND VISITS ULYSSES S. GRANT ADVANCING TOWARDS PETERSBURG, JUNE 1864

During the spring of 1864, I had an intense desire to see Grant. We had had such bad luck with McClellan and others; everything seemed to depend upon Grant. So when the Baltimore convention met to nominate Lincoln, I was sent to that convention. I was on the committee to inform Mr. Lincoln of his re-nomination. Then I went to [Secretary of War Edwin M.] Stanton and told him I wanted to see Grant. I told him I wanted to see the man in whose hands seemed to be the destiny of the nation. He replied that I could not go. But I said, "Mr. Stanton, I have come all the way from California and I don't want to go back without going to the front." "Well, if you really want to go, you shall. I will make you a bearer of dispatches." The next morning I went to take the steamer down the Potomac, and found that a good many others had passes to go down on the same steamer, and even some of our California delegates. This struck me as very strange, I could not understand it. I went on

---

[8]JB-91, pp. 26–28.
[9]Ibid., pp. 13–14.

board and presently there came an order for every man to go ashore. Every one did go except me; I was the bearer of dispatches. We went down to the White House and it so happened that Lieut. Wells had arrived bearing dispatches to Washington. I took his horse and started with about a dozen soldiers. Where I was going I did not know, but finally came to Grant's tent. I did not see an army. Grant took my dispatches. He asked me to dinner, and in about half an hour he told Quartermaster-General [Rufus] Ingalls that we would start in half an hour. In 15 minutes, every tent, everything was out of sight and in the wagons. I asked Grant how far it was to the front. He said about half a mile. "How far is it to where Lee is encamped?" "They are about 40 feet from our advanced line." We mounted and were off. We went about 15 miles but in such a cloud of dust that we could scarcely see ourselves. But I could see Grant's shoulders and kept watch of him. At sundown we came to a stop; did not see the army then. We built a camp-fire and lay there until 5 in the morning. The baggage wagons had not come up yet. About one o'clock they arrived and in fifteen minutes every tent was in its place. I slept in Grant's tent that night in an iron bedstead. In the morning he arranged for me to go back. He told the quartermaster to hurry up or the troops would take the road from us. Finally the troops came along. Grant knew just where each column was. During that night I don't think he slept more than 15 minutes at a time. Dispatches were arriving constantly. His composure under those circumstances led me to have great confidence in him, altho' he was so entirely different from what I had expected.[10]

### Securing Honey Lake Valley against rebel sympathizers

A Gentleman from Honey Lake Valley, reports that immigrants and others of disloyal sympathies, are bold and defiant—that they frequently display the rebel flag, hurrah for Jeff. Davis, and boast they are going to vote or fight. The loyal people there feel alarmed. There is a Cavalry Company organized under the laws of this State, from good and loyal material, but no arms have been furnished them. I deem it important that they should be supplied at the earliest moment. When at Susanville, Oct. 20, loyal citizens informed me that the Company (U.S. Vols) stationed there was so divided in political sentiment that they could have no confidence in them in case of an emergency. I know nothing myself. Honey Lake Valley is the key to the travel, trade and immigration from and into northern California. It seems important to keep it guarded. If the Arms & Accouterments for the Honey Lake Guards, the Militia Company before alluded to, be sent, it should be done immediately, as the mountains may be closed to travel any day—by snow.

I have written hurriedly, will keep posted if possible and advise you from time to time.[11]

---

[10]Ibid., pp. 28–29.
[11]JB to Major General Irvin McDowell, San Francisco, 1 November 1864, Indian War Papers of State Adjutant General, 1850–1880, California State Archives, Sacramento.

## Elected to U.S. Congress

My loyalty to the Union gave me, I think the nomination for Congress in '64. I took my seat in '65 and my term expired in '67. I was elected against one of the best men we ever had in this state—Jackson Temple. He was democratic. I was always outspoken and in favor of the Union.[12]

## On Slavery and Racial Equality

Ever since the rebellion began no man has felt more desirous than myself to see every vestige of slavery swept from the land. The war was the result of injustice to an unfortunate and downtrodden race. I have believed, and still believe, that our only safety for the future is to plant ourselves on the enduring rock of equal and exact justice—by that I mean equal protection and civil rights—to all citizens, the high, the low, the rich, and the poor. Every line of distinction is purely arbitrary and despotic in principle and in tendency, and wholly inconsistent with the fundamental principles of democratic republican government.[13]

## Congress Must Protect the Emancipated Slaves

... In answer to your request I will frankly state to you,—I cannot be a candidate for reelection to Congress. I would make the gubernatorial race if I could. But it is too early for me or anyone, I fear, to say so. Too many things may conspire to render the situation untenable. I am here to do a duty. I may not be able to come out unscathed from the most important field the country has ever seen—save the war for the Union, now happily closed; but the consequences not closed.

The President is not, I fear, in harmony with Congress—we try to claim that he is, but I fear the contrary is true. During the war it was easy to be right—it was then country or no country, the issue was clearly defined. We were running in a deep groove that held all loyal men, beyond the possibility of error or escape, to their country's cause. The course would still be clear but for the course which the executive has seen proper to pursue. He seems to ignore Congress altogether in the work of reconstruction.

If his policy is carried out I really believe we shall have trouble. The freedmen would be reduced by State laws to a condition worse than slavery. The feeling against the Union in the South is as bitter now as it has ever been. The President's policy giving immediate and unconditional control to the States, would silence the Union sentiment in the South, which is in the minority, and drive every school teacher from the southern plantations. I feel it to be the duty of Congress to insist upon adequate protection to the freedmen and the right to instruct and elevate them. The Copperheads are opposed to the freedmen's Bureau—and everything that will give them a chance to be free and useful. I shall not waver—governor or no governor—I would rather be right than be governor. ...

---

[12] JB-91, p. 28.   [13] *Congressional Globe*, 39th Congress, 1st Session, p. 1575.

P.S. . . . One word as to the duty of the Union party. They who have saved the Union must sustain the efforts to meet and arrange the logical consequences. They must labor to make intelligent the freedmen, that their presence may be the less pernicious, and protect them against the prejudice that would keep them degraded. The Copperheads and traitors will howl, "negro equality"—Let them do so. The issues must be met with an unbroken front. They would deny the colored man the means to intelligence and then degrade him because he is ignorant. Our party will be sure to triumph if we meet the question boldly, and on the principle of equal justice.[14]

### Fighting in Congress to secure the Idaho trade for Chico

You are right, and say just what I have known for the last two and one half years. The [California and Oregon] railroad must be hurried up the valley and the [Idaho] stage line put on before the [Central] P[acific] R.R. gets beyond a certain point. Why the land holders in the vicinity of Chico should remain dormant in view of the grand prize now almost within their grasp, but if lost never to return, is and has been, beyond my comprehension.[15]

I had to make a fight for a mail contract for some one—and, [John] Mullan [of the California and Idaho Stage and Fast Freight Company] edged himself in continuously, so that I could not strike anywhere without hitting him—and the Nevada delegation were fighting me so that I could not get an amount as large as it should be, for carrying the mail. But it [$45,000] was the best I could do. Other parties wanted about $100,000 for carrying a daily mail—and I believe I could have managed it, but for the peculiar disadvantages under which I had to labor. Now Mullan must succeed—everything must be done to aid him, without incurring pecuniary liability.[16]

It is life or death with us. If this does not succeed, then everything is to be drawn away from our section of [the] country to the [Central Pacific Railroad's] Dutch Flat route. All our hopes are with Mullan, not because of the man, but of the great end to be attained through him or not at all.[17]

### Bidwell blames the Big Four for Chico's loss of the Idaho trade

Our farming had come to that point that we needed a more extended market. We had heard of the discovery of gold in Idaho and of the silver mines in Nevada, and we wanted to get a road across the mountains to get a market for our produce. I started to find a road. . . . In 1862 I made 100 miles of wagon road across the Sierra Nevada Mts. The costs must have gone up to $50,000. I did it in the interest of trade. We also had a stage line running from Chico to Idaho, and I got $40,000

---

[14]JB, in Washington, D.C., to George A. Gillespie, 29 January 1866, George A. Gillespie Papers, HUNT.
[15]JB, in Washington, D.C., to D. D. Harris, 29 January 1866, JB-CSUC, b. 3.
[16]Ibid., 28 April 1866, JB-CSUC, b. 3.   [17]Ibid., 4 July 1866, JB-CSUC, b. 3.

for carrying the mails. The C[entral] P[acific] R.R. absorbed everything. They determined that I should not have the mail route on that road. We went before the Postmaster General. They got [Senator] Reverdy Johnson [of Maryland] and William Stewart, U.S. Senator from Nevada, to go in opposition to me, and I won my case alone, with nobody to help me. I won the case and got my mail route established from Chico to Idaho, via Susanville. Then they put their spies on the road, and finally succeeded in breaking the road up. If I had been in congress still, I would have given them a pretty hard battle. The road is still one of the principal ones across the mountains.[18]

### BIDWELL AND THE CONNESS BILL ON CALIFORNIA LAND TITLES, 1866

The only thing that engaged my attention there [in Congress] especially was the settlement of California land claims. The state had passed laws in reference to lands to which it was entitled under the act of admission. Those laws were in conflict with the laws of the United States, and therefore there were constant conflicts. A man would buy state script [sic] expecting to hold it under the state title. Another would jump it and expect to hold it under the U.S. laws. The governor and men generally interested in land claims posted me in regard to the matter and how important it was to have it settled. I found the land office at Washington against me. Could not do a thing. Judge [James M.] Edmunds [Commissioner of the U.S. General Land Office] would not listen to any propositions. He declared that the state laws were subordinate to the U.S. laws. Would not give me any satisfaction. I tried to draft a bill that would suit the wishes of the land office, but anything that suited them would not do us any good. Finally I went to the commissioner and told him I was going to introduce this bill again; he had reported adversely upon it. "You may introduce and pass a hundred bills if you like, but it won't do you any good." I went to work to introduce my bill, had it printed. Went to Justice [Stephen J.] Field and he helped me very much, and we got the bill in the best possible shape. Joe Wilson [Edmunds' predecessor and successor] had been commissioner of the land office whenever there was a vacancy. He was chief clerk [of the land office] and had been for a quarter of a century. In fact he was indispensable in the land office. One night he delivered a parlor lecture, and invited some ministers and senators, and I also received an invitation which was rather out of the common. A member of congress was not a very big man in those days, and had very little influence except in certain directions. As a rule they did not receive much attention. He delivered a very good lecture and I took the occasion to compliment him. I said: "Mr. Wilson, you must have read a good deal." "No, sir, I am a man of very few books." He called me aside and said that he had some good news for me. Said he: "The land office have surrendered; they have agreed to everything you want, but they have given the

---

[18]JB-91, pp. 63–65.

bill to Senator Conness to introduce." Said I : "Wilson, I am glad, but don't you think it is treating me unfairly to give it to him to introduce. He has taken no interest in this at all." He replied: "Never mind; Conness and Edmunds are on good terms with each other and while he would not give it to you he would give it to Conness, and in order to get it through, just let it stand." When I met Judge Field, he told me the same thing. I asked him if it were not treating me badly. "Don't you say a word," he replied, "for the sake of your State, don't say a word."

Conness took occasion to introduce the bill. He had changed it considerably. I had gotten a copy of the original bill. Edmunds did not like it that the bill was changed, and they quarreled. Finally, it would [end] up Edmunds' going before the committee and explaining it all. Conness got mad and destroyed the bill. I got hold of the same bill and introduced it in the House. At that stage of the game the Californians were so anxious in regard to the land bill that they sent out the [State] surveyor-general [James F. Houghton]. He said there must not be any quarrels: we must have the bill. He and I introduced it in the House and Conness introduced it in the Senate where it was hurried through, because bills were hurried through very quickly there. It got to the House before my bill, and that was the bill that was passed and they called it the Conness bill. I think I deserve something for what I did. It was one of the greatest measures that was ever passed for the benefit of California.[19]

### BIDWELL SUPPORTS CONNESS' RAILROAD BILL, 1867

The State of California is already falling into the grasp of monopolies, and some of those interests in these monopolies reside in New York. They have power enough to influence the New York delegation here. But I hope it will not be the disposition of this House to place California entirely at the mercy of a monopoly. I say, give every interest and every enterprise an equal chance.... The defeat of the bill is to postpone this necessary measure and to place it practically in the hands of another company [the Central Pacific Railroad].[20]

### ARGUES FOR EXTENDING THE 1862 MORRILL LAND GRANT COLLEGE ACT TO THE FORMER CONFEDERATE STATES

And I will embrace this occasion to say, Mr. Speaker, that when all citizens shall have an equal opportunity to become intelligent and understand the real issues that have drenched this nation in blood, and labor shall be duly respected, there will be no more traitors within the length and breadth of this then glorious and happy country.... To me it seems that whatever may be denied the States recently in rebellion, they should not be denied the means of intelligence. Give them that with a bounteous hand, and surround them with a flood of light to light their future pathway to allegiance and good government.[21]

---

[19] JB-91, pp. 29–31.  [20] *Congressional Globe*, 39th Congress, 2nd Session, p. 1699.
[21] *Congressional Globe*, 39th Congress, 1st Session, p. 1575.

John Bidwell, ca. 1866.
Reprinted with permission by Special Collections, Meriam Library, California State University, Chico and Bidwell Mansion.

"IF I WAS EVER CONSERVATIVE—I AM RADICAL NOW"

Your kind favor of May 30, was duly received. The haste and confusion incident to the closing scenes of a Session of Congress, are the only plea I have to make for not rendering an earlier acknowledgment.... Now as to the Gubernatorial race. First I do not desire, above all things, to do aught to distract the Union party. That political organization which carried the emblem of our country's unity, its glory and its freedom through the dark and bloody war of the rebellion, must be preserved. Every principle involved in the war, and of our future prosperity, and even the perpetuity of free government—the capacity of man to be free—the past—the present—the future, alike demand that this government should not be surrendered into the hands of the late rebels, rebel sympathizers, or inert northern Copperhead democracy. No act of mine shall knowingly impair the Union organization.

The rest is in your hands. If I can be an available candidate, I am willing to make the race, and my friends must be the judges, and you among the first. If any other man can make the race and harmonize the party better, then I am not in the way. I really consider the preservation of the Union party, at this time and for some time to come, of more real consequence to the future of our country than I am able to express through the media of words and language.

Fortunate indeed may we be if we can carry out the true policy, dictated by wisdom and tempered with firmness and justice—not too severe, but severe enough—not too lenient, but lenient enough—not hang too many rebels, but still hang enough—in a word, to that which shall redound to freedom and the perpetuity of free government, without having to drench the land again in blood and conquer a second rebellion. If I was ever conservative, I am radical now. No lukewarm policy can preserve the Union party. Its principles must be as fervent as loyalty itself. The present so called democracy are trying to please unrepentant rebels, the rebels accept because at present they cannot do any better—and both are going to style themselves the "National Union Party", thus stealing the living of the court of Heaven to serve the devil in. But this is all that I have space or time to say. I commit my case to you and my other friends—I know you will do right. I am, with the warmest emotions of my heart, very truly Your friend.[22]

### FRUSTRATIONS OF A FRESHMAN CONGRESSMAN

I saw many things in congress that I wanted to do, but was unable. I did learn a good deal while I was there but did not learn as much as I wanted to. I found out that there was deep rascality in the postal department, especially in regard to the mail contracts in California. I went to the second-assistant postmaster in regard to the matter, but could get no satisfaction. Yet this was going on and the government was being robbed all the time.

I tried to get a sutlership for one of my friends. I could not do it. Those things were surely bought and sold. You could no more touch one of them. I did want to investigate those things, but found it was impossible. In two years you do not learn anything until your term is nearly over. You do not learn to be useful until you have had experience.[23]

### BIDWELL DISILLUSIONED WITH CONGRESS

I thought that if I could be sure of an election year after year like Thad Stevens, and such men who have risen to prominence, I should like it. But I lost all taste for politics after being in congress the first year. In the first place, I was head of the committee on agriculture. I had a set of men on my committee that were so far below mediocrity that I was unable to do anything. We were appointed to make investigations into the agricultural department which had become full of corruption, and the head of the board at that time was a politician and had some of the members of my committee fully under his influence and I was unable to make a report. I became sick of what I saw there and intended never to go back.[24]

### DECIDES TO RUN FOR GOVERNOR

... This letter is not written for publication—I merely allude to the facts for

---

[22]JB, in Washington, D.C., to George A. Gillespie, 31 July 1866, George A. Gillespie Papers, HUNT.

[23]JB-91, pp. 31–32.   [24]JB-91, p. 8.

the purpose of saying that I cannot, with any degree of self composure, attempt to collate anything in favor of myself. I have thus far written a number of letters, none however for publication, but all of a tenor similar to the one I wrote you. So that the whole question is in the hands of my friends to do as they may deem best. I cannot now, if I would, retract—and having said that I would accept the nomination, I do not desire to be beaten.

My friends I know, will not advise me to do anything that would be unfair or dishonorable. I shall expect them to keep me advised, and when they are agreed upon a course of action I expect to abide their counsel. I can see that with all the conflicting aspirations, there may be dangerous combinations against us. But we can meet successfully any unfair schemes by being vigilant, bold in the sight, and reliant upon the people who have the real interests of the State at heart.

I would regard the position as one of honor. But to do justice to the State it would also be a task. Hence I could not afford to compromise or abridge my usefulness by pledges made in advance. I cannot declare in favor of any man for my public position—if I do, then I array all the combinations against me. I do really hope the Union Party will remain undivided. This is of more importance than the success of any one candidate. But I shall be with the party and add my efforts to preserve and enhance its integrity.

But I have written more at length than I intended. I shall bear in mind your suggestions, and comply with them as far as in my power. One thing I ought to say—the State Convention ought not to be held before the middle of June—first of July would be better. Having been away from home for so long, I must of necessity devote two or three months to my personal affairs. Two months will be long enough for a campaign. When we begin we must be active to the very day of election. It will take two or three weeks to close up my business here after the adjournment. But I will make the time as short as I can.[25]

## Views on Reconstruction

... The character and purposes of the present national administration, the bitter feelings of regret on the part of many Democrats, because they did not succeed in destroying our government, and their undisguised hostility to those who opposed and defeated them; the obstacles they are now interposing to embarrass reconstruction; the hopes they entertain of yet succeeding in repudiating the national debt and thereby accomplishing by legislation what they failed to do by war—the utter ruin of the nation; and other questions and facts of general interest, are as well known in San Francisco as in New York. I concede that men may sometimes honestly differ in opinion. But in questions of principle and patriotism where the facts are known to all alike, some things are so palpa-

---

[25]JB, in Washington, D.C., to George A. Gillespie, 19 January 1867, George A. Gillespie Papers, HUNT.

bly wrong as to carry them beyond the sphere of opinion. Slavery is wrong and every man knows it. It is treason to take up arms against our country. National repudiation would be national ruin. Those who so lately attempted to destroy the government, cannot be safely entrusted, at present, with its control. These and many others are too glaring to be made matters of opinion. The southern rebel is as much in favor of slavery today as he ever was. He would reestablish it if he could. His hostility to those who abolished it is unmistakable, but it is not the armed hostility of rebellion. He will not soon resort to that again for he has been whipped nearly enough to dissipate every shadow of feasibility.

> "What though the field be lost
> All is not lost; the unconquerable will,
> And study of revenge, immortal hate,
> And courage never to submit or yield"

This is his condition, but he is not going to make open war soon, in my opinion. I cannot, therefore, share with you the anxiety you entertain that the "great battle is yet to be made before the country is safe." The disaffection in the late rebel States is natural. Under all the circumstances I do not know that anything else could be expected. It is not the storm, but the rolling billows which last long after the storm has passed. I know that wisdom, prudence, firmness are required on the part of the government. But a new rebellion I do not apprehend. It would instantly kindle all the patriotism of the country. Millions of loyal soldiers would fly to arms—the struggle would be short, but overwhelming and general confiscation would be inevitable to pay all the expenses of the war. All loyal people (including all the patriotic portion of the Democratic party) would rally under one standard. The result would be the complete and practical vindication of the principle, which ought, and I believe will be conceded without further war, that the conquerors have the right to prescribe the terms of peace....

But I am not, and never have been, in favor of pursuing a vindictive policy towards the late rebel States. I have no sympathy with those who would do anything for revenge. I am in favor of restoring to them all the rights enjoyed by the loyal States, as soon as it will be safe to do so. But in view of the attitude of the administration, it will not do to be in a hurry now. It is not possible, in my judgment, to bring all of the seceded States into the Union in time to participate in the presidential election of 1868. But it depends entirely upon the States themselves. The rebellious element must go down or be overwhelmed, it must not rule in any State. The work of reconstruction must be thorough. Some of the more honest and fearless of the Democratic party of this State do not disguise their sentiments. Secession, repudiation, and slavery, will, I trust, be forever silenced on this coast at the pending judicial election.[26]

---

[26]JB to James Warren, 27 September 1867, James L. L. Warren Papers, BANC, b. 1.

## Waving the "Bloody Shirt" at California's Copperheads

... My sympathies are with the loyal people who stood by their country in its darkest hour. To their hands, and their hands alone, can the affairs of Government be safely intrusted. They, I maintain, who preserved the ship of state during the storm of rebellion, are the faithful pilots to whose keeping alone we can now confide her destiny. Let us hope to see harmony restored, that we may be able to say to the Copperhead party of this State, by an overwhelming majority on the 4th of September, "Gentlemen, please continue to occupy back seats. You richly deserve them, and your rights to them we propose to maintain for an indefinite period."[27]

... To me it is no matter of surprise to learn you are in the field as an active supporter of the Union cause. Your ardent nature will always carry you where the battle rages the fiercest. The issues upon national questions are clear and well defined, and scarcely less important than they were during the late slaveholder's war....

The Copperhead candidates sing the same old song that cheered on the pro-slavery rebellion.... The fact is, the Copperhead party is almost as out of date in their political thesis and teachings as Noah's Ark. They are entirely behind this progressive age of freedom, and must and will be defeated in this State. I plant myself unequivocally with the loyal masses. They must present a united front to defeat this misnamed Democratic Party; and I say to friends everywhere, this is our only hope.[28]

### 1867 Gubernatorial Campaign:
#### Distracted by Courtship and Conversion

I read and re-read your letters on account of their Christian advice. They never fail to melt me to tears, but my heart at times, and too often, becomes more cold and worldly, if possible, than ever.... The coming political campaign in my state intensively occupies my thoughts.

I regret almost that I consented to become a candidate for further political honors. Nearly all the papers are beginning to talk about me; most of them are very friendly, too much so. One [is] very unfriendly, stating things absolutely false, infamous. Herewith I enclose examples. Now I hope to be so fortified in Christian principle that I shall return good for evil. I will not I hope ever descend to abuse my enemies and if I shall be elected to preside over the affairs of State for a term, I do hope I shall have wisdom from above to guide me in the discharge of my high duty. But I do not intend to set my heart on the result of the election. Popular favor is very uncertain. I may be defeated,

---

[27]JB to C. M. Patterson, Secretary Yuba County Central Committee, 11 July 1867, in Sacramento *Union*, 11 July 1867.
[28]JB to Major William Gouverneur Morris, 25 July 1867, in Sacramento *Union*, 25 July 1867.

but if I am, I do not intend it shall cause me the slightest pain. I will not bend to intrigue and abuse.[29]

... Sunday evening I intended to go somewhere, but did not know what church to go to. While looking over the paper to see what Presbyterian church, if any, could be reached in time, an acquaintance came in, and talked about Railroads and everything worldly, politics even, and kept me from attending church. Oh! how I wished that I had courage enough to say to him that I was determined to become a Christian, that I could not see him then, but would be glad to see him any other day! But alas, I could not do it. I had called to see him the day before. This was his return call, because I did not find him at home. He is a very influential man, represents large moneyed and other interests. His company wields great political power! So I permitted him to talk all the Sunday evening away. I felt very badly about it....[30]

... I am now sorry that I ever consented to be a candidate for office again. I fear it will interfere with the all important business of preparing for eternity. That is certainly the most important thing that can engage the mind of mortals in the world....

To be a politician and succeed in such contests requires management, and often crooked schemes and combinations, for which I have no more talent or disposition. I am in by no means the right mood. As I said before, I regret that I agreed to go into the contest. If an honorable course will relieve me, then I shall so relieve myself. I do not look upon life as I used to. If I had a certain person to care for, (you know whom I mean), I should, doubtless, be ambitious. I would brave anything, suffer everything perhaps to attain distinction. But as I am, I have nothing to live for. I feel a loneliness which I never felt before I saw you. I hope you will not fail to remember me in your devotions. I regard you as the only *real* friend I have in the world.[31]

For two weeks I am going to be much engaged in political matters. Yesterday our primary elections were held. I have not heard a word as to the result, as to whether the expression will be favorable to me.... If I am defeated, it will be by trickery to which I persistently refuse to descend. Others may do it for the sake of office—I will not. Friends have appealed to me, saying "money must be used"—"if we expect to win we must have money in San Francisco, otherwise we will lose the city"—"we must take the world as we find it, money always has been, and always will be used in elections" etc....

Oh, if I could only be near you, to see your example, to receive your Christian

---

[29]JB to AB, 7 March 1867, quoted in Linda Rawlings, ed. *Dear General: The Private Letters of Annie E. Kennedy and John Bidwell, 1866–1868* (Sacramento: California Department of Parks and Recreation, 1993), pp. 22–23.
[30]JB, in New York City, to AB, 28 March 1867, in Ibid., p. 38.
[31]JB, aboard steamship *Constitution*, to AB, 17 April 1867, in Ibid., p. 50.

advice! What am I to do for two weeks now among politicians and conventions! Can I ever escape the temptations? In all such gatherings there will be drinking, swearing, and heretofore, it has been the custom and will of course be expected of me, to keep open rooms well supplied with liquors of all kinds, cigars, etc!! I am sorry from the bottom of my heart that I ever agreed to run again for office. It seems like swapping off heaven for a few fleeting earthly troubles![32]

### Defeated at Union Party Convention by Gorham and Railroad, betrayed by Conness

This note must necessarily be a short one, for in order to go by the next steamer it must go down on the stage today. So when I see the stage coming I must close, abruptly as it may seem.

The great political struggle is over, and I was defeated for governor—defeated while 19 out of the 20 of the Union people of the state were in my favor—defeated by money, fraud, and the vilest trickery ever known to political contests on this coast—defeated because I would not stoop to corruption. But you know what my determination was. I have kept my purpose, and I feel grateful that I had the firmness to do so. At one stage of the game, when two votes would have saved me, I could have received ten votes if I had promised a single appointment! But I refused all bargains. Even Senator [John] Conness found it necessary to join my enemies in order to save his own waning cause; and to aid him (who has become indispensable to the monopolists of this coast) more than ten millions of dollars were invested in the issue. In San Francisco 63 delegates were elected principally by copperhead votes. And 21 in Sacramento, making 84. These were by management and unfair ruling, admitted against me. Then several delegates absolutely instructed for me were bought off. But after all, I was only beaten by two or three votes. The convention was really mine by a large majority. There is scarcely a paper in the state which does not admit it. After the nomination for governor was made, I was solicited to accept a nomination for Congress, which I could have obtained without a struggle, but I declined....

I am now really glad that I am out of politics—honorably out of the excitement and temptations. Some tell me that I must go to the U.S. Senate. But I will not indulge such a thought. Money of unscrupulous men would in all probability be used to defeat me—Oh how I wish you could be near to give me advice....[33]

### Vents anger at Gorham and Conness

Not a single paper advocated the claim of my opponent—but he was a cunning trickster, a successful wire-puller—a man of some cunning, but no breadth—just the one to be used by schemers and speculators, men who live by plundering the State and want anything but an honest man for governor. I made up my mind

---

[32] JB to AB, 2 June 1867, JB-CSL, b. 45, f. 18.
[33] JB to AB, 18 June 1867, quoted in *Dear General*, pp. 80–81.

that I would not be guilty of intrigue to obtain any position. It seemed up to the very last moment, that nothing could prevent my nomination. I believe money was used freely to purchase votes—every promise was made, every corruption was practiced—by the most open fraud and unfair ruling, of a certain man (who obtained a nomination for office for his odious act). 84 delegates elected by Copperheads were admitted—these of course all voted against me—many others sold themselves outright—and after all they only beat me by 2 or 3 votes!

The nominations made are received so coldly throughout the state that I fear the Union party may be defeated. If the candidates were men of honor or sensibility they would receive the manner in which their names have been received as a most withering rebuke. I will enclose herewith a few random slips cut from the best newspapers published in the State—showing the public feeling.

I did everything except to practice corruption, which I deemed that it would be right for me under the circumstances to do. Some friends blamed me because I would not do as my opponent did—use money, buy votes, promise offices etc. etc. they said that no man could succeed without it—that we must take the world as we find [it], not as we would like to have it. Since all is over, I feel grateful that I had the firmness to hold out against such fearful struggle as I had, and I sincerely trust that no earthly honor will ever cause me to swerve from the path of rectitude. Some now say that there are parties that would spend millions of dollars in gold to keep me *out* and Senator [John] Conness *in*. He was against me in the recent struggle and is indispensable to certain monopolies on this coast. He is, as I think, a morbidly sensitive and selfish man.

I have tried to forget and forgive—fear I have not succeeded entirely, but I intend to do so.... The exciting, corrupting political convention. Oh how I wish I had never gone into it! I have tried to forget and forgive all those who inspired me—but they keep doing it, and in such an aggravating way. After having beaten me by intrigue and corruption, they now demand that I shall come out and stump the State for the ticket, the head of which I loathe. I read the letter last night saying that if I did not come out in favor of a certain candidate (the governor) that he would publish such and such things, all of which was false. My first impression was to treat such a letter with silent contempt. Then, conscious of having done nothing to deserve such ingratitude, I resolved to write him simply—"I deny, defy, spurn and scorn you."

Were I to do this would call for a rejoinder—perhaps a hostile one—a challenge. It would not be right to provoke combat for I do not believe in fighting duels. The time once was when I might do such things, but I must now try to live a better life. I am trying all I can. I am afraid I have committed some great sin. I believe I ought to have been baptized, that I ought to join some church, but I would not dare to do it now. I pray constantly and try to do it fervently. The great trouble is with me is I can not feel humble enough—meek and lowly of heart. If these political matters were banished from my mind, I could become reconciled. I can forgive all that is passed, but they keep adding fresh insults day by day. Publishing and republishing the most monstrous falsehoods! It seems that in order to build up a chance of a prospect for my opponent and justify the corruption used to nominate him, he deemed it customary for a candidate when beaten, to come out and declare in favor of his opponent who has been successful. In this case, however, there was so much corruption that it could not consistently be brought within the pale of any just rules. I could not declare in favor of any such man as my opponent, after obtaining the nomination the way he did, without being guilty of hypocrisy.

My business in my absence as I examined further and further into it, I found had been badly, very badly managed. This with the political strife, so often alluded to—all conspire to annoy me. But I am determined to press on and not give up. . . .[34]

### BIDWELL DECLINES NOMINATION OF ANTI-GORHAM REPUBLICANS

Having been a candidate before one convention, I desire to say to those friends who adhered to me during the struggle for the nomination, and who labored earnestly for and were favorable to my nomination, and to all others, that I feel profoundly grateful to them, but that I cannot consent to enter the field again and attempt to make the race for governor. To do so would be tantamount to giving aid to the so-called democratic party, the success of which, at this juncture of affairs, would be a calamity both to the state and nation, and ought not to be thought of by any loyal man. As far as I am concerned, I am trying to lay aside all personal feelings and considerations; in fact, I have done so, so far as human nature is capable under similar circumstances. . . . A new ticket cannot be substituted, at this late hour, with any certainty of success. We must then stand by this or let the copperheads take the state. I say, therefore, to my friends everywhere, let us rally and prevent such a calamity, by taking the only course that seems within our power.[35]

### FINDS VINDICATION AND CONSOLATION IN GORHAM'S DEFEAT

. . . You are right, I am entirely reconciled, am really glad that I am out, honorably out, of politics. Had any good loyal man received the nomination, he could have been elected governor by 5,000 to 10,000 majority. It does not become me to say what I could have done. Democrats have said that had I been nominated, their party would not have deemed it advisable to make any nomination—not that the Democrats like me, for they do not—but because they knew or believed they could not beat me. The fact is the *people* were with me—it was too plain. All the Union papers of the State with the exception of a few perhaps half a dozen or a dozen—raised my name before the convention—it was conceded all over the State that I was to be the nominee—and when they bought the convention away—deceived the people—the announcement fell like a pall—the result

---

[34]JB to AB, 5 July 1867, JB-CSL, b. 45, f. 21.
[35]JB to G. N. Swezy, 24 July 1867. Quoted in Winfield Davis, *Political Conventions in California*, pp. 262–63.

was a complete and overwhelming rebuke to Senator Conness and his clique. But I must close—the stage is waiting....[36]

### ACCUSES AARON SARGENT OF COLLUSION WITH GORHAM FORCES AT 1867 CONVENTION

... we were as a party demoralized and defeated by a ring of intriguers in the interests of monopoly and corruption ... intriguers whose ambition is sleepless and boundless, who hesitate at no means to gain their ends, who have little or no sympathy or interest in common with the people of this State—as dangerous to the public good, and to such extent that no one can be even friendly with them without suspicion of taint.... there was a time when Mr. Sargent could have done me a real service, had he not been absent [from the convention vote]—and, where I have believed him ever since to have been, in the friendship and confidence of the ring who defeated me in 1867.[37]

### A LATER ACCOUNT OF HIS DEFEAT

I have been voted for at several State Conventions. Votes were cast for me the same year Stanford was nominated at the Convention of the Union party, and also at the Republicans Convention when Gorham was nominated. I did not solicit the compliment on either occasion, except that in the latter case I wrote a few letters to political friends, and was in Sacramento at the time the Convention came off. I lost the nomination through Gorham and the railroad company. Whole delegations from all parts of the State pledged to me, but my opponents managed to take them away in some manner, I don't know how. For instance, delegates would rush in to me almost breathless (I do not care to specify more particularly), and say, "You are going to lose this nomination unless you have the vote of our delegation." "Well, what's to be done. I would ask." "We can save you on certain conditions." "Name the conditions." "We want ten appointments and $5,000 in cash, and the arrangements for the payment of the money must be made at once." To this I simply replied: "Gentlemen, tell your delegation that I do not want their support, and will not have it on any such terms as you name." So I lost the nomination. From the approaches made to me, I thought I had a right to infer that there was a good deal of money in active circulation, some of which was used to accomplish my defeat.[38]

### BIDWELL QUITS THE MASONIC ORDER

I did at one time belong to the Masons, but have never joined any other fraternal society, and if I knew as much about that organization as I do now, I never would have joined it. In a new country Masonry and other fraternal societies have a mission. I think if a man is good, and is willing to help his fellow men to the

---

[36]JB to Joseph Kennedy, 17 October 1867, BFP, b. 1.
[37]Chico *Northern Enterprise*, 21 October 1871.   [38]San Francisco *Chronicle*, 14 July 1875.

extent of his ability, [he] ought not to belong to those societies, for the reason that it takes too much time to attend the meetings. Then again, I have noticed that many men belong to these societies simply for gain. For instance, if a man is a merchant, he would join the Masons, so as to get as much of the Masonic patronage as possible. Then again, I have seen men, who would be temperate under certain conditions, go out to the saloon, drink, gamble.

One reason why I decided to leave the Masons was that my wife and her people are much opposed to masonry, and then when we came to this state, she did not want me to go out in the evening. She wanted me at home and my inclinations were to be at home. While I always paid my lodge dues as regularly as convenient, it sometimes happened that I fell behind. There is another thing I did not like about the Masons and that was the peremptory notice one received if he fell behind in his dues. The wording of the whole thing was very tyrannical. Well, I happened to fall behind, and was suspended. I thought they might be a little patient with me. I had given two or three thousand dollars toward the lodge when it was established in Chico. So I never went near them again.[39]

### WARNS OF MONOPOLY BEFORE COMPLETION OF FIRST TRANSCONTINENTAL RAILROAD

Our great hope is centered on the completion of the Pacific Railroad. But if possible to avoid it, we ought not to be obliged to wait for that event, or be entirely dependent upon it when it shall be completed. The difficulty lies in this, that all the principal channels of travel are in the hands of monopolies, and are likely to continue to be so. It requires quite a fortune for a laboring man to make the journey from Europe to California. It takes as much to pay for the passage of a single man from New York to San Francisco as it does to purchase a farm of one hundred and sixty acres from the Government of the United States after he gets here. If there is any legitimate remedy for the obstacles in the way of immigration it should be sought for and applied. Agriculture and all our industrial interests are involved in this vital question.[40]

Even after the Pacific Railroad shall have been completed—aye, and after the Northern Pacific and Southern Pacific Railroads shall span, as they surely will, the Continent, and be coterminous with the northern and southern borders of this great country, from the Mississippi Valley to the Pacific Ocean—the danger will still remain. The railroad and steamship companies can and will combine to gauge their tariffs of charges by their own—I was going to say consciences, but corporations have no consciences—I will say by their own will, limited only by their love of money and their ability to extort it from the people at the expense of the prosperity and all the material interests of the whole country. The carrying business between the Atlantic States and the Pacific Coast is destined to be immense beyond

---

[39]JB-91, pp. 48–49.   [40]CSAS 1867, pp. 429–30.

computation. Shall it be suffered to go permanently into the grasp of unrestricted monopolies?[41]

### MONOPOLIES ARE DANGEROUS AND CORPORATIONS SOULLESS

We know that monopolies are always onerous and dangerous to the best interests of a people. They may be less dangerous, perhaps, in a free country like ours, where exorbitant charges will, in most cases, diminish patronage, beget opposition, curtail resources, and thus wound, in the most vital part, soulless corporations. Excessive prosperity may produce extravagance, extravagance beget indebtedness, and indebtedness dissolution.[42]

### FAVORS FEDERAL REGULATION OF TRANSPORTATION SYSTEMS

The prosperity of agriculture, of mining, of manufactures—in a word, of all interests, hinges upon the proper regulation of commerce among the several States....

This question does not concern California alone; the States upon the Atlantic slope will soon demand it. The monopolies so combine to fix the prices of freight—and the travel is inseparably connected with the commerce—that the farmer of Illinois is often obliged to sell his corn at a mere nominal price for fuel, when it would bring seventy-five cents to one dollar per bushel in New York....

Agriculture and all the industrial interests of California, and of all the States, are deeply concerned in seeing commerce among the several States freed from all odious and unjust obstructions, and prosperity regulated by the only power having competent authority to do it, namely, the Congress of the United States.[43]

Just and liberal encouragement ought to be given to laudable enterprises and investments of capital. It is necessary, every one will admit, that there should be accumulations of capital. I am in favor of them; we are all in favor of them. Without them no great undertakings could be begun and executed. But we cannot favor the building up, at the expense of the people and prosperity of the whole country, monstrous moneyed oligarchies, powerful enough to control Conventions, Legislatures and even Congress, and contaminating our whole political system. Human laws limit the interest on money—why not fix limits to the earnings of capital invested upon the highways of commerce under the express authority given to regulate commerce among the several States? In a word, the channels of commerce among several States ought to be redeemed from the grasp of the grandest monopolies, perhaps, the world has ever seen, and be regulated with an eye single to the public welfare, before they become so potential as to virtually own the Government itself.[44]

### ON THE IMPEACHMENT OF PRESIDENT JOHNSON

... The impeachment of the President will begin soon—but there is really no

---

[41]Ibid., p. 431
[42]CSAS 1867, pp. 429–30.
[43]Ibid., pp. 430–31.
[44]Ibid., p. 432.

excitement about it. If Andrew Johnson had as much ability and patriotism as he has of stubbornness, he would be the greatest man living. As it is, he is blindly rushing along the giddy verge of ruin, and will sacrifice anybody or anything, in order to crush the party who elected him to office. He cannot succeed. But I cannot add more in the way of politics except to say; that men of all classes are glad the President cannot carry Gen. Grant from the path of duty; and consequently there is no danger of war should the President in his stubborn blindness to carry his points, attempt to use the military power.

Grant now in this important crisis stands between the President and the people. The ambition of men has ever been the bane of popular liberty—ambition triumphant results in monarchy—oppression. Is not human nature the same in all ages? How fortunate it is that under our form of government there are so many checks to the Executive power. How favored are we as a people that the President cannot offer Grant any higher position. Grant is as high as he can be <u>under</u> any President—the only higher step he can take is to be President himself.

If Andy Johnson could make Grant obey him and not the law, he would carry his points at all hazards—who knows what he might do? But I must close—I never know when to stop, when I get on politics—for I cannot help taking an interest in public affairs—though I never intend to enter the arena of politics as a politician in the common acceptation of the term....[45]

### Playing Patronage Politics, 1868

Yours of the 26th is before me. First, I beg leave to thank you most sincerely for your unvarying friendship, and to say that it is a wish very near my heart to be able someday to show that I am not ungrateful nor forgetful. What the future may have in store, we know not.

Now to the subject of your letter. I am opposed to the selection of John Conness as member of Grant's Cabinet, because he is not a fair representative of the masses who have won our recent but hard-contested victory. To be sure, he wisely staid away—for with his presence the State would have been lost. Nor can he claim any credit on account of Gorham, who did not have sense enough to stay away—and thereby lost us several thousand votes. Still it was necessary for some such move to be made in order that Gorham might claim to have carried the State in the interest of Conness. Otherwise there would be no hope for those chosen instruments of speculators and the ring—for both seem to be sailing in the same boat at present.

But to the point—Whom will the leading Republicans of the State and coast recommend for a position in the new Cabinet? Conness is playing every card he can, but the Union masses ought to be heard—they have been true in every trial—they fought and won the victory for Grant & Colfax.

---

[45]JB to John Kennedy, Rancho Chico foreman, 12 March 1868, BFP, b. 1.

I cannot be a candidate, but will consult with you and others and join in a recommendation of the best man on whom we can agree. I am not playing Seymour when I decline—I have the best of reasons. On account of nearly three years absence my business became embarrassed. I must give it close attention for a year or two—or lose more than ten times the salary of a cabinet officer. As matters stand, I do not believe it would be possible for me to succeed, for I am so circumstanced that I cannot go to Washington during the winter or spring, or give the matter any attention. How would Judge O. C. Pratt of San Francisco do for Secretary of the Interior? How would Gov. [George L.] Woods of Oregon do? and if so, would it do to recommend him considering that Oregon has not gone for Grant & Colfax? How will Fred[erick] Billings answer? He is now in New York, but he is only temporarily there, as I understand. We want a positive man and a live man—one who has not been doubtful in the past, and can under all circumstances be relied on in the future.

You were right, Gillespie, about [state senator Chancellor] Hartson. [State senator Lansing B.] Mizner would have made a better run [for Congress]. The fact is (confidentially) Hartson is the poorest stumper I ever saw, besides the minds of the people could not be disabused of the idea that he was unobjectionable to the "ring"—the speculators—and Gorham and Conness, and of course that was enough to defeat him—especially when added to the settler influence.[46]

### "A NEW ORDER OF THINGS"—
### THE ENORMOUS IMPACT OF THE TRANSCONTINENTAL RAILROAD

... Since the completion of the overland railway, a new order of things exist—we hardly know ourselves what to do to adapt ourselves to the new circumstances by which we are surrounded. Salaries & wages may continue high, or they may go way down very low....[47]

The year eighteen hundred and sixty-nine has been made memorable by the completion of the great transcontinental railway, and we are suddenly brought into more intimate relations with the Atlantic States and Europe. The mystery and romance of our isolation have been snatched away and we now stand face to face with the world.[48]

### SOME WASHINGTON GOSSIP

... In the overland cars today, among the passengers were R. J. Stevens & family. He was always an ardent friend of mine, or pretended to be. But during this last winter he has been very thick with Gorham and other very contemptible men who are my enemies and live by political corruption. As to his wife she is the daughter of Senator Baker—but that is all of which she can boast. There

---

[46]JB to George Gillespie, 2 December 1868, George A. Gillespie Papers, HUNT.
[47]JB to AB, 9 August 1869, JB-CSL, b. 48, f. 19.    [48]CSAS 1869, p. 320.

was so much scandal in regard to her intimacy with a certain prominent man in the House, that I wonder how she could have the face to go into the presence of decent people. All of this is of course strictly confidential.[49]

### RIGHT-OF-WAY POLITICS: LOCATING THE CALIFORNIA AND OREGON RAILROAD LINE

... In regard to the Railroad, on its location it is reported on the streets that it is located—but where no one knows. I fear it will be to the west of us—for these monopolists do just about as they please. All the laws in this State, having been passed at their dictation and for their benefit enable them to run their roads anywhere—through houses even, and other valuable improvements—without paying a dime, provided they can prove that the property is worth more <u>with</u>, than <u>without</u> the railroad. Though they may destroy half the property a man possesses, yet if they can prove that the remaining half [will be] worth as much or more in consequence of the building of the road, he can collect nothing. Nor can they be made to pay for the right of way—except one (1) dollar, the consideration named in the deed! Lawyers and men who have built other roads all tell me so—But, dear Annie, I will do all in my power, except to fight against impossibilities....[50]

Today I had a long talk with Mr. [Charles] Cadwalader [construction engineer for the Central Pacific Railroad] about the location of the Railroad. He has several lines run—but which the company will adopt he does not know.[51]

The ride down was rather cold—the air in fact felt like snow. My seat was on the outside above the driver, so that I was not troubled by dust—which was not bad, of course, but still there was some—and the north wind carried it towards us. On the way down met Mr. Cadwalader going up in his buggy. He says the railroad bridge near Marysville is completed—and that about 10 miles of the grade are completed—also that men are at work on the grade near Dry Creek, which is about half way between Marysville and Chico—or if any difference nearer to Chico.

There is no mistake about the thing we have long and so much desired—the event is soon to be realized—and we are to be connected, by railroad, with the "world & rest of mankind." But I feel that all is not beyond a peradventure respecting the line in the vicinity of Chico—and that much will depend on the disposition of Mr. Cadwalader. We ought to make him and Mrs. C. our fast friends. No opportunity should be allowed to pass. Of course it would not do for you to say anything to Mrs. Cadwalader about the railroad. But do not therefore, I beg of you, omit an occasion to forward our purposes so far as is possible, and con-

---

[49]JB to AB, 29 June 1869, JB-CSL, b. 47, f. 33.
[50]JB to AB, 11 August 1869, Ibid., b. 48, f. 21.
[51]JB to AB, 12 August 1869, JB-CSUC, b. 17, f. 20.

sistent with your sense of right and propriety. You might have them (he & wife) take dinner with us sometime....⁵²

### STRANGE BEDFELLOWS: DOING BUSINESS WITH THE NEW RAILROAD

Arrived here [San Francisco] at 8—now nearly 9 P.M.... Just as I arrived at the corner near this hotel I met two friends Mr. Mizner (you remember him do you not?) and P. B. Cornwall. Both told me that it was in the Union (or some other perhaps) that I was guest of C. Crocker last night! They must be hard up for items to get hold of such a thing—and so soon. But perhaps they are trying to insinuate that I am weakening in my opposition to corruption and monopoly—and that I have forgotten my defeat for Gov[ernor] brought about by R.R. Com[pany] of which Crocker is such a prominent member.

But they need have no fear—for I shall I hope ever be opposed to corruption, oppression and wrong. I have important business relations with these men. Their building the railroad to Chico and through my (our) land, brings me unavoidably in business contact with them. My interests have become, to the extent of freight I may have, blended with those of the Com[pany].—they want freight—that is what the road is for. I can be courteous and gentlemanly with men whom I politically despise.⁵³

### EXPIRATION OF BIDWELL'S RAILROAD PASS

...Mr. D. C. Haskin, one of the principal owners of the Cal. Pacific R.R., was in the cars all the way from Marysville to Vallejo. When I gave my ticket to the conductor he said, "I thought I gave you a pass"? You did Sir, but it expired a year ago, was my answer. But he did not offer me another. He wanted me to set a price on our whole ranch. I told him I could not, for we never intended to sell....⁵⁴

### THE U.S. SENATE ELECTION OF 1871: BIDWELL INFORMS SENATOR CORNELIUS COLE OF HIS EFFORTS ON COLE'S BEHALF AGAINST CHALLENGER AARON SARGENT AND THE BIG FOUR

Yesterday I called to see [W. N.] D'Haven [a Republican assemblyman from Butte County]. I feel sure he is right and will support you. He did not tell me so, but said enough to establish the most important point, to wit: that he is opposed to [George] Gorham, Sargent & Co. and all their schemes and combinations. He will be useful too in keeping [Republican state senator David] Boucher from falling into the hands of the "ring". I shall lose no opportunity in using all fair means to defeat corruption and trickery.⁵⁵

Yours of the 8th to hand. You are certainly right. Merit is not to be relied on

---

⁵²JB to AB, 25 November 1869, JB-CSL, b. 48, f. 35.
⁵³JB to AB, 29 June 1870, Ibid., b. 49, f. 5.
⁵⁴JB to AB, 30 December 1870, Ibid., b. 49, f. 10.
⁵⁵JB to Cornelius Cole, 4 October 1871, Cornelius Cole Family Papers, b. 3, UCLA.

wholly—but vigilance, sleepless and widespread—to defeat the corrupt combinations.

There is to be a Republican paper established here [in Chico]. The editor [Watson Chalmers], who knows well my sentiments (on all political matters at least) asked me to aid him. I at once offered to do so to a small extent—say $250. But today I took occasion to show him the article in the Oakland paper—in your favor—and suggested he might copy it in his first issue—when he showed his hand, by saying he did not believe there was any combination between Sargent & Gorham—and that he intended to recommend Sargent as a candidate for the U.S. Senate! I told him if he did so that I not only would not aid him—but forbid him from ever sending me a copy of his paper.

I have conversed with two prominent Republicans on this subject, and both agreed with me—as I think this region generally will. Having tried to keep aloof from politics, I find a disposition in some instances to ignore my wishes while they rely on my aid—but I can't stand that. Will keep you posted.[56]

Yours at hand—but no time till now to reply. Sure enough, [Watson] Chalmers [editor of the newly established Chico *Weekly Review*] came out for Sargent. Before his first number was issued I told him not to send it to me—but he did send—and I returned it.

Enclosed is his editorial on the subject. I do not usually notice such things, but in this instance I have; and my statement (written very hastily today and by no means a full reply) will appear in the N. Enterprise tomorrow.

In regard to [state assemblyman] J[oshua]. N. Turner [of Butte County] I have not seen him since the election—and cannot say that I have the least influence with him. The same of [state senator George C.] Perkins. But I will not fail to let them know, when I have the opportunity, how I feel on the questions of the hour. Everybody in this region knows how I have stood since 1867, and before, except for Mr. Chalmers.[57]

When I wrote a few days ago I did not expect to trouble you again so soon. I have just learned that Sargent & [former state senator] L. M. Foulke spent the day (Sunday)(yesterday) and left [Chico] this morning. Although I passed through the town more than I usually do I did not see them or expect their presence. I understand that Sargent went down to see Boucher, and that he was closeted part of the day with D'Haven. I believe D'Haven is unapproachable—and also Boucher. Still would it not be well for you to accidentally see some of these men. Sargent & Foulke have, I understand gone after Perkins & Turner—at least my informant told me they were going on cars to Oroville today.

---

[56] JB to Cornelius Cole, 10 October 1871, Ibid.
[57] JB to Cornelius Cole, 20 October 1871, Ibid.

I see Senator [Oliver] Morton [of Indiana] is in the State and your guest. Could not you come up here with Morton and stay a day if no more—we would be very happy to have you so.

P.S. Herewith a few scraps, which may amuse you, and explains why Sargent did not call on me!![58]

Yours of the 25th duly to hand—last night—I say "duly" because it must have been on the same train, and delayed by the accident, when Senator Morton was on board. But the envelope—a very thin one (I enclose it) was torn open sufficiently to have enabled any one to take the letter out and put it back. I do not know if any one read it, but it looks suspicious! The rent extended about from A to B—and had I thought of it in time would have sent it just as I found it. I suspect no one in the P.O. here.

Chalmers still gives me the benefit of all the venom of which he is capable— he is a very weak man—and I do not think I shall ever notice him again.[59]

### SENATE ELECTION OF 1871: BIDWELL DESCRIBES TO ANNIE HIS CONTINUED EFFORTS ON COLE'S BEHALF

... Sacramento, 9 P.M. arr'd here about 2 1/2 hours ago. Have just had a long talk with the principal editor of the *Sacramento Union*—he is beginning to fear the combination between Sargent & Gorham, and I hope to see the powerful influence of his paper thrown on the right side of this, as it is on most all important issues, Chalmers to the contrary notwithstanding....[60]

... I have been greatly annoyed all day by the telegram from Sen. Cole and others to come immediately to Sacramento to help defeat Sargent.

Of course I want him defeated—but I will not mix in the political strifes going on, farther than to give friends a friendly word now and then. I really fear that Sargent will be elected for he has all the corruption and intrigue and R. Road influence on his side. But a day of political reckoning is coming. Woe to the members of the Legislature who sell themselves, or permit influences, or bad judgment, to cast them on the side of railroad monopoly. That question is one of overshadowing importance, and should be dealt with promptly and wisely now—at this very time or it may, ere the people are aware, jar this nation from center to circumference. They must be one of two things—<u>free</u>, or vassals to its power....[61]

I have but a very few minutes to write—returned home last night. Sacramento yesterday was swarming with politicians—I had almost literally to run

---

[58] JB to Cornelius Cole, 23 October 1871, Ibid.
[59] JB to Cornelius Cole, 28 October 1871, Ibid.
[60] JB to AB, 20 November 1871, JB-CSL, b. 49, f. 35.
[61] JB to AB, 5 December 1871, Ibid., b. 50, f. 5.

the gauntlet on the sidewalks in order to do my business and get away. Sargent has all the corruption in State on his side, the very same element namely—R.R. monopoly, unworthy office seeking, moneyed power which defeated me in 1867 is working for him now. I greatly fear he will win. Weak members of the Legislature cannot stand such an assault as is being made—our man D'Haven is a very weak man I fear. He told me what no man of prudence would tell—that he had been offered $20,000 for his vote. If true he ought to have resented such an approach—and not doing so he ought to have been ashamed to mention it . . .[62]

. . . You know [George F.] Jones has always had unbounded influence over D'Haven and, though a Democrat, Jones still has—and what do you think—why Sargent has promised to send [his son] Albert Jones to West Point in case Sargent be elected to the U.S. Senate and D'Haven shall vote for Sargent!!! This is the way the story goes—we shall see—Republicans elected D'Haven. Sargent to be Republican U.S. Senator but distribute his favors to Democrats who can purchase or influence weak and purchasable Republican members of our Legislature!!!! . . .[63]

### Defending Chico Creek against railroad and lumber interests

. . . D'Haven has actually introduced a bill to enable flume companies to do certain things—just to meet the wishes of Allen and others who want to use Chico Creek for floating lumber down. If they succeed they will ruin the creek. That they can pass the law there is but little doubt, for the railroad company will probably be in favor of anything that will bring lumber or other freight for their road. My only hope will be to defeat them by a lawsuit and show the law to be unconstitutional.[64]

### Playing local politics in Chico

In the *Enterprise* I see the names of those who have signed a petition to have the Act of Incorporation repealed. It is believed that Jones is at the bottom of it, for he is very sore on account of his defeat as one of the Trustees at the Election. On that day Jones spent a good deal of money—and consorted with the vilest elements of the town, he was seen walking arm in arm with a noted rowdy who keeps a low disreputable house and sort of saloon & gambling trap, to the disgust of all decent people. Even his fellow Democrats who are respectable, are down on him for it. The struggle was a hard one, but the "whiskey ring" was beaten, and Jones is very vindictive about it. The rowdies are opposed to incorporation, because they fear police regulations. The names of some men who ought

---

[62]JB to AB, 8 December 1871, Ibid., b. 50, f. 7.
[63]JB to AB, 19 December 1871, Ibid., b. 50, f. 9.
[64]JB to AB, 2 February 1871, Ibid., b. 50, f. 39.

to know better are on the list asking for repeal—for instance, Mr. Mason, Sandy Young, Jo Wood, &c.[65]

### Presidential Election of 1872: Bidwell backs Ulysses S. Grant over Horace Greeley

I believe the people are more generally for Grant than they were in 1868—at least I hope so. It will be a little against Grant that the Central Pacific R.R. monopoly, Gorham, Sargent &c &c support him—but even that circumstance cannot make any true Republican swallow Greeley.[66]

### Farmers must organize against monopolies

In my opinion there is but one way for the farmers to succeed in the accomplishment of these objects, and that is through the organization of local clubs, and the steady support of the State Club in its efforts in their behalf. If the farmers in all portions of the State will come together and form local clubs and put themselves in correspondence and business relations with the State Farmers' Union, in such a manner as to authorize the officers of this association to act for and bind them under necessary moral and financial obligations, in my opinion the relief which they seek can be obtained, to a great degree at least, and industrial prosperity may become general throughout the State. But while the farmer remains aloof from his neighbors—while he continues to act on selfish individual policy—other classes, such as importers and manufacturers of sacks, common carriers, grain dealers, commission merchants and money loaners, will unite for the advancement of their interests and ends, and will take undue and unjust advantages of the farmer; will oppress, prey upon him and eat out his substance and keep him poor and dependent. Farmers now, unorganized are weak and in a great degree helpless, and they have but little courage to make an effort to free themselves or better their conditions; but let 100,000 farmers of this State unite together and act as one man, through an honest and reliable organization, demanding only common justice, but exacting this to the last degree and with a firm and united front, and there is no power in the land that can prevent the attainment of their demands. The farming interests of the country need some wholesome legislation to place them on an equal footing with other occupations and to relieve them from the exactions of heartless monopolies.... I repeat, and I wish I could sound it in the ears of every farmer in the State, the only salvation of the agricultural interests, the only safety to the individual interests of the farmer, is in union of interest and union of action.[67]

---

[65]JB to AB, 3 March 1872, Ibid., b. 51, f. 2.
[66]JB to Cornelius Cole, 13 August 1872, Cornelius Cole Family Papers, b. 3, UCLA.
[67]Charles C. Royce, *John Bidwell: Pioneer, Statesman, Philanthropist: A Biographical Sketch* (Chico: n. p., 1906), JB speech to Farmers' Union, San Francisco, April 8, 1873 in *Pacific Rural Press*.

### Farmers and Transportation Monopolies

I can say for myself, and I speak the sentiments of the farmers generally, as I believe, in the following declarations: . . .

That transportation is indispensable to agricultural prosperity, and that it is our duty, as farmers, to promote the construction of roads, canals, vessels and all modes of conveyance calculated to facilitate the movement of agricultural products.

That the charges on lines of transportation should be regulated by law, and not left to unlimited monopoly; and if such regulations be found impractical on existing lines, they should be made applicable to all future lines, until reciprocal relations shall be fully established between the producer and the common carrier.[68]

### Denounces Free Railroad Passes

We declare that farmers and all others should be equal before the law; that all laws should be enacted without bias, and executed without partiality; and to this end we declare that neither farmers or others ought to furnish legislative, executive, or judicial officers with free passes, or in any manner do anything calculated to improperly influence them in the discharge of their public trust; and that no officer, or candidate for office, ought to accept, nor shall any officer, with our consent, be hereafter elected who will accept of a free pass, or other gift.[69]

### Bidwell Accepts Free Railroad Pass and Regrets It

. . . I have done one thing which perhaps I ought not to have done. Mr. [A. N.] Towne [of the Central Pacific Railroad] insisted that I should come free this morning to this place. So I bought no ticket, but I really felt as if I had lost my independence. He has always shown me kindness and attention. But in (the) future I must not thus give away my self respect. If it were in my power to reciprocate, then I would not feel embarrassed—as it is. Had I known how it would affect me I would have resisted even Mr. Towne. We must return in some way this kindness and then not again incur obligations of this kind. . . . The free pass system I deprecate, denounce, as demoralizing. It is not extended to the needy. Public patronage pays for it, and it is intended to win favor from some and thereby strengthen the grasp and perpetuate the lease of oppression.[70]

### The People Should Rise Against Railroad Monopolies

. . . I believe at this time the people should rise, and before it is too late, regulate the great question of monopoly. There is no candid man in this State, be he capitalist or railroad man, who, if he could see the issues just as he ought to see them, would not be willing to allow the people of the State to regulate fares and

---

[68] Ibid., JB speech to the Farmers' Union Convention, Jan. 3, 1873 in *Pacific Rural Press*.
[69] Ibid.
[70] JB in Sacramento to AB, 20 June 1874, JB-CSL, b. 127, f. 10.

freights, and to regulate everything which may be monopolized, because his true interest would permit the people to have control of these questions, without which they cannot have of their own destinies.[71]

### HIGHLIGHTS OF THE DOLLY VARDEN PLATFORM COAUTHORED BY BIDWELL, 1875

*Why a third party is needed*
... the so-called national parties in California have fallen into the control, in a large measure, of the more worthless elements of society, managed in the interest of certain powerful corporations and associations of individuals, who systematically seek to accumulate wealth at the public expense, through and by means of the machinery of government, until affairs have reached a point where the people can no longer safely trust the political control of the state to either of them. ...[72]

*Overall goals*
... the people's independent party seeks ... the regulation and control of all corporations exercising franchises of a public nature, the reduction to reasonable rates of fares and freights on railroads, as well as steamboats operated in conjunction with railroads; and the prevention and punishment of unjust discriminations by railroad and other corporations against localities and against individuals; the securing from the power or possibility of monopoly the natural waters of the rivers, streams, and lakes of the state, and revesting them once more in the people; the rescue of the inhabitants of our cities and towns from the oppressive power of water and gas companies, and other kindred monopolies. ...[73]

*Transportation empire of the Big Four*
... Through improvident and inconsiderate legislation, the funds generously appropriated by the nation, and materially increased by our state, its cities and counties, to aid in constructing the Pacific railroad, have been so employed that a small number of individuals, acting in corporate capacity, now own and control the only transcontinental railroad in the country, together with almost the entire railroad system of the state, as well as the river steamers and ferry boats plying upon our interior waters, thereby practically monopolizing not only the entire overland traffic, but likewise the general carrying trade of the state and coast. ...[74]

*No possible relief from competition*
... it is apparent that there can be no final relief from the excessive charges and unjust discriminations of the railroad corporations through competition, because

---

[71]Sacramento *Union*, 19 July 1875.
[72]Winfield Davis, *Political Conventions in California*, p. 342.
[73]Ibid.
[74]Ibid., p. 343.

of their vast wealth and power, which are invariably used to break down all rival enterprises, and to ruin the projectors, and failing in that, then to combine with them against the people. . . . [75]

### The Big Four's corruption of politics

. . . the railroad corporations have . . . systematically intermeddled with and corrupted the politics of the state, using their wealth and influence to elevate scheming men, and in many instances their interested partisans, and to place them in the legislature and other stations of trust where they could vote away the people's rights, until the domination of the railroad and other corporations in our politics and government has become an intolerable evil; . . . [76]

### Unjust transportation rates

. . . the rates of freight and fare charged and collected upon the railroads of California, and upon the steamboats owned and operated in connection with them, in most places where there is no competition, are unjust, unequal, and excessively high.[77]

### Key railroad planks

. . . the people's independent party hereby pledges its nominees for office throughout the state, to reduce said rates of freight and fare, by law, to a just and fair standard, based upon the actual cost of the road and the expenses of operation; and also to the enactment of laws to prevent and punish all manner of unjust discriminations against individuals or localities, and generally to reduce the railroad corporations to the supervision and control of the laws of the land.[78]

. . . we seek by all lawful means to drive the railroad corporations out of politics, and to protect the people by wise and calmly considered laws from extortion and unjust discrimination at their hands, . . . [79]

. . . we favor the construction of all independent lines of competing railroads, to connect the Atlantic states with California, provided they be built and operated in the interest of the people, and not solely in that of the monopolists, as is the case with the railroads now existing in this state.[80]

### Water belongs to the people

. . . the waters of the lakes and rivers of the state should be and remain forever in the ownership and control of the public, and never allowed upon any pretence to become the subject of private monopoly.[81]

. . . the fresh water in the rivers and lakes of this state, as well as the rains

---

[75] Ibid., pp. 343–44.
[77] Ibid.
[79] Ibid.
[76] Ibid., p. 344
[78] Ibid.
[80] Ibid., p. 345.
[81] Ibid.

that descend from the clouds, belongs of right to the whole people, and that any ownership or monopoly of it by any corporation or person, beyond what they shall put to some beneficial use, is a wrong to the entire community.[82]

## State must promote irrigation

... the legislature should speedily enact proper laws to encourage and favor irrigation in the agricultural districts of the state wherever needed, and to prevent the monopoly by speculators of the natural waters necessary thereto, at the same time having due regard for the wants of the mining localities, and fostering and protecting the just rights of those engaged in mining pursuits.[83]

### PRAISES CITIZENS OF SAN BERNARDINO FOR STANDING UP TO THE BIG FOUR

I can say to you, judging from the unmistakable signs of the times, that the Independent movement of this State is deep in the hearts of the people of southern California, and that everywhere we were met with welcomes that gave us encouragement, and I come to you now with the cheering news that we have nothing to fear in southern California. Even as far south as San Bernardino we met the spirit of this movement, it is true almost unorganized, but it existed there. One act will demonstrate to you that they are not going to submit to dictation or oppression from any quarter. This is said to be a good Democratic locality, but when the railroad approaching that point demanded $100,000, or it would leave the town off the line, they neither submitted to the exaction, nor did they submit to their charges. The railroad company exhibited its oppression, as in other places, by laying out another town and trying to crush out this center of Southern California by building up a rival town [Colton] within three or four miles just because a subsidy was not granted. What did the people do? Would they stand the exorbitant charges? Oh, no. They started fifteen mule teams to the sea coast, a distance of ten miles, by the side of the railroad, because they saw they could haul freights by mule teams and horse teams, and for aught I know, ox teams, cheaper than they could do it by rail. That is a little of the spirit that animated our fathers to get up the Boston tea-party. They would not submit to oppression there, nor would the people of San Bernardino submit to it even for the privilege of riding upon a railroad....

Standing here as we do, we may say in the face of the whole world, having to compete with all other people, we must have these facilities, or we cannot go on prospering, developing this grand State, managing our own destinies, and reaching that degree of prosperity, which is ours if we can only control these necessary elements. How many people are there in California who are willing to kneel down to a gigantic monopoly which aims at nothing less than supreme control, the sur-

---

[82]Ibid., pp. 346–47.
[83]Ibid., p. 345.

rendering [of] all liberties of the people, all their future into the hands of those who wish to use them for their own purposes. We little thought, my friends, when first the people granted millions upon millions to aid in the construction of the overland railway, that the gentlemanly and amiable individuals composing that company would use that very means which we had given them to oppress us....[84]

### BIDWELL DENOUNCES HIS DEMOCRATIC OPPONENT, 1875

The nominee for Governor on the Democratic ticket, Hon. William Irwin, is objectionable on many points. One is, that during the last Legislature he was a member of a very important committee, that of Corporations, to which important bills were referred, bills proposing to limit and regulate fares and freights within proper and reasonable limits.... He was, more than any other member of that Legislature, responsible for the defeat of a bill to regulate freight and fares. I assert here without fear of contradiction that the whole history of the last Legislature proves it.[85]

### BIDWELL RECALLS THE DOLLY VARDEN CAMPAIGN OF 1875

When the great railway corporation became oppressive, and corrupt, interfering in politics in every way possible, determining to gain and hold power for its selfish ends, the people became aroused, and formed a new party, the Anti-Monopoly party, and gave me the nomination for governor. That was in 1875.

[State Senator] Henry Edgerton [of Sacramento], the most effective stump speaker and one of the best orators that the Pacific Coast has ever had, agreed to stump the state for us, and we believed we had the state with us, and had it not been for this great railway monopoly, its money and powerful influence, we would have been successful.... In '75 I did not go into the campaign. Did not meet any of the candidates except [William] Irwin. Irwin and [James A.] Johnson [the Democratic candidate for Lieutenant Governor] were elected. T[imothy] G[uy] Phelps was candidate on the Republican ticket. After '75 I was an independent republican. The Republican party, I think, have never regarded me as a republican. I regard myself as as good a republican as at any time as far as the principles of that party are concerned, but I contend that I have graduated and have gone beyond.[86]

### NEW STATE CONSTITUTION OF 1879

New Constitution said to be adopted and all good people greatly disappointed.[87]

### ON THE ELECTION OF 1879 AND THE WORKINGMEN'S PARTY

The election here went against [George] Crossette—he is not popular—is

---

[84]Sacramento *Union*, 19 August 1875.
[85]Ibid.      [86]JB-91, pp. 34–35.
[87]JBD, 8 May 1879.

too bitter a partisan—even abusive. See how he has defamed President Hayes—a man who was legally placed in the presidential chair by the Electoral commission—and acquiesced in by the vote of a Democratic House of Reps.—who commands the respect of even the Democrats everywhere else. And yet Crossette uses every mean opprobrious epithet he can command against him! It was simply impossible to concentrate the vote for him by any plea of local interest or otherwise.... As yet we can tell nothing about the Gubernatorial vote, but hope [Republican George C.] Perkins is elected.

P.S. Enclosed I send a sample of the Butte County W.P.C. ticket—a barbarous, brutal thing.[88]

### STILL HATES GORHAM THIRTEEN YEARS LATER

The papers say Gorham is coming to California to stump the State for Garfield. If he does, Garfield's majority will be reduced. Gorham will hurt any cause he advocates.[89]

### STILL HATES GORHAM TWENTY-FOUR YEARS LATER

At the session of the legislature previous to my [campaign for the] nomination they had lobbied through the legislature a bill granting to the C[entral] P[acific] R.R. an immense amount of bonds. I think $2,700,000 to help in the construction of the C.P.R.R. Geo. C. Gorham was their lobbyist, a shrewd, tricky politician. They wanted him for Governor, as they could trust no one else.

The people were unanimous in favor of my nomination for Governor. That was in '67. Gov. [Frederick F.] Low had vetoed that bill and the state was wild with rejoicing. Wherever he went he was met with the plaudits of the people. Gorham went to Low and told him that if he did not sign that bill, he (Gorham) would; he would be the next governor and would sign it. The bill was vetoed, and the railroad company wanted Gorham nominated. I did not go to Sacramento until the last day [of the convention]. The railroad company were able by their trickery and bribery to nominate Gorham. The Republican party was greatly split up. They wanted me to take the nomination of the Independent party, but I refused, and they nominated [Caleb] Fay of this city [San Francisco]. Gorham was beaten by [Henry] Haight.[90]

### ADVOCATES FEDERAL OWNERSHIP OF THE RAILROADS
### AND OTHER TRANSPORTATION SYSTEMS

It is in my judgment a necessity that the channels of internal transportation be made cheap, and be held and controlled in the interests of agriculture, and all other

---

[88] JB to AB, 4 September 1879, JB-CSL, b. 54, f. 42.
[89] JB to AB, Ibid., b. 55, f. 10.
[90] JB-91, pp. 34–35.

industrial pursuits. There is an inseparable connection. And this is no fancy picture. These ways must be either owned and controlled by the Government, or they will own and control the government, and its agriculture, and all its manifold industries. Please do not understand me to mean any attack on railroads or other ways of travel, or anything like confiscation or destruction of their rights or property. By no means. I would not confiscate a hair that honestly belongs to any man or company of men; nor would I incite others to do an unlawful act. I am utterly opposed to agrarianism, communism, and nihilism in all their lawless forms and tendencies. But I am in favor of the General Government's obtaining control by lawful means and paying a fair compensation; because no other power can grapple with the mighty question; it has passed beyond the stage of State or local issues. It must be a national, because trade and commerce are questions of national regulation under the Federal Constitution....

Equal and exact justice alone will be a permanent solution of the question. This is a question of greatest moment, and it is evident to my mind that the rights are not all on one side. It has not been possible, at least thus far, to divest my mind of the idea that the people have some rights in these great public highways. I contend that they were not only made for the people, but that the people made them. It was their prior enterprise, in the various fields of production and invention, that created the demand for and made them possible. The people were the real moving power which brought them into existence. Their industries alone sustain and perpetuate them; the people are indispensable to them; they are indispensable to the people; they alone can protect and prosper them; without the people they would vanish from the earth.[91]

I can see no future for this country unless the government will own and control the great transportation lines in the interest of the people. Monopoly can never be controlled by competition, because competition is the nearest neighbor to combination. It is so easy for people at this time to organize. In fact we are born with the elements of organization in us. Now we are able to form combinations here that threaten almost to absorb the vitality of this country. Everything is being monopolized.[92]

It is the duty of the government to enable people to go and come as cheaply as possible. I cannot see why this government, if it can carry a letter for two cts. thousands of miles, cannot manage to transport things cheaply. I think it can be done. Some say the government has enough to do. So it has, the way it is organized, but it can do more. If the Australian government can run and own railroads, why can't we do it. They say they are well managed. The Canadian Pacific is not a rapid railway, but is well conducted. I think it is an exceedingly

---
[91]CSAS 1881, pp. 36–37.
[92]JB-91, p. 35.

safe road. In stopping at the unimportant stations, the time they lose is almost nothing. They only stop long enough for a passenger to step off and the instant he is off they begin to move. When they lose time they cannot make it up. It is against the law. That is in the interest of safety. Roads conducted on that principle, I think, are a lesson to us. Under government control we would have fewer accidents. Transportation of course would have to become a department of the government by itself. As all the people would be interested in its safety, if adopted by the country, it would soon receive the attention necessary to make it efficient in all respects.[93]

### Presidential Election of 1884, Hopes for Large Prohibition Vote

Tomorrow will be election, and I think Blaine is to lead Cleveland—at least that is my desire. But the election of neither is as important as the giving of [Prohibitionist John P.] St. Johns a large vote.[94]

If Blaine is defeated it will not hurt the cause of prohibition, but greatly promote it. The burning of St. John in effigy in Kansas, will also help prohibition. Such persecution always reacts.[95]

### Bidwell Defines His Politics as of 1888

My politics are intensely Republican, in the sense of that term as used to bring that party into existence, and in its mission to preserve the Union, but I am more than a Republican, I am a Prohibitionist, a native American and anti-Chinese in the sense of wholesome restriction of all foreign immigration and an anti-monopolist in the truest sense of the term.[96]

### Bidwell Reaffirms His Support of Nativist American Party, 1891

I believe in American party principles. I stand firmly for the American party platform. I can endorse almost every word of their platform.... We must have the right of controlling immigration. It is humiliating to see a city like Milwaukee demand that the laws shall be printed in the German language. If a person does not think enough of our country to learn our language, we want to restrict immigration. I am not only in favor of restricting Chinese immigration, but all dangerous immigration, and have been for years. The American Party is essentially different from the "Know-Nothing" party. The American Party is not opposed to foreign immigration, but it is opposed to this wholesale immigration. It is opposed to the liberty taken by foreign governments to deposit upon our shores the pauper and criminal classes. We have no prejudice against foreign nations. We

---

[93] JB-91, pp. 47–48.
[94] JB to AB, 3 November 1884, JB-CSL, b. 57, f. 43.
[95] JB to AB, 8 November 1884, Ibid., b. 57, f. 45.
[96] "Butte County," *Resources of California* (April 1888), p. 3.

are made up of foreigners ourselves, but we have a right to restrict our immigration. I think I am in favor of the absolute repeal of the naturalization laws. I think it has come to that point where a man can afford to live in this country 21 years before he has the right to vote. I don't know but what I would carry it as far as to say "you must be born in America." I do not want to be an extremist, but sometimes we cannot take a middle ground.[97]

### Bidwell confesses his anti-Catholicism

I believe in the Bible as it is interpreted by the Protestant denomination. I have really a good deal of prejudice against the Catholics and against the church, for its grasping power. I think it is dangerous. I think its influence is to break up the American school. The Catholic church as it existed in California under the Mexican regime was demoralizing, so much so, that its influence among the Californians was not much.[98]

### Disillusionment with politics, 1891

I remember when I was a boy I used to dream that I would like to be President of the U.S., and yet since I have grown up, I have been entirely cured. I do not say that I did not want to be governor of this state. I did, and the reason was that the people wanted me, but the railroad company with its money and its corruptions defeated me. After one term in Congress, I began to see the shallowness of such ambitions.[99]

### Bidwell endorses the Australian ballot

The Australian ballot system to me is the most important: I believe that no political party at this time appreciates its value. To me it is a matter of amazement that the system of balloting has been in England, transferred from there to Canada, and again to Australia, and New Zealand and other British provinces, and the United States, so superior in many things, should be so far behind in its system of balloting. All we had to do was to transfer it right across the Niagara Falls, but it was too near. It was too common. It had to go to Australia. An intelligent American had to see the advantages of it there, and then had to write about it here. So strange that we did not accept that system instead of our own. I almost believe that system is so important that the existence of our country depends upon it. I believe that if the people can express themselves, if they can exercise their intelligence, let it be intelligence small or great, if they can only exercise that intelligence—the intelligence itself will grow. What does any ballot mean here? Here's a democratic ballot. Not one man in 20 cares a fig for all the names. Every one perhaps has a favorite. A few very intelligent men may want to vote their own ticket and see every one elected, but if a man does not care anything

---

[97]JB-91, pp. 36–37.   [98]JB-91, pp. 49–50.
[99]JB-91, p. 8.

about those names and puts in the ticket simply because it is the party ticket, how much of an expression of his will is that?

Under the Australian ballot, a man is obliged to exercise his intelligence. He reads the first name. He knows whether it is republican or otherwise, because the party name is printed right opposite. He knows there are one or more candidates, but he is intelligent enough to know that he can vote for but one. While he marks his ticket he is in a little room by himself. He does not see a ticket until he comes to the polls and gets one. He has to be intelligent enough to know his own number, and when the clerk has found it, he is entitled to a vote. There is but one ticket and that is handed to him. All are represented on that ticket. He goes in a room by himself, and he exercises his own good judgment in regard to the men he wants to vote for.

Under the present system, the law says the ticket must be kept a hundred feet from the polls. Here we find little tables, with the different party tickets spread out upon them. A man may not want to vote a whole ticket; he may want names from certain other tickets than his own party. He is afraid to go to the different tables, because everyone is watching. He must go and get his republican or democratic ticket, and bring it to the polls and put it in. Under the Australian ballot, we get the expression of the people. They may say a man cannot read and write. Let one of each party go with him in a special room, and let the ticket be filled out and examined in the presence of all three. I would be willing to trust one man to go with him. It would take but a short time and the man could say for himself whom he wanted to vote for.[100]

## Prohibition and Female Suffrage

My conviction has resulted from what I know. Miss [Frances] Willard [President of the Women's Christian Temperance Union] mentions an instance in Arkansas. That state was terribly cursed by whiskey, resulting in a great deal of poverty, in crime, destitution among the families, and abuse perpetrated by drinking husbands upon the families. The legislature passed a law to this effect: that whenever the majority of the inhabitants in a certain district should petition the county judge to exclude saloons, distilleries, and places where liquor was sold, it should be the duty of the judge to carry the law into effect. The western and southern people have a direct way of dealing with such things when they undertake it. That law was deemed a necessity. The wisdom in that law, in my opinion, was shown in this, that the women over the age of 18 had the same right as the men to sign the petition, and the women almost unanimously signed them. They were the mothers. Such was the result of the law when it was carried into execution, that in one or two years, fifty-two counties in the state of Arkansas did not have a saloon or distillery. The men never could have done it, but the women, united

---

[100] JB-91, pp. 37–38.

with that portion of the male population who were in favor of the law, made it a success. Now, take that for an example. If a woman can do so much good and make her influence felt in that way, what is the difference if she expressed her will by the ballot. If she is capable of the one thing, why not the other. In questions that effect [*sic*] the family, a woman's instinct would be almost invariably right, and hence I argue that she ought to have an opportunity to exert that influence. We see the influence everywhere in our lives. There is hardly a man so indecent anywhere, that in the presence of women will use profane language. Her very presence is restraining, and is in favor of order and propriety. I think we should give woman the opportunity to exert her influence for the good and the home. That means everything....

Few men appreciate the extent of the liquor trade of this nation. In the east vast amounts of liquor have accumulated. It has been put into bonded warehouses, the receipts have been pledged at the banks, securities pledged upon this very liquor traffic, which is such a curse in our country, which is the direct and indirect cause of half the burdens which the people bear, in sustaining courts, jails, insane asylums, etc. Now to think, that the organized money power of this country should be so largely based on this death curse. Yet I know that if women had the ballot, that question would be solved. That is my conviction and hence I hold it to be a duty to give women the ballot. I think the sentiment is growing everywhere. England will give women the ballot first, if America does not look out....

Another reason why men interested in the liquor curse do not give women the ballot, is that they know the thing will receive its death blow, when women have a chance to vote upon it. They know, too, that their business would be at an end unless they can keep the great army of drinkers recruited from the boys growing up. They must have it reinforced, or else their business is gone.[101]

### Highlights of Bidwell's letter accepting the Prohibition Party nomination for President, 1892

...I am formally notified that the National Prohibition Convention in session in the city of Cincinnati, adopted a platform of principles for the coming political campaign, and thereupon conferred upon me the distinguished honor of its nomination for President of the United States.

In accepting the nomination, which I do with misgivings as to my ability to meet the just expectations of the people, permit me to thank you ... and the friends of Prohibition and Reform throughout the country whom you represent, my grateful acknowledgements.

It is scarcely necessary to add that I am overwhelmed with a keen sense of the responsibility which I assume.

Mistakes are possible, but I trust the cause may not suffer in my hands. All

---
[101] JB-91, pp. 45–47.

I have to plead is unswerving devotion to those great principles and needed reforms which have brought into existence the Prohibition party of the nation.[102]

## The curse of monopolies and the liquor traffic

There are well founded apprehensions that this nation which we love—this mighty empire of sovereign states—cannot survive unless redeemed from the dangers that jeopardize its existence, prominent among which are that immeasurable evil, the monstrous liquor traffic, and the numerous forms and phases of monopolistic combinations, creating immense wealth in the hands of the few and impoverishing the many. The same causes and processes which have created increasing numbers of millionaires will, if unchecked under the rule of the old political parties, in time turn over the entire nation into the hands of an aristocracy of monster billionaires.

Labor creates the wealth of the country. Without labor there can be no development of resources, no national prosperity. The liquor traffic robs, impoverishes and demoralizes labor, thereby sapping the very foundations of the national fabric.

... But it is not necessary further to enumerate; suffice it to say, the liquor traffic is a standing curse; a danger to public health; the prolific source of untold political corruption, crimes, diseases, degradation and death; a public nuisance and a public immorality; in a word, it is an unmitigated and measureless evil without a redeeming feature.

Every consideration of justice, the public welfare, protection to labor, all cry out against this great wrong. The only adequate remedy lies in the entire overthrow of the liquor traffic in every State and Territory.

The liquor power leads, corrupts and dominates both the old political parties. Without the liquor support neither could make another political fight or win a victory.[103]

## Women's suffrage

The family is the unit of civilized government. Protect the home and the nation will be protected.

In the name of right and humanity then, let not free, enlightened and Christian America longer injure and degrade woman by withholding from her that which is her inalienable right, that which will elevate American womanhood, that which will enlarge her usefulness; that which will impart to her greater ability to be the helper and co-worker with man under all circumstances and conditions; that which alone will make woman man's equal before the law and place in her hands the most efficient weapon with which to defend her rights and protect her home. I allude, of course, to that priceless heritage, the ballot.

---

[102]Charles C. Royce, *John Bidwell: Pioneer, Statesman, Philanthropist: A Biographical Sketch* (Chico, Ca.: 1907), p. 71.
[103]Ibid., p. 72.

In doing this Americans should lose no time. Americans, of all people under the sun, are the most nearly ready. Our women know what the ballot is and its power; they are brave enough to ask it because it is their right. They are as a class intelligent, virtuous, self-reliant, womanly, modest.

If we delay, England will take the lead in the emancipation of woman.

The nation that first gives woman equal rights with man will earn a crown of imperishable glory.[104]

### Favors federal income tax

An income tax can do no injustice, work no opposition; for where there is no income there will be nothing to pay; the rich will pay most and the poor least or nothing. This mode of revenue is no experiment in this country. During the great rebellion, when every source of revenue was strained to sustain the armies of the Union an income tax was resorted to and it worked like a charm.

It helped then to save the Union and will help to save the nation now in another rebellion—the classes against the masses.

Some men, of course, will always try to evade the payment of their just taxes. But no honest man, I think, can ever make any reasonable objection to a well regulated income tax.

The effect of this mode of raising national revenue cannot fail to be beneficent. It will relieve the poor without oppressing the rich. Perhaps no other measure possible to be devised will work greater reform or give greater impetus to general prosperity than a wisely regulated income tax. One of its results would be to favor the equal distribution of wealth; it would go far to heal the growing discord between labor and capital.[105]

### Federal control of the railroads

There is perhaps no one issue in all the broad array of Prohibition principles embraced in our national platform of more vital concern to the material prosperity of our whole country, than that of transportation. Hence we declare in favor of government control of "Railroad, telegraph and other public corporations", in the interest of all the people. If railways cannot otherwise be so controlled, then it becomes the imperative duty of government to acquire and exercise absolute ownership, especially of the great trunk lines, for we mean practical and efficient control—nothing less.

So essential is this instrumentality to our national life and prosperity in this stage of rapid transit, that whatever powers own and control the railways of the United States, intimately associated as they are with other great monopolistic interests, will have it within their sway virtually to own and control the government.

It is well known that railways and their natural affiliations (the great mon-

---

[104]Ibid., pp. 72–73.   [105]Ibid., p. 76.

eyed and other corporate powers) have already a most dangerous influence in all elections and in every department of the government. They are absolutely corrupting. We boast that ours is the freest and best government, and so it is.

But the question comes home to every thoughtful mind: Is it safe for the people to surrender their rights into the hands of great corporations? ...

For these considerations, transportation must be controlled—owned if necessary—by the government of the United States.[106]

*English as the national language*
In the interest of national unity there should be a national language—and that of course the English.

No other should be the language of the public school. A knowledge of the national language so far as to read and write the same fairly well, should, in addition to good moral character, be made a condition of naturalization and the inestimable right of suffrage.[107]

*Immigration restriction*
In 1776 we needed immigration. The complaint against England was that immigration had been obstructed. But times have changed. We make no war against foreigners as such. This is a world of competition. Every nation is competing with all other nations. Some are favored nations. Ours is one. All the world has been and still is coming to us.

But we must now begin to close the doors in self-defense. We do not want the world faster than we can Americanize the world. We have already quite enough of imported nihilism, anarchism and pauperism.

We do not ask foreigners coming to this land of freedom to change their faith. We do not propose to Protestantize or Romanize or in any manner sectarianize them. But we do insist that they shall not destroy our liberties by any attempt to foreignize, or anarchize us or our government; that they should appreciate our liberties and privileges; that as a condition of citizenship they should learn to speak our national language and to read and write it fairly well.[108]

### ON SUSAN B. ANTHONY, FEMALE SUFFRAGE, AND EQUALITY BETWEEN THE SEXES, 1871

....Miss Susan B. Anthony [gave speech at Wood's Hall]—the power of the ballot was her theme—and I must say she handled the subject very ably. She was very argumentative—her reasoning was good—and though she was not a Cicero or Demosthenes in eloquence—she was almost eloquent....[109]

The burden of Miss S. B. Anthony's lecture last night was, that woman ought

---

[106]Ibid., pp. 76–77.
[107]Ibid., p. 78.
[108]Ibid., p. 80.
[109]JB to AB, 1 December 1871, JB-CSL, b. 50, f. 1.

to rely on herself, and not on man for support and protection—that she can never rise to her proper sphere without the ballot—that she is simply the slave of man, a mere appendage to ornament his parlor and do his bidding—that in many if not most cases instead of husband and wife being bound by the cords of love there was really no love, but simply the golden chain which bound her to the man, and she accepted it rather than starve because man deprived her of the ballot and thereby of the means to command respect and equality in wages and compared her with the southern slaves, the Chinese, and other disfranchised classes.

But I can tell Miss Anthony this: If she succeed in making the women of America like herself—fired with an ambition to enter into political discussions—to run for office and hold political power—to learn the rough ways of ambition and practical outdoor employments—she will succeed in multiplying indefinitely the number of her sex who will have to tramp the lonely paths of single blessedness, for no man of taste and refinement will marry them. The fact is, a man ought not to be a woman—nor a woman a man. The all wise Creator never so designed them. But enough of women's rights....[110]

---

[110] JB to AB, 2 December 1871, JB-CSL, b. 50, f 2.

# 6

# Bidwell and the California Indians

During John Bidwell's hotly contested congressional and gubernatorial campaigns, opponents tried to portray him as a hypocrite who had championed abolition and black equality only to enslave the Indians who worked his ranch. In 1864, the *Yreka Semi-Weekly Union* accused Bidwell of establishing a "slave pen" at Chico where Indian workers were beaten with clubs. "As you are such a stickler for freedom of the slaves, why not set an example and comply with the request of your neighbors by giving freedom to your (Indian) slaves?" the paper rhetorically asked.[1] Such charges inevitably led Bidwell's defenders to respond by casting him as the friend, protector, and civilizer of the Indians. According to the Chico *Enterprise*, "the landlord of Rancho Chico is a gentleman of broad humanity, the true philanthropist, and the promoter of man's freedom."[2]

The sharply contrasting views of Bidwell's contemporaries each found their champions among twentieth-century historians. Bidwell's hagiographer, Rockwell Hunt, claimed that "Bidwell's personal attitude toward the Indians was not simply that of consideration and friendship; it was that of unselfish love...."[3] Dolores Huff, however, stated flatly that "Bidwell had Indian slaves," and she condemned him for authoring "the Act for the Protection and Governance [*sic*] of Indians that formalized the legal sanction of Indian slavery..." in California.[4]

The more complicated truth, of course, lies somewhere in between. While Bidwell was clearly not the unselfish saint depicted by Hunt, he

---

[1] James J. Rawls, *Indians of California, The Changing Image* (Norman: University of Oklahoma Press, 1984), p. 95.
[2] Chico *Enterprise*, 6 Aug. 1875; Hunt, p. 318.
[3] Hunt, p. 141.
[4] Chico *Enterprise-Record*, 12 March 1993. Huff is a professor of Ethnic Studies at California State University, Fresno. For a similar interpretation, see *The Maidu Mechoopda Indians* (Chico: Mechoopda Indian Tribe, 1995), p. 7.

certainly was not a slave owner and his role in the enactment of the notorious Indian law of 1850 has been grossly misinterpreted by Huff and others.[5] In actuality, Bidwell's attitudes and behavior towards Indians seem to have been governed by a complex blend of curiosity, humanitarianism, and pragmatic self-interest. When viewed against the incredibly racist and violent backdrop of Gold Rush California, Bidwell's interactions with Indian people appear remarkably tolerant, compassionate, and enlightened.

The discovery of gold at Coloma set in motion a series of events which resulted in profound changes for California's aboriginal inhabitants. Many Indians fell victim to smallpox and other epidemic diseases carried by the immigrant miners. Others, forced out of their traditional economies, initially became an important source of labor in the gold fields. However, the large numbers of newly arrived Anglos who headed into the foothills starting in 1849 showed little interest in employing Indians. Instead, they saw the native residents as threats, competitors, or potential slaves. In any event, as far as most miners were concerned, the land had become theirs by right of conquest. For years, miners and other whites in northern California shot Indians on sight or tried to force them into involuntary servitude. Some northern California communities actively sought to rid the region of Indians by paying bounties for Indian heads and scalps.[6] After having already declined from 300,000 to 150,000 under Spanish and Mexican rule, California's Native American population fell another eighty percent between 1850 and 1870 to a mere 30,000![7]

Although his own success as a miner and a rancher depended heavily upon Native American labor, Bidwell never adopted the abusive practices of John Sutter and the Mexican rancheros who utilized conscription, peonage, and military force to control their Indian workers. In fact, while serving as *alcalde* at Mission San Luis Rey during the Mexican War, Bidwell used his authority to strike a blow at the peonage system by refusing to return runaway Indians to their ranchero employer-creditors. Bid-

---

[5]See, for examples, Rawls, p. 89; Rosaline Levinson, "Bidwell's Relationships with Minorities: The Altruistic-Pragmatic Mix," in *Ripples Along Chico Creek: Perspectives on People and Times* (Chico, Ca.: Butte County Branch, National League of American Pen Women, 1992), pp. 81–83; and Tomas Almaguer, *Racial Fault Lines: The Historical Origins of White Supremacy in California* (Berkeley: University of California Press, 1994), p. 137.

[6]Theodora Kroeber, *Ishi, In Two Worlds* (Berkeley: University of California Press, 1961), pp. 56–79; Rawls, pp. 171–201.

[7]Sherburne F. Cook, *The Population of the California Indians, 1769–1970* (Berkeley: University of California Press, 1976), pp. 43, 44, 59, 65.

well ruled that American law forbade compulsory servitude based on indebtedness.[8]

Nevertheless, as an employer himself, Bidwell had a vested interest in maintaining the supply of Indian workers during the early years of the Gold Rush when white labor was scarce and wages high. Consequently, his alleged authorship of the exploitive Act for the Government and Protection of Indians in 1850 has been interpreted as an attempt to preserve the rancho labor system under American rule. That, indeed, was precisely what the law accomplished. As finally enacted, the bill permitted local authorities to release Indians convicted of crimes "punishable by fine" into the custody of private employers who agreed to pay the fines in exchange for the Indians' labor. The scope of this labor leasing system was vastly expanded by an anti-vagrancy clause that subjected unemployed Indians to arrest "upon complaint of any resident." Convicted Indian vagrants could then be auctioned off to private employers for terms of up to four months. In addition, the new law also established a system of indentured servitude that, in effect, legalized the enslavement of Indian children and young adults. The ability to "apprentice" Indian workers fostered the growth of a brutal traffic in slaves that flourished in California until 1863, when the system was finally abolished in the wake of President Abraham Lincoln's Emancipation Proclamation.

The Indian law enacted by the legislature was not, however, the bill that John Bidwell originally drafted and introduced as a member of the first California state senate. Indeed, Bidwell's legislation never even came to a vote. Instead, it was tabled by the senate in favor of a rival assembly bill introduced by ranchero Elam Brown of Contra Costa County. With the Brown bill thus established as the basis of further debate, the senate appointed a select committee comprised of Bidwell, Mariano Vallejo, and David Douglass of San Joaquin County to review the legislation. Three days later, the committee brought forth a slightly amended draft which passed both houses of the legislature and was signed into law by Governor Peter Burnett on April 22, 1850.[9]

Bidwell's opinion of the law is not known. The select committee's deliberations and vote were not recorded, and Bidwell did not vote on the bill

---

[8]JB-77, pp. 183–84; Hunt, p. 124.
[9]Albert L. Hurtado, *Indian Survival on the California Frontier* (New Haven: Yale University Press, 1988), pp. 128–130; Rawls, pp. 88–90; California Legislature, *Statutes of California Passed at the First Session of the Legislature, 1850*, Chapter 133, pp. 408–410. Brown, a native of New York who emigrated to California in 1846, had known Bidwell back in Missouri where the two men had boarded together for a brief period. See Bidwell, "The First Emigrant Train to California," *Century Magazine*, 41 (November 1890), p. 111.

when it passed the legislature on April 19. While Vallejo and Douglass cast aye votes, Bidwell appears to have been absent from the senate chambers. Whether he was absent or abstaining, the fact remains that Bidwell never voted to enact the 1850 Indian law, which differed dramatically from his original proposal. Bidwell's draft, for example, did not include the notorious anti-vagrancy clause and, while it permitted the indenture of Indian children, it also required that such contracts receive the prior consent of the child's parents or relatives, and that compensation be provided to Indian servants upon the completion of service.[10]

A remarkable document, Bidwell's failed draft contains the clearest and most comprehensive statement ever written by its author regarding his vision for establishing harmonious Indian-white relations in California. Though the violence and turbulence of the Gold Rush would soon make his plan appear hopelessly naïve, Bidwell remained convinced throughout most of the 1850s that a peaceful coexistence could be fashioned between the races. At the heart of his plan lay a system of shared governance designed to protect and guarantee fundamental Indian rights. In a sharp break with established American customs, Bidwell proposed that all legal matters involving whites and Native Americans, including labor contracts and child indentures, be subject to the purview of special "Justices of the Peace for Indians." These judges, whose sole concern was to be the administration of Indian laws, were to be elected annually not only by white voters but by adult male Indians as well.[11]

In addition, Bidwell's proposal contained strong language that recognized the right of Indians to remain in the villages that they had possessed "from time immemorial," even when these villages were located on land subsequently claimed by whites as private property. Indeed, in all such cases, white property owners had to share the land in common or concede to resident Indians a village land allotment equal to at least one acre per person, along with free access to timber and grazing rights sufficient to support herds averaging one horse and one cow per person.[12]

Whether they resided on private lands or the public domain, Bidwell's proposal also recognized the right of Native Americans to continue their

---

[10]California Legislature, *Journal of the Senate of California, First Session, 1850*, pp. 217, 224, 228, 257–258, 337–338, 366, 369, 384–387; *Journal of the Assembly of California, 1850*, pp. 1205, 1233, 1284. Bidwell did vote against a motion to indefinitely postpone action on the Brown bill when it came up for its second reading in the Senate on April 17. See *Journal of the Senate, 1850*, p. 343.

[11]John Bidwell, "An Act Relative to the Protection, Punishment, and Government of Indians," 16 March 1850, California State Senate, Old Bill File, California State Archives.

[12]Ibid.

"usual avocations" of hunting, fishing, and gathering seeds and acorns. With the important exception of range and woodland burning, all traditional Indian subsistence practices were to be respected.[13]

Bidwell realized that, even under his generous terms, the Indians of California would never retain enough land to remain self-sufficient hunter-gatherers. On the contrary, he expected them to accept the inevitability of American conquest and to respond accordingly by gradually taking up farming and animal husbandry. In the meantime, Indians would compensate for lost resources by seeking gainful and instructive employment from whites and thereby provide California with a reliable and badly needed supply of wage labor. Bidwell apparently calculated that the demand for Native American labor was so great that, if properly monitored by the justices of the peace and other government authorities, the free market would treat the Indians well. Whites would have to compete for their services, and the Indians would gravitate toward "him who treats them best." Bidwell did not believe he was indulging in wishful thinking. Based on his own experience with Indian workers and his observations of successful models elsewhere, Bidwell had concluded that, as long as they were dealt with fairly, the Indians of California would "naturally and voluntarily domesticate themselves."[14]

The practicality of Bidwell's approach was never tested. Instead, legislators opted for more familiar and coercive measures, rejecting Bidwell's call for limited Indian suffrage and diluting every specific guarantee he attempted to enact into law. In the end, the chief accomplishment of Bidwell's proposal was to mark its author as an unusually fair-minded man, quite out of step with the majority of his white contemporaries.

The unorthodoxy of Bidwell's position was underscored the following year when the federal government tried to assert its own Indian policy in California. While the legislature gutted Bidwell's Indian proposals and violence rapidly escalated against Native Americans in the gold fields, Congress authorized President Millard Fillmore to appoint three com-

---

[13]Ibid.

[14]JB to Congressman Joseph W. McCorkle, 20 December 1851, in *Letters Received by the Office of Indian Affairs, 1824–1881, California Superintendency, 1849–1880*, Roll 32 (Washington, D.C.: The National Archives and Records Service, 1958), pp. 761–67. Michele Shover argues that Bidwell's optimistic views on Indian-white relations were deeply influenced by the example he encountered at Mission San Luis Rey during the Mexican War. Shover makes the interesting case that the humanitarian legacy of Fr. Antonio Peyri provided Bidwell with a more satisfying and personally compatible role model than did the abusive John Sutter. See Shover, "John Bidwell: Reluctant Indian Fighter, 1852–1856," *Dogtown Territorial Quarterly*, 36 (Winter 1998), pp. 33–34.

missioners to meet with the various California tribes and to establish reservations for them within the state. Between January 1851 and January 1852, the commissioners negotiated eighteen treaties with representatives of 139 different lineages and clans. Altogether, these agreements reserved nearly eight million acres of land, much of it located in the rich Central Valley, for California's hard-pressed Native Americans. Though ample in size, the reservations were not large enough to support the traditional hunting and gathering economies of the California Indians, nor were they intended to do so. Like John Bidwell, the commissioners expected the Indians to adapt to their new circumstances by becoming farmers and herdsmen. To enable them to make this fundamental transition, the treaties promised each tribe a specified allocation of farming tools, plows, and livestock, along with a team of farmers, carpenters, blacksmiths, wheelwrights, and schoolteachers to train and assist them.[15]

Among the eighteen protocols was a treaty signed on August 1, 1851, at Rancho del Arroyo Chico. Playing host and advisor to federal commissioner Oliver M. Wozencraft, John Bidwell provided food for the 300 Indians who assembled on the ranch and secured for the commissioner the assistance of one of his employees, a twelve-year-old Maidu boy named Rafael, who acted as interpreter. The ensuing deliberations resulted in an agreement that permitted the tribes of Butte County to remain in possession of a wide swath of their ancestral homeland. Covering some 227 square miles, the proposed reservation stretched southeast from Rancho Chico to the Feather River and Bidwell's Bar. Although Kulmeh, the headman of the Konkow Maidu, refused to sign, nine other local leaders, including the Mechoopda chief Luccayan, affixed their marks to the document, which also bore Bidwell's signature.[16]

Though he signed the treaty as a witness, Bidwell had serious misgivings about both the document itself and Wozencraft's interim policy for ensuring Indian cooperation. Until the agreement took effect, the commissioner promised free beef rations to the Indians encamped on Bidwell's ranch and nearby properties. Since this included the Mechoopda and others whom he often employed, Bidwell suddenly found it difficult to obtain willing workers. Fearing that rations would undermine his labor supply as well as the effort to guide the Indians toward agricultural self-

---

[15]Bean, pp. 167–168; George H. Phillips, *The Enduring Struggle: Indians in California History* (San Francisco: Boyd and Fraser, 1981), pp. 47–51; Dorothy J. Hill, *The Indians of Chico Rancheria* (Sacramento: Ka Ca Ma Press, 1978), pp. 20–23.

[16]Hill, *The Indians of Chico Rancheria*, pp. 20–23, 89–90.

sufficiency, Bidwell protested strenuously, and federal handouts on Rancho Chico soon ended.[17]

As for the actual treaty, Bidwell believed that the reservation established by Wozencraft was insufficient, both in size and quality of soil. Indeed, Bidwell remained skeptical of the entire reservation system proposed by the federal commissioners, arguing that forced geographic segregation would never work in California, where the white and Indian populations had already become too interspersed. In a lengthy letter to Congressman Joseph McCorkle, Bidwell spelled out his objections in great detail and offered some alternatives for crafting a more humane Indian policy better suited to California's unique conditions. Most of his suggestions fell along the same lines as those he had proposed to the state legislature in 1850.[18]

Unfortunately, Bidwell's ideas did not win the approval of Congress, but neither did the eighteen treaties concluded by Wozencraft and his colleagues. Instead, a storm of indignation erupted from white Californians who, unlike Bidwell, complained that too much valuable land had been surrendered by the commissioners. In response, the state legislature overwhelmingly passed a series of resolutions condemning the treaties and demanding that Congress refuse to ratify them. Bowing to popular demand, the United States Senate voted to reject all eighteen documents on July 8, 1852. When the federal government finally did enact a reservation policy for California later in the decade, it proved far less benevolent than anything Bidwell or the commissioners had ever envisioned. Beginning in 1853 with the Sebastian Agency at Fort Tejon near Los Angeles, Congress authorized the establishment of a series of smaller reservations scattered throughout the state. These included the Nome Lackee Agency near Red Bluff and the Nome Cult (Round Valley) Reservation in Mendocino County.[19]

---

[17]Deposition of John Bidwell, U.S. Court of Claims, San Francisco, *Samuel Norris vs. U.S., 1858*, in U.S., House of Representatives, *Documents*, 36 Congress, 2 Session, 1860, Report C.C., no. 257, pp. 9, 75, 79.

[18]JB to McCorkle, 20 December 1851; JB in *Norris vs. U.S.*, p. 74. Both Albert Hurtado and Michele Shover see Bidwell's letter to McCorkle as a self-serving reversal of position and a betrayal of the Indians who had joined him in signing the Rancho Chico treaty. Such an interpretation, however, assumes that Bidwell's signature constituted an endorsement of the agreement and the reservation system. Actually, the text of the document indicates that Bidwell, together with three U.S. Army officers who were also present, signed the treaty merely as witnesses, not as representatives of the contracting parties. See Hurtado, *Indian Survival*, pp. 138–39; Shover, "John Bidwell: Reluctant Indian Fighter," pp. 42–44; Hill, pp. 21, 91.

[19]Rawls, pp. 141–148; Hurtado, pp. 132–142; Robert F. Heizer and Alan Almquist, *The Other Californians: Prejudice and Discrimination Under Spain, Mexico, and the United States to 1920* (Berkeley: University of California Press, 1971), pp. 67–79.

In the meantime, Bidwell, unable to shape Indian policy at the federal or state levels, proceeded at Rancho Chico to implement his own views on Indian-white relations. Here, Bidwell's dealings with the local Mechoopda attest to the fact that his liberal stance on Indian affairs was not merely rhetorical. Bidwell's close relationship with the Mechoopda and other Butte County native peoples had begun during the Gold Rush when he and two partners recruited Indians to work for them at Bidwell's Bar. Together they employed anywhere from twenty to fifty or more Indian laborers during the mining seasons of 1848 and 1849. Paid in-kind with food and clothing, the Indian miners enabled Bidwell to amass the fortune with which he purchased Rancho Chico. When he moved onto the property in 1849, no Indians resided there. The local Mechoopda were instead concentrated in several rancherias south of Chico Creek. Badly in need of labor to develop his estate, Bidwell invited the tribe to move onto the ranch. There, on the north bank of the creek, just one hundred yards west of his own residence, the Mechoopda established the village of Mikchopdo, later known also as Bahapki. The resulting arrangement proved mutually beneficial. Bidwell secured the workers he needed, and the Mechoopda obtained a sanctuary that enabled them to live safely in Butte County at a time when Indians throughout California were literally being enslaved, exterminated, or, at best, herded onto reservations far from their ancestral homelands.[20] Unlike so many California tribes, the Mechoopda were to be spared the ravages of war and the sorrows of exile.[21]

And, while farm work necessarily required a significant change in their traditional way of life, Bidwell did not use his authority to launch a private *Kulturkampf* against the Mechoopda. That, regrettably, was the doing of his wife, Annie. Until her arrival in 1868, however, the Mechoopda kept their culture largely intact. Many hunting and gathering activities not only continued but were extended, in the form of gleaning rights, to the ran-

---

[20]Hill, pp. 12, 16–17, 25, 30; Rawls, pp. 86–201; Henry Azbill, "Some Aspects of Mechoopda Indian Culture" (Association for Northern California Records and Research, and California State University, Chico Oral History Program), Azbill interviewed 11 January 1966 by Jim Neider. Sometime after 1860, as more Indians from other tribes sought refuge at Mikchopdo, residents began referring to the village as Bahapki, the Maidu word for "unsifted or mixed." Henry Azbill, "Bahapki," *Indian Historian*, 4 (Spring 1971), p. 57.

[21]As the cultural resources representative of the Mechoopda recently acknowledged, "... the protection afforded them by John Bidwell, whether provided to the Mechoopda for reasons of philanthropy or personal gain, ... was essential for their survival." See Rodney Clements, "The Mechoopda, 1860–1900: When Lives Changed Forever," Chico *Enterprise-Record*, 29 October 1999.

cho's orchards and fields. While the Mechoopda came to include the products of the farm and ranch in their diet, traditional food ways were sustained by fishing, acorn harvesting, and communal grasshopper drives. For the Mechoopda, these activities successfully coexisted with their employment as *vaqueros*, teamsters, harvest workers, and plowmen, activities which drew both cash and in-kind compensation from Bidwell and other local ranch owners, with whom they actively negotiated wages.[22]

Among themselves, the Mechoopda continued to speak their native tongue and were free to practice their own religion, which centered around the ritualistic spirit dances of the Kuksu cult conducted in the village *kum* (assembly hall or roundhouse).[23] Though western work clothes were required during the hours of labor, native dress remained the style of the village, and visitors in 1855 still found the men "nearly naked." According to observers in 1855 and 1868, traditional bark and earthen housing continued to typify village construction, though visitors to Rancho Chico reported in 1857 that at least some of Bidwell's Indian workers "live in a cluster of substantial adobes, arranged in the form of a cross." The census of 1860 suggests that this "cluster" comprised three large structures that housed nearly fifty unmarried adult Mechoopda, who were segregated by sex. The rest, however, lived in fifteen to twenty Maidu "hutwees" or "ooyehs."[24]

Ironically, the harmonious *modus vivendi* struck on Rancho Chico did not prevent larger circumstances from forcing Bidwell to become, in the apt words of Michele Shover, a "reluctant Indian fighter" during the 1850s.[25] By settling in the Sacramento Valley and befriending the Mechoopda and nearby Wintu, Bidwell was inevitably drawn into the violent inter-tribal conflicts that pitted his native clients against the so-called "Mountain Indians." These included the Nimshew, "Tigers," and Konkow Maidu to the east and, to the north, the particularly aggressive Yahi, a Yana Indian tribelet who whites referred to as the Deer Creek

---

[22] Hill, pp. 61–65. Regarding Indian wage negotiations, see quote excerpted below from JB to AB, 21 June 1869. See also George M. Gray, "Reminiscences," *Sandy Gulch News*, 16 March 1939.

[23] Azbill, "Some Aspects," p. 3. The *kum* was also referred to as the Dance House or Sweat House.

[24] Annie Bidwell, "The Mechoopdas, or Rancho Chico Indians," *Overland Monthly*, 27 (February 1896), p. 205; Hill, pp. 24, 28–29, 52–61; Hurtado, p. 204; CSAS, 1857, p. 20; Azbill, "Some Aspects," p.3; Letter to authors from Craig D. Bates, Curator of Ethnography, Yosemite Museum, Yosemite National Park, 1 March 1995. The eleven females listed in the 1860 census were all identified as day laborers. Most of the men were described as farm laborers, though five were identified as gardeners, three as herders, one as a *vaquero*, and another, sixty-three-year-old Yummarine, as chief. See Hill, p. 29.

[25] Shover, "John Bidwell: Reluctant Indian Fighter," pp. 32–56.

or Mill Creek Indians.[26] Their periodic raids on the more prosperous tribes of the valley were, after the Gold Rush began, increasingly directed against white settlers as well, and Bidwell proved no exception.[27]

In October 1850, following a violent encounter that left one male Mechoopda dead, Bidwell set out on his first Indian campaign. Leading a group of twenty whites and Mechoopdas, Bidwell pursued the attackers up into the hills and overtook them along a narrow trail between Butte Creek and the West Branch of the Feather River. In the ensuing struggle, Bidwell's party killed seven or eight Indians, including two or three women, and lost one man of their own.[28]

Two years later, Bidwell took the field again after Indians raided Rancho Chico in June 1852, making off with several head of cattle. Hoping to avoid violence and not wishing to injure an innocent party, Bidwell patiently waited for over a month until, after capturing two suspects, he was satisfied regarding the identity of the actual culprits. Then, rather than launch a bloody punitive raid, the typical white response to such cases during the Gold Rush, Bidwell determined to content himself by apprehending the responsible parties and bringing them to trial. Accord-

---

[26]The terms Deer Creek and Mill Creek Indians must be interpreted with some caution. A decade of violence, disease, and dislocation had taken a severe toll upon the Yana groups so that by 1860 "Mill Creeks" had become a generic reference applied to any Indians hiding out in southern Yana territory, whether they were Yahi, Maidu, or mixed bands of refugees. Anthropologists Stephen Powers, Thomas T. Waterman, Alfred Kroeber, and Theodora Kroeber all equated the Mill Creeks with the Yahi. See Powers, *Tribes of California* (1877. Reprint ed., Berkeley: University of California Press, 1976); Waterman, "The Yana Indians," *University of California Publications in American Archeology and Ethnology*, 13 (27 February 1918); Alfred L. Kroeber, *Handbook of the Indians of California*, Bureau of American Ethnology, Bulletin 78 (1925), pp. 336–46; Theodora Kroeber, *Ishi in Two Worlds: A Biography of the Last Wild Indian in North America* (Berkeley: University of California Press, 1961). In contrast to these early anthropologists, linguist Jeremiah Curtin believed the Mill Creeks were renegade bands of "fugitives; outlaws from various tribes." Curtin's contention is supported by contemporary accounts and by the recent works of Steve Schoonover and Michele Shover. See Curtin, *Creation Myths of Primitive America* (Boston: Little, Brown and Co., 1898); D. F. Crowder, "The Eventful Yesterdays: The Story of Early Chico," Chico *Enterprise*, 22 January 1918; H. H. Sauber, "Hi Good and the 'Mill Creeks,'" *Overland Monthly*, 30 (August 1897), p. 122; Schoonover, "Captured by the Mill Creek Indians," *Dogtown Territorial Quarterly*, 22 (Summer 1995), p. 51; and Schoonover, "Who Were the Victims at the Three Knolls?" *Dogtown Territorial Quarterly*, 16 (Winter 1993), pp. 12–13, 46–47; Shover, "The Politics of the 1859 Kibbe Campaign: Northern California Indian-Settler Conflicts of the 1850s," *Dogtown Territorial Quarterly*, 38 (Summer 1999), pp. 4–8.

[27]Mansfield, pp. 185, 188, 217; Theodora Kroeber, *Ishi*, pp. 14–15, 24–28, 50.

[28]Mansfield, p. 185; Shover, "Reluctant Indian Fighter," p. 42. Years later, Bidwell failed to recall this first campaign when he incorrectly described a subsequent venture in 1852 as "the only Indian expedition I ever engaged in." Actually, he led at least three between 1850 and 1865. See JB-91, p. 21.

ingly, on July 15, Bidwell left Rancho Chico with a posse of thirty Indians and a handful of whites who agreed to respect his wishes for a measured pursuit of justice.

Unfortunately, Bidwell's careful plan went awry soon after he had tracked his quarry to an Indian encampment at the head of Chico Creek. Instead of making a few quiet arrests, Bidwell suddenly found himself under attack and ordered his men to retreat down Chico Creek canyon. At least eleven Indians were killed during the engagement, which also cost the life of Amos Frye, one of Bidwell's most trusted employees. As news of Frye's death spread among the white settlements of Butte County, a wave of criticism broke over Bidwell, who was condemned for his failed attempts at peaceful restraint.[29]

Indeed, Bidwell's defeat seemed to give greater encouragement to the mountain Maidu, who soon launched a second, and far more serious raid on Rancho Chico at the end of August. Attacking one night while Bidwell was away from home, members of the Sulamshew and other bands swooped down and struck with a vengeance. Though no lives were lost, Rancho Chico suffered considerable damage. The attackers burned a stable and four buildings containing farm equipment, lumber, dry goods, and 3,000 bushels of grain. Bidwell put his estimated total losses from the raid at a staggering $25,650.[30]

Remarkably, Bidwell does not appear to have attempted any retaliatory response to this devastating attack, nor did he reply to two subsequent incidents at Rancho Chico. In the summer of 1853, another Maidu nighttime raid resulted in the near-fatal shooting of Dupah, a Mechoopda worker who was pierced through the chest by an arrow. Three years later, in January 1856, a Maidu assassination attempt aimed at Bidwell led to a pitched battle on Rancho Chico in which five mountain Maidu perished after killing James Schaeffer, Bidwell's grain miller.[31]

Bidwell's reluctance to seek personal justice in these cases stood in marked contrast to the behavior of white settlers residing on the more exposed mountain frontiers of eastern Butte and Tehama counties. Running northwest in a great arc from Yankee Hill above Oroville to the lower

---

[29]JB-91, pp. 20–21; Shover, "Reluctant Indian Fighter," pp. 44–47.
[30]JB-91, pp. 18–19; JB, Petition to James Y. McDuffie, U.S. Superintendent of Indian Affairs for California, 5 December 1859, in *Letters Received*, Roll 37, pp. 891–912. Bidwell's petition also included a $200 claim for the four head of horned cattle taken by the Indians in June 1852.
[31]Annie Bidwell, *Rancho Chico Indians*, Dorothy Hill, ed. (Chico: Bidwell Mansion Cooperating Association, 1980), pp. 70–71; Mansfield, p. 188; Shover, "Reluctant Indian Fighter," pp. 48–51.

reaches of Antelope Creek outside of Red Bluff, the pale of white settlement was the scene of repeated clashes and interracial violence between 1850 and 1870. In this rugged mountain terrain, settlers residing on isolated farmsteads and mining claims lived in constant fear of Indian attack.

The anxiety-ridden frontier starkly revealed the inadequacy of Bidwell's Rancho Chico model for managing Indian affairs in all parts of California. Here, topography encouraged Indian resistance by blunting the technological and demographic superiority of the whites. At the same time, climate and geography ruled out extensive agriculture and, with it, the possibility of sustaining a permanent economy large enough to meaningfully integrate the Indians into the wage earning labor force on terms that they, like the Mechoopda, might find acceptable. Given its limited resource base, the mountain frontier could only breed competition. Consequently, race relations in the foothills swiftly degenerated into a dreary annual round of spring and summer Indian raids on livestock, sometimes accompanied by violence, and almost always followed by savage counterattacks mounted by hastily assembled white posses.[32]

Indeed, with their lives and property even more insecure than Bidwell's at Rancho Chico, whites along the Butte-Tehama frontier soon came to insist upon "total solutions" to the so-called "Indian problem." In effect, this meant either the complete removal of the Indians to distant reservations or, as many whites advocated, their total extermination. Led by draconian avengers like Manoah Pence, settlers waged a war of bloody reprisals against even the slightest Indian "depredation." Pence, a Butte County supervisor who owned a large ranch just below Yankee Hill, once hanged a Konkow chief for stealing cattle, even though he had successfully retrieved

---

[32] Given Bidwell's friendship with the Mechoopda and the Mechoopda's rivalry with the mountain Maidu, it is important to keep in mind that the fundamental racial division between Indians and whites was blurred by significant interracial alliances and intraracial tensions. Indeed, in her analysis of white attitudes toward the mountain Maidu, Michele Shover posits a schism between pro-Indian miners and valley ranchers like Bidwell who suspected the argonauts of aiding and abetting Maidu thefts of horses and cattle. However, while it is true that the mining districts included a considerable number of "squawmen" who cohabited with Indian women and interacted easily with members of the mountain tribes, only a minority of the gold seekers could be described as pro-Indian. Throughout the 1850s and 1860s, miners suffered from frequent Indian attacks and responded with the same violence employed by local ranchers. Thus, in describing the white community, it is probably much more accurate to dispense with occupational labels and to simply speak instead of a large anti-Indian majority confronted by small and divided groups of settlers who somehow managed to maintain close commercial and social ties with the various Indian tribes. In the end, most Butte county ranchers and miners remained united in their desire to see the Indian problem eliminated. See Shover, "The Politics of the 1859 Kibbe Campaign," pp. 9–10, 14–19.

his missing livestock. Two years later, in 1853, Pence was elected captain of a seven-man posse that pursued a band of "Tiger" Indians suspected of taking livestock from one of his neighbors. Pence and his company seized one straggler, hanged him, and then overtook another, whom they left dead in the road. Finally, they came upon a camp of about thirty "warriors" armed only with bows. In the ensuing slaughter, twenty-five Indians were killed while Pence's unit suffered just one man wounded.[33]

Despite this and other similar successes, Pence's reputation as an "Indian tamer" was soon eclipsed by the martial exploits of Robert A. Anderson and Harmon "Hi" Good, the most celebrated Indian fighters of the Butte-Tehama frontier. As neighbors residing along Deer Creek, Anderson and Good became the nemeses of the Mill Creek Indians and played a leading role in the virtual extermination of the Yahi tribe by 1871.[34] Beginning in 1857 when they first rode together, Anderson and Good led at least ten campaigns against the Mill Creeks that culminated in the infamous Three Knolls Massacre of August 1865.[35] Along with killing scores of Native Americans, Good and Anderson could boast that they never lost a single man to their enemies. Indeed, their campaigns offer ample proof to support the famous contention of historian Hubert Howe Bancroft that, with the possible exception of the Modoc conflict in the 1870s, California "cannot grace her annals with a single Indian war bordering on respectability. It can boast, however, a hundred or two of as brutal butcherings, on the part of our honest miners and brave pioneers, as any area of equal extent in our republic." As Bancroft correctly observed, and as events in Butte and Tehama demonstrated, the California Gold Rush was not merely a grand and adventurous search for wealth and opportunity, "It was one of the last human hunts of civilization, and the basest and most brutal of them all."[36]

For their part, both Anderson and Good were blunt in their advocacy of genocide, though they differed in some important details. Anderson, who as late as 1909 could still publicly refer to dead Indians as "good Indians,"

---

[33] Wells and Chambers, pp. 138, 170, 174, 217–18, 251–52.
[34] Regarding the grim fate of the Yahi and other Yana groups, see Waterman, "The Yana Indians," pp. 35–70; Theodora Kroeber, *Ishi*, pp. 56–100; Curtin, *Creation Myths*, pp. 517–20; Powers, *Tribes of California*, pp. 275–81; Anne Hunt, "The Allen and Jones Massacres and the Extermination of the Yana," Shasta County Historical Society *Covered Wagon* (1960), pp. 40–52.
[35] Steve Schoonover, "The Three Knolls Massacre," *Dogtown Territorial Quarterly*, 15 (Fall 1993), pp. 4–5, 48–50, 54–55.
[36] Hubert Howe Bancroft, *History of California*, 7 (San Francisco: The History Company, 1890), pp. 474, 477.

recalled that "I had often argued with Good regarding the disposition of the Indians. He believed in killing every man or well-grown boy, but in leaving the women unmolested in their mountain retreats. It was plain to me that we must also get rid of the women."[37] A crude and violent man, Anderson seemed to thrill in the hunt of Indians which he placed on a par with other blood sports. During one campaign, Anderson warned his men that the Mill Creeks "are just like ground squirrels, hard to kill."[38] On at least two other occasions, Anderson actually interrupted his pursuit of the Mill Creeks in order to shoot grizzly bears that his party chanced upon. Both times, Anderson and his companions killed four of the animals and left their carcasses on the ground to rot, but only after making sure to carefully remove their gallbladders, "which we knew we could sell to Chinamen."[39]

Despite his reluctance to kill females, Good was actually more sanguinary than Anderson. Sim Moak, who campaigned at least twice with the duo, recalled that Good always exercised the right of the captain to claim all scalps taken in combat. Though Anderson was selected captain as often as was Good, the latter still managed to amass a personal collection of forty scalps which he suspended from a poplar tree outside his cabin. Before returning home from the Three Knolls Massacre in 1865, Good collected the scalps cut from the slain and stitched them together on a leather string that he attached to his belt. Dangling all the way down to his ankle, the grisly trophies attested to Good's prowess and helped secure his reputation as, in Moak's admiring words, "one of California's Grand Men."[40] Moak's reverential assessment was echoed by Dan Delaney, another of Good's companions. Like Moak, Delaney praised Good as "one of God's noble men," whose "self-sacrificing defense of the lives of the people in Butte and Tehama ... against the ravages and depredations of savage Indians, will form a bright page in the history of these counties...."[41]

Such sentiments were not restricted to Good's followers or to those

---

[37] Robert A. Anderson, *Fighting the Mill Creeks: Being a Personal Account of Campaigns Against Indians of the Northern Sierras* (Chico: Chico Record Press, 1909), pp. 24, 80.

[38] Sim Moak, *The Last of the Mill Creeks and Early Life in Northern California* (Chico: n.p., 1923), p. 26.

[39] Anderson, *Fighting the Mill Creeks*, pp. 12–13, 64–66.

[40] Moak, *The Last of the Mill Creeks*, pp. 23, 31, 33.

[41] Dan Delaney, "The Adventures of Captain Hi Good," Chico *Northern Enterprise*, 7 June 1872. Few Native Americans would have agreed with Delaney or Moak. John Clark, the grandson of a Konkow chief, recalled in 1918 that most of Butte County's Indian hunters "were nothing less than assassins" and that "Hi Good, in particular, was held in the most bitter hatred among the Indians." Interestingly, however, Clark remembered Anderson as "a just man, albeit an Indian-fighter." See Mansfield, p. 210.

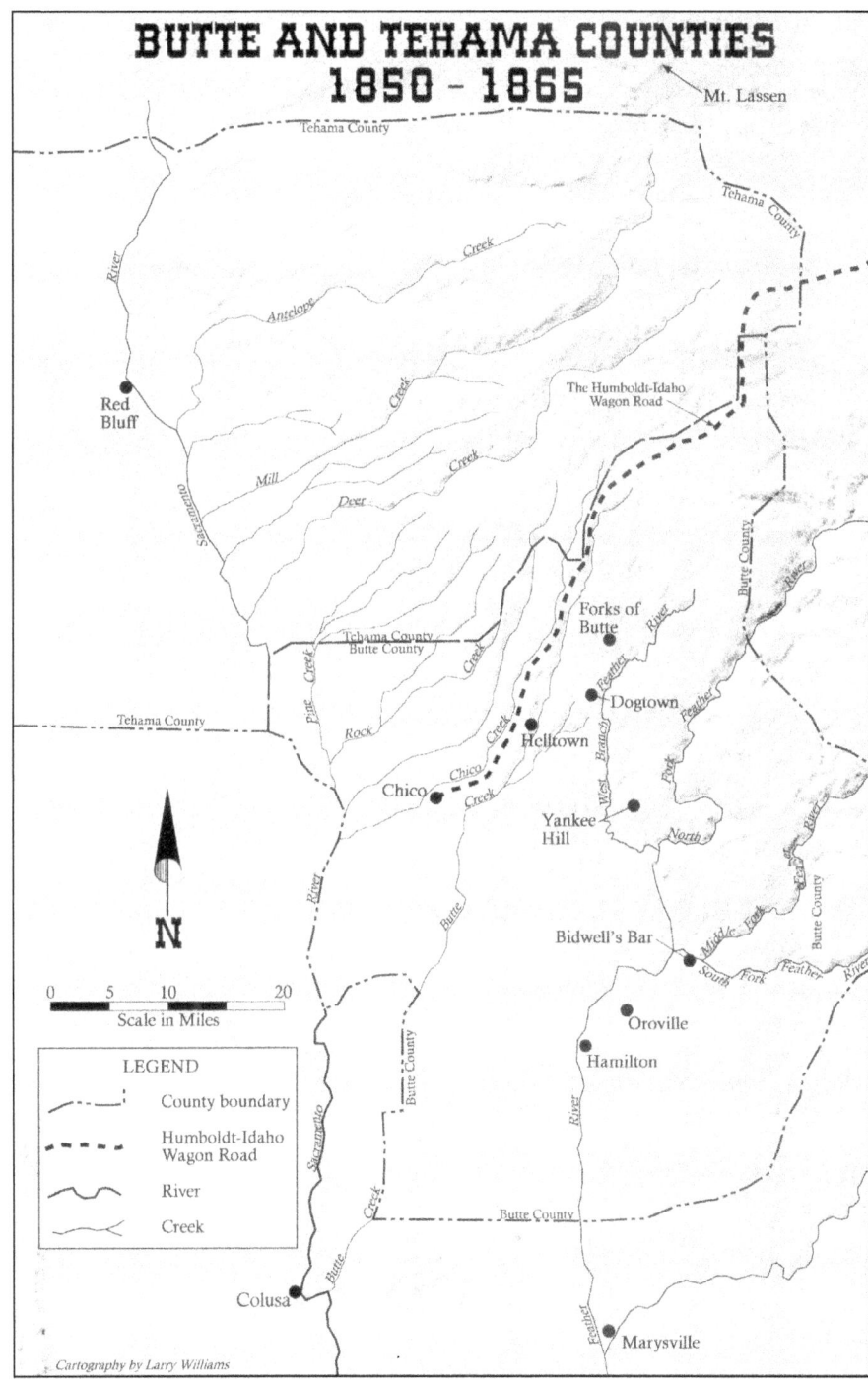

settlers living in the foothills. Good's popularity extended throughout Butte and Tehama counties and reached upwards into the most "respectable" elements of local society. When Good was finally murdered in 1870 at the age of thirty-four by an Indian boy employed on his ranch, Chico *Northern Enterprise* editor W. N. DeHaven eulogized him as "one of the most distinguished personages in this section. Years since, when the savages brought mourning into several of our families by murder and rapine, Mr. Good gallantly led the little band who avenged the wrongs inflicted and ever since he has been a terror to the savage and a protector to homes of hundreds of defenseless women and children. He was a noble-hearted man...."[42]

Remarkably, Good's reputation actually grew with the passage of time so that, by the end of the century, his exploits had become the stuff of popular fiction. In 1897, public schoolteacher Halbert Sauber, the scion of a pioneer Tehama County family, published the first of two sensationalized accounts of Good's campaigns. In Sauber's fanciful reconstruction of local lore, Good assumed almost superhuman strength, stealth, and courage. On one nighttime pursuit of the Mill Creeks, for instance, Sauber describes Good advancing swiftly but silently through the forests "like a weird phantom . . . possessed of supernatural sight" and guided by "unerring instinct." As Sauber informed his readers, Good was nothing less than "the Boone of the Sierra," a fierce and determined frontier warrior "whose whole life seemed devoted to the destruction of the renegades and the protection of the helpless."[43]

Like Good, Robert Anderson too received his share of adulation but, since he was not destined to die young at the hands of an Indian, failed to achieve Good's legendary status. Instead, Anderson went on to become a prosperous rancher near Chico and a prominent member of the local Republican party who, in 1890, would be elected to the first of two terms as Butte County's sheriff.[44]

The high esteem with which Anderson and Good were regarded indicates clearly the degree to which racism, hatred, and fear came to govern white attitudes towards Indians. With their remarkable capacity to ignore

---

[42] Chico *Northern Enterprise*, 14 May 1870.

[43] Sauber, "Hi Good," pp. 122–27. See also Halbert H. Sauber, *Adventures of a Tenderfoot* (San Francisco: The Whitaker and Ray Company, 1899), pp. 62–65, 113–30. Sauber, who graduated from Chico State Normal School in 1893, went on to become a high school principal and, in 1922, won election to a four-year term as Tehama County superintendent of schools.

[44] Mansfield, pp. 634–37; Chico *Enterprise*, 14 November 1890, 19 November 1892.

the fundamental fact that they were trespassers on Indian land, most whites held few qualms about resorting to genocidal policies, especially after Mill Creek "depredations" came to include the kidnapping and murder of women and children. This ominous turn of events began in Butte County in June 1862 with the brutal killing of three children belonging to the Hickok family near their home on Rock Creek, just north of Rancho Chico. With similar atrocities recurring each summer for the next four years, the general level of violence escalated dramatically during the 1860s.[45]

It was in this context that Good and Anderson emerged as local heroes and that the white community embraced the opinions expressed so frankly in 1866 by attorney A. W. Bishop, owner and editor of the Chico *Courant*. Following a Mill Creek attack on "friendly" Maidu at Big Meadows in Plumas County, the enraged newspaperman recommended that "The whites of that vicinity should turn out en masse and slay every Mill Creek Indian in the country.... Let the whites and the Big Meadows join forces and exterminate the Mill Creeks."[46] Fed up with "Indian troubles," Bishop declared that "it has become a question of extermination now. The man who takes a prisoner should himself be shot. It is a mercy to the red devils to exterminate them, and a saving of many white lives. Treaties are played out—there is only one kind of treaty that is effective—cold lead."[47]

Such was the political climate in which John Bidwell had to maneuver in order to ensure the safety of Rancho Chico and the village of Mikchopdo, a dangerous and hostile environment in which, as local pioneer Jacob Patterson remembered, many whites held Indian life "in little more regard than the life of an animal."[48] As the target of Indian raids himself, Bidwell shared the concerns of his white neighbors and had an obvious interest in seeing the Indian question resolved once and for all. He could not, however, endorse extermination as a solution. Not only was such a strategy morally reprehensible, it also posed an immediate and grave danger to Mikchopdo, whose residents had every reason to fear the unleashing of genocidal passions among the whites who surrounded them.

Bidwell and the Mechoopda were well aware that their relationship was deeply resented by whites who envied Bidwell's access to Indian trade

---

[45]Mansfield, pp. 196–225.
[46]Chico *Courant*, 11 August 1866.
[47]Ibid., 28 July 1866. For a similar opinion in another local paper, see the Red Bluff *Independent*, 1 July 1862.
[48]Mansfield, p.193.

and labor. In 1864, while assessing the potential for renewed violence in Butte County, Capt. James Van Voast of the United States Army reported that "It appears that some farmers and other persons who do not make use of the Indians in the cultivation of the land, look with more or less jealousy upon those who employ such labor, believing that it brings with it such advantages that to compete with it is impossible. This is therefore one of the causes of jealousy which exists against the Valley Indians, and one reason why some desire their removal. . . ."[49]

Van Voast also noted another and more ominous cause of resentment against Bidwell and the Mechoopda. ". . . [A]s is always the case on the borders of civilization where Indians are found, there occurs annually to a greater or less extent Indian robberies and depredations committed by a few wandering, irresponsible, and bad Indians. Such is the case in a section of country about Chico. It is supposed by many, or at least they pretend to believe, that when these thefts and robberies are committed that the Valley Indians are cognizant of the matter, and are in some way connected with the guilty parties. This, therefore, is another cause of jealousy against the Valley Indians, and often the spirit of revenge leads to the murder of the innocent for the crimes of the guilty. It is the old and repeated story, and of necessity often yet to be repeated."[50]

Prominent among those who habitually suspected the guilt of the Mechoopda was George H. Crosette, the influential editor of the Butte *Record*. In his memoirs composed in 1880, Crosette complained that "the Indians came and went as they desired" on Rancho Chico. "Often the mountain Indians came down into the valley. They found a ready welcome at the Bidwell rancheria and being received and welcomed under the protection of Bidwell they felt safe in fomenting strife and laying their plans for depredations. This was well known to many of the settlers. They saw no reason why an elysium should be granted to the outlaws." Adding to the settlers' frustration was Bidwell's apparent indifference to their fears. While most viewed Indians as inherently untrustworthy and dangerous, "Bidwell on his part thought all Indians good."[51]

The widespread perception of Bidwell as an indulgent landlord who

---

[49]Van Voast to Col. Richard C. Drum, 24 June 1864, *The War of the Rebellion: A Compilation of the Official Records of the Union and Confederate Armies*, Series 1, Vol. 50 (Washington, D.C.: Government Printing Office, 1897), Part 2, pp. 874–76.

[50]Ibid.

[51]Crosette, "From the Memoirs of George H. Crosette, Written in 1880," Chico *Enterprise*, 25 January 1918.

provided a safe haven for Indian intrigue placed Rancho Chico's proprietor in an increasingly delicate political position. Following his failed attempts to promote the Rancho Chico model in 1850 and 1852, Bidwell appears to have adopted a more modest stance in regard to the shaping of Indian affairs in California. This retreat was no doubt hastened by the embarrassing pair of setbacks he suffered in the county supervisorial and state senate campaigns of 1855. With his political fortunes at a low ebb, Bidwell was in no position to be assertive on the volatile Indian issue.

Instead, Bidwell compromised with the harsh realities that confronted him. Abandoning his hope of duplicating the Rancho Chico model throughout California, Bidwell confined himself to the protection of the Mechoopda and the preservation of Mikchopdo, which became his paramount objectives. As for the rest of California's Native Americans, only two options had ever been politically viable. Compelled by circumstances to finally choose between the stark alternatives of extermination or removal, Bidwell opted for the lesser evil. Thus, between 1855 and 1863, Bidwell abandoned his earlier opposition to the federal reservation system and gradually became one of its most forceful advocates.

By endorsing the removal of recalcitrant tribes to federal reservations, Bidwell sought to achieve a very complex set of goals. First of all, he wanted to establish a permanent peace without resorting to genocide. Second, by taking a strong and popular stand in solidarity with his neighbors and against their common foes, the mountain Maidu and Yana, Bidwell aimed to revive his sagging political stock and, at the same time, undermine white antipathy toward the Mechoopda. Finally, Bidwell hoped to steer Indian policy away from the caprice of violent locals and to place it securely in the more distant and restrained hands of the United States Army and the federal Office of Indian Affairs.

Towards these sometimes conflicting ends, Bidwell resumed his close cooperation with state and federal Indian officials beginning in 1859. That spring, renewed Indian raids sent Hi Good and Robert Anderson back on the hunt as members of a ten-man posse headed by John Breckenridge. For two months, supported by $3,000 of privately donated funds, they ranged over the entire sweep of Yana territory and beyond, from the Pit River to Butte Creek, killing at least twenty-nine Indians and taking a dozen women and children as prisoners.[52]

---

[52]Anderson, *Fighting the Mill Creeks*, pp. 9–43; Shover, "Politics of the 1859 Kibbe Campaign," pp. 16, 25.

John Bidwell does not appear to have contributed to this local effort, however, choosing instead to support a large-scale military expedition organized and led by Adjutant General William Kibbe, the head of the California state militia. Dividing his forces into three separate commands, Kibbe launched his grand offensive in mid-August and remained in the field for the next four months, campaigning not only against the Maidu and Yana but the Pit River (Achumawi), Hat Creek (Atsugewi), and Paiute tribes residing to the north and east of Mt. Lassen. As they fanned out from Red Bluff, Kibbe's troops encountered some heavy fighting in the Pit River region but failed completely to locate the elusive Yana. Meanwhile, the Maidu offered little resistance and Kibbe's men quickly rounded up approximately 300 Konkows, Kimshews, and "Tigers" who were, along with some 900 other captives, eventually sent to the Round Valley and Mendocino reservations.[53]

Though he did not participate directly in the fighting, Bidwell helped provision Kibbe's troops by advancing over $1,500 worth of food, clothing, ammunition, and services to the state militia between August 22 and December 14.[54] Whether he felt he got his money's worth is highly debatable, however. Despite the fairly quiet removal of 300 troublesome mountain Maidu, Bidwell could not have been fully satisfied with the results of Kibbe's campaign. The 200 Native Americans killed along the Pit River testified eloquently to the fact that the critical line between exile and extermination was not only thin, but easily dissolved in the face of Indian resistance. Furthermore, as the pivotal events of 1862 and 1863 would soon demonstrate, Bidwell's cooperation with the militia did nothing to allay his neighbors' suspicion of the Mechoopda.

The shocking murders of the Hickok children in June 1862 capped a violent month of Yana and Mill Creek raids in Tehama and Butte counties that also claimed the lives of three white men near Chico. Outraged citizens had already gathered at Forks of Butte to demand retribution, and now similar assemblies were convened near Red Bluff and, on June

---

[53] William C. Kibbe, *Report of the Expedition Against the Indians in the Northern Part of this State* (Sacramento: State Printer, 1860); Crowder, "Eventful Yesterdays," Chico *Enterprise*, 16 and 17 January 1918; Steve Schoonover, "Kibbe's Campaign," *Dogtown Territorial Quarterly*, 5 (Winter 1994), pp. 10–11, 44–49.

[54] Among the important services Bidwell provided was the hiring of teams and teamsters, along with bearers of military dispatches. He also allowed Kibbe to use Rancho Chico as a headquarters during the early stages of the campaign, and then as a collecting point for Maidu prisoners of war. See U.S. Senate, 53rd Congress, 2nd Session, *Executive Document 84*, Vol. 4, 20 April 1894, pp. 8, 65–66; Shover, "Politics of the 1859 Kibbe Campaign," pp. 24–25, 32.

26, in Chico. At the Chico meeting, which took place right after the funeral of the two Hickok girls and before Frank Hickok's body had been recovered, "excitement ran high" and "some very radical and fiery speeches were made advocating the killing of every Indian that could be found in the valley and hills."[55] Sharing in their anger but hoping to deflect attention away from the Mechoopda, Bidwell donated fifty dollars to assist the stricken family and put up one hundred more as a reward for the recovery of Frank Hickok, "dead or alive."[56] As Bidwell undoubtedly anticipated, most of his money ended up in the pockets of Hi Good, whom the citizens' meeting hired to pursue the Mill Creeks. Leading a small party into the hills, Good retrieved young Hickok's body and returned it to Chico for burial alongside those of his sisters.

Meanwhile, Bidwell and the cooler heads in the community worked to prevent a local bloodbath by appealing to Governor Leland Stanford for state military intervention. Rather than call out the militia, however, Stanford relayed their petition to U.S. Army General George Wright at the San Francisco Presidio, where Bidwell journeyed to meet personally with the commander on July 18. Wright immediately ordered cavalry units from Fort Crook and Fort Humboldt into the field but, unfortunately, they moved too slowly and troops did not begin to arrive at Red Bluff until August.[57]

The army's tardy response led impatient settlers to once again call upon the services of Hi Good. According to Robert Anderson, ". . . the feeling against the Indians was so bitter that it was proposed to make a general clean-up, even of the friendly Indians, of which there were camps at Bidwell's, at [James] Keefer's [on Rock Creek], and at the [Frederick] Phillips place on Pine Creek; but Mr. Hickok, the bereaved father, forbade this being done on his behalf, and, of course, at such a time, his wishes were respected."[58]

A less sentimental factor was also at work, however, to spare the "friendly Indians." On July 22, Hi Good issued a public appeal to the "Citizens of Butte and Tehama Counties," requesting funds so that he could "carry out my plans to punish the incarnate fiends" who had committed "the Rock Creek Massacre" and previous murders. Good promised that, "if

---

[55]Crowder, "Eventful Yesterdays," Chico *Enterprise*, 17 and 19 January 1918.
[56]Sacramento *Union*, 2 July 1862.
[57]JB to Leland Stanford, 19 July 1862, Indian War Papers of the Adjutant General, California State Archives, item 619; *War of the Rebellion*, 50, Part 1, pp. 1162–63; Part 2, pp. 27–28, 46.
[58]Anderson, *Fighting the Mill Creeks*, p. 55.

sustained," he would "pursue the inhuman foe ... until the stolen scalps are returned, and the guilty are exterminated." Authorizing Dr. Willard Pratt to take up the collection in Butte County, Good raised $356 from thirty-four Butte contributors. Heading the list with the two largest donations were James Keefer and John Bidwell who, respectively, made contributions of forty and one hundred dollars.[59]

Needless to say, Good did not attack the Indians at Keefer's ranch or Rancho Chico. Instead, he directed his efforts against the suspect Mill Creeks, whom he pursued for the next two months, despite his failure to obtain an official militia commission from Governor Stanford. Fighting several engagements in the canyons of Deer, Mill, and Antelope creeks, Good's sixteen-man posse killed at least twenty-one Indians and collected twenty-four prisoners before they finally ran out of funds.[60]

The first of two such devil's bargains, Bidwell's backing of Hi Good marked the ethical low point of his life, a compromise that graphically illustrated the moral precariousness of the middle ground he was trying to occupy. Ironically, it occurred just two months prior to one of Bidwell's more noble acts: his decision in October to open the gates of Rancho Chico and provide shelter to some of the same mountain Maidu who had once raided his estate.

At the end of September 1862, all 350 Konkow and Atsugewi living at Round Valley fled the reservation where they had been confined for the past three years. Driven out by disease, food shortages, and the massacre in August of twenty-four Wailaki Indians by local homesteaders, the refugees headed back toward the Sacramento Valley. Knowing that "if the Indians returned to their old homes they would all be killed," George Hanson, the federal Indian superintendent for northern California, desperately wrote to Bidwell asking him to provide a temporary refuge on Rancho Chico. Bidwell quickly agreed, allowing the Indians to establish a camp on the Sacramento River at Bidwell's Landing. Under the supervision of Hanson's assistant J. F. Eddy, the Konkow and Atsugewi supported themselves by fishing, gathering acorns, and hiring themselves out as farm laborers to local ranchers at one dollar per day. They also received nearly $2,000 worth of flour, beef, and other provisions advanced to the federal government by Bidwell between October 1862 and June 1863.

---

[59] Butte *Record*, 26 July 1862; Oroville *Union*, 11 October 1862.
[60] Red Bluff *Beacon*, 7 and 21 August 1862; Oroville *Union*, 16 August and 11 October 1862; Good to Adj. Gen. William Kibbe, 13 July and 8 August 1862, Indian War Papers, items 607 and 608.

Though they made it safely through the winter and following spring, the Round Valley refugees had unwittingly returned to a Butte County that would soon become more violent than ever before, and far more dangerous than the place they had just left behind.[61]

Hostilities commenced early in 1863 with the hanging at Helltown of five Nimshew Maidu suspected of stealing an ox. When a white sheepherder above Pence's ranch was shot and wounded in retaliation, Bidwell decided to intervene personally and, in early March, led his third and last Indian foray. With a company of twenty men, Bidwell rode off in pursuit but apparently came back empty-handed.[62] Nevertheless, things remained quiet until July, when an explosive series of events brought Butte County's Indian wars to a dramatic and tragic climax.

On July 12, an Indian raiding party consisting of about ten men attacked and wounded a white man near Forks of Butte and killed two or three "domesticated squaws." Moving south toward Dogtown and Pence's ranch, they struck three more times over the next two days, injuring another two whites and killing two more, including a young child. Finally, on July 15, the raiders came upon rancher Samuel Lewis's three young children as they walked home from school. Killing the eldest, eleven-year-old James, the Indians seized his sister Thankful, aged nine, and brother John, aged six. Taking the children back north toward Chico, four of the Indians paused briefly to beat John to death when he failed to keep pace with the fast moving group. Later that evening, a terrified Thankful Lewis made a daring and successful escape down Chico Creek canyon. Like the murders of the Hickok children the year before, the story Thankful Lewis had to tell electrified a white community that was already thoroughly alarmed.[63]

Retributions followed quickly and indiscriminately. State militia Captain H. B. Hunt of the Oroville Guards immediately took the field and seized three innocent Maidu employed at a butcher shop. Despite the protests of their employer, Hunt executed all three. Oroville *Union* editor Thomas Wells cheered him on and said of the Guards "May unbounded

---

[61]James Short to George Hanson, 25 September 1862, *War of the Rebellion*, 50, Part 2, pp. 163–64; Hanson to Bidwell, 28 October 1862, JB-CSUC, b. 1, f. 8; Hanson to William P. Dole, U.S. Commissioner of Indian Affairs, 17 June 1863, *Letters Received*, pp. 246–47; Augustus G. Tassin, "The Con-Cow Indians," *Overland Monthly*, 4 (July 1884), pp. 10–12.

[62]Butte *Record*, 7 March 1863.

[63]A. Thankful [Lewis] Carson, *Captured by the Mill Creek Indians* (Chico: n.p., 1915); Schoonover, "Captured by the Mill Creek Indians," pp. 10–11, 45; Mansfield, pp. 200–16; Wells and Chambers, p. 220.

success attend them, and [may] they never take one male prisoner." Making his intentions quite clear, Wells listed the crimes and victims of the July raid and then pointedly asked, "What will those say to this catalogue of outrages, who are opposed to killing off these 'devils of the forest'?"[64]

Fueled by such rhetoric, a virtual "open season" on Indians took effect in Butte County by the end of July. In the terrible last week of that month, an angry mob of citizens descended on Yankee Hill where a large number of Maidu had assembled under the protection of Michael Wells, the justice of the peace for Concow Township. For over two hours, Wells pleaded the innocence of the Maidu and finally convinced the mob to back down, but only after they had selected four alleged "bad Indians" for execution. The condemned were granted an opportunity to flee for their lives, but only two managed to get away.[65]

Next it was John Bidwell's turn to face an armed mob, this one led by Samuel Lewis, the grieving father of the murdered children. Arriving in Chico intent upon revenge, Lewis and several of his neighbors seized two Indian suspects in town, tied them to trees, and shot them to death. Then, joined by local townspeople, they marched to Rancho Chico and confronted Bidwell on his doorstep. For half an hour, Bidwell protested on behalf of the Mechoopda and the other Indians residing on his property.[66]

Though he turned the crowd away, Bidwell was not able to prevent the subsequent murder of five of the Konkow refugees camped at the Landing. The victims—three boys, a woman, and a ten-year-old girl—had been hired out as laborers on the ranch of former state senator Isaac Allen, who employed the boys on his threshing crew. On July 27, while returning home to Rancho Chico, the Konkows were seized and killed "in open day light," despite the fact that they bore visibly displayed safe conduct passes issued to them by Allen and Indian agent Eddy.[67]

Meanwhile, that very same day, a mass meeting of white settlers convened at Pence's ranch to determine a final solution to Butte County's Indian troubles. Fearing a popular call for mass slaughter, Bidwell and Eddy had telegraphed Superintendent Hanson in San Francisco on

---

[64] Oroville *Union*, 25 July 1863.
[65] Butte *Record*, 25 July 1863; Wells and Chambers, pp. 164, 219–20, 304; Tassin, "The Con-Cow Indians," pp. 12–14; Mansfield, pp. 209–10.
[66] JB-91, pp. 14–15; Moak, *Last of the Mill Creeks*, p. 14; Carson, *Captured by the Mill Creek Indians*, p. 15.
[67] JB to John P. Usher, Secretary of the Interior, 4 December 1863, *Letters Received*, p. 719; J. F. Eddy to George Hanson, 30 July 1863, *Letters Received*, p. 285.

July 25, urging his "immediate presence." Traveling by steamboat, railroad, and stagecoach, Hanson managed to reach Chico by 10:00 P.M. the following day. Arriving at the Pence ranch meeting with Bidwell at his side, Hanson "found about 300 of the most infuriated men I ever met." Once again Bidwell proclaimed the innocence of the Mechoopda before a hostile audience. As George Crosette recalled, "Hot words flew back and forth and the [settlers'] spokesman finally shook his fist in Bidwell's face and said 'shut your mouth. If you open it again in defense of those outlaws, I'll strike you.'" Hanson's reception was not much better. Urging caution, the superintendent asked that efforts be made to identify the perpetrators of the July raid and to demand justice from their tribes. His appeal was angrily swept aside with Bidwell's, however, and the assembled settlers went on to adopt six resolutions requiring "the removal of every Indian" from Butte County "to some distant reservation." The Indians were granted a grace period of thirty days during which they were to surrender themselves and be collected for evacuation. Those "found in this county after the expiration of thirty days will be killed at sight," and "any Indians who shall, after their removal, return to this county, will do so at the risk of their lives." The settlers made it quite clear that their resolutions applied to the Mechoopda, stating "That what we mean by 'every Indian' is, those that are roaming in our mountains, as well as those upon the ranches in the valleys." To carry out their plans, citizens' committees were appointed to notify the tribes and to collect funds for financing the removal effort.[68]

While a mass roundup looked unavoidable, Bidwell and Hanson had no intention of leaving the removal in the hands of the irate locals, nor did they plan to permit the eviction of the Mechoopda. As soon as they returned to Chico, Hanson telegraphed General Wright requesting troops to supervise the roundup and to protect Rancho Chico. This time, the army responded promptly. On July 31, Captain Augustus Starr arrived with forty troops and, on the following day, established Camp Bidwell on the grounds of Rancho Chico. Additional troops continued to arrive throughout the next month following a meeting in Sacramento between Bidwell and Wright in mid-August. Thus, by the time Lt. Col. Ambrose

---

[68]Hanson to William P. Dole, 4 August 1863, *Letters Received*, pp. 283–84; Crosette, "Memoirs," Chico *Enterprise*, 25 January 1918; Butte *Record*, 1 August 1863; Moak, *Last of the Mill Creeks*, p. 14; Mansfield, pp. 208–09; Oroville *Union*, 1 August 1863.

Hooker assumed command on August 26, Camp Bidwell contained over 100 enlisted men.[69]

Though Bidwell would always insist that the troops were brought in solely to control secessionist sentiment during the Civil War, it was clear that the army's primary concerns were to guard the Mechoopda while supervising the removal of the mountain Maidu tribes. As a delegation of Bidwell's neighbors soon discovered when they came to meet with the officers in charge, "Bidwell's Indians were not going to the reservation, and . . . we had better keep quiet or some of us might get a chance to pack sand or live in the guard house."[70]

Even with the presence of troops, however, the situation at Rancho Chico remained dangerous. At a second public meeting held at Pence's ranch on August 28, the settlers reaffirmed their pledge to remove all Native Americans from the county and voted to raise a volunteer force of 150 men to deal with those who resisted. The delegates threatened that those Indians who "will not consent to . . . removal shall be exterminated," and they vowed to "effectively drive the Indians from our borders, or make the last redskin bite the chaparral of his native hills in his death struggle." The following day, Superintendent Hanson warned Bidwell that "the lives of your Indians are not only in danger, but also the life and property of yourself."[71]

Still, the restraining influence of the army put a halt to the atrocities of the previous month. By the end of August, 435 Maidu had been taken from the mountains by the settlers and forwarded to Bidwell's Landing without major incident. There, they came under the jurisdiction of the army and the Office of Indian Affairs, which had jointly agreed to relocate them to Round Valley, along with the refugees who had fled that reservation the previous fall. Altogether, a total of somewhere between 600 and 800 Indians would be sent from Chico to Round Valley over the course of the next two months.[72]

The mass evacuation over California's "Trail of Tears" began momentously on September 4, 1863, when Capt. Augustus Starr and twenty-three

---

[70]John H. Guill in Chico *Chronicle*, 16 July 1886. See also Richard C. Drum to Capt. Augustus Starr, 1 August 1863, *War of the Rebellion*, 50, Part 1, p. 550; Butte *Record,* 19 and 20 July 1886; Crosette, "Memoirs," Chico *Enterprise*, 26 January 1918.

[71]Mansfield, pp. 212–13; Hanson to JB, 29 August 1863, JB-CSUC, b. 2, f. 2.

[72]Butte *Record,* 19 September 1863; Hanson to JB, 19 September 1863, JB-CSUC, b. 2, f. 3; Hanson to William P. Dole, 21 and 22 August 1863, *Letters Received*, pp. 297–301; JB to John P. Usher, 4 December 1863, *Letters Received*, p. 719.

mounted troops set out from Rancho Chico with a wagon train carrying 461 Native American men, women, and children. Having been appointed a Special Indian Agent by Superintendent Hanson, John Bidwell had played a key role in preparing the train by hiring a physician and advancing food, teams, and wagons to federal authorities.[73] Unfortunately, despite careful planning, the slow and difficult one-hundred-mile journey across the valley and through the Coast Ranges took a heavy toll on the Indians, many of whom were ill when the trip began. Thirty-two died en route, and Starr had to leave another 150 old and sick behind with sub-agent Eddy at Mountain House, the half-way point where wagons gave way to pack animals and foot travel. Following the loss of two more who escaped from the train, Starr finally arrived in Round Valley on September 18 with just 277 Indians. For even this greatly reduced number however, Starr discovered Round Valley poorly prepared. As Hanson had tried to warn his superiors, not enough food was available, and housing facilities were either not ready or poorly constructed. Nevertheless, there was simply no other place for the Indians to go.[74]

Though far reaching, the removal of 1863 did not end all conflict in Butte County. Some Maidu apparently escaped the net, and roving bands of "Mill Creeks" remained at large in Yahi territory, no doubt reinforced by refugees fleeing the extermination campaigns waged against the Yana in Shasta and Tehama counties the following summer.[75] Thus, minor outbreaks of Indian trouble continued to occur sporadically throughout 1864 and the first half of 1865. Several citizens' posses went out in apparently fruitless pursuits, as did the soldiers garrisoned at Camp Bidwell, who made a sweeping tour through Maidu territory in August 1864 and another across Yana country the following April. Though guided on the latter patrol by Hi Good, the army returned with nothing to show for its efforts.[76]

As the Civil War came to a close, the lingering Mill Creek threat increasingly worried John Bidwell, who clearly wanted it resolved while federal troops remained available. Addressing Indian and military matters with enhanced authority following his appointment as Brigadier Gen-

---

[73]Hanson to William P. Dole, 8 September 1863, *Letters Received*, p. 305; Hanson to JB, 9 September 1863, JB-CSUC, b. 2, f. 3; JB to John P. Usher, 4 December 1863, *Letters Received*, p. 719.
[74]Hill, pp. 38–42; Bleyhl, "Camp Bidwell," pp. 4–5; Pamela A. Conners, *The Chico to Round Valley Trail of Tears* (Willows, CA: Mendocino National Forest, 1993).
[75]Hunt, "The Allen and Jones Massacres and the Extermination of the Yana," pp. 40–52.
[76]Butte *Union Record*, 5 and 12 March 1864; B.B. Brown to JB, 26 and 29 February 1864, JB-CSUC, b. 2, f. 8; Bleyhl, "Camp Bidwell," pp. 7–12.

eral, Bidwell pressed the army to continue pursuing the Mill Creeks, whom he had come to see as a "hostile, roving, murderous band" that constantly disrupted the peace and frustrated efforts to establish friendly relations between whites and other Indians. Viewing the Mill Creeks as utterly incorrigible, Bidwell urged that they be banished to a remote reservation on the coast or to "some island," presumably Alcatraz or one of the Channel Islands off southern California.[77]

Still, Bidwell stopped short of endorsing extermination, the fate that ultimately befell the Mill Creeks. In June 1865, just two months after the end of the Civil War, U.S. troops abandoned Camp Bidwell and left Butte County. Then, on August 7, less than two months later, Indian raiders suddenly struck Robert Workman's ranch in Concow Valley above Yankee Hill. Having left to labor on his mining claim, Workman escaped the Indians who severely injured his wife after killing and mutilating his sister-in-law and a male field hand.[78] Like the murders of the Hickok and Lewis children, the Workman Massacre enflamed the passions of the white community and imperiled the lives of every Native American in the county. Again, the Mechoopda fell under instant suspicion and a posse mustered at Concow set out towards Rancho Chico, only to be intercepted by Robert Anderson, who convinced its members to go after the Mill Creeks instead.[79]

While it is not clear whether Anderson was already working with him, it appears that, in the absence of regular troops to better control the situation, John Bidwell was once again willing to buy protection for the Mechoopda and to appease public opinion by joining forces with Anderson and Good against the Mill Creeks. Assembling a seventeen-man force that included the volunteers from Concow, Good and Anderson advanced into Yahi territory, carrying forty pounds of bacon and forty pounds of crackers given to them by Bidwell.[80] Two days later, at dawn on August 14, 1865, they ambushed and routed between twenty-five and fifty Indians encamped at Three Knolls on upper Mill Creek, killing nine and wounding several others. Apparently satisfied with the result, Anderson and Good led their company

---

[77] JB to John P. Usher, 4 December 1863, *Letters Received*, p. 719; JB to Major Gen. Irvin McDowell, 6 May 1865, *War of the Rebellion*, 50, Part 2, pp. 1221–22.
[78] Moak, *Last of the Mill Creeks*, p. 18; Wells and Chambers, p. 221; Mansfield, pp. 218–20.
[79] Anderson, *Fighting the Mill Creeks*, pp. 71–73; Crowder, "Eventful Yesterdays," 21 January 1918.
[80] Daniel Klauberg, "A Trip in the Mountains and Fight with the Indians," Oroville *Union Record*, 26 August 1865.

back home after stopping once to execute a wounded and uncooperative female prisoner.[81]

When word reached Chico that the expedition had emerged from the hills, Bidwell immediately dispatched two of his teams to greet the returning members of the Concow posse and carry them back into town, where they were treated to dinner at the Chico Hotel. Bidwell instructed the proprietor, Ira Wetherby, to charge the entire meal to his account, and then had his teams convey the Concow men homeward as far as Pence's ranch. Though it is not clear whether he was acting as a private citizen or in his official capacity as Brigadier General, Bidwell's largess gave a very public stamp of approval to the recently concluded campaign.[82]

A major turning point in local Indian warfare, the Three Knolls Massacre put the Mill Creeks on the defensive, and they never again attacked a white person in Butte County. For the next five years they remained on the run, until Tehama County rancher Norman Kingsley and three armed companions tracked most of them to a cave on Mill Creek and annihilated nearly every last one, leaving just a handful of survivors that included the ill-starred Ishi.[83]

By then, the concerns of John Bidwell and the white residents of Butte County had already shifted beyond the Sierra to the Paiute wars raging in the newly admitted state of Nevada. The completion of the Humboldt Wagon Road and its extension into southern Idaho brought the communal interests of Chico into direct conflict with the Paiutes, who almost immediately began attacking white travelers and settlers along the road in the spring of 1865. For nearly a year, Paiute raids against civilians alternated with bloody punitive campaigns waged by California and Nevada volunteers commanded by U.S. Army officers. Operating out of several remote garrisons scattered throughout the deserts of northwestern Nevada and northeastern California, the army finally resolved on a sustained wintertime offensive that effectively ended the Paiute threat.[84] As Lt. Col. Ambrose Hooker bluntly informed Bidwell in a confidential letter from his new post at Fort Churchill, "I have inaugurated a *winter* campaign

---

[81] Anderson, *Fighting the Mill Creeks*, pp. 73–83; Moak, *Last of the Mill Creeks*, pp. 19–23; Klauberg, "A Trip in the Mountains and Fight with the Indians"; Schoonover, "The Three Knolls Massacre," pp. 4–5, 48–50, 54–55.

[82] Moak, *Last of the Mill Creeks*, p. 24; Klauberg, "A Trip in the Mountains and Fight with the Indians."

[83] Waterman, "The Yana Indians," p. 59; Theodora Kroeber, *Ishi*, pp. 84–85.

[84] Sessions S. Wheeler, *Nevada's Black Rock Desert* (Caldwell, Idaho: Caxton Printers, 1985), pp. 86–136.

against the hostile savages, and arranged that the troops from the different stations in Northern Nevada shall cooperate with each other in exterminating or subjugating them (the first in my opinion preferable)...."[85]

What Bidwell thought of Hooker's preference is not known, but his correspondence with Hooker's superiors remained limited to repeated requests for increased army surveillance over the Humboldt and Idaho roads. As Brigadier General in the state militia, and later as a member of Congress, Bidwell sent a steady stream of letters and telegrams to generals Wright and Irvin McDowell. These missives included petitions from settlers demanding protection, as well as Bidwell's own recommendations that army posts be located at strategic sites on or near the Idaho route. These appeals were not ignored. McDowell and Wright eventually established six garrisons between Susanville and Boise, including Fort Bidwell in the Surprise Valley region of northeastern California.[86]

Beyond regular policing by U.S. troops, Bidwell apparently planned to deal with the Paiutes by confining at least a few of them to reservations. Thus, while serving in Congress, he continued to argue for the federal policy he had once rejected. In May 1866, Bidwell introduced legislation designed to resolve the still festering conflicts between whites and Native Americans in Round Valley. Bidwell's proposal, which unfortunately did not pass, would have authorized the federal government to buy out all private property and homestead claims in the valley, thereby enlarging the reservation while, at the same time, entirely removing whites from the area. With an expanded capacity and a secure environment, Bidwell hoped that Round Valley would become an effective refuge for other California Indians facing death and dispossession in their ancestral lands. The failure of his bill did not end Bidwell's efforts to promote the reservation system. In September 1867, shortly after leaving Congress, Bidwell endorsed an attempt to create a reservation on the Pit River for an estimated 2,000 Achumawi, Atsugewi, Yana, and Paiutes.[87]

---

[85]Hooker to JB, 20 January 1866, JB-CSUC, b. 3, f. 2.
[86]Wright to JB, 30 April 1864, *War of the Rebellion*, 50, Part 2, p. 833; McDowell to JB, 7 February 1865, Ibid., pp. 1129–30; JB to Wright, 27 March 1865, Ibid., pp. 1171–72; JB to Wright, 21 April 1865, Ibid., pp. 1205–06; JB to McDowell, 28 April 1865, Ibid., pp. 1214–15; JB to Wright, 17 June 1865, Ibid., pp. 1264–65; Patera, "Chico Route to Idaho," pp. 14–15.
[87]House Bill in Relation to Round Valley and Other Indian Reservations in Northern California, *Letters Received*, p. 656; Petition to Allow Establishment of a Reservation in the Northeast Corner of California, September 1867, Ibid., pp. 583–90. Regarding the situation in Round Valley, see Lynwood Carranco and Estle Beard, *Genocide and Vendetta: The Round Valley Wars of Northern California* (Norman: University of Oklahoma Press, 1981).

Meanwhile, throughout the entire turbulent and dangerous decade of the 1860s, Bidwell steadfastly pursued his Indian policy ideal on Rancho Chico, where Mikchopdo continued to flourish despite all the threats to its existence. Nevertheless, conditions did not remain static on Rancho Chico, and life began to change dramatically for the Mechoopda following Bidwell's marriage to Annie Kennedy in April 1868. Perhaps the first to feel the change was chief Luccayan's daughter Nopanny, whose life reflected the complex and evolving state of Bidwell-Mechoopda relations during the second half of the nineteenth century.[88] A single woman in her late twenties or early thirties, Nopanny had worked for many years as Bidwell's cook and head housekeeper. With her unique culinary repertoire, Nopanny lent a distinctive Maidu influence to daily life in Bidwell's old adobe, serving grasshopper meal pancakes that Bidwell apparently savored and shared with guests.[89]

Shortly after she arrived to occupy the newly completed Bidwell Mansion, Annie Bidwell encountered some unexpected resistance from Nopanny when she asked the Mechoopda housekeeper to hand over her set of keys. According to Henry Azbill, a Native American who grew up in Mikchopdo, Annie later recalled that Nopanny had refused, saying "No, me Mrs. Bidwell number one, you Mrs. Bidwell number two. You go!" Annie backed down, and Nopanny kept the keys until she died.[90]

Azbill's intriguing account is the source most frequently cited by those who insist that Nopanny was not merely a domestic servant but, in fact, was John Bidwell's first wife by Mechoopda rite.[91] However, despite this and similar tales that have become embedded in Mechoopda and antiquarian lore, the case for Bidwell's alleged miscegenation is a weak one.[92] As skep-

---

[88]"Nopanny" is Bidwell's spelling of her name, which is variously rendered in other sources as Nupani, Nopani, Napani, and Nopaney.

[89]Margaret Ramsland, "Napani, Unsung Heroine," Butte County *Bugle*, 1 March 1973; Hill, p. 29; Gray, "Reminiscences," *Sandy Gulch News*, 23 June 1938.

[90]Azbill, "Some Aspects of Mechoopda Culture," pp. 26–27.

[91]See Ibid.; Ramsland, "Napani"; Craig D. Bates to Michael Gillis, 14 December 1992, copies in authors' possession.

[92]According to Craig Bates, Curator of Ethnography at Yosemite National Park, Azbill also claimed that Bidwell and Nopanny had a son who died sometime early in childhood, and that Bidwell was involved with two other Mechoopda women, one of whom he identified as Wesumto, the mother of Amanda Wilson, who later became Annie's Bidwell's maid and the wife of chief Holi Lafonso. Some of Wilson's descendents apparently claim that she was Bidwell's daughter. Bates to Gillis, 14 December 1992. For a biography of Bidwell's alleged Indian daughter, see Craig D. Bates and Brian Bibby, "Maidu Weaver: Amanda Wilson," *American Indian Art Magazine*, 9 (Summer 1984), pp. 38–43.

tics are quick to point out, no documented evidence has ever been found to corroborate claims that Bidwell ever married or cohabited with Nopanny or any other Native American woman. While it is perhaps no surprise that John and Annie's extant papers are silent on the subject, more telling is the utter lack of comment from the many visitors who left written accounts of Rancho Chico. Casting even greater doubt on the Nopanny claims is the unusual reticence of Bidwell's numerous and vituperative political opponents. Had an intimate relationship with Nopanny existed, it is hard to imagine that Bidwell could have kept it secret or that his enemies would have forfeited the chance to brand him with the damning epithet "squawman."

Still, given Bidwell's age and circumstances prior to 1868, the possibility of a marital union with Nopanny cannot be dismissed as entirely unlikely. Marriages between white men and Indian women were common on American frontiers, where they served a number of important functions besides providing companionship. For hunters, trappers, and other frontiersmen with commercial ambitions, marriage into a local tribe provided physical protection, access to natural resources, and an exclusive clientele. Any one of these considerations might have motivated young John Bidwell, who began doing business with the Maidu three years before he finally received a federal Indian trading license from Oliver Wozencraft in 1851. By taking Nopanny as his bride, Bidwell would have been following a familiar and effective strategy for cementing his alliance with the Mechoopda.[93]

In any event, whether or not she was ever actually "Mrs. Bidwell number one," Nopanny had occupied a prominent position on Rancho Chico during Bidwell's bachelor years. Even after Annie arrived and replaced her at the mansion with a staff of Chinese cooks and Irish Catholic servant girls, Nopanny continued to wield considerable authority as "a sort of squaw high priestess."[94] In fact, despite her initial confrontation with Annie, Nopanny soon began a close collaboration with the new Mrs. Bidwell, converting to Christianity and helping Annie to carry out her Indian reform program.[95]

---

[93]Wozencraft to Luke Lea, Commissioner of Indian Affairs, 4 August 1851, *Letters Received*, p. 435. Regarding the prevalence and importance of intermarriage and cohabitation in Gold Rush California, see Hurtado, *Indian Survival*, pp. 63–65, 114, 173–76, 187, 207–08.

[94]John Rodney Gleeson, "'Lost Indians' Easily Traced," Stockton *Record*, 26 March 1911, quoted in Robert Heizer and Theodora Kroeber, *Ishi the Last Yahi: A Documentary History* (Berkeley: University of California Press, 1979), p. 77.

[95]Margaret D. Jacobs, "Resistance to Rescue: The Indians of Bahapki and Mrs. Annie E. K. Bidwell," in Elizabeth Jameson and Susan Armitage, eds., *Writing the Range: Race, Class, and Culture in the Women's West* (Norman: University of Oklahoma Press, 1997), pp. 235, 237.

A devout Presbyterian and zealous proselytizer, Annie exercised a powerful influence over her husband and his Indian tenants. Taking up the plight of the Native American as one of her chief political causes, Annie sincerely believed that the best strategy for the Indian people lay in their complete assimilation into mainstream American culture. That meant adopting western dress and customs, learning English, and most importantly, embracing Protestant Christianity. Towards these goals she dedicated her work among Rancho Chico's 250 Mechoopdas, whom she adopted as her personal flock. Directing most of her efforts towards the women and children, Annie aggressively set out to transform the residents of Mikchopdo.[96]

First, however, she transformed Mikchopdo itself. Supposedly disturbed by the loud wailing that accompanied Mechoopda mourning rites, Annie effected the removal of the village away from the creek to a new location one mile west of the Bidwell Mansion in March 1869. The rebuilt rancheria, dominated by small wood frame houses, presented a sharp contrast to its predecessor, though three traditional dwellings were put up and a new roundhouse constructed.[97]

In 1875, Annie began offering sewing lessons to the Mechoopda women and opened a school for their children. The following year, Annie won her first adult Indian male convert to Christianity and, in 1879, received an official appointment from the Presbyterian Church to preside as pastor over the Mechoopda village. The Bidwells built a chapel there in 1882 but Annie's congregation quickly outgrew the small structure. In 1886, it was replaced by a larger edifice erected near the mansion in a walnut grove. Nine years later, the Bidwells moved the church back to the village and added a vestibule, belfry, and tower. The church buildings doubled as Annie's "Industrial Mission School" until the Bidwells succeeded in convincing the Chico public school system to accept Indian children in 1890.[98]

Annie's reform agenda received explicit endorsement from her husband in 1885 when John Bidwell issued his "Proclamation of Rules Made for Rancho Chico Indians." These included strict Sabbath observance,

---

[96] For a careful and generally favorable assessment of Annie Bidwell's career as an Indian reformer, see Valerie S. Mathes, "Indian Philanthropy in California: Annie Bidwell and the Mechoopda Indians," *Arizona and the West*, 25 (Summer 1983), pp. 153–166. For a more recent and much more critical evaluation, see Jacobs, "Resistance to Rescue," pp. 230–51.
[97] Hill, pp. 56–58; Hunt, pp. 138, 390–391; Azbill, "Bahapki," p. 57; Mathes, pp. 155–156.
[98] Hill, pp. 68–71; Hunt, pp. 390–392; Annie Bidwell, "The Mechoopdas," pp. 206–208; Mathes, "Indian Philanthropy," pp. 159–160.

mandatory church attendance, and a complete ban on alcohol consumption. For the first time, apparently, Bidwell also interfered directly in village governance by installing Holi Lafonso as chief in place of the rightful heir "Mike," "whom dissipation robbed of his birthright." Unlike Mike, all Indians, including the chief, were required to be "industrious," and had the right to work for Bidwell or any other nearby employer whenever work was available. However, in order to prevent Mikchopdo from becoming a haven for transients, Bidwell threatened to permanently ban any Indians who left the village to seek employment outside the local area.[99] Still, despite the increase in restrictions effected by the new code, it is apparent that Bidwell continued to exercise some restraint over his wife's reforming zeal and to display a measure of the tolerance that had once dominated his relationship with the Mechoopda.

The village roundhouse, for example, remained standing as long as Bidwell remained alive, and *Kuksu* spirit dances and sweat ceremonies continued to be performed there. Henry Azbill recalled that Bidwell "realized that these ceremonies were the backbone of the Indian people and he encouraged them to retain it [the roundhouse]. Otherwise he would never have allowed the sweathouse to be built when he moved them to where they are now.... But of course Mrs. Bidwell didn't have that sort of idea." Indeed, Annie believed "this use of the sweathouse was a heathen form of worship" and she "always did try to get [the Mechoopda] to do away with the sweathouse after she built the church." Nevertheless, she did not get her way until after the deaths of John Bidwell in 1900 and chief Holi Lafonso in 1906. Mechoopda tradition dictated that the roundhouse be demolished after the chief's death and that a new structure be built. It was a sign of Annie's ultimate success, therefore, when only the first half of this custom was observed. When the roundhouse was finally razed in February 1907, nothing rose in its stead. A new era in Bidwell-Mechoopda relations had begun.[100]

---

[99] Hill, pp. 73–74; Gleeson, "'Lost Indians' Easily Traced," p. 77.

[100] Hill, pp. 79–80; Azbill, "Some Aspects," pp. 22–25; Mathes, "Indian Philanthropy," p. 160; Craig D. Bates and Brian Bibby, "Collecting Among the Chico Maidu: The Stewart Culin Collection at the Brooklyn Museum," *American Indian Art Magazine*, 8 (Autumn 1983), p. 48. For the subsequent history of the Mechoopda village, see Anne H. Currie, "Bidwell Rancheria," *California Historical Society Quarterly*, 36 (December 1957), pp. 313–325; and Currie, "Bidwell Rancheria," Butte County Historical Society *Diggin's*, 4 (Fall 1960), pp. 4–8.

## *Remarks on the California Indians*

### Overall relations with Indians

Now with the Indians I never had any trouble. Some men could not go long among the Indians without having trouble with them.... I seem to have a sort of intuitive insight into the Indian character.... But there is one thing I can say, I have never justified any abuse or wrong treatment of the Indian. I had for them a regard, a sympathy—knowing that their lands had always been taken from them without any compensation. I have never justified the cruel treatment of them which I know very frequently was unjustifiable.[1]

### Encounter with Indian raiders after Sierra Crossing, 1841

...I came to the camp which I had left the previous morning. The party had gone, but not where they said they would go; for they had taken the same trail I had followed, into the canon [canyon], and had gone up the south side, which they had found so steep that many of the poor animals could not climb it and had to be left. When I arrived the Indians were cutting the horses to pieces and carrying off the meat. My situation, alone among strange Indians killing our poor horses, was by no means comfortable. Afterward we found that these Indians were always at war with the Californians. They were known as the Horse Thief Indians, and lived chiefly on horse flesh; they had been in the habit of raiding the ranches even to the very coast, driving away horses by the hundreds into the mountains to eat. That night after dark I overtook the party in camp.[2]

### Indian wages in Mexican California, 1841

You can employ any number of Indians by giving them a lump of Beef every week, and paying them about one dollar for same time.[3]

The wages of white men are about $25 per month, Mechanics get $3 per day. Indians hired from 4 to 6$ per month but they are very indolent.[4]

### Condition of the Mission Indians in 1841

Missions—Missions are nearly all broken up; but few pretend to preach or teach, and those, that still remain, are fast declining—whether the missions have ever been the means of doing the Indians much good, I cannot say—but I do not like this manner of civilizing the Indians, who still live in filth and dirt, in mud houses without floors or fireplaces. Whenever an offense is committed, like stealing, they are plunged into the prison houses, laden with irons and made to

---
[1] JB-91, pp. 17–19.
[2] Bidwell, "First Emigrant Train to California," pp. 128–29.
[3] *Journey*, p. 38.        [4] Ibid., p. 42.

toll a bell every minute in the night, this was the case at St. Joseph when I was there on the 16th of November last.

Missions, that have ceased their labors, have distributed the cattle and horses among the Indians, after reserving a large share for the priests, etc. And artful men have taken advantage of the times and purchased the cattle and horses from the Indians for a small quantity of ardent spirits or some trifling articles leaving them destitute—all the missions were once very rich in cattle etc. but they are now very much reduced, there are about 22 missions in Upper California. The mission of San Gubler [Gabriel] had 100,000 head of cattle, that of St. Joseph [Jose] 18,000, that of Santa Clara 30,000, many others had intermediate numbers—these missions likewise had horses, sheep etc. in proportion.[5]

### Indians speaking Russian at Fort Ross

My first occupation in California was at Bodega and Fort Ross, taking charge with Robert T. Ridley, who preceded me there, of the Russian property still remaining at those points, and removing the same as fast as practicable to Sutter's settlement at Sacramento, whither everything was eventually transferred. All the Indians on the coast at that time in the vicinity of the Fort, spoke the Russian language, the Spanish [language] gradually superseding it.[6]

### Origins and use of the term "digger Indians"

Most people speak of California Indians as "diggers." That is a misnomer. There was no such tribe in California. The name digger does not apply to one Indian any more than to another. There was a tribe in the Rocky Mtns who were always friendly to the whites. They with other tribes lived large on what was called the Camas root which grew wild in the mountains. It was customary with them to dig up quantities of it and store it away for the winter. The neighboring tribes called them what meant in the Indian language "diggers," because they dug in the ground so much. Then the trappers who went among the hostile tribes, marrying among them at times, got to calling these Indians "diggers." They used to call the Californians diggers, but there was no reason for it. The California Indian perhaps was not as intellectual perhaps as some other tribes, yet they were more intelligent than one would suppose who is not acquainted with them. In our little village my wife has done so much toward civilizing them. Their friendship for her is really remarkable, and would be for any one who is kind to them.[7]

. . . ignorant people began to call all Indians "diggers." Surely no intelligent man should now call Indians "diggers." In the first place there is no such tribe as a "digger" tribe, and there never has been. It is reported that Major Powell

---
[5]Ibid., pp. 40–41.
[6]Bidwell, "Early California Reminiscences" (February 1904), p. 184.
[7]JB-91, pp. 21–22.

said that no such tribe has ever been found. Prof. Henshaw suggested to me that the name "digger" may have started from some Indian name or word of similar sound. We never ought to call Indians "diggers" because the name is untrue, as well as unkind, and because it implies reproach or degradation. The Indians in California, many of them at least, are well behaved. Most of them can read and write and some are Christianized.[8]

### INDIAN KILLERS FROM OREGON AIDED BY SUTTER

In 1843 a company came by land from Oregon, composed partly of the immigration which had gone to Oregon the year before from across the plains. This party had with it men, two at least, who might be styled "Indian killers," and on the way they frequently fired at Indians seen in the distance. The better portion of the company tried to dissuade them from this, but with only partial success.

On arriving at Red Bluff, the company camped early in the day, intending to remain during the night, but left hastily owing to this event. One of the Indian-shooters, seeing an Indian on the opposite bank of the river, swam over, carrying a butcher knife in his mouth. The Indian allowed him to approach till he was very near, but at last ran. The man with the knife threw a stone and crippled him, and then killed him with the knife. The company, fearing the Indians, concluded to travel on.

After a few miles an Indian was seen following them—no doubt out of curiosity, not having heard of the killing. One of the Indian-killers, seeing the opportunity, hid in the brush till the Indian came up, and then shot him. . . .

The day after, the company camped and reached water at a place now called Colusa. The excitement among the Indians preceded them, and a considerable number of them were gathered on the opposite bank of the river. When the horses were led down to water, in an almost famished condition, the Indians fired at them with arrows. No one was hurt or hit. For some unaccountable reason, when the party reached Sutter's establishment a few days later and reported what happened, Sutter came to the conclusion that the Indians where the arrows had been shot across the river were hostile and should be punished. . . .

I heard the story of the emigrants. Some thought the Indians where the shooting was done were hostile, but most of them, and the best informed among them, did not blame the Indians in view of the previous occurrences.

Sutter, however, concluded to punish them, and went with fifty men and attacked the Indians at daylight. His forces were divided, part having gone above and crossed on the Indian bridge, so that they would be ready simultaneously at daybreak to begin the attack. The Indians fled and mostly jumped into the river, where they were fired on and great numbers of them killed. After that time the

---

[8] *Pioneers*, p. 24.

Indians in that part of the valley were never known to be hostile to the whites. I do not believe there was sufficient reason for considering them hostile before. At any rate I remember of no hostile act on their part, having gone among them almost alone a year after, twice at least, and once, with only five men with me, camped all night near a village without molestation.[9]

### Encounter with Colusa Indians
### while locating Larkin Rancho Grant, 1844

We saw deserted Indian villages, deserted because the springs had dried up. (I should mention the fact that the summer of 1844 was a very dry one, because the previous winter had been almost rainless.) We were in our saddles by daylight, making our way toward the high mountains that lay to the southwest, feeling sure of finding water there. About 10 or 11 o'clock in the morning, from the top of a ridge, we saw a glorious sight, a large, clear, flowing stream. This we reached as soon as possible and our nearly famished horses plunged into the middle of it. We saw at the same time a great number of Indians, men, women, and children in a state of flight, running and screaming. Unsaddling our horses under a wide-spreading oak, they began to eat the wild oats, which were abundant. We were absolutely obliged to give them rest.

In less than an hour, the Indians that we had seen fleeing from us, the men I mean, were seen coming towards us from many directions. The Indian with me became alarmed. I had a gun, but he had none. By certain signs, I gave them to understand that they must not approach us, but still large numbers had come very near. We saddled our horses, jaded as they were, so as to be ready if obliged to retreat.

Four or five of the Indian chiefs, or head men, came nearer than the others. They understood no Spanish, but my Indian, who came originally from the country between Sonoma and Clear Lake, was able to understand a few words of a very old Indian. They asked what we came for. They said they had not seen white men before....

I should mention that before, at our first talks with the Indians, I tried to present each of the chiefs with a few beads and fancy cotton handkerchiefs (things I always carried for that purpose when among them).[10]

I remember one instance where self-possession served me: Thos. O. Larkin asked me to find a good tract of land that he could ask a grant of from the Mexican government for his children. I started out to explore. I struck across the mountains to the west of the Sacramento valley, thinking there might be valleys of good land there. The season was very warm and we traveled in the night. All the Indian villages were deserted because the springs were dried up. We did not

---
[9]Bidwell, "Early California Reminiscences" (March 1904), pp. 285–87.
[10]Bidwell, "Early California Reminiscences" (April 1904), pp. 377–78.

reach water until late the next day, and there on the banks of the stream, it seemed as if all the Indians in the country had congregated. They all went off when they saw us. We had to stop there, as our horses were very tired, and we had to turn them out to grass. After giving them water, we could see the Indians approaching us, and they were too numerous to make it comfortable. I had but one Indian with me and he could not speak the language of the others. He was very much frightened, but I had to keep cool and calm. I saw there was danger but I had to pretend that I was very brave. I found an old Indian who could understand a few words of the language of my man. He told us that the Indians intended to kill us. I told my Indian to say to them that if they attempted to do anything wrong, I would kill every one of them. Then they had a great talk; wanted to know how I would kill them. (They had never seen a white man before.) I told them I had come into the mountains to kill grizzly bears; furthermore that I had killed a bear down in the valley, and fortunately I carried the feet along. I pointed to them, and they became alarmed. They had great dread of grizzly bears, thinking they were a kind of powerful and bad omen against which they were helpless. I managed to make them understand that I thought they were very good Indians, and would not kill them unless it was necessary. I had some beads and a few fancy things which I gave to the chief, and they became friendly. I passed 17 temporary villages. It seemed to me the place was alive with Indians. As I came to the different villages, I found that they had a place all prepared for me, with plenty of provisions, thinking that I had come there for that purpose, but I managed to tell them I was not hungry. I did eat some of a sort of powder they made of Juniper berries, for they were very sweet. At one place, I selected a spot for the night and told the Indians that they must not come near me that night, as I intended to sleep up there. Not one of them approached. The next day we came to the last village on the stream. That was the only place I had ever seen trees cut down by stone axes. They had cut the trees down to build their large sweat houses. They questioned me a good deal, but all I had to do was to point to the bear's foot. They believed that the bears were bad people.[11]

    Let me say here that the Indian village on the present site of Colusa was one of the largest in the valley, but there were many other villages on both sides of the river in the vicinity of the Colusa village, and both above and below it. I believe I can truthfully say that the number of Indians within ten miles of that point amounted to not less than 1,500 or 2,000. They lived largely on fish, mostly salmon, which they caught in great numbers in the river. For the purpose of fishing they had formed a fish-weir at a point some miles above Colusa, by using willow poles, the ends of which were rounded and sharpened and then in some manner made

---
[11]JB-91, pp. 15–16.

to penetrate the sandy bottom to a depth sufficient to resist the force of the current. By the use of cross-sticks lashed with grapevine, the structure formed a bridge not less than eight or ten feet wide, for men to pass and repass upon. At this point the river was very wide and the bottom very sandy, and the water was perhaps not more than four or five feet deep.[12]

At noon we came to the largest of all the permanent villages. There the Indians had built a large dance-house in the usual Indian style, using long poles for rafters, and were finishing the roof, the house being circular in form, by covering with earth in the usual way.

Here for the first and last time in my life I saw that the Indians had procured poles for the rafters of the house by cutting down cottonwood and willow trees with stone axes, leaving the stumps a mass of bruised woody fibers resembling well worn brooms. The stone axes bruised rather than cut.[13]

### Trappers kill Colusa Indians

On my return to Sutter's Fort and describing the country seen and the streams of the Coastal Range Mountains, the trappers believed that it was a good country in which to trap beaver. A man named Jacob Myers raised a company of twenty or more and went to trap the beaver.

The first thing they did, however, was to become alarmed at the number of Indians, and, considering them hostile, without proper cause, made war on them and killed a great number. I asked why they shot the Indians who were so friendly to me, and he said that they wore white feathers in their head-dresses or caps, and that they made a great noise, and that he considered these a sign of hostility. He said he had seen an Indian with a white feather and had shot him. I told him they ran and screamed and showed white feathers when I was there, but no one showed any signs of hostility. I was sorry he felt obliged to kill them. They caught some beaver, but not many on account of the Indians.[14]

### Indian helps Bidwell cross Sacramento River

Crossing Antelope Creek, and following the trail of the Oregon party, we came to the Sacramento river opposite the present site of Red Bluff. Here the company had crossed the river and were encamped on the opposite bank. They had no wagons, simply pack animals. The stream at that time was considerably swollen, deep, swift, and cold. With simply a small hatchet, scarcely larger than a tomahawk, I set about making a raft to cross, which was no easy task to construct of a dry willow brush and such dead sticks as we could secure with our means.

At last it was completed, being sufficient merely to hold me up above water;

---

[12]Bidwell, "Early California Reminiscences" (March 1904), p. 286.
[13]Bidwell, "Early California Reminiscences" (April 1904), pp. 378–79.
[14]Ibid., p. 379.

however, to secure a dry passage if possible, a second story was built on it, consisting of dry fine brush, tied securely. In size it resembled somewhat a small load of hay. Fearing I could not manage it alone, I persuaded a wild Indian to get on with me. He consented to go with great reluctance, but a few beads and a cotton handkerchief were so tempting he could not resist. The only things we could get to propel the raft were willow poles, and none of them long enough to touch the bottom when we got into the stream; so we had to use them as paddles. We were high and dry when we started, but the displacement of the water by the brush was so little, and the material became so quickly waterlogged, that the raft was soon under water. The swift current carried us so rapidly down that it was with difficulty we got over at all, but we finally got across one-and-a-half or two miles below. The most of the time we were up to our arms in cold water, and only knew by the brush under our feet that we were on the raft at all. If men ever labored for their lives we did.[15]

### Colusa Indian Sweathouse

The sweat-house was a large house where they all congregated to take their baths, something after the style of a Russian bath. It was large enough to hold all the Indians in the village. It was made of poles, covered over with earth, with a large pole at the tipe [sic]. In the center a great fire was built, so hot, that almost the moment you were in, you would be in a rain of perspiration. After being thoroughly warmed, the Indians would throw themselves upon the frozen ground and lie there for half an hour. Then [they] would put their clothes on and be all ready for a hard days work. The Indians advised a man named [Robert] Ridley (my predecessor at Bodega) to try the sweat-house, saying that it would cure his rheumatism. We both tried it. It did him some good perhaps, but he afterwards caught cold.[16]

### First Encounters with Butte County Maidu

When I came to survey this and other Ranchos in this part of California, the Indians were almost as wild as deer and perfectly naked, save the women, who always wore a sort of apron of tule of varying length and width, fastened to a belt or to a handle thrust under the belt: I have never seen a woman, no matter how untidy or degraded not thus clothed, which recalls [African explorer] Mungo Park's assertion that in all his travels he had never received a rude answer from a woman showing that among the most savage, woman's sense of refinement is greater than that of a man.

When I began surveying, not having enough white men, I had to use Indians. In clearing brush and brambles it became necessary to furnish them some-

---
[15] Bidwell, "Early California Reminiscences" (February 1904), p. 188.
[16] JB-91, pp. 16–17.

thing in the way of clothing including shoes, pantaloons, and shirts; these were often discarded when they were not at work. In fact it was not uncommon for the men when the weather was not cold, to take them off as soon as they were done work, carry them home to their village, and in the morning bring them back in their hands, and put them on to resume work. And for many years afterwards it was customary for them in stormy weather to carry their shoes in their hands to and from work, wearing them only while at work under shelter—as in mill or barn.

But soon they learned to wear the clothes all the time, even slept in them, until worn out. At the same time they became quite skillful in the use of soap and water to cleanse such things as were made of cotton goods. They also became skillful—both men and women—in converting calico and other cotton goods into garments. It was a wonder to me how soon the women would have skirts after receiving a piece of calico, and how soon the men would be wearing pantaloons after receiving cloth that could be used for such purpose. [They would] get paid Saturday night in goods, and by Monday morning have pantaloons and shirts made, and really credible imitations. Still there were many peculiarities about the wild Indians. One was, that if he had a choice of receiving payment in clothing, or material of which to make it, or [glass] beads, he would often choose the latter, no matter what the state of the weather. This trait had its counterpart in some of the Mexicans, especially that class which had some indications of mixed origin: for instance, if these people, who were generally poor, had an opportunity to choose something useful or a peculiar expensive ornament, worn around the hat, called 'toquillo' (to-keel-yo) made of silk, silver or gold thread, they would choose the ornament for the hat, or strings to tie their leggings of like value, though they might be almost naked. These ornaments frequently cost from ten to twenty dollars.

Whenever we had work to do the Indians were employed, and at first paid entirely in clothing, food and beads. They would take almost all their wages in beads. They were great gamblers with certain kinds of sticks [bone gaming pieces], which they concealed in their hands under dried piles of grass, tossing the grass about while they chanted wildly and exchanged the sticks from hand to hand, suddenly ceasing, when the guesser must instantly indicate in which hand he thinks the prize.[17]

### BIDWELL SAVES INDIAN MINERS FROM WILLIAM DICKEY'S VIGILANTE "JUSTICE"

The Indians very soon learned that there was value in the gold. While I was gone to wash a panful of earth I left an Indian to wash another panful. When I went back I spoke to him but received no reply. When he was compelled to speak,

---

[17] Annie E.K. Bidwell, *Rancho Chico Indians* (Bidwell Mansion Association, 1987), pp. 4–7.

I found he had his mouth filled with gold. My Indian boy reported he had seen some of [the] other Indians with gold. Mr. Dickey was for shooting them right away. I said "No, I'll settle that." I asked the Indians if they had any gold. They brought some in. I gave them a handful of sugar and they gave me their gold. They liked the exchange and gave up cheerfully all the gold they had for sugar.[18]

EXCERPTS FROM BIDWELL'S UNSUCCESSFUL INDIAN BILL, 1850

*Voting rights for Indians*

Sec. 1. The Court of Sessions of each county in this State shall make an order dividing the County into not less than two, nor more than ten districts; in each of which district shall be elected by the qualified electors of county officers, and the male Indians of the district over the age of eighteen years and natives of California, a Justice of the Peace for Indians, whose duty it shall be to hear and determine in a summary manner all suits and matters in controversy which may be brought before him, wherein an Indian is a party, except where otherwise provided in this act....

Sec. 4. Inspectors of Elections under this act, shall be appointed by the Court of Sessions of each County, and shall discharge the same duties as inspectors of County elections, and shall also procure one or more interpreters to be at the polls during the election, who shall ask every indian who is entitled to vote, whom he prefers for Justice for the Indians the ensuing year, and his vote shall be recorded for the person he prefers....

*Indians to retain village sites and hunting, fishing, gathering, and pasturing rights*

Sec. 5. Proprietors and persons in possession of lands, on which indians are residing, shall permit such indians and their descendants, peaceably to reside on such lands unmolested; and no person shall molest such indians in the pursuit of their usual avocations of hunting, fishing, gathering seeds and acorns for the maintenance of themselves and families. Provided however that the proprietors or white persons in possession of such lands, may apply to the Justice of the Peace for Indians of the district in which the land or most of it lies, to set off to such Indians a certain amount of lands in a body, including the site of their village, if they so prefer it. In such case it shall be the duty of the Justice to set-off a certain amount of land in a body not less than one acre to each indian properly residing on such tract of land; but in no case shall indians be forced to abandon their village sites where they have lived from time immemorial....

Sec. 16. Indians residing on lands held by a white person, by virtue of a Spanish or Mexican grant or lands belonging to the United States and in possession of white persons, and who may desire to remain and be employed by the person

---

[18]JB-91, p. 56.

so holding such lands, shall not be molested by any other person, and shall be entitled to have suitable lands so held to cultivate for the maintenance of their families, and necessary and suitable fire-wood and fencing timber and the pasturage for horses and cattle, not exceeding for a village, an average of one horse and one cow for each Indian: Provided, indians so residing upon lands, shall be free to go and work for, or be employed by any other person than the owner of or claimant of the land, if they shall desire to do so.

## *Bidwell's version of Indian indenture*

Sec. 8. If any person shall obtain a minor indian from the parents or relatives of such indian, to keep and raise; the person so obtaining such indian shall go before the Justice of the Peace for Indians of the District, with such parents or relatives, and the Justice may question them relative to the matter, and being satisfied that no compulsory means have been used to obtain the child, shall enter on record in a book to be by him kept for that purpose, the name, sex and probable age of the child, and the name (if any) given by the person taking the child, and shall give to such persons a certificate, authorizing him or her to have the care, custody, control and earnings of such minor, until he or she shall attain the age of majority.

Sec. 9. Every male indian shall be deemed to have attained his majority at the age of eighteen years, and every female indian at the age of fifteen years.

Sec. 10. Every person having minor indians in employ, care, custody or control, shall, if desirous of keeping them, within six months after the passage of this act, go before the Justice of the Peace for Indians of the District, and have the sex and name and probable age recorded as provided in section eight of this act, and the Justice shall insure and deliver a certificate to the applicant as is therein provided.

Sec. 11. Any person who shall obtain a minor indian in the manner provided in Sections eight and ten of this act; shall be entitled to the care, custody, control, earnings and labor of such indian until he or she shall attain the age of majority.

Sec. 12. Any person having an indian in his care or control by virtue of the eighth, tenth and eleventh sections of this act, and who shall neglect to comfortably clothe and suitably feed such indian, or shall inhumanely or barbarously treat him or her, shall on conviction thereof be fined not less than fifty nor more than two hundred dollars, and such Indian may return to his or her parents or relatives, or the Justice may place the indian in the care of some suitable person, who shall be liable to the same duties towards the Indian and entitled to the same rights over him or her, as had the person from whom he or she was taken, prior to the removal. . . .

Sec. 38. When minor Indians attain their majority, and desire to leave the persons who have had the care of them, such persons shall pay to such Indians in useful property the value of fifty dollars if a female, and one hundred dollars if a male, and two good suits of clothes.

*Indian contractual obligations*
Sec. 24. Indians shall not be held liable on any contract made with a white person, except where the same shall have been made with the consent of the Justice of the Peace for Indians of the District, or by him certified. . . .

Sec. 36 . . . It shall be the duty of every person desirous of employing indian labor in the mines, to go before the Justice of the Peace for Indians of the District where such Indians reside, with the Indians or their chief, and have the contract ratified: but no such justice shall authenticate any contract against the will of the Indians, . . .

*Restrictions on sales of Indian land to whites*
Sec. 37. No person shall purchase or exchange other lands, for any lands belonging to or set off to Indians except by consent of the Court of Sessions, to the entire satisfaction of the Indians.[19]

RESERVATIONS IMPRACTICAL IN CALIFORNIA

Comm. of Indian Affairs [Luke Lea]　　　　　　　　　　Feb. 6th 1852
Dear Sir,

Enclosed you will find the letter of Maj. Bidwell of Ca. is relative to our Indians & their management. Maj. "B" is an "old Californian" and understands the Indians of that Country better than any man in it, & as you will discover from his letter to me (intended to be private) a humane, honest & conscientious man.

From these years of observation I am satisfied that his opinions & suggestions in regards to the Indians are just & true & I hope you may find in his remarks the germ of a system, which when adopted will work for the benefit, as Maj. B. remarks, of both the whites & Indians.

　　　　　　　　　　　　　　　　Respectfully,
　　　　　　　　　　　　　　　　Jos W. McCorkle

　　　　　　　　　　　　　　　　　　Chico 20 Dec. 1851
Dear Mac [Congressman Joseph W. McCorkle]

I ought to have written to you much earlier,—indeed it was my intention to have done so—and I have no excuse to plead—but a kind of submission to procrastination, which is the thief of time.

Our own circumstances in California, are, as you well know by actual experience and observation, in very many respects *peculiar*. There are bands and tribes of Indians on the whole frontiers of the Atlantic States—But here we have not

---

[19]John Bidwell, "An Act Relative to the Protection, Punishment and Government of Indians," 16 March 1850, California State Senate, Old Bill File, California State Archives.

only Indians on our *frontiers*, but all *among* us, *around* us, *with* us—hardly a farm house—a kitchen without them. And where is the line to be drawn between those who are domesticated, and the frontier savages? Nowhere—it cannot be found. Our white population pervades the whole entire State and Indians are with them everywhere. The farmer no sooner settles down, that he is surrounded by them, with their families; and children will leave the villages alone to cling around his house; and if he be a humane man and treat them always consistently, they naturally and voluntarily domesticate themselves. They look up to the white man with a filial obedience to his commands, and expect from him a kind of parental protection. When he wants them to work he tells them to go into his fields—when they want food they invariably come to him—also clothing, and whatever their necessities require. And it would be cruel indeed to force these harmless creatures from the places of their ancient habitations. The system pursued by the UStates Govt. towards Indian tribes on the Atlantic side may be adapted to circumstances there—but they must learn that all Indians as well as all frontier territories are not alike—and that the same system will by no means apply here. The nature of our state is such that the Indians cannot be all collected together on one body of land reserved for them—because the valleys are already covered with a white population that cannot be disturbed—the large ones are shingled over with Spanish Grants: And these timid and defenseless beings cannot be thrown into the rugged and barren mountains with only here and there a little valley of a few acres, affording not a hundredth part of the grass required for the animals of the miners who traverse and occupy every nook, glen, corner and ravine of our almost boundless mountain regions.

The Indian Commissioners have seen so far—that they could not all be placed upon *one* reserve—and the only thing that surprises me is that men who should have been selected for their practical knowledge of Indian affairs in this country—could see no further.

When you begin to lay plans, for removing the entire Indian population to any one body of country, the impracticability, the injustice to the Indians, the expense, and the impossibility of executing such a law all become too apparent, and forbid it as cruel & impolitic. If you vary the plan, and make a number of reserves instead of one, the same objections exist with undiminished force, until you increase that number of reserves to as many as there are Indian villages in the State—then you have it exactly right—that is—*let the Indians alone*—make laws *to protect* them against the brutal treatment which is so often inflicted upon them. Let them cultivate a garden, and have a reasonable quantity of land for pasture right where they live, and work in their vicinity to obtain food & clothing &c. for whom and where they please. They are sure to cling around and shelter themselves under the protection of him who treats them best.

The UStates can enact laws for their protection and appoint an Indian Agent to be constantly employed, and always on hand, to be present at the trial and punishment of Indians when they have been accused of crime and see that they have justice done them—that punishments are not inflicted in a cruel manner. Make it a provision of the law that the Ind[ian] Agent be notified on all such occasions. In this manner chastisements would have a salutary effect. The Indians would see the reason & justice of it. Make the shooting of Indians, which has heretofore been as common as the shooting of wolves, a heavy penalty—and teach the malicious and brutal vagabonds who have shot thousands of these innocent creatures, because a horse happened to be missing, or some imaginary offense was committed, thereby destroying all the confidence the poor Indian had reposed in the white man, and thereby exposing the industrious and well disposed miner to dangers and death.

If the UStates cannot be persuaded to enact a law to protect and govern the Indians where they now are, even in our midst, they should permit our State Govt. to do it—under such restrictions as they may deem wise. In making small reservations of a few acres in the localities of their villages, or adjacent to them, no injustice could be done to any one, whether he be owner of Mexican or Spanish Grants or not; for every such title contains a provision, protecting the Indians, in the use of the land where they live, and from molestation by the Grantee in the occupation of their villages. I have to regret that such a provision was not engrafted in the law passed by the last Congress for the "settlement of land claims in California." But it is not too late now. I for one intend to donate lands for the Indians in this neighborhood—whether Congress makes such provision or not.

You will believe me candid, when I tell you that I have no other object in setting forth these views, than the real good of the Indians as well as that of the white population. I am a permanent settler—and anything that disturbs the Indians in the neighborhood affects me more or less—so it is with every citizen all over the State. I do solemnly declare that the action of the Indian Commissioners here in California is an outrage upon the citizens of the State, both the old settlers and the new comers, an abuse and an idle perversion of the spirit of the law under which they are acting, a great expense to the Govt., and has and will be productive of no benefit to the Indians, on the contrary its tendency is to injure and degrade them, and to render them pilfering vagabonds.

The Commissioners have been feeding the Indians during the summer on the beef of the Govt. at a time when they need no such assistance—and the very means too which the law promises them to enable them to move to the reserves made for them, and begin to cultivate for themselves—and this too before the

Treaties made have been ratified, by the President & Senate, or even an attempt to set them to farming.

I must close this now for want of time, but I shall address you on various subjects, and shall be very happy to see you have the honor of bring[ing] about many measures that will be for the benefit of the country. I have written this very confusedly, and it is now late in the evening.

I am very truly yours,<br>J. Bidwell

P.S. Don't fail to send the *Documents* etc. I have not time to write to Doct. [William M.] Gwin [U.S. Senator from California]—Please show him this letter if you deem proper.[20]

### 1858 DEPOSITION REGARDING INDIAN TREATY OF AUGUST 1, 1851

*Treaty negotiations*

Q When did you first come to California, and where have you resided since?
A In 1841, and have resided since in different parts of California, but principally in the Sacramento valley, and for the last seven or eight years at Chico, in the county of Butte.

Q Since your residence in California, have you or not had much intercourse or acquaintance with the California Indians; if so, with the Indians of what section of California in particular?
A I have been acquainted with the Indians all over the State to a considerable extent, and have had considerable to do with them in the southern part of the State, and still more in the Sacramento valley, and consider myself well acquainted with the Indian character of California.

Q Where were you residing during the years 1851 and 1852, and in what business were you engaged?
A I resided in Chico, and was farming.

Q Were you present at the making of a treaty by O. M. Wozencraft, as the representative of the United States, with the Mi-chop-da, Es-kuin, Holo-lu-pi, To-to-sa-nus, Chero, Bat-si, Yut-duck, and Suir-sa-un tribes or bands of Indians, on or about the first of August, 1851? If so, please, state where said treaty was made, and whether you assisted in any manner at the making of said treaty.
A I was present at the making of said treaty with said Indians; it was at my ranch; I collected the Indians together by request of Dr. Wozencraft.

---

[20]JB to Joseph W. McCorkle, 20 December 1851, enclosed in McCorkle to U.S. Commissioner of Indian Affairs Luke Lea, 6 February 1852, *Office of Indian Affairs, Letters Received, 1824–1881, California Superintendency*, RG 75, National Archives (Microfilm Publication M234, roll 32: 761–67).

Q  Please state how large were these tribes or bands with whom said treaty was made.
A  They were different sizes, but I would say they would average about a hundred—men, women, and children—to each tribe; but they were not all present.

Q  About how many were present?
A  I think there were three hundred, perhaps, or more.

Q  Were any of them Indians who lived and had their rancherias upon the ranches of white settlers in the Sacramento valley, and worked for said settlers upon said ranches?
A  Yes, sir.

Q  Had there been, previous to the making of said treaty, or was there afterwards, during the year of 1851, any "sanguinary war," or any hostilities whatsoever between said Indian tribes or bands, or between any of the Indian tribes or bands of the Sacramento valley and the whites?
A  There was not, to my knowledge.

Q  Had there been, previous to the making of said treaty, or was there afterwards, during the said year 1851, any scarcity of their usual and accustomed food among said Indians, or among any of the Indians in Sacramento valley?
A  There was no extraordinary scarcity, so as to produce want or suffering among them.

Q  What was the accustomed food of said Indians?
A  Fish, acorns, various kinds of seeds and roots, wild fowl, and sometimes game, such as deer, antelope, rabbits, &c.

Q  Did that food exist in its usual abundance in the Sacramento valley in the year 1851?
A  I think it did; I do not remember that there was any scarcity.

*Poor condition of land in proposed reservation*
Q  Was any reservation made by O. M. Wozencraft for said Indian tribes with whom said treaty was made; if so, where was it situated or provided?
A  Wozencraft located or described one [a reservation] in the treaty which he made with the Indians, embracing a long, narrow strip of country to the east of my ranch and those of Hensley and Neal, being five or six miles wide and some twenty or twenty-five miles in length, the land being principally barren and worthless.

Q  Did he require them, immediately after the making of said treaty, to remove from their former haunts or houses to said reservation, and to reside thereon, and did they so remove?

A   They did not remove there; he told them, as near as I can remember, that as soon as the treaty was ratified they were to remove there, but they were not required to remove there immediately.

## *Wozencraft's flawed plan for the Indians*

Q   Please give a concise narrative of the proceedings of Wozencraft, from the time of his arrival at your ranch, on Chico creek, until his departure therefrom, including the collection of said Indians, his talk with them, and the negotiation of said treaty.

A   Wozencraft requested me to collect the Indians together for him, which I did. I furnished him an Indian boy, some twelve years of age, who understood the Indian language well, and the English tolerably, as an interpreter; in making the treaty he promised the Indians that they should have plenty of beef to eat, and that when they removed to the reservation they should have, I think, two hundred head of cattle, and some twenty-five head of mares, I think, to raise stock from, several hundred blankets, shirts, pantaloons, &c.—I do not recollect the number; and that a person would be placed with them to teach them how to farm, &c.; he told them in the meantime they would be in my charge, and that I would furnish them with beef whenever they wanted it. The Indians asked him when they were going to get all these things, and my impression was that they understood these things to be present in the baggage wagons which belonged to the escort under Major Fitzgerald; he told them in a short time; by this Mr. Wozencraft meant in a few months or a year or two; I supposed as soon as the treaty could be ratified in Washington; but I do not think the Indians so understood it; and I mentioned the same to Dr. Wozencraft at the time, and suggested that he should speak to the Indians, through the boy, in simple concise sentences. He stated to me very promptly that he understood his duty, and was conversant with the Indian character; from what occurred immediately after I was convinced the Indians did not understand, for they commenced a great clamor for the blankets, shirts, pantaloons, &c., which he had promised them; and when they found that there were none there they left the ground without much ceremony, and started off in spite of the doctor's solicitations to remain and have a further talk. He wished the boy to call them back, but the boy could not stop them; most of them left and went away. Wozencraft had a few jackets which he intended for the chiefs, but the other Indians wanted something as well as the chiefs; there is not much difference between chiefs and other Indians in this country; the chiefs possess but little dignity; they said they wanted pantaloons and shirts, too; that was not enough to pay them for coming so far, and some of them threw the jackets down.

*Feeding the Indians*

Q   What were said Wozencraft's instructions to you in reference to the feeding of said Indians with beef, and in what manner and to what extent were they carried out by you?
A   He told me to feed the Indians with just as much beef as they wanted, and that he had made arrangements with Mr. Norris for beef, and that it would be subject to my order. Some Indian tribes came in some days afterwards, who did not get there in time to be present at the making of the treaty, and I killed some beeves for them, I cannot remember precisely, but not to exceed three or four head. After I received these instructions from Doctor Wozencraft I did not kill over three or four head of cattle.

Q   Were these three or four head all the cattle you ever killed for the Indians under those instructions?
A    They were; there was a fellow of the name Patrick O'Brien, who was in Norris's employ, who commenced killing cattle for the Indians, and did kill some; I don't know how many—there might have been six or seven head; he continued until I strongly protested against it, because I conceived it to be an injury to give the Indians beef when not employed, because they had enough of their native food. I thought it would have a tendency to make them more idle and vicious.

Q   Why did you not fully carry out said Wozencraft's instructions in regard to the feeding of said Indians with beef?
A   Doctor Wozencraft's ideas were all wrong about the Indians; he had an idea that they could be employed in the mines, and I told him there were no mines there—that it would be impossible to do it; and I only promised him that I would kill a beef when I conceived the Indians needed it. I made no further promise at the time.

Q   Did he wish you to become an Indian trader under him, and did he say anything to you in regard to there being any speculation in it, and in feeding beef to the Indians? If so, please state what he said on these subjects.
A   He did desire me to become an Indian trader, and gave me a certificate of appointment as Indian trader, to be fulfilled by the execution of a bond which I never executed, and never acted as Indian trader under that. He intimated that the Indians could be profitably employed by sending them into the mountains to dig gold; I told him it was entirely impracticable, and I never sent them.

*Effect of treaty on Indians*
Q   What was the effect of the proceedings of Wozencraft, and the feeding of

the Indians with beef, so far as it was done in your vicinity; and was it beneficial or injurious?

A   The effect of the treaty, in my opinion, was injurious—it was all injurious; the effect of the treaty was injurious, because it seemed to destroy my authority over the Indians, and no one else had any. There was not beef enough fed to them to do much injury.

Q   Did Wozencraft, while there, in his conduct and instructions to you, manifest and express a desire to have as little beef as would answer the necessities of the Indians fed to them, or the opposite wish?

A   He did not say anything about a little beef; he said give the Indians what they wanted; and he himself, while there making the treaty, was, I thought, extremely bountiful.

Q   Did not the whole of this proceeding—that is, of Wozencraft's proceeding—in your opinion, render these Indians less valuable to you as laborers on your ranch?

A   I did not cultivate much in 1851; I had a number of Indian boys constantly with me that belonged to that village [Mikchopdo]; the grown Indians did not work much for me except for a week or two in harvest, which was over at the time the treaty was made; . . . Wozencraft's proceedings rendered these Indians less valuable to me as laborers, and a greater nuisance to the community generally.

Q   Do you understand the Indian language?
A   To some extent.[21]

### BIDWELL'S EXPEDITION AGAINST THE MOUNTAIN MAIDU, 1852

I never went on an Indian killing expedition except on one occasion. The Indians came to my place and stole cattle. I had a few domesticated cattle of a better breed, bought from emigrants, and they were very valuable and of course they were easily driven off. I wanted to punish the Indians and communicated the fact to my neighbors. They were all willing to help me, but I did not want to kill. I wished to arrest them and have them punished according to law. For some time I was unable to get any one to assist me unless I would, as they expressed it, "wipe them out." Finally about a dozen men volunteered and promised to do just what I said. I waited a month perhaps before I made any move, for I wished to find out as near as possible who took the cattle. Finally two mountain Indians came down. I seized them, and locked them apart so they could not talk to

---

[21] Deposition of John Bidwell, U.S. Court of Claims, San Francisco, *Samuel Norris vs. U.S., 1858*, U.S., House of Representatives, *Documents*, 36th Congress, 2nd session, 1860, Report C.C., no. 25.

each other. Asked each one if he knew who stole the cattle, and one of them replied the Indians had, and gave me the exact names. The other did likewise, withholding only his own name. Then I said we would go and get those Indians. I thought we could surround the village at night and wait until daylight. We had the two Indians with us, and had agreed that their lives would be safe if they helped us to catch the others. Just as it was getting light, one of our men accidentally discharged his gun. Then the Indians were roused and they ran in all directions. I had stationed a man on the outside to see that none of the Indians escaped. In the excitement he was shot. The men were greatly excited and wanted to kill the Indians. I would not allow it, and we returned home, without the thieves. I was blamed for the loss of a white man's life, in comparison with which 1,000 Indians were nothing. That was the only Indian expedition I ever engaged in.[22]

### BIDWELL PETITIONS FEDERAL GOVERNMENT REQUESTING COMPENSATION FOR LOSSES SUFFERED IN 1852 INDIAN RAID

Your Petitioner represents that in the [year] 1850 he commenced Farming and trading at his residence aforesaid on Chico Creek in said Butte County, and in the year 1852 the wild Indians inhabiting the Mountains adjacent to the Residence of your Petitioner, came down in the Month of August 1852 in the night time, and burned and destroyed Buildings & a large amount of personal property belonging to your petitioner at his residence aforesaid on Said Chico Creek. A list of which said property so destroyed is as follows, to wit

| | |
|---|---:|
| 800 Bushels of Wheat, at 7.50 | $5,800.00 |
| 2,200   "      " Barley, 5.00 | 11,000.00 |
| One Grain House | 1,500.00 |
|   "   Stable | 500.00 |
| 5,000 feet of Sawed Lumber, $70.00 | 350.00 |
| Three buildings used as Store House, Carpenter Shop, Kitchen and Dwelling House all joining together containing a great quantity of Provisions Blankets and other dry goods, Farming & other utensils, Kitchen Household furniture and many other things at present impossible to specify to the value of at least the sum of | <u>$6,500.00</u> |
| Amt forward | 25,650.00 |
| Also 4 head of horned cattle that were stolen & driven away by said Indians during the year 1852, of the Value of the sum of | <u>200.00</u> |
| | $25,850.00 |

---

[22]JB-91, pp. 20–21.

Your Petitioner therefore prays that the same may be enquired into, and that he may be heard in proof of the claim against the United States Government and that he may be paid the value of property destroyed by the Indians aforesaid.[23]

### Trade between mountain and valley Indians leads to battle on Rancho Chico, 1856

The valley Indians never made their own bows, simply the arrows, and bought the bows of the mountain Indians. Once in several years the old Indians would arrange a meeting for the purpose of trade, under a flag of truce. As soon as they parted, they were enemies. It so happened that these hostile Indians came down to my ranch and because the weather was cold, came right into the village into the Indian houses. The matter was reported and we went over and surrounded the sweat-house. While we were fastening it up, the Indians escaped. Before they broke out, they shot a miller who was among our party. Then there was a good deal of shooting and three or four Indians were killed. . . .[24]

### Protects Rancho Chico Indians from a vengeful posse led by Samuel Lewis, 1863

Another time, a band of Indians took a little girl [A. Thankful Lewis] prisoner, after having killed her brother. She managed to escape and finally reached Chico. I had gone up into the mountains. The Indians that worked for me were in no way connected with these mountain Indians—in fact, they were always at war with them. The men in town wanted to kill my Indians and in fact the Indians everywhere. The rebel sentiment was abroad at that time also. The people became thoroughly alarmed and sent for me. They overtook me 75 miles in the mountains. I turned about and reached home in one day. When I reached home, I found the door locked, and rather than disturb the family, I wrapped my blanket about me and lay down on the door-step. I was so tired. The next morning the men came over furious. They had already caught two strange Indians and shot them. Every one expected they would shoot me down, but I talked to them, and in half an hour they went off.[25]

### Defends Mechoopda from false charges of murdering Lewis children, 1863

Indian labor has never to me been profitable; but I have always protected them and given them work in preference; idle Indians are a nuisance. As a matter of justice I kept them from being driven away. Malicious people have tried to drive

---

[23]John Bidwell, in Oroville, petition to James Y. McDuffie, U.S. Superintendent of Indian Affairs for California, San Francisco, 5 December 1859, *Letters Received by the Office of Indian Affairs 1824–1881, California Superintendency, 1849–1880*, Roll 37, 1859–1860 (Washington, D.C.: The National Archives and Records Service, National Archives Microfilm Publication M234, 1958), pp. 898–99.

[24]JB-91, p. 21.   [25]JB-91, pp. 14–15.

them away, because they imagine they were a benefit to me—that their labor was cheap and profitable.

This letter of Mr. John H. Guill is malicious. He knows that the Indians on Rancho Chico were innocent of the murders [of the Lewis children] and trouble he mentions—and yet he and others would have murdered or driven them away. Infuriated, drunken men make no distinction between innocent and guilty Indians. I do not say that Mr. Guill drank—but at the time ... many did drink and but for my interference and the Indians escaping to and across the river, these Indians would have been murdered. He now blames me for protecting them. The soldiers came to keep the rebels in check, Mr. Guill was a rebel sympathizer.[26]

### SUPPORTS REMOVAL OF MOUNTAIN MAIDU TO ROUND VALLEY, 1863

The [foothill] Indians conceived a great hostility toward me. They seemed to think that if I were out of the way, they would have a free pass to do almost what they wanted. I seemed to be in their way. They set my place on fire several times in the night, but we always put it out. On one occasion, however, I was absent in the city, and they burned me out. My life was in danger there for years until I had the Indians moved over into the Round Valley Indian reservation. Even the miners up there would sometimes pretend to be friendly to the Indians and not to me, because they were afraid of them.[27]

### BIDWELL RECALLS INDIAN REMOVAL TO ROUND VALLEY, 1863

... In October 1862 part of the Indians (between 300 & 400) were driven from the Round Valley Reservation. They made their way over the high snow capped mountains (Coast Range) into the Sacramento Valley on their way to their former homes.

Superintendent Hanson brought them to my farm and made a contract with me to furnish supplies, ... During the winter many of the Indians were hired out on neighboring farms, some fished, gathered acorns etc., which materially reduced the expense. In the month of July last the Mill Creek Indians, who are a hostile, roving, murderous band living in the Sierra Nevada Mountains, 40 to 50 miles north of this place, made a raid in this direction and committed several murders in this vicinity, the whole country was excited and bad men tried to direct the excitement against all Indians, and exterminate indiscriminately those on my farm as well as others living quietly on other farms in the vicinity where they had always lived.

Five of the Indians who had been at work in the harvest field for wages on the farm of a neighbor were murdered by white men in open day light, while returning to my place. In this state of affairs the Indians, though innocent and

---

[26]Charles C. Royce, *In Memoriam: John Bidwell*, Vol. 3 (1905), CSL. Comments by John Bidwell written in margin of Chico *Morning Chronicle*, 16 July 1886, that contained Guill's letter.
[27]JB-91, pp. 18–19.

peaceable, were compelled to cease to work out. Other Indians were collected here for safety preparatory to returning to the Reservation, numbering at one time about 800. All these had to be furnished provisions, which was done by Col. Hanson's order. It being the sickly season many were dying daily and it was desirable to send them as soon as possible to the Reservation. But teams for transportation could not be procured unless I would go security—they would not trust Col. Hanson—I did so and have paid the bills.... The Indians were fed, taken care of and finally sent to the reservation—all at my expense....[28]

### Brigadier General Bidwell Advocates Removal of the Mill Creek [Yana] Indians, 1865

Judge C. C. Bush, judge of Shasta County, has written me representing the necessity of military aid to suppress Indian troubles in that county.... The Indians who are the authors of the troubles alluded to are, in my judgment, the same hostile tribe which have for years been the scourge of the eastern border of the Sacramento Valley from the vicinity of this place to Pit River, a distance of eighty or ninety miles. They are generally known by the name of Mill Creek Indians. The number is small, but they are, from the peculiarity of the region they inhabit, capable of great mischief. From the nature of the country exposed to their ravages, the white settlements are sparse and isolated. My knowledge of these Indians leads me to believe that no such thing as a treaty or pacification is possible, and the only effectual remedy will be their capture and removal to some reservation on the coast or some island, where their return would be impossible. But they must first be caught. The rocky and abrupt places they inhabit are such that the very paucity of their numbers is what renders it difficult to find them. They are never seen but as enemies, and never approach habitations but to steal and murder. They are peculiarly relentless in their hostility. The aged and the young alike meet with the same fate at their hands. A temporary campaign could do but little good. I think a force of forty men with suitable guides would be sufficient, but they should enter upon the task with the instructions to continue as long as necessary, and even till snow drives the Indians toward the valley if they cannot be captured before.[29]

### Bidwell Argues in Favor of Bill to Expand the Round Valley Reservation, 1867

The Government of the United States ... have never purchased a single acre

---

[28] JB to John P. Usher, Secretary of the Interior, Washington, D.C., 4 December 1863, *Letters Received by the Office of Indian Affairs 1824–81, California Superintendency, 1849–1880* (The National Archives and Records Service, General Services Administration, Washington, 1958), Roll 39, 1863–1864, pp. 719–721.

[29] JB to Major General Irvin McDowell, 6 May 1865, *War of the Rebellion, Official Records of the Union and Confederate Armies*, Series I, Vol. L (50), Part II, Correspondence etc., Operations on the Pacific Coast, July 1, 1862–June 30, 1865, pp. 1221–1222.

of land, to my knowledge, from the Indians of California. On the contrary, the white settlements have been extended throughout the entire State, almost into every valley, however secluded, in the mountains of that State; thereby taking from the Indians their hunting grounds and every possible means they have in their power for their support.

I say, therefore, notwithstanding the immense sums which the Government may have heretofore appropriated for the maintenance of the Indians in California, it is still an obligation upon the Government to properly provide for them. Here is a valley in the mountains of the coast range, distant from the settlements, and large enough to support a considerable portion, if not all of them, of the Indians in northern California. That valley at this time is partially occupied by a reservation on which a large number of Indians are located; it is also partially in the occupation of settlers.

The object of the bill now before the House is this: to enable the Government to acquire possession of the entire valley. . . . I may state here that in California one of the great obstacles to the management of the Indians there is the existence of a class of loose people, men of bad morals, who congregate around the Indian reservations, furnish the Indians with liquor, teach them every vice, and induce them to run away from the reservations. Now to prevent these troubles it is necessary to get a location for them distant from the settlements. This Round valley . . . seems to be peculiarly fitted for a reservation for Indian purposes. It possesses a fertile soil, a salubrious climate, and it is ample in its extent. . . .

It is the duty of this Government to come to a decision and say whether it intends to make that entire valley a reservation. It is inconsistent with the interests of the Indian Department, the proper management and control of the Indians, that white settlements should be in juxtaposition with the reservation; and I say that the Government ought either to take possession of the whole valley and make it a suitable reservation or abandon it altogether.[30]

I feel the more anxious about this, because I know the people of that portion of the State are depending upon me to see that this question is properly adjusted; and that the settlers who occupy a portion of this valley should be purchased out, so that it may be used for the purposes of an Indian reservation. . . .

It is not designed to disturb the Indians upon any of the reservations in California, but simply to provide a place where Indians may be taken as soon as it is found necessary to remove them to a reservation.[31]

BIDWELL SEEKS MILITARY PROTECTION FOR
HUMBOLDT AND IDAHO WAGON ROADS, 1865

Having just returned from Susanville, I embrace the occasion to explain the

---

[30] *Congressional Globe*, 29 January 1867, 39 Congress, 2 Session, p. 843.
[31] *Congressional Globe*, 5 February 1867, 39 Congress, 2 Session, p. 1023.

condition of affairs in the vicinity of Honey Lake and beyond. Two principal routes diverge from Susanville, one to Idaho through Surprise Valley, and the other to the Humboldt mines. Both are exposed to the ravages of Indians. On the latter the keeper of the Granite Creek Station, and on the former the expressman, have been murdered by Indians during the winter. Also a large amount of stock has been driven off and slaughtered. This intelligence is authentic, as I have it from many persons, who all concur, with several of whom I am acquainted and know to be reliable. The anxiety is great among all the people to have troops sent immediately. The work of breaking a road through the snow was more than I anticipated, but it is now done. I began it something like seven weeks ago, and have prosecuted, through storms almost unprecedented, the task, till there is now a passable road for sleighs, not for wagons. There is now no route in the State where wagons can cross over the Sierra Nevada mountains, nor will there be till at least the 1st of May, and I believe this route will be traveled or in a traveling condition earlier than any other. By a little effort I believe troops can be got over this road now. They would have to haul their baggage over the snow belt on sleds, and then take their wagons on sleds too, or purchase wagons on the other side, which can be done. I represented to the people the difficulties of conveying baggage in wagons. Several told me that they would furnish flour and take the same quantity in return when the roads became passable for wagons. I am of the opinion that there will be a large travel (beginning in April, which is at hand) to the Idaho mines the present season through this route. To protect the Humboldt and Surprise Valley roads will require troops at some point beyond, but not distant from Honey Lake or Willow Creek Valley, and another station or post between Surprise and the Owyhee River. I do not believe that troops stationed at or near Goose Lake will answer the purpose, being off the direct route. I desire to add that all of the officials of Lassen County, of which Susanville is the county seat, concur in these views and the necessity of immediate military protection. I will see that no tolls be charged troops or freight for the military service on this road, and will render any assistance in my power.[32]

The petition which I have the honor to inclose herewith is signed by the officers and others of Siskiyou County, and was sent to me with the request that I would have Governor Low, Comptroller Oulton, and other State officials sign it, and then personally present it to you. But this is not necessary. You already comprehend the situation. Surprise Valley is in Siskiyou County. I indorse the petition, and believe a military post is required at that point not only in summer, but in winter, too. Post route No. 14903 will pass through that valley. I inclose a slip from the Morning Call, containing the said route advertised. Should the route via Fort Crook and Pitt River be traveled the coming summer, it will inter-

---

[32]JB to Gen. George Wright, 27 March 1865, *War of the Rebellion*, 50, Part 2, pp. 1171–72.

sect the main route (Susanville to Boise) at or near Surprise Valley. Passenger trains have been running regularly via Susanville to Idaho since April 3.

No Indian troubles have as yet occurred, but I am in constant apprehension. Stages are to be put on the route as soon as the snow is off, when the regular mail will begin. With a full company at Smoke Creek or a point a little farther west, to range on the road to Surprise Valley and on the Humboldt road as far east as Black Rock and the station prayed for in this petition at or near Surprise, present emergencies so far as I can see would be met. Beyond Surprise, however, there is a distance of 150 miles entirely unsettled. The Indians may not be hostile, or there may be few or none there. Time will show.[33]

Feeling satisfied that a great stream of travel is to go to Idaho Territory the present season, and that most of it, if not all, will go by Smoke Creek, Deep Hole, Granite Creek, and Pueblo to the Owyhee, and knowing the danger from Indians between Smoke Creek and Pueblo and between Pueblo and Owyhee River, where the travel must pass, I feel obliged to submit to your favorable notice the propriety of having a company of troops sent to Pueblo, to range in three directions, namely, toward Owyhee, Surprise Valley, and Granite Creek; or, if deemed better, have the company stationed at Surprise Valley range to Pueblo and thence toward Owyhee, and the company at Smoke Creek range as far as Pueblo via Granite Creek, as in the judgment of the commanding officers circumstances might require. Whatever is done should be done without delay. Teams are to leave here on Monday without fail with a large freight for Idaho. I have heard no contradiction of the attack and massacre by Indians at Pueblo, stated in a former letter. On the contrary, a confirmation as follows: The last stage from Susanville says three men were prospecting near Pueblo; one escaped (the other two being killed) toward Pueblo, and when near the place saw it surrounded by a large number of Indians, and he believes all the white people there (seven or eight instead of twenty) must be killed. Now, these freight teams have to pass directly through that region. Others have been going in that direction for some time. Besides, Capt. E. D. Pierce is with a party of men going on removing obstructions from the road. The travel that was going by Surprise is now taking the Granite Creek route.[34]

### BIDWELL REVEALS A BIT OF HIS OWN RACISM

Speaking generally, I don't believe the Indian has as high a regard for life as the Christian white people.[35]

### PROTECTS FEMALE INDIAN WORKERS

I have had men threaten to shoot me and have had them shoot at me. There

---

[33] JB to Gen. Irvin McDowell, 28 April 1865, *War of the Rebellion*, 50, Part 2, p. 1214.
[34] JB to Gen. George Wright, 17 June 1865, *War of the Rebellion*, 50, Part 2, p. 1264.
[35] JB-91, p. 22.

was a fellow who was making himself too familiar with some Indian women I had working for me. I lost my temper for once and seized a willow stick and wore it out on the fellow's head. He went out, got his revolver, and shot at me but missed. I can't stand any nonsense about men that way.[36]

### INDIAN LABORERS SUCCESSFULLY BARGAIN FOR HIGHER WAGES, 1869

... Ten Indian boys came up a short time ago to say that they wanted a dollar and a half per day for work through harvest! As labor is scarce I shall have to give it I fear—If I do not my neighbors will, and thus entice them away.[37]

### MAN CAUGHT SELLING LIQUOR TO INDIANS, 1872

... Mr. Cochran has detected a man selling liquor to the Indians, so I will make him feel the weight of the law—get him fined probably $50. . . .[38]

### VISIT FROM SMITHSONIAN ETHNOGRAPHER JEREMIAH CURTIN, RECORDS STORY OF SAM NEAL CUTTING DOWN REVERED INDIAN OAK TREE, 1884

This morning a Mr. Jeremiah Curtin—a learned man, just from the Smithsonian to learn points in Indian history &c&c. He came with a letter from Judge Sharpstein who is on the Supreme bench of this State. Mr. Curtin has with him his wife, a very fine looking and agreeable lady. He has been Secretary of Legation at St. Petersburg—understands Russian (and other European languages I infer, from his extensive travels abroad, and his having translated some work from the French &c&c.) He says it will be two weeks tomorrow since they (he & his wife) left Washington.

I took him to the Rancheria. Nopanny & Tonoco came here this A.M. And (after dinner with me) Mr. Curtin & wife went to the rancheria and took notes nearly all the afternoon. Then I gave them a drive. They are to come again tomorrow, having another appointment with the Indians. Old Sahweeco is on a visit to Tehama. So Nopanny had to bring Tonoco today being the only available savant.

Among the things I learned from him and Nopanny who interpreted was this story. Yapo-ne (the great Chief or Spirit) who came when all was water—no land—and (as told by Sahweeco) made the land through the agency of that wonderful turtle, planted the first oak tree in the world. It stood near the Esquin rancheria on Butte creek. It was the largest and the oldest oak in the world. The Indians covered it with feathers and other ornaments used in worshipping the Great Spirit who planted it.

But Sam Neal cut the tree down, and as he was cutting the blood ran out of the tree! All the Indians saw the blood. And because that tree was cut down the

---

[36]Ibid., p. 14.     [37]JB to AB, 21 June 1869, JB-CSL, b. 47, f. 26.
[38]JB to AB, 17 February 1872, Ibid., b. 126, f. 85.

Indians have been dying ever since! That is the reason there are so few Indians now living.

Whether Sahweeco would corroborate this history I cannot say. Jack was here this evening and says that Tonoco knows more than Sahweeco, for Lafonso says so....[39]

### INDIANS UPSET ABOUT YOUNG MEN BEING ARRESTED

... Nopanny was here this morning in a great way about Soosook (Mike) who is under arrest at Sacramento, being accused of putting timber across the RR. track—once at bridge and once near the rancheria. She of course believes him innocent—thinks it pure persecution. Soosook is a relative—cousin—no—his mother was Nopanny's half sister. So she is to go to Sacramento tomorrow to see him. She says that Sahwee'-co is nearly crazy about it, and threatens to go off and kill himself—in fact, did go off to the mountains this morning—said he could not stand it to see all the young men taken away.[40]

### PROCLAMATION OF RULES MADE FOR RANCHO CHICO INDIANS, 1885

1st    Lafonso is chief, and is always to be respected and obeyed as such; and it is his duty to see that these rules be also respected and obeyed.

2nd    Billy Preacher is hereby made chief teacher in temperance and good behavior, and [you] are directed to pattern after him and to learn to be as good as he.

3rd    Luccayan was a great and good chief. He was Nopanny's father, and ought to be remembered by all and his memory respected, because he was good.

4th    This Rancheria is the home of these Indians, and of all Indians who may wish to come and live here, on condition: namely

*First*, That they obey these Rules.

*Second*, That they drink no whiskey or other liquor.

*Third*, That they obey Lafonso as chief and pattern after Billy Preacher and be good like him.

*Fourth*, That all must be temperate, industrious and good.

*Fifth*, That all Indians—men, women, and children—must (unless in case of sickness) attend church every Sunday when there is church.

*Sixth*, That parents must send their children to school when old enough, keep them clean, and teach them to be polite.

*Seventh*, That these things are wrong and therefore forbidden, namely; to swear; to quarrel; to steal; to fight; to hunt or fish on Sunday; and to play ball or other sporting games on Sunday.

---

[39] JB to AB, 7 October 1884, Ibid., b. 57, f. 27.
[40] JB to AB, 28 November 1884, Ibid., b. 57, f. 56.

5th     All Indians who now live here or have their families here, and all Indians who may hereafter come to live here, are to have work when I have work for them to do, and they are to have full pay for all the work they may do or earn; but if they go away and work elsewhere, they lose the right to live here; for this place must not be a harbor for tramps or idle or otherwise not useful people.

6th     All who do not know or who may forget these Rules, or any of them, must ask Lafonso, or Billy Preacher, or ask Mrs. Bidwell, and have the Rules read, until all shall know them from the least to the greatest.

                Witness my hand this 21st day of June, A.D. 1885

                              John Bidwell[41]

---

[41] John Bidwell, "Proclamation of Rules Made for Rancho Chico Indians," 21 June 1885, JB-CSUC.

# 7
# Bidwell and the California Chinese

Except for the Southern Pacific Railroad monopoly, nothing aroused the political passions of late-nineteenth-century Californians more than the "Chinese question." Involving as it did the separate but intimately related issues of Asian immigration and labor, the Chinese question helped define and shape California politics during the three decades that followed the Civil War. For John Bidwell, the contentious subject was more than the mere passing interest of a sometime candidate for public office. Instead, Bidwell's continuous employment of Chinese workers on Rancho Chico drew him repeatedly into the heart of social conflict after 1870, and brought the threat of violence to his very doorstep on more than one occasion. Ironically, the explosive issue had its roots in the same event that had made Bidwell a wealthy man: the California Gold Rush.

Between 1849 and 1882, over 200,000 Chinese immigrants journeyed to America, nearly all of them bound for golden California. The overwhelming majority of these Asian immigrants were natives of Guangdong (Kwangtung) province in southeastern China, and hailed from small peasant villages in the Pearl River Delta region adjacent to Canton and Hong Kong. Driven from their homes by chronic poverty, overpopulation, and land scarcity, these immigrants also sought to escape the ravages of nearly constant warfare in the Guangdong countryside. Beginning with the First Opium War against Great Britain in 1839–1842, a series of armed conflicts spread havoc across the province for the next twenty-five years. The great T'aip'ing Rebellion (1845–1864) and the Second Opium War (1856–1860) were coupled in Guangdong by the local Red Turbans uprisings and the Punti-Hakka war of the 1850s and early 1860s.[1]

---
[1]Elmer Clarence Sandmeyer, *The Anti-Chinese Movement in California* (Urbana: University of Illinois Press, 1973), pp. 12-15; Sucheng Chan, *This Bittersweet Soil: The Chinese in California Agriculture, 1860–1910* (Berkeley: University of California Press, 1986), pp. 16–23, 37; Gunther Barth, *Bitter Strength: A History of the Chinese in the United States, 1850–1870* (Cambridge, MA: Harvard University Press, 1964), pp. 9–31.

Overseas migration was nothing new to the entrepreneurial people of Guangdong which, in several important respects, was quite unique among the provinces of China. Between 1757 and 1842, the isolationist Chinese government had designated Canton as the nation's sole international port. Consequently, Canton became the hub of a vigorous maritime trade and her merchants developed strong commercial ties with traders from all over the world, including the United States. The peasants of Guangdong followed suit, and increasingly shifted away from rice and subsistence production toward more lucrative cash crops aimed at regional and international markets.

Meanwhile, international trade gave a renewed stimulus to emigration as opportunity-seeking merchants and laborers fanned out across southeast Asia, following the familiar routes plied by commercial junks and joining well-established Chinese émigré communities that, in some cases, dated back to the fifteenth century. Ever on the lookout for new possibilities, these hard-working and hard-pressed sojourners quickly began to direct their attention eastward after James Marshall discovered gold at Coloma.[2]

The sudden attractions of far-off California presented an alluring contrast to the miseries of home. Fabulous rumors from "Jinshan" ("Gold Mountain") had reached Guangdong by 1849 and, within three years, a large trans-Pacific migration had begun. Despite the Chinese government's ban on emigration, China suddenly became, for the first time, a major source of American immigration. By 1852, some 25,000 Chinese citizens, mostly adult males, had poured into California. Representing roughly one-tenth of the state's total non-Indian population, the Chinese comprised California's largest foreign-born minority group.[3] Their ranks swelled to almost 35,000 by 1860, and reached nearly 50,000 ten years later. In 1880, California's nineteenth-century Chinese population finally peaked at just over 75,000, nearly nine percent of the state's total.[4] Throughout the same period, Butte County contained one of the largest Chinese communities outside

---

[2]Yong Chen, "The Internal Origins of Chinese Emigration to California Reconsidered," *Western Historical Quarterly*, 28 (Winter 1997), pp. 521–46.

[3]According to Census Bureau figures, only forty-six Chinese immigrants resided in the entire country between 1820 and 1850. U.S., Department of Commerce, Bureau of the Census, *Immigration, Immigrants by Country: 1820–1945*, pp. 35–36; Walton Bean, *California: An Interpretive History*, 2nd ed. (New York: McGraw-Hill, 1973), p. 164.

[4]Post-1880 Census estimates suggest that California's Chinese population might actually have reached as high as 104,000 by 1883, thanks to a sudden surge of immigration just prior to the passage of the Chinese Exclusion Act of 1882. See Chan, *Bittersweet Soil*, pp. 41 and 46; California, Bureau of Labor Statistics, *First Biennial Report of the Bureau of Labor Statistics, 1883–1884* (Sacramento: 1884), pp. 166–168.

of San Francisco. Between 1860 and 1880, Butte County's Chinese population rose from 2,177 to 3,793, figures representing eighteen and twenty percent, respectively, of the county's total number of residents. It is important to note that, since most Chinese immigrants were adult male laborers, these percentages actually understate their importance in the county and state work forces. As one historian has estimated, Chinese workers may have comprised fully one-quarter of the state's wage labor supply by 1870.[5]

As California's placer gold fields began to play out after the mid 1850s, displaced Chinese miners shifted to new occupations. A large number managed to remain self-employed in a variety of different callings, but most became unskilled wage earners. Joined by a steady stream of new arrivals from their homeland, Chinese immigrants successfully competed for jobs in California's rapidly expanding economy. Major employers in both the agricultural and industrial sectors turned eagerly to Chinese work crews following the triumphant demonstration of their efficiency by the Central Pacific Railroad. Rushing to complete the western half of the nation's first transcontinental rail line, the Central Pacific employed over 10,000 Chinese laborers between 1865 and 1869 to build its way across the Sierra Nevada mountains and the Great Basin deserts beyond. By the time the Golden Spike was driven at Promontory Point in Utah, Chinese workers made up eighty percent of the Central Pacific's entire payroll.[6]

In the meantime, the increased availability of Chinese labor was ensured by the inauguration of regular steamship service between San Francisco and Hong Kong by the Pacific Mail Steamship Company in 1867. Together with the Burlingame Treaty of 1868, which ended the official Chinese stricture against emigration, Pacific Mail steamships greatly strengthened the growing human ties between China and the United States. Like the other white employers who followed their lead, the Big Four would have no difficulty locating Chinese job applicants when they began building California's second transcontinental link, the Southern Pacific Railroad, in the mid 1870s.[7]

Though often at odds with the Big Four, John Bidwell shared their enthusiasm for Chinese laborers who found seasonal and permanent employment on Rancho Chico for over thirty years. Bidwell's employment of Chinese made him an obvious and convenient target for those

---

[5]Chan, *Bittersweet Soil*, pp. 48–50; Alexander Saxton, *The Indispensable Enemy: Labor and the Anti-Chinese Movement in California* (Berkeley: University of California Press, 1971), p. 7.
[6]Chan, *Bittersweet Soil*, pp. 38 and 52.
[7]Ibid., pp. 26–28, 37–39.

who blamed these Asian immigrants for California's social problems and periodic economic depressions. Anti-Chinese attitudes came from many different quarters and took many different forms. Some critics claimed that the so-called Six Companies that financed Chinese immigration and contracted Chinese labor out of San Francisco were essentially slave traders who ruthlessly exploited their fellow countrymen. Such critics were not far off the mark. The large majority of Chinese workers who came to California during the nineteenth century arrived as semifree or indentured emigrants bound to the Chinatown merchants who had arranged and paid for their passage. Under the harsh terms of the notorious credit-ticket system, the emigrants had to work for their merchant-sponsors until they had completely retired their debts. This was no easy task, since their financial obligations included interest payments set at ferocious rates ranging from four to eight percent per month! In the meantime, the immigrants remained in a state of debt bondage, completely "at the mercy of their bosses" who either employed them directly or hired them out to white employers in need of cheap labor. Given these circumstances, much of the criticism leveled at Chinese labor was completely justifiable and certainly understandable.[8]

Less defensible were the numerous racial arguments employed by whites against California's growing Chinese population. These included the familiar notion that the presence of Chinese in the community threatened Christian virtue and posed a menace to children. Prostitution, opium smoking, and a general lack of sanitation in local "Chinatowns" were seen as threats to the health, safety, and morality of the larger white community. Such widely held perceptions were commonplace in Butte County. According to the Butte *Record*, for example, the Chinese in Oroville were "filthy in their habits, grossly immoral, and have no attachments for our institutions. Great licentiousness exists among them."[9] Racial incompatibility or "unassimilability" was another common theme sounded during periods of anti-Chinese unrest. Local newspapers, including the *Record* and the Chico *Enterprise*, encouraged racist rhetoric by publishing xenophobic editorials and anti-Chinese hate mail sent as letters to the editor.[10]

---

[8] Barth, *Bitter Strength*, pp. 2–3, 51–68, 76–80, 99–100, 137–38, 212–13; Chan, *Bittersweet Soil*, pp. 21–22, 25–26.

[9] *Butte Record*, 13 May 1876. In regards to the famous Chinese Six Companies of San Francisco, see Richard Dillon, *The Hatchet Men: The Story of the Tong Wars in San Francisco's Chinatown* (New York: Coward-McCann, 1962), Chapter 4.

[10] *Butte Record*, 1 June 1867, 23 Dec. 1875, and 29 Jan. 1876; Chico *Enterprise*, 17 Nov. 1875, 18 Feb. 1876, and 27 April 1877.

The most common and influential anti-Chinese arguments, however, were those emphasizing the threat of economic competition. Many Americans believed that Chinese labor undermined wages and forced white laborers into poverty. The alien Chinese became convenient scapegoats during times of economic recession, and the press of California was more than willing to fan the flames of racial fear and hatred in the midst of hard times. The Chico *Enterprise* warned its readers that unless the Chinese were stopped, they would "fasten upon our soil, impoverish our mines and degrade labor, erect their pagan temples, and convert our favored state into a semi-Celestial province...."[11] Given the climate of local opinion in Butte County, John Bidwell's prominence as an employer of Chinese labor frequently placed him at the center of heated controversy and sometimes exposed him to financial and even physical danger.

As it did throughout many California communities, the divisive Chinese issue split Chico along class lines, pitting major employers against working class whites fearful of losing jobs to the despised Asian "coolies."[12] In prosperous times, whites tolerated the Chinese presence as long as it remained confined within Chico's two small Chinatown sections.[13] Similarly, Chinese workers venturing beyond their ethnic enclaves were respected so long as they toiled at occupations not coveted by whites. Consequently, Chinese cooks, laundrymen, domestic servants, and vegetable peddlers became very familiar local figures.

Unfortunately, prosperity traded places all too frequently with depression in late nineteenth-century America's turbulent boom and bust economy. In the absence of labor unions strong enough to stop them, California employers typically discharged white workers and resorted to cheaper Chinese labor when confronted by falling prices and profit margins. With an economy based on the seasonal industries of agriculture and lumber manufacturing, Chico was particularly vulnerable to the

---

[11] Chico *Enterprise*, 17 Nov. 1875.
[12] Most whites did not bother to distinguish between the three very distinct forms of unfree Chinese immigrant labor that prevailed in the nineteenth century. The notorious coolie trade, which flourished in many Caribbean and Latin American nations after the abolition of African slavery, was little different from the involuntary system it replaced. Meanwhile, though harshly exploited, Chinese contract laborers and credit-ticket debtors toiled under agreed-upon conditions that made their status more comparable to indentured servitude. See Barth, *Bitter Strength*, pp. 51–52; Chan, *Bittersweet Soil*, pp. 21–25.
[13] Located on the east side of Chico's downtown business district, Old Chinatown centered upon Flume Street between Fifth and Sixth streets. New Chinatown sat on the west side of Chico fronting Cherry Street between Seventh and Eighth streets. See Chico *Enterprise-Record*, 2 October 1972.

Chinese New Year Procession on Main St. near 2nd St. in Chico.
Reprinted with permission by Special Collections, Meriam Library, California State University, Chico and Bidwell Mansion.

vagaries of the business cycle. It is therefore no surprise that the town's largest employer, Sierra Flume and Lumber Company, anxiously turned to the "Chinese solution" when hard times struck in the late 1870s, mid 1880s, and early 1890s.[14]

So too did John Bidwell. Despite the risks involved, Bidwell found the advantages of Chinese farm labor irresistible. Echoing the sentiments of growers throughout the state, Bidwell lauded the Chinese as extremely industrious and reliable workers who were easily managed as well. Laboring in disciplined gangs recruited and supervised by a single Chinese contractor or foreman, they planted fruit and nut trees, pruned vineyards, and built roads. With strong rural roots of their own, many of them were already skilled and experienced horticulturalists whose services were proving critical to the successful development of California's emerging orchards and vineyards. This was particularly the case with important California "spe-

---

[14]On the lumber industry in Chico and Butte County, see William H. Hutchinson, *California Heritage: A History of Northern California Lumbering* (Santa Cruz, Ca.: The Forest History Society, 1974).

cialty crops" like oranges, peaches, pears, plums, and persimmons, all of which flourished in the Pearl River Delta.¹⁵

They were also exploitable. Regardless of whether they were free or still ensnared by the credit-ticket system, all Chinese immigrants were reduced to a vulnerable second-class status by both state and federal laws. They could not vote, become citizens, or even testify in court against whites who committed crimes against them.¹⁶ And, because they labored to support families they intended to rejoin back home, Chinese workers measured their prosperity against the decidedly lower standard of living that prevailed in Guangdong. As a result, they willingly accepted wages equal to just two-thirds of those paid to whites. Between 1870 and 1894, Chinese field hands earned average monthly incomes that ranged from twenty to twenty-five dollars per month with board, an amount roughly equal to one dollar per day. Whites, meanwhile, drew an average of over forty-six dollars per month in 1869. The gap narrowed during the general price deflation of the ensuing two decades which lowered white wages while Chinese incomes remained static. Nevertheless, a sizeable differential existed on the eve of Chinese exclusion in 1882, when white farm labor in California averaged over thirty-eight dollars per month.¹⁷

Outside the Bay Area and the Sacramento-San Joaquin Delta region, the enactment of exclusion did little to substantially improve the bargaining position of Chinese farm workers who could still be replaced by whites if they demanded too much. Thus, the dual wage rate endured until the depression of the 1890s, when its demise would be brought about by the collapse of white wages rather than the elevation of Asian incomes. Until then, however, whites continued to insist upon and receive

---

¹⁵Barth, *Bitter Strength*, pp. 15, 20; Chan, *Bittersweet Soil*, pp. 19, 84; and Chen, "Chinese Emigration," pp. 533, 536.

¹⁶They were not completely helpless or "docile," however. Backed by the resources of the Six Companies and the Chinese consulate in San Francisco, residents of California's Chinese community proved quite adept at asserting what rights they did have by aggressively pursuing justice in the federal court system. See Charles J. McClain, *In Search of Equality: The Chinese Struggle Against Discrimination in Nineteenth-Century America* (Berkeley: University of California Press, 1994); Christian G. Fritz, *Federal Justice in California: The Court of Ogden Hoffman, 1851–1891* (Lincoln: University of Nebraska Press, 1991); Ellen D. Katz, "The Six Companies and the Geary Act: A Case Study in Nineteenth-Century Civil Disobedience and Civil Rights Litigation," *Western Legal History*, 8 (Summer/Fall 1995), pp. 227–71; and Lucy Salyer, *Laws Harsh as Tigers: Chinese Immigrants and the Shaping of Modern Immigration Law* (Chapel Hill: University of North Carolina Press, 1995).

¹⁷Chan, *Bittersweet Soil*, pp. 327–330; and California, Bureau of Labor Statistics, *First Biennial Report of the Bureau of Labor Statistics of California, 1883–1884* (Sacramento: 1884), pp. 166–168.

higher wages because there were never enough Chinese to drive them out of the market. During the late nineteenth century, Chinese workers probably never comprised more than one-third of California's total farm labor force and certainly not more than one-half. Concentrated in the orchards and vineyards of northern California where they were most highly prized by employers, Asian workers divided the agricultural job market in a tense *modus vivendi* with their more numerous white counterparts.[18]

Rancho Chico fully incorporated California's racial divisions of farm labor and wages after 1869, when John Bidwell took on his first Chinese employees. In May of that year, Bidwell hired Yang Tie, a "Chinese boy," and Ah Wing, paying the latter twenty-five dollars per month. Apparently working through Chico Chinatown merchant Ah Sun, Bidwell expanded his new Asian labor force and, by November 1872, had erected a "China house" in his vineyard.[19] The location of this domicile was significant, for it was in Rancho Chico's vineyard, nursery, and garden (truck farm) departments that Chinese majorities soon emerged. However, except for sizeable minorities employed at the dairy and almond orchard, Chinese hands were conspicuously absent from the remaining divisions of Bidwell's estate, where whites continued to prevail. Of the 150 long-term employees hired by Bidwell between 1870 and 1875, only twenty-five (less than seventeen percent) were Chinese.[20] This racial balance remained essentially unchanged a decade later. In 1886, the Chico *Enterprise* esti-

---

[18]Chan, *Bittersweet Soil*, pp. 278–279, 302–319, 332–333; Varden Fuller, *Hired Hands in California's Farm Fields: Collected Essays on California's Farm Labor History and Policy* (Davis: Giannini Foundation of Agricultural Economics, University of California, 1991), pp. 11–12. California, Bureau of Labor Statistics, *Second Biennial Report of the Bureau of Labor Statistics of California, 1885–1886* (Sacramento: 1886), pp. 46–47, 80; William C. Blackwood, "A Consideration of the Labor Problem," *Overland Monthly*, 3 (May 1884), pp. 452–453. The percentage of Chinese in California's farm labor force has been grossly exaggerated in several important studies. See, for example, Carey McWilliams, *Factories in the Field: The Story of Migratory Farm Labor in California* (Boston: Little, Brown, and Co., 1939), pp. 66–67; and Linda Majka and Theo Majka, *Farm Workers, Agribusiness, and the State* (Philadelphia: Temple University Press, 1982), p. 32. For a careful critique of their sources and figures, see Chan, *Bittersweet Soil*, pp. 281–82.

[19]JBD, 5 and 19 May 1869; 19 February and 16 December 1871; 12 March 1872; 21–23 November 1872. Although his diaries give no earlier indications, Bidwell may have employed Chinese on Rancho Chico prior to 1869, since he had already hired many of them during the construction of the Humboldt Wagon Road in 1863–1864.

[20]John Tubbesing, "Economics of the Bidwell Ranch, 1870–1875" (MA Thesis, CSUC, 1978), pp. 28–44. It should be noted that Tubbesing's analysis actually overstates the Chinese presence since wages paid to Indian laborers were usually not recorded in the ledgers that provided the data for his study.

mated that only "about one-fifth of the hands employed on Rancho Chico are Chinamen," almost all of whom were assigned to Bidwell's garden and orchard departments.[21]

Like their compatriots elsewhere in rural California, the Chinese on Rancho Chico received wages that were significantly lower than those earned by whites doing the same kind of work. Indeed, during the first half of the 1870s, Bidwell took full advantage of the state's dual wage scale, paying his Chinese hands at average rates equaling just one-half to two-thirds of those he paid whites. Only in the vineyard did the monthly earnings of Chinese come close to those of whites. There, Asian hands drew $25.36, over eighty-one percent of the white monthly average of $31.27.[22]

On the rare occasions when he was challenged, Bidwell made it clear that the dual wage system was non-negotiable. During the 1880s, for instance, a group of Chinese almond harvesters went on strike for higher wages just one day after having signed a contract to work for three cents per pound. Rather than give in to their demands, Bidwell retaliated by calling upon the Mechoopda to break the strike. Bidwell directed orchard foreman George M. Gray to "Go down and talk with Nopenny [see Chapter Six] and see if the Indians will do the job; the men can knock them [the almonds] and the boys and girls pick them up and the squaws hull them." According to Gray, the Mechoopda "were glad to take the job and they did good work and we got the work done at just a little more than we were to pay the Chinamen." An unusual occurrence for Rancho Chico, the almond strike represented the only serious dispute Bidwell ever had with his Asian employees.[23]

Most of the time, the Chinese lived up to their reputation as dependable and cooperative employees, a reputation that depended heavily upon the Chinese contractors and foremen who directly supervised their work and maintained discipline. From 1878 to 1886, the "boss Chinaman" on Rancho Chico was Ah Louey, who was fondly remembered by George Gray fifty years later. Gray recalled that "Old Louie was a fine Chinaman" whose service was invaluable, especially during the harvest season. After the picking and drying of peaches and plums, "The Chinamen used

---

[21]Chico *Enterprise*, 26 February and 12 March 1886.
[22]Tubbesing, "Economics of the Bidwell Ranch," pp. 28, 31–32, 35, 38–40.
[23]George M. Gray, "Reminiscences of the Life of General John Bidwell, (Chico) *Sandy Gulch News*, 16 March 1939.

to gather, cut and pack into boxes from the trays both kinds [peaches and plums] for 2 １/₂ cents per pound, then [Ah Louey] and myself would go around from one gang to another; he would put the name of the gang on the end of the box and we would take the load to the warehouse and weigh it and he would put it on his book and I on mine and I never heard one word of complaint from any one of the workers."[24]

Unfortunately, these uncomplaining harvest hands caused others nearby to complain very bitterly. To the white working-class households of Chico, the ominous prospect of Chinese competition for harvest season jobs posed a very serious threat. Most families, even those headed by wage earners with stable year-round employment, depended upon the local harvest to provide summertime jobs for wives and children. For many, the supplemental income earned laboring in Chico's fields and orchards proved essential to maintaining a decent standard of living.[25]

With his diversified and large-scale production, John Bidwell was the community's single largest provider of harvest season jobs. Commencing each spring with the picking and packing of cherries in mid May, the harvest at Rancho Chico progressed steadily for the ensuing five months. Apricot picking began around the second week of June, followed by peaches, plums, and almonds during the height of the season in July and August. By the time September arrived, the pear harvest had already begun, and workers were kept busy until the close of the season in mid October.[26]

During the entire period, as many as 350 people, mostly women and children, labored in the orchards and packinghouses, preparing fresh fruit and nuts for shipment. Job opportunities on Rancho Chico increased after 1875 when Bidwell, eyeing the new possibilities created by the transcontinental railroad, began sending dry and canned fruit back east. Bidwell erected his first drying house in 1877, and a new cannery followed five years later. The two establishments each employed up to 200 workers during a typical season, and the cannery alone paid as much as $1,200 per week in wages.[27]

---

[24]Gray, "Reminiscences," *Sandy Gulch News*, 9 and 16 March 1939. Gray must not have been privy to a letter John Bidwell received from former employee Ah Kun. While praising Bidwell for the "kind treatment" he had always afforded Ah Kun and his fellow countrymen, Ah Kun complained bitterly about "Ah Lui who acts very mean." Ah Kun claimed that Louey frequently cheated his men by shorting the weight of their boxes. See Ah Kun to John Bidwell, 19 January 1884, John Bidwell Papers, Meriam Library, CSUC.

[25]See, for example, Chico *Enterprise*, 13 October 1882 and 8 March 1890.

[26]Chico *Chronicle-Record*, 8 June 1895.

Until 1894, the vast majority of these jobs, and the earnings that went with them, belonged to white workers rather than the much maligned Chinese.[28] Whites dominated the drying houses and held every single position within the cannery.[29] Out in the fields and orchards, whites heavily outnumbered Chinese laborers.[30] Indeed, a careful analysis shows that between 1870 and 1875, Chinese employees comprised just thirteen percent of Rancho Chico's short-term seasonal labor pool.[31] Nevertheless, the Chinese minority on Bidwell's estate became a source of bitter resentment and controversy in 1876 when Chico's first major anti-Chinese movement began.[32]

The local crisis grew directly out of the prolonged nationwide depression triggered by the financial Panic of 1873. Toward the end of 1876, the

---

[27]Chico *Enterprise*, 15 July 1887 and 8 March 1890. Fruit harvest employment fluctuated dramatically during each season, as well as from year to year depending on overall yields. In June 1886, for example, sixty hands were at work in the cannery earning a total of $300 per week. By the end of July, the cannery employed 125 workers, while another 172 laborers were busy picking and packing fruit. See Chico *Enterprise*, 2 and 30 July 1886.

[28]The significance of Chico's resident white workforce highlights a serious deficiency in the historiography of California farm labor and rural social conflict. Because scholars in the field have been so preoccupied with the compelling and poignant struggles of immigrant and migratory farm labor, the saga of resident, non-Hispanic white farm workers remains one of the great untold stories of rural California's social history. At best, the vital contributions of these working people receive only passing mentions in the leading historical accounts. See, for examples, Chan, *Bittersweet Soil*; McWilliams, *Factories in the Field*; Majka and Majka, *Farm Workers, Agribusiness, and the State*; Walter Goldschmidt, *As You Sow* (New York: Harcourt, Brace and Co., 1947); Lloyd Fisher, *The Harvest Labor Market in California* (Cambridge, Mass.: Harvard University Press, 1953); Cletus Daniel, *Bitter Harvest: A History of California Farm Workers, 1870–1941* (Ithaca: Cornell University Press, 1981); Walter Stein, *California and the Dust Bowl Migration* (Westport, Ct.: Greenwood Press, 1973); James Gregory, *American Exodus: The Dust Bowl Migration and Okie Culture in California* (New York: Oxford University Press, 1989); and Devra Weber, *Dark Sweat, White Gold: California Farm Workers, Cotton, and the New Deal* (Berkeley: University of California Press, 1994). For an important recent exception, see Richard Steven Street, "Tattered Shirts and Ragged Pants: Accommodation, Protest, and the Coarse Culture of California Wheat Harvesters and Threshers," *Pacific Historical Review*, 67 (Nov. 1998), pp. 573–608.

[29]Chico *Enterprise*, 2 July 1886 and 15 July 1887.

[30]As late as 1886, for example, only 15 of 100 pickers harvesting Bidwell's cherry crop were Chinese. Butte *Record*, 1 June 1886. Indian harvesters also outnumbered the Chinese, especially in the almond orchards. See JB to AB, 20 August 1888, Annie K. Bidwell Collection, CSL, box 60, folder 15; and CC Parry, "Rancho Chico," pp. 568–569.

[31]Tubbesing, "Economics of the Bidwell Ranch," pp. 28–44.

[32]Chico had experienced a previous outbreak of anti-Chinese sentiment in 1868 when the advancing Central Pacific Railroad succeeded in short circuiting the town's trans-Sierra wagon trade with Idaho and Nevada, triggering a local economic slump. The crisis gave rise to an anti-Chinese newspaper, the *California Caucasian*, which flourished briefly before folding in March 1869 due to insufficient support. See Wells and Chambers, *History of Butte County*, p. 196 and Michele Shover, *Chico's Lemm Ranch Murders and the Anti-Chinese Campaign of 1877* (Chico: ANCRR, 1998), p. 13.

economic slump began to seriously affect California businesses. Struggling to cope with hard times, the Sierra Flume and Lumber Company decided to cut costs by hiring Chinese workers to fill most of the 200 jobs created by its new sash and door factory in Chico. Then, in December, Sierra Flume leased its entire Chico operation, including its mill, yard, and factory, to a San Francisco firm that brought in an all-Chinese work crew.[33]

Mass protests quickly erupted among displaced white workers and their angry supporters, who rallied together and formed a series of militant anti-Chinese organizations. The Order of Caucasians sponsored public demonstrations and sent delegations to Sierra Flume, Bidwell, and others demanding that they replace their Chinese workers with whites. The Order also launched a boycott of Chico's six or seven Chinese laundries and encouraged customers to patronize a newly established but short-lived white laundry using female labor.[34] For the next two months, the Order kept up a constant agitation and mobilized its supporters for the upcoming municipal elections. On February 6, 1877, the Caucasians seized control of the town government by winning a majority on the Chico board of trustees and capturing the office of town marshal.[35]

Meanwhile, the stubborn refusals of Sierra Flume and Bidwell to back down before the Order's earlier demands led impatient workers to launch a more aggressive organization known simply as the Labor Union. The Union in turn gave birth to the conspiratorial Council of Nine. Together, the two newer groups initiated a local "reign of terror" by resorting to arson, death threats, and other forms of intimidation. Bidwell himself received numerous death threats and, while they were never carried out, arsonists successfully torched two barns on Rancho Chico. Then, on January 27, 1877, arsonists struck again, this time destroying a former soap factory in town that Bidwell had rented to Yee Kee, a Chinese butcher. Bidwell offered a $500 reward for the arrest of the incendiaries, but to no avail. The wave of arsons continued unabated throughout February

---

[33] Shover, *Lemm Ranch Murders*, pp. 16–17.

[34] Ibid., pp. 13–16. Interestingly, despite its name, the Order of Caucasians also took up the cause of Chico's forty or fifty black residents. Like their working class white neighbors local blacks felt directly threatened by Chinese competition. Scattered evidence suggests that blacks and whites cooperated against the Chinese in 1877 and against both the Chinese and Japanese in 1894. See Peter Jackson, et al. to John Bidwell, 16 May 1885, John Bidwell Papers, Meriam Library, CSUC; Mansfield, *History of Butte County*, p. 276; *Chico Anti-Chinese League Minute Book, 1894–1895*, 12 May 1894, 4 and 11 June 1894: Shover, *Blacks in Chico, 1860–1935: Climbing the Slippery Slope* (Chico, Ca.: ANCRR, 1991), pp. 23–26, 37.

[35] Shover, *Lemm Ranch Murders*, p. 26.

and March when three Chinatown homes, a barn, a laundry, and Sierra Lumber's flume were set ablaze.[36]

Finally, on March 13, 1877, the campaign of violence reached its climax when four Chinese laborers—Ah Lee, Ah Gow, Sue Ung, and Ah Yuen—were murdered and two others wounded at Christian Lemm's ranch just east of Chico. The victims had been hired to clear some land on the ranch and Lemm had built a small cabin for their use. On the night of the murders, five men and a boy broke into the cabin and robbed the Chinese workers of approximately five dollars, and then opened fire on them. One of the wounded victims, Wo Ah Lin, successfully managed to feign death until his assailants left. He then reported the attack to Lemm who, fearing for his own life, decided to do nothing until the next day.[37] Although wounded and bleeding, Wo Ah Lin made his way into town arriving at about midnight when he reported the murders to Benjamin True, the night watchman for Chico's Chinatowns.[38]

Both the Order of Caucasians and the Labor Union publicly condemned the murders and denied any connection to them. Meanwhile, fed up with the unwillingness and inability of local law enforcement officers to stem the escalating tide of violence, John Bidwell and others resorted to a non-violent vigilante campaign to reestablish civic peace and order. Meeting in the Masonic Hall on March 16, they organized the Citizen's Committee of Safety and offered rewards totaling $2,800 for the arrest and conviction of those responsible for the murders and arson fires. Joining the effort were the Chinese Six Companies of San Francisco which contributed another $1,000 to the reward fund and dispatched a pair of detectives to aid in the Citizen's Committee investigation. Within days one of the leading suspects was arrested while trying to mail threatening letters. Upon interrogation he confessed to the killings and identified others involved in both the murders and the previous acts of arson. Twenty-eight more arrests swiftly followed and jury trials began toward the end of April. Five men were eventually convicted of murder and given life sentences in prison. Another six were found guilty of arson and sentenced to prison terms ranging from five

---

[36] Chico *Enterprise*, 2 and 9 March 1877; Wells and Chambers, *History of Butte County*, p. 230; and Shover, *Lemm Ranch Murders*, pp. 17–25, 30–34.
[37] Chico *Enterprise*, 16 March 1877; *Butte Record*, 15 March and 2 June 1877; Chan, pp. 372–373.
[38] Shover, *Lemm Ranch Murders*, pp. 35–38.

to twenty-five years. Among them were Hank Wright and Hayden Jones, who received twelve- and twenty-year sentences for burning Bidwell's soap factory.[39]

Bidwell's reward for helping catch the criminals was to have his life threatened again and to have a mob gather outside his mansion vowing to burn it down if he did not immediately discharge his Chinese workers. Infuriated by the threats and the subsequent burning of Rancho Chico's carpenter shop, Bidwell quickly placed an order for a box of repeating rifles and left no doubt he would put them to good use if necessary. He also rebuilt his soap factory, only to see it burned to the ground a second time the night before it was scheduled to reopen.[40]

Peace eventually returned to Chico in the summer of 1877 but only temporarily. Throughout 1878, the lumber industry remained in the doldrums while Chico's economy suffered a series of shocks. That year, the Sugar Pine and Lumber Company failed, as did Jason Springer and Company, a door and sash factory that employed fifty workers. Then, in July, Sierra Flume and Lumber went bankrupt. When it reemerged in October as Sierra Lumber Company, officials began a drastic reorganization and downsizing program.[41]

As the economic recession thus deepened, anti-Chinese resentment continued to fester. In March 1878, local dissidents hoping to capitalize on the previous year's election victory organized a branch of the Workingmen's Party of California (WPC). Founded six months earlier by trade unionists and unemployed workers in San Francisco, the WPC rallied to the motto of its inflammatory Irish immigrant leader Denis Kearney. "The Chinese," he thundered, "must go!" Given the strength of anti-Chinese sentiment in Chico, local Democratic and Republican party chieftains were understandably alarmed by the appearance of the WPC. Putting aside their differences, the traditional rivals closed ranks to ward off the threat from below. In the bitterly contested elections of June 1878, the joint "Non-Partisan" slate triumphed over the WPC, which managed to poll only twenty-three percent of the ballots cast in Butte County. The Workingmen held on but never fully recovered from this defeat. In the subsequent gubernatorial campaign of 1879, the WPC failed to field a local ticket, and its gubernatorial

---

[39]Chico *Enterprise*, 16 March 1877; JBD 16 March 1877; Wells and Chambers, *History of Butte County*, pp. 229–230; Mansfield, *History of Butte County*, pp. 273–275; Shover, *Lemm Ranch Murders*, pp. 40–55; Chan, p. 373.
[40]JB-91, pp. 52–54; JBD, March 17, 1877; Chico *Enterprise*, 8 June 1877; Chan, p. 373.
[41]Hutchinson, *California Heritage*; Shover, *Lemm Ranch Murders*, p. 6.

candidate, William White, finished a distant third in Butte County. White captured a mere seven percent of the county's vote, despite a special campaign appearance on his behalf by Denis Kearney. Bidwell, who skipped Kearney's address, contemptuously noted the event in his diary: "Kearney, the communist, made his harangue at the Chico Hotel."[42]

The demise of the WPC brought an end to the anti-Chinese crisis in Chico, and employers like John Bidwell could resume business as usual. Seven years later, however, the Chinese issue flared up again, though this time without violence. In January 1886, a new Anti-Chinese Association launched a general boycott of employers and products of "Asiatic slave labor."[43] Prominent among the Association's leaders was Chico attorney E. J. Emmons, who singled out Bidwell as the boycott's number-one target. Emmons publicly condemned Bidwell as "... the very essence of Chinese lovers in this community. Why not attack him first? He is the richest man in the county and if we fetch him first, the other employers of Chinamen will quickly follow."[44]

The boycott officially commenced on February 22 and quickly started to take its toll, especially on the sale of flour from Bidwell's mill. Though he vehemently denied several reports of Rancho Chico flour being returned by merchants in San Francisco and nearby Cherokee, Bidwell was definitely feeling the pinch. Coinciding with a tremendous glut on the California flour market, the boycott forced Bidwell to shut down his mill by the second week of April, throwing twenty to twenty-five employees (all white males) out of work.[45]

Bidwell fought back against the boycott with a strategy of simultaneous attack and retreat. To appease public opinion and relieve some of the pressure against him, Bidwell had begun a policy of attrition back in January that steadily lowered the number of Chinese workers on Rancho Chico from forty to just fourteen by the end of March.[46] At the same time, Bidwell took the offensive by organizing the Law and Order Committee of One Hundred. Jolted into action by the receipt of a death threat sent to him in the mail, Bidwell attempted to rally "the most intelligent

---

[42]Butte *Record*, 29 June 1878 and 20 September 1879; JBD, 17 August 1879.
[43]Rockwell D. Hunt, *John Bidwell, Prince of California Pioneers* (Caldwell, Idaho: Caxton Printers, 1942), p. 218.
[44]Chico *Enterprise*, 26 February 1886; Michele Shover, "Fighting Back: The Chinese Influence on Chico Law and Politics, 1880–1886," *California History*, 74 (Winter 1995/96), pp. 417–418.
[45]Chico *Enterprise*, 12 and 26 February 1886; Hunt, p. 222; Sacramento *Record-Union*, 24 April 1886.
[46]Chico *Enterprise*, 26 March 1886.

and conservative class of the community" against the boycotters and to prevent a replay of 1877's violent turn. Composed primarily of Chico's leading merchants, landowners, and professional men, the Committee of One Hundred eloquently expressed the fears of California's propertied elites toward the emerging labor movement, as well as their hatred of Denis Kearney, who continued to stand as a symbol of labor radicalism and violence despite the collapse of the WPC six years earlier. With Kearney still very much on his mind, Bidwell, as chair of the One Hundred's committee on resolutions, temporarily forgot his American history and helped draft a declaration of principles that condemned the boycott as "a new invention, born of tyranny and nourished in wickedness—a recent importation from desperate and distracted Ireland." Warming to the task, Bidwell and his coauthors went on to denounce boycotting as "an unmitigated wrong . . . illegal in its every principle, act, and tendency . . . inhuman, cruel, merciless . . . cowardly and hypocritical."[47] Such glaring hyperbole clearly revealed the great depth to which the Chinese issue had once again divided the local community.

With the Committee of One Hundred now shoring up the home front, Bidwell ventured to Sacramento one week later to represent Butte County at a state anti-Chinese convention organized by boycotters in the capital city. Bidwell's purpose in attending the convention was to prevent the unification of various local boycott efforts into a massive and coordinated statewide crusade. He was not well received. When he attempted to address the convention delegates, "they booed and hissed me for half an hour, but I stood and looked them in the face."[48] Finally Denis Kearney, who came to the convention hoping to revive his political career, stepped forward and shouldered Bidwell aside. Seizing the podium, Kearney began to whip up the already howling crowd. Bidwell stubbornly held his ground and confronted the immigrant labor leader saying, "All right, Mr. Kearney, let's send the Chinese [away]. Next thing is, the Irish will have to go!"[49] The delegates continued to boo and hiss Bidwell until he at last gave up and left the stage. Interviewed by a newspaper reporter two weeks after the convention adjourned, Bidwell described the meeting as "the wildest, most disorderly gathering he had ever seen."[50] Five

---

[47]Ibid., 5 March 1886.
[48]JB-91, p. 53.
[49]Hunt, p. 221.
[50]Sacramento *Bee*, 29 March 1886.

years later, still bitter about the episode, he condemned the entire incident as the work of "extremists . . . and the socialist element."[51]

Bidwell returned home from the convention even more determined to break the back of the boycott. In April, he finally began carrying out threats to sever commercial ties with all those honoring the boycott and to fire any employee on Rancho Chico who dared support the anti-Chinese movement.[52] By the middle of May he had also managed to locate enough customers to reopen his flour mill and to market one of the largest cherry crops ever harvested on Rancho Chico.[53]

Such firm resolve contributed to the subsequent collapse of the boycott, which ultimately fell victim to a bold gambit orchestrated by Colonel Frederick A. Bee, an attorney who represented the Chinese Six Companies while serving simultaneously as the Imperial Chinese government's consul in San Francisco. Vowing to "make some trouble for your boycotting fellow citizens," Bee informed Bidwell in a confidential letter that he was dispatching "U.S. Marshal" H. J. Burns to Butte County. With Burns' help, Bee promised Bidwell that "I will make it hot for them."[54]

Though it remains unclear whether Burns actually was a "deputy federal marshal," he nevertheless presented himself as one when he arrived in Oroville and Chico. Discreetly avoiding any mention of his connections to Bee and the latter's Chinese clients, Burns announced to the local press that he had just visited Folsom Prison where preparations were being made to house thousands of boycotters who would soon be convicted and imprisoned under "pending" federal statutes. His purpose in visiting Butte County, claimed Burns, was to identify prominent boycotters in order to expedite their arrest as well as the seizure of their property by the federal government. Burns' pronouncements had their desired effect. The boycott came to an abrupt end and members of the Anti-Chinese Association abandoned their fraternity in haste.[55]

Despite the opposition's collapse, John Bidwell still felt the pressure of hostile public opinion and tried to balance his defense of Chinese labor with support for tight restrictions on further Asian immigration. As he

---

[51]JB-91, p. 53.
[52]Chico *Enterprise*, 12 March 1886; Chico *Record*, 10 April 1886; Shover, "Fighting Back," p. 419.
[53]Chico *Enterprise*, 14 and 21 May 1886, and 25 June 1886.
[54]Bee to Bidwell, 3 May 1886, John Bidwell Papers, Meriam Library, CSUC; Shover, "Fighting Back," p. 416; McClain, *In Search of Equality*, pp. 64–65, 86.
[55]Chico *Enterprise*, 7 and 14 May 1886; Shover, "Fighting Back," pp. 419–420.

attempted to explain, "I don't want to be over-run by the Chinese. . . . I am anti-Chinese in a certain sense, but not in a sense that abuses them."[56] Bidwell's concession on the immigration issue represented a pragmatic accommodation to political reality. The outcry against the Chinese in California had grown so loud that Congress finally responded by passing the Chinese Exclusion Act in 1882. Originally designed as a ten-year moratorium, the act was renewed in 1892 and made permanent a decade later. Though complete enforcement proved difficult, the continued supply of cheap Chinese labor had finally come to an end.

Even with an immigration ban, Bidwell, like many farmers in the Sacramento Valley, was still determined to hire resident Chinese workers whenever practical, regardless of public feeling. Indeed, Bidwell once kept a gang of Chinese on his payroll even after they had completed their contract because, as he explained, "If I had discharged them, it would have been interpreted by the anti-Chinese element as fear on my part."[57] For several years after the 1886 boycott, however, Bidwell proceeded cautiously and avoided any actions that might reignite controversy. Then, in the wake of the nationwide financial Panic of 1893, an unrepentant Bidwell suddenly resumed hiring Chinese labor, once again arousing the ire of his white neighbors in the midst of hard times.

Caught fast between mounting debts and plummeting prices for fruit and grain, California growers aggressively slashed wages in a desperate attempt to reduce production costs. Though the cuts affected all farm laborers, white workers suffered the most dramatic losses because, at least for the moment, the dual wage structure that had elevated them above the Chinese suddenly collapsed. On Leland Stanford's Vina Ranch just north of Chico, and on the nearby Glenn estate as well, farm wages that had ranged from twenty-five to forty dollars per month with board fell to uniform rates of just seventy-five cents per day.[58] Such drastic cuts were bound to encounter resistance from whites, and growers reasoned that the easiest way to implement the reductions was to hire as many Chinese as possible. Locating and securing them became the great challenge of the moment.

To meet the challenge in time for the harvest of 1894, John Bidwell and his new manager, Colonel Charles C. Royce, deployed a revolutionary strategy that dramatically altered the racial balance on Rancho Chico.

---

[56]JB-91, p. 53.
[57]Ibid., p. 51.
[58]Chico *Chronicle-Record,* 25 March 1894.

In so doing, however, Bidwell and Royce directly precipitated Chico's third and final confrontation over the explosive Chinese issue. Adopting what had become a widespread practice in northern California's fruit industry, Bidwell quietly began leasing his orchards to Chinese tenants. They, in turn, hired their own crews of Chinese and, in yet another important new development, Japanese laborers brought in from Sacramento and San Francisco. Several of Bidwell's neighbors, including prominent grower Benjamin F. Allen, followed suit.[59] Soon, local newspapers began to report that "The Chinese now have possession of the large majority of the orchards about Chico." They also relayed ominous rumors that "300 coolies will be brought to Chico to do the work this year that has heretofore been done by white people."[60] Such reports made it clear that, for the first time in Chico's history, the local harvest would be gathered by mostly non-white hands.

Public reaction was swift and furious. On May 10, 1894, a crowd of 1,300 gathered at Armory Hall to denounce "the coolie invaders" and demand an immediate end to "the importation of Mongolian laborers for fruit picking or other purposes." The mass meeting resulted in the formation of the Chico Anti-Chinese League, which immediately established an employment bureau to register job-seeking whites and blacks who were willing to replace Asian workers. The League dispatched visiting committees to leading employers, urging them to hire from the bureau rolls, which contained eighty names by the end of its second day.[61]

Delegations met with Sierra Lumber Company, Benjamin Allen, and, on July 10, John Bidwell. Like the others, Bidwell expressed a preference for white labor but pleaded its scarcity at prevailing wage rates. After making vague promises to replace his Asian workers, Bidwell, ignoring the hiring practices of his new Chinese tenants, disingenuously asserted that he had "but three Chinamen in his employ." He also told the League committee that he had rented only half his orchards, and that those still under his direct control "were pruned and cared for by white labor." This was true at least of his cherry crop, which he had sold on the tree to the J. Z.

---

[59] On the spread of Chinese tenant farming in California's orchards, see Chan, *Bittersweet Soil*, pp. 225–264. Prospective Chinese tenants had approached Bidwell about renting his orchards as early as 1881, but he apparently showed little interest prior to 1894. See JBD, 30 September 1881.
[60] Chico *Chronicle-Record*, 5 and 12 May 1894.
[61] Chico *Chronicle-Record*, 12 and 19 May 1894; *Chico Anti-Chinese League Minute Book*, 10–12 May 1894. A separate Ladies Anti-Chinese League was also formed in Chico. See *League Minute Book*, 28 May 1894 and Chico *Chronicle-Record*, 4 August 1894.

Anderson Fruit Company of San Jose. Working in cooperation with the League's employment bureau, Anderson's representative on Rancho Chico, I. D. Howe, hired over 300 whites to pick and pack the crop. As for his Chinese tenants, Bidwell claimed that since "no white people offered to rent his orchards" he had no choice but "to rent to Chinamen."[62]

Bidwell's answers did little to soothe public opinion, especially when large numbers of Chinese continued to arrive in town throughout July with "their destination being the same in nearly all cases, the Rancho Chico." By the middle of August, threats of renewed violence began to surface. The editor of the Chico *Chronicle-Record* warned that "the people here are at fever heat on this Chinese question. The matter has reached that shape where only a spark is needed to make serious trouble.... There is a storm brewing, ... whether it shall be calmed now or grow into a tempest that will sweep everything before it is a matter for the employers of Chinese labor to decide, and they want to decide it quickly."[63]

As in 1877, the failure of nonviolent tactics resulted in mounting frustration and growing support for more extreme measures. On August 10, angry militants met at the Chico Hotel and organized the United Labor League (ULL). One week later, the ULL issued a public proclamation ordering all Chinese farm workers to vacate Chico by September 1. Though members of the ULL denied any intentions of backing their demand with force, the implication of violence was clear enough.[64]

In the context of the times, the threat posed by the ULL was not an empty one. Beginning in 1885 with the forced evacuation of Eureka, California's Chinatown and the massacre of Chinese coal miners in Rock Springs, Wyoming, "abatement by violence" had become the preferred method of anti-Asian extremists. In dozens of towns throughout California and the West, Chinese laborers were routed from their homes and jobs by rioting mobs of white workers. The expulsion campaigns of 1885 and 1886 set the precedent for a second round of violent evictions in 1893 and 1894. In San Bernardino, Redlands, Fresno, Vacaville, Ukiah, and at least ten other rural California communities, angry mobs expelled their Chinese neighbors *en masse*. Certainly there was no reason to believe that the same thing would not happen in Chico.[65]

---

[62]*League Minute Book*, 9 July–6 August 1894; Chico *Chronicle-Record*, 9 and 26 May 1894, 2 June 1894, 9 and 16 July 1894.
[63]Chico *Chronicle-Record*, 28 July and 11 August 1894.
[64]Ibid., 11 and 18 August 1894.
[65]McWilliams, *Factories in the Field*, pp. 74–79; Sandmeyer, *Anti-Chinese Movement*, pp. 97–98; Saxton, *Indispensable Enemy*, pp. 176–177, 210–213, 229–232.

Fortunately, and in sharp contrast to the situation in 1877, local authorities acted quickly to prevent violence. On the eve of the September 1 deadline, the Butte County sheriff served ULL leaders with papers ordering them "to desist from any attempt to intimidate or forcibly expel the Chinese." The sheriff's timely intervention quashed the ULL campaign and the organization soon disintegrated.[66] So too did the Anti-Chinese League, which gave up the fight after Bidwell once again leased his orchards to Chinese tenants for the upcoming season. Bidwell had won. As the anti-Chinese *Chronicle-Record* lamented, "the matter has ceased to be a sensation." The League held its last meeting on February 23, 1895, and was never heard from again.[67]

Meanwhile, John Bidwell had actually expanded the scope of his Chinese leasing program. For 1895, Bidwell rented almost all his orchards to a syndicate of wealthy San Francisco Chinese merchants with close ties to the Six Companies. In addition to Rancho Chico, the syndicate leased several other northern California orchards and, in yet another blow to the local economy, arranged to have its entire harvest packed and canned by the Pacific Fruit Packing Company of San Francisco.[68]

Thus, with the exception of the cherry crop, which Bidwell had again sold to Anderson Fruit Company, the orchard produce of Rancho Chico was almost completely harvested by Asian labor in 1895. For the first time, Chinese workers also dominated the drying houses, where their presence sparked a violent racial altercation with white employees toward the end of August. Their entry into local canning, the only sector of specialty crop agriculture still beyond their reach, was prevented solely by the fact that Bidwell had closed his cannery in 1890. Its successor, the Chico Canning Company, continued to employ an exclusively white work force.[69]

Bidwell, however, stuck with the Chinese, even after the return of prosperity toward the end of 1896. In December of that year, as he edged further into retirement, Bidwell began leasing his prized fruit and almond orchards to a small group of eight Chinese tenant farmers.[70] Signing yearly agreements secured by chattel mortgages on Rancho Chico's growing crops, each of these enterprising but landless growers obtained the right to use one or more of Bidwell's orchards as if it were his own. Each enjoyed

---
[66]*League Minute Book*, 27 August 1894; Chico *Chronicle-Record*, 1 September 1894.
[67]*League Minute Book*, 22 October 1894 and 23 February 1895; Chico *Chronicle-Record*, 2 March 1895.
[68]San Francisco *Call*, 23 February 1895; Chico *Chronicle-Record*, 2 March 1895.
[69]Chico *Enterprise*, 8 and 25 March 1890; Benjamin, *John Bidwell*, pp. 26–27; Chico *Chronicle-Record*, 11 May 1895, 3 and 24 August 1895.
[70]The eight tenants were Yet Poy, Quong On, Joe Hong, Bock Sing, Go Sen Yen, Gee Sing, Wah Sing, and Him Moon.

a considerable degree of individual autonomy, coupled with the chance to profit directly, and substantially, from the labor he invested in Bidwell's mature and bearing trees.[71]

There were significant strings attached, however. In exchange for the use of his orchards, the Chinese promised to pay Bidwell annual cash rents ranging from $1,000 to $3,500 deducted from their harvest proceeds. Portions of the contracted figure that went unpaid for any reason bore ten percent interest, as did any funds borrowed from Bidwell to meet operating expenses during the growing season. These could be considerable, since the tenants agreed to bear all the costs of gathering, curing, and delivering their harvested crops to Bidwell, who retained the exclusive right to market them on his and the tenants' behalf.[72]

The presence of these Asian renters on Rancho Chico testified eloquently to the anti-Chinese movement's failure to dictate John Bidwell's hiring and management practices. Despite periodic threats and violence, Chinese labor remained essential to Rancho Chico's prosperity right up to the end of Bidwell's life. As he had done with the Mechoopda Indians, John Bidwell had successfully played the roles of both protector and exploiter of Chinese immigrant labor.

## *Bidwell's Remarks on the Chinese*

### CHINESE INCLUDED IN MANSION WORK FORCE

This is our first day under the administration of Hannah & Wong and everything is better—at least so it seems. There is a decided improvement in the cooking—and I think there is all round. Johnny's Chinaman in the garden still holds out a faithful fellow. And I have permitted another one to be hired for the garden. The force in that department now consists of—John Harry, Capt—Edward, 1st Lieut—2 Chinamen, 2nd & 3rd Lieuts—rank & file, about 6 to a dozen aborigines of the female persuasion—with Wong and the adobe Chinaman as skirmishers around the castle. Jackson (African) spy! . . .[1]

---

[71] See Butte County, *Index to Chattel Mortgages,* Book 1, 1852–1915. At least one of the eight renters, Go Sen Yen, also received permission to live on Rancho Chico as a resident tenant. See Butte County, *Chattel Mortgages,* Book J, p. 109.

[72] Butte County, *Chattel Mortgages,* Book G, pp. 351, 354, 375, 393, 418, 431; Book I, pp. 76, 198, 415, 417, 420, 423; and Book J, pp. 106, 109, 112, 115, 118, 121, 124, 151. The combination of cash leases secured by chattel mortgages had become a common arrangement between white orchardists and individual Chinese tenant farmers in late nineteenth century California. See Chan, *Bittersweet Soil,* pp. 235 and 420.

[1] JB to AB, 19 June 1869, JB-CSL, b. 47, f. 25.

### Wong "is a perfect treasure"

...Wong keeps the verandah very clean—oh ever so much better than Thomas did! and makes no noise or fuss about it. He is a perfect treasure and as neat as a pin. As I write he is going to and fro carrying two buckets at a time to water plants &c.[2]

### Some Chinese are "spoiled"

...Wong is no longer here, but of his going I wrote you. The new China boy—whose name is Seng—is not a success, though he does the best he knows—is steady and honest—but young. One good sign is, however, that he is not handsome, and understands very little English. All the handsome Chinamen with fluent tongues are "spoiled boys". The rule holds good with all the dark and yellow races....[3]

### Hires Chinese to prune orchards, 29 March 1876,

Hired six Chinamen to go & prune for one month @ 27 [dollars], they board themselves.[4]

### Advises Chinese facing threats and discrimination

...Yesterday a delegation of 7 well dressed Chinamen called on me. They are apprehensive that the meetings held in Chico by anti-Chinese men, who treat them insolently and threaten to drive them away, because they compete with them in many kinds of labor—and notably because some 60 or 70 Chinamen are employed by the Sash factory—may result in a collision—that is, that the Irish and others may attack them! Some of the men were from Oroville—and some from San Francisco. I could not give them much comfort. My advice was, for them to be good, industrious, quiet people, then they would have right on their side and gain, the good. Then also the law would have a better chance to protect them....[5]

### Soap factory burned by anti-Chinese arsonists

...The Caucasian (anti-Chinese) influence in this town is becoming unbearable. Something over a week ago somebody set fire to our soap factory building, because, I had it rented to Sun Kee's brothers. They kept hogs there but did not kill them there. But the Chinaman there succeeded in putting the fire out. He saw a man run after the fire started. About four or five days ago, the man who sold the lot to McMillan began suit against the Chinamen to abate the keeping of hogs there as a nuisance, and the trial was to come off tomorrow. Feeling an

---

[2] JB to AB, 10 July 1869, Ibid., b. 47, f. 43.
[3] JB to AB, 23 August 1869, Ibid., b. 48, f. 24.
[4] JBD, 29 March 1876.
[5] JB to AB, 21 December 1876, JB-CSL, b. 53, f. 14.

interest in the matter because they rent the building from me, and wishing to have the matter settled without a suit (if it really was a nuisance), I went and examined it, and had others to do it, and we found it to be far less offensive than the making of soap was—in fact it was not offensive at all—on the contrary it was neat—no killing going on, there was no offal—nothing to give offense—and all so thought and said.

But the <u>finale</u>. Just as our prayer meeting tonight concluded, the fire bells rang. The soap factory building was set on fire by several men—(a sort of mob of a dozen or so men, the Caucasians or men influenced by them no doubt)—and the building with $600 worth of hogs all burned!

As Petersen belongs to that Society I ought to discharge him without further delay—will do so as soon as I can find a man to take his place. The danger is that these fellows may do more and greater damage. Petersen has shown at times a most malignant temper. He is not the mild tempered man he used to seem—he is mild in work though! . . .

The burning of the soap factory last night was done by men who prevented the Chinamen from putting out the fire or even saving their hogs alive! I know the men, but I have no certain proof as yet which will convict them. I have offered $500 reward for such evidence as will lead to their arrest and conviction. . . .[6]

### ANTI-CHINESE MOVEMENT CARRIES CITY ELECTION AND INFILTRATES RANCHO CHICO

. . . The election in town the other day was an anti-Chinese victory—and it throws [F. C.] Lusk out as Clerk and Attorney for the town; and he was greatly disgusted, and said he wanted 'to go and live in St. Petersburg—where no man ever voted.'!!!!! . . . Our new coachman (William Kirkwood) seems to do very well. For a person who has not been long here, I think he is as good as could be expected. But learned one thing about him which I do not like—he belongs to the [Order of] Caucasians! And for this I may let him go. But I think it is probable he is a new member, inveighed in by Petersen—because I hear William Hansen also belongs to that order, and if so, it must have been through Petersen of course![7]

### CHICO CHINATOWNS SET ABLAZE, 9 AND 10 MARCH 1877

Both Chinatowns were set on fire last night. . . . Called at Chico Record office and talked about anti-Chinese movement—counseled against it.[8]

### LEMM RANCH MURDERS, 14 MARCH 1877

. . . a great anti-Chinese excitement arose all over California. I think it was in 1877. About 2 miles from Chico a neighbor of mine had given six Chinese a

---

[6]JB to AB, 7 February 1877, Ibid., b. 54, f. 5.
[7]JB to AB, 9 February 1877, Ibid., b. 54, f. 6.
[8]JBD, 9, 10 March 1877.

job to clear some land off. Six men, with their faces blacked, went into their cabin one night, and each put his revolver at the head of a Chinaman and fired, 5 were killed instantly. One, badly wounded, crawled into the bushes and the next day he was able to crawl nearly half a mile to the house of his employer, and gave the notice. There was much excitement against the Chinese, but that crime roused the good people. They met, appointed a committee to find the perpetrators of the outrage. Almost every man in Chico received anonymous letters that if he did not discharge his Chinese his property would be burned, etc. The first thing I did was to telegraph to S.F. for ten Winchester rifles.

The Chinese who had been clearing the land for me were not discharged; I kept them for nearly a month. If I had discharged them, it would have been interpreted by the anti-Chinese element as fear on my part. I have never had as many Chinese working for me as white men.

I was appointed by the committee to watch the post office, as this was in one of my buildings. I did it through some young men in my employ. If a local letter was dropped into the office it was marked. A letter was dropped in, one day, addressed to a person unknown to the watcher. The receiver of the letter went off into the woods and was followed. The letter was of a threatening nature. He was arrested and put into the town hall. No one was permitted to speak with him, and in about 24 hours he became thoroughly frightened. He was not threatened, but he suspected a good deal.

He confessed everything; told the names of the murderers of the Chinese. They were arrested. We employed ex-Gov. Wood to assist our district attorney, also an expert detective. The men were all convicted and sent to the penitentiary. We followed them up until we got them, because it would not do to allow such things to transpire.[9]

### CITIZENS JOIN SEARCH FOR MURDERERS, 16 MARCH 1877

Meeting of citizens committee in Masonic Hall against the murders of the Chinese on Lemm ranch . . . offer reward for murderers of the Chinese.[10]

### BIDWELL PREPARES TO ARM RANCHO CHICO, 17 MARCH 1877

. . . wrote for (Henry's) Rifles . . . [local merchant Charles] Stilson sent over box of Henry's rifles.[11]

### A THREATENING NOTE, 24 MARCH 1877

To General Bidwell—

Sir; You are given notice hereby to discharge your Mongolian help within ten days from date, or suffer the consequences. Let this be enough.

signed Committee[12]

---

[9]JB-91, pp. 50–51.
[11]Ibid., 17, 21 March 1877.
[10]JBD, 16 March 1877.
[12]Butte *Record*, 24 March 1877.

### "If the law cannot protect us, we must protect ourselves"

... The grand jury indicted several of the murderers and conspirators yesterday; but, owing to some of the Jury being "Caucasians" themselves, and perhaps some of the officers being affected with that mania and wishing to conciliate as far as possible so as to make votes for a reelection, several of the worst men arrested as conspirators, were turned loose! The people are talking of taking the law into their own hands. Abram [Bidwell] just came in much haste to say, I had better not go out this morning. Of course I shall not take that advice. It is with us a common defense. If the law cannot protect us, we must protect ourselves....[13]

### "Caucasian element an insignificant minority"

It is astonishing how deep and general the sentiment is against the Chico murderers and incendiaries,—and the swift justice which was meted out to the latter receives warm and unanimous commendation. I had no idea how earnestly the people were watching our movements. Am now satisfied we have not only the moral power of the State with us—as well as the law on our side—but a vast majority of the people. In other words, the 'Caucasian' element is really an insignificant minority.[14]

### Bidwell exposes Caucasian Society and receives more threats

I got hold of the by-laws of the Caucasian Society, the organization that did all the mischief. I had them published throughout the state to show what men could do. The members were under the most binding oaths to persecute every man who employed Chinese; those who taught Chinese any of the arts of civilization were put on the list as perpetual enemies and were to be persecuted in every way possible except to kill. Another thing that was worse than that. Some of the Caucasian Society who were not averse to killing, formed a new club and called it the Labor Union Society. An old convict was the president. They held their meetings at midnight in a certain grove. They were put under oath to execute the orders of their captain; if he said murder, they had to murder. Knowing that it was my habit to post my letters late at night, they determined to assassinate me as soon as opportunity offered.

I have never yielded to any of those bad influences. I have stood my ground. At one time it was reported that the anti-Chinese had carried the town of Chico. There came up from San Francisco and San Jose a set of three or four hundred ruffians. They came to my ranch and asked of a man "Who does this place belong to?" "Gen. Bidwell." "Are you working for him?" "Yes." "Is it possible that he employs anybody but Chinese and niggers?"[15]

---

[13]JB to AB, 5 April 1877, JB-CSL, b. 54, f. 13.
[14]JB to AB, 2 May 1877, Ibid., b. 54, f. 3.
[15]JB-91, pp. 51–52.

### BIDWELL SEEKS GOOD RELATIONS WITH CHINA, AND A MARKET FOR CALIFORNIA WHEAT AND FLOUR

We have a treaty with China, and, as I understand, we have ample control of Mongolian immigration. All is satisfactory. Why may we not lay hold of China and convert that vast empire of more than four hundred million people into a boundless and never-failing market for all our surplus flour? I do not mean to compel the Chinese to swallow our bread at the cannon's mouth—far otherwise. But lay hold of China by the stronger and more enduring ties of friendship. I can see no reason why we should perpetuate the senseless abuse and prejudices for which politicians and demagogism have in the past, as I think, been so largely responsible. We, on this coast, are too needy, and our country is too powerful and too magnanimous, I trust, to give any uncertain sound on the question of such vital moment to her Pacific border. The Mongolian becomes degraded by the use of opium; but do not let us in any way help to degrade him (by abuse or otherwise) and then blame him because he is degraded. Let it not be said that Mongolians came in contact with Christian civilization and were made worse. Genuine friendship alone can elevate.

It has been said that the people of China eat rice, and will not, therefore use wheat flour. But they do use wheat flour. The shipments of flour from San Francisco were: In 1878, two hundred and nine thousand six hundred and eleven barrels ... in 1880, two hundred and thirty-five thousand and three hundred and three barrels. These shipments began with ninety-six thousand barrels in 1865, and have steadily increased till the present time; and thus far this year they have been at the rate of nearly three hundred thousand barrels....

I may err; but to me this flour business with China seems susceptible, by a just and wise policy, of almost indefinite expansion. But China takes more than flour from California. Last year the merchandise exports amounted to three million three hundred and twenty-four thousand seven hundred and 66 dollars.

During the last month (August, 1881) the exports of merchandise from San Francisco by sea were larger to China than any other foreign country except England.[16]

### BIDWELL BLAMES ORGANIZED LABOR FOR ANTI-CHINESE AGITATION

It would be no more than just that the Chinese should revenge themselves in their own country, but it is not likely that they will. The eminity [sic] against them came about in this manner. In early days, we had to manufacture many things ourselves. We could not wait to have them brought from the east it was too expensive, and so manufactories were established. It was not long before the journeymen began to dictate to the employers, because they employed the boys.

---

[16]CSAS 1881, p. 34.

They made a rule allowing one apprentice to every seven men. Finally they made so much trouble that Chinese were employed, because they were easily managed and industrious. After a while nearly all the manufacturing was performed by Chinese labor, and then it was this that was made a political issue, and the candidate for office who was not in favor of this movement, would not get the votes, especially of the foreign element. I have never taken any stock in such business. I don't want to be over-run by Chinese. I am anti-Chinese in a certain sense, but not in a sense that abuses them. For a long time the two leading political parties vied with each other to see who could hit the Chinese the hardest in their platforms. The democrats could always go it a little stronger than the republicans, and possibly they got the larger portion of the anti-Chinese vote.[17]

### Bidwell denounces anti-Chinese movement, 1886

Dear Sir [Weekly Butte *Record*],                    13 February 1886

As for China labor, I care very little for it. If raising fruit or garden products cost more by white labor, then the people must pay more for them. But I am utterly opposed to the unlawful, cruel and outrageous treatment going on in this State against the Chinese.

Very truly,<br>John Bidwell[18]

### Another threatening letter

Get rid of your Chinese help <u>now</u> or youl [*sic*] see fire over your heads when you leest [*sic*] expect it. We positively mean business and don't you forget it. Last call, last notice.[19]

### Bidwell, representing the Committee of 100, denounces anti-Chinese boycott, 1886

It has ever been the pride and boast of America that our country should be a refuge for the oppressed of every land. Under this benign theorem we can now look back over more than a hundred years of unexampled prosperity.

Our invitation has been to all the world, and the world has been coming to us. But now we find that, vast as is our imperial domain, it will not hold all the world, and we must not longer invite all the world to come.

In any modification of our past policy and in taking to an extent a new departure, let us be just—let us do no wrong or violence to any people.

That we may not be misunderstood we declare, once and for all, that we are in favor of so amending treaties, and of such just and efficient action by our government as shall, at the earliest period practicable, effectually prevent further

---
[17]JB-91, pp. 53–54.
[18]Weekly Butte *Record*, 13 February 1886.
[19]Anonymous to JB, 1 March 1886, JB-CSL, b. 126, f. 8.

immigration of Chinese and of all other foreigners who may be deemed or found detrimental to labor or any other American interests.

That we further declare and recognize the fact, that industry alone is true wealth; and that labor—expressly intelligent labor—is the only sure foundation for the prosperity of communities and States. And we openly and publicly affirm that we are, as all good citizens must be, the friends of labor. . . .

That at this period of unusual excitement, of well known and admitted lawless acts, of persecutions, and of threatened injuries against peaceable citizens; against the friends of law, order and the best interests of the State; against all hoped-for prosperity and business prospects; and surely against the true interests of the laboring man; which lawless acts are largely, if not wholly, the result of violent harangues and race prejudice begun and persistently fomented by designing demagogues and reckless agitators, evidently for political and ulterior purposes. In view of these facts the conclusion is irresistible that the people, moved to such acts, have been, and are being, purposely misled, and it is to be hoped, and we confidently believe, that on sober second thought all right-minded men will abandon methods that can lead only to ruin. . . .

And what is one of the great instrumentalities they propose to use in the satanic work of destroying business and prosperity, ruining credit, starving families, persecutions, invasions of private rights, destruction of public credit, and trampling under foot the Supreme law of the land? BOYCOTTING. And what is it? and what its real purport? Why, it is a new invention, born of tyranny and nourished in wickedness—a recent importation from desperate and distracted Ireland—and has, no doubt, the full endorsement of the San Francisco sandlot, and of those concentrations of human fiendishness known as "dynamiters." Boycotting began its career as a desperate remedy for a desperate state of things—a fit instrument for a star chamber, and for organized tyranny and revenge. In a word, it is a perilous parasite on the life of free America; the introduction of which into this land of freedom was without cause or excuse, and should be branded as a crime.

Boycotting is an unmitigated wrong, and should not be countenanced, or have an abiding place in this country; because its mission is to menace, to coerce, to injure.

It is illegal in its every principle, act and tendency; because it is a law-defyer and law breaker, and appeals to no law except the law of power, of passion, of prejudice and of brute force.

It is inhuman, cruel, merciless; because it persecutes and oppresses the weak and helpless and all who dare disobey its tyranny—and makes homeless and starves families without cause.

It is dangerous; because a fit instrument for the use of complotters in their dark designs of revenge, sedition or organized conspiracy.

Boycotting is cowardly and hypocritical; because in the garb of loyalty, innocence and pretended regard for labor, it is an enemy in disguise and seeks, by indirection, to commit injury and compass ends which no man would dare attempt in a fair, honest, open and legal manner.

In a word, boycotting is the thumbscrew of a modern inquisitorial machine, which may be used in a multiplicity of ways for sinister purposes, and which aims to *rule*, but whose mission (if tolerated) is to *ruin* America....[20]

### BIDWELL DESCRIBES THE 1886 ANTI-CHINESE CONVENTION IN SACRAMENTO

... Convention here is boisterous—a vast majority extremists—will no doubt sanction boycotting and everything else they dare do to persecute the Chinese. Was greatly surprised that L. H. McIntosh [of Chico] should've voted with the enemy. I have lost all respect for him. [Former U.S. Senator Aaron A.] Sargent made a much more conservative speech than I expected from him. He is opposed to boycotting. Mr. [William] Earll [of Chico] is right and so far is with me in everything. The great battle will be on the report of the committee on Resolutions. [California Republican party leader Morris] Estee is on the wrong side—and can never again have my confidence or support for any office.[21]

### BIDWELL CHALLENGES ANTI-CHINESE BOYCOTTERS, MARCH 1886

To the People ...

"Boycotting," as you know, has begun expressly to injure me. This I sincerely regret, because it cannot fail to injure also you; and because it will surely injure, if not destroy, all business and prosperity. I ask, then, can any good man or citizen afford to stand neutral and not raise his voice against the course of ruin already begun against your best interests?

The pretense this time is the Chinaman; next time it will be something else—it means trouble; it means ruin, and only ruin.

Having been misrepresented far and near, let me say, once for all: No Chinaman is, or ever has been, employed in my home, or in farm work, or in my harvest fields, in my flouring mill, or elsewhere on my premises, except, in part, in the garden and orchards, picking and drying fruit.

On the contrary, almost all my berries and small fruits are picked by women, girls and boys from town, and they also comprise almost my sole help in the cannery.

If it were not for these industries, their time might be spent in idleness, or worse pursuits.

---

[20]Chico *Enterprise*, 5 March 1886.
[21]JB, in Sacramento, to AB, 11 March 1886, JB-CSL, b. 58, f. 29.

To the good men in my employ, let me say a word; I believe you to be faithful to your interests. If you stand firm against those who have banded together to prevent me from raising money to pay you, I shall feel grateful. Those who do not stand by me cannot, of course, expect me to employ them, or keep them in my employ.

And, "boycotters," a word to you: I trust you will have the decency not to come or drive on my premises as long as you are trying to injure me.

John Bidwell[22]

### BIDWELL DISGUSTED BY SUFFRAGIST LAURA DE FORCE GORDON'S STAND AGAINST CHINESE

This is simply a line—as I was up last night at the [Anti-Chinese] Convention till after 2 A.M. Mrs. Laura de Force Gordon [attorney and feminist leader] was invited last night to speak at the Convention for a few minutes while waiting for a committee's report. I never want to hear her again. She made a very unwomanly speech. Among other things she said, "our mothers had no Chinamen to help them and raised a good deal larger families than they do now"! She may not have meant anything, but it brought down the house! But I did not like any thing she said. . . . Your letter of last night I received at Sac. You are right about L. H. McIntosh—he is utterly unreliable.[23]

### BIDWELL RECALLS THE 1886 ANTI-CHINESE CONVENTION

Another Chinese excitement broke out all over the coast in '86. Few knew how it was started. I have a theory, not based on hearsay, as to its cause. There is evidence of the cause in the archives at Washington. There were men foolish enough to contemplate the destruction of government records of titles of property in all the Pacific Coast states. Their leader [Denis Kearney?] was a man of nihilistic ideas. They began the excitement by raising the cry against the Chinese. They started a convention in Sacramento on that one question. All the counties were requested to send delegates. They also asked all anti-Chinese societies to send their delegates. So-called societies were formed of only three or four members in order that the delegates might be sent to Sacramento. Our county did not intend to do anything but so much was published about the matter that just about a week before the convention's meeting, our supervisors thought it best to send delegates. They selected a dozen men, myself among the number. I told them I had no business in an anti-Chinese meeting, but the others said they would not go unless I did. It was thought to be so important that I finally consented. All the socialistic element was there. There were about 80 conserva-

---
[22]JB, 3 March 1886, in Chico *Enterprise*, 12 March 1886.
[23]JB, in San Francisco, to AB, 12 March 1886, JB-CSL, b. 58, f. 30.

tive men out of the four or five hundred present. When I got up to speak, they hissed me for half an hour, but I stood and looked them in the face. Nothing could be done of course, and the matter was referred to Congress;—the matter being a national question and beyond the jurisdiction of the State government.[24]

ANTI-CHINESE ACTIVITY FLARES ONE MORE TIME IN CHICO, 1894

Women's Anti-Chinese League Procession tonight.... The Hobo anti-Chinese Committee notified Chinese yesterday to leave by first of Sept.! ... Anti-Chinese Meeting at Armory Hall tonight. ... Great anti-Chinese procession tonight. Speaker—Rev. Mr. Fen, Rev. Mr., Gibson, Dr. Murray, music. etc.[25]

---

[24]JB-91, pp. 52–53.
[25]JBD, 10 May, 23 June, 14 July, 11 August 1894.

# A Bidwell Bibliography

### Manuscripts

*Bidwell Mansion State Historic Park, Chico, California*
    Bidwell, Annie E. K. *Personal Diary, 1888–1911*
    Bidwell, John. *Personal Diary, 1864–1900*
    Reminiscences of A.G. Eames, March 1938

*Bancroft Library, University of California, Berkeley*
    Bancroft Land Case Maps. These include *diseños* drawn by Bidwell of the following: Larkin's Children's Rancho; Rancho del Arroyo Chico; Rancho Boga; Rancho de Farwell y del Rancho Arroyo Chico; Rancho de los Coluses; Rancho Llano Seco; Rancho Rio de los Molinos; Ranchos de Butte County; Mapa de los Valles del Sacramento y San Joaquin; Mapa del Valle de Sacramento, 1844; Rancho del Nueva Flandria, 1844.
    Josiah Belden Papers
    Bidwell Family Papers, 1851–1918
    John Bidwell Letters, 1895–1899
    John Bidwell Letters to E. W. Haskell, 1867
    Nicholas Dawson Papers
    Robert Underwood Johnson Papers
    Thomas O. Larkin Papers, 1822–1858
    Mott-Von Schmidt Family Papers
    New Helvetia: Diary of Events, 1845–1848
    Alice M. Reading Collection
    Edwin Allen Sherman Papers
    James L. L. Warren Papers

*California Historical Society Library, San Francisco*
    John Bidwell Papers
    Henry William Cleaveland Papers
    Albert Peri Papers

*California State Archives, Sacramento*
    Records of the State Legislature. State Senate. Old Bill File.

*California State Library, Sacramento*
    Annie E. K. Bidwell Papers, 1842–1918

John Bidwell Diary, 1864–1900
John Bidwell Papers, 1841–1900
John Bidwell, Sutter's Fort Pioneer Collection
George McKinstry Papers
Warren Sexton Collection

*California State University, Chico, Meriam Library, Special Collections*
Annie E. K. Bidwell Diaries and Papers, 1855–1913
Annie E. K. Bidwell Estate Papers, 1920–1939
John Bidwell Diaries and Papers, 1844–1900
Frank Durkee Collection
Waterland, John S., a.k.a. Old Timer. *Historical Articles on Butte County in Chico* Record, 6 volumes plus index, 1939–1940.

*Henry E. Huntington Library, San Marino*
George A. Gillespie Papers
Samuel Holladay Papers
Grace Nelson Papers
John Townsend Papers

*Holt-Atherton Center for Western Studies, University of the Pacific*
John Muir Papers

*Society of California Pioneers Library, San Francisco*
John Bidwell Papers
Nancy Kelsey File

*Sutter's Fort State Park, Sacramento*
Reminiscences of A. G. Eames, March 1938

*University of California, Los Angeles, University Research Library, Special Collections*
Cornelius Cole Family Papers
Archibald H. Gillespie Papers
William S. Rosecrans Papers

OTHER UNPUBLISHED PRIMARY SOURCES

Azbill, Henry. "Some Aspects of Mechoopda Indian Culture." ANCRR and CSUC Oral History Program, 1966.

Bidwell, John and Annie E. K. Bidwell. "Recollection, 1897." In Annie E. K. Bidwell Papers. CSL.

Bidwell, John. "California 1841–1848: An Immigrant's Recollections of a Trip Across the Plains and of Men and Events in Early Days, Including the Bear Flag Revolution." Dictation to Seth Sprague Boynton for Hubert H. Bancroft, 1877. Bancroft Library, University of California, Berkeley.

_____. "Dictation From General John Bidwell: An Autobiography." Dictation for Hubert H. Bancroft Collections with some corrections in Bidwell's handwriting, 1891. Bancroft Library, University of California, Berkeley.

Bolt, Rebecca French. *Recollections of General and Mrs. Bidwell.* Chico: ANCRR and CSUC, Oral History Program, 1972.

English, Ruby. *Recollections of Ruby English as Mrs. A. K. Bidwell's Maid, 1914–1918.* ANCRR and CSUC, Oral History Program, 1964.

Gage, Helen Sommer. *Recollections of Life in Early Chico and of General and Mrs. Bidwell.* ANCRR and CSUC, Oral History Program, 1972.

Rice, Charles. *Rancho Chico as Seen by a Youthful Employee, the Chico Gas and Water Companies, and the Town of Chico as it Developed between the 1880's and the 1890's.* Chico: ANCRR and CSUC, Oral History Program, 1964.

Royce, Charles C. *In Memoriam: John Bidwell.* Three-volume scrapbook, 1905. CSL.

Wilson, Thelma. *News Items Primarily Concerning Gen. John Bidwell Taken from Newspaper Files.* Vols. 1–3. CSUC, Meriam Library Special Collections.

_____. "A Mechoopda Descendant Relates Her Family's History." Chico: ANCRR and CSUC Oral History Program, Northeastern California Project, 1972.

## Published Primary Sources

Anderson, Robert A. *Fighting the Mill Creeks: Being a Personal Account of Campaigns Against Indians of the Northern Sierras.* Chico: Chico Record Press, 1909.

Bidwell, Annie E. K. "The Mechoopdas, or Rancho Chico Indians." *Overland Monthly*, 27 (February 1896): 204–210.

_____. *Rancho Chico Indians.* Edited by Dorothy Hill. Chico: Bidwell Mansion Cooperating Association, 1980.

_____. *An Example of Indian Civilization.* Philadelphia: Women's National Indian Association, 1891.

_____. "The Character of General John Bidwell: Two Letters Written by His Widow, Mrs. Annie E. K. Bidwell." *Annual Publication of the Historical Society of Southern California,* 11 (1919): 53–55.

Bidwell, John. *A Journey to California, with Observations about the Country, Climate, and the Route to this Country....* Independence, Liberty, or Weston [?], Missouri: n.p., 1842.

_____. *A Journey to California, with Observations about the Country, Climate, and the Route to this Country.* Introduction by Herbert I. Priestly. San Francisco: John H. Nash, 1937.

_____. *A Journey to California, 1841. The First Emigrant Party to California by Wagon Train. The Journal of John Bidwell.* Introduction by Francis P. Farquhar. Berkeley: Friends of the Bancroft Library, 1964.

_____. "Earliest Explorations of Colusa County." In *Colusa County: Its History*, by Justus H. Rogers. Orland, California: n.p., 1891. Pp. 37–54.

_____. "Early California Reminiscences." Dictated to O.B. Parkinson of Stockton, California. *Out West*, 20, 8 parts: (January 1904), pp. 76–78; (February 1904), pp. 182–188; (March 1904), pp. 285–287; (April 1904), pp. 377–379; (May 1904), pp. 467–468; (June 1904), pp. 559–561; (July 1904), pp. 79–80; (August 1904), pp. 193–195.

_____. *Echoes of the Past About California*. Chico: Chico *Advertiser*, 1914.

_____. *Echoes of the Past About California*. Reprint edited by Milo M. Quaife. Published with *In Camp and Cabin* by Rev. John Steele. Chicago: R. R. Donnelley and Sons, 1928.

_____. *Echoes of the Past*. Reprint. New York: Citadel Press, 1962.

_____. *Echoes of the Past*. Reprint. New York: Arno Press, 1973.

_____. *Echoes of the Past*. Reprint. Sacramento: California State Department of Parks and Recreation, 1987.

_____. *In California Before the Gold Rush*. Introduction by Lindley Bynum. Los Angeles: Ward Richie Press, 1948.

_____. "The First Emigrant Train to California." *The American Progress Magazine*, [n.v.] (May 1910): 5–13.

_____. "The First Emigrant Train to California." *The Century Illustrated Monthly Magazine*, 41 (November 1890): 106–130.

_____. *The First Emigrant Train to California*. Introduction by Oscar Lewis. Palo Alto, California: Lewis Osborne, 1966.

_____. "The First Emigrant Train to California." *American History Illustrated*, 20 (April 1985): 36–47.

_____; Bancroft, Hubert Howe; and James Longmire. *First Three Wagon Trains: To California, 1841; To Oregon, 1842; To Washington, 1853*. Portland, Oregon: Binfords and Mort, 1956.

_____. "Life in California Before the Gold Discovery." *The Century Illustrated Monthly Magazine*, 41 (December 1890): 163–183.

_____. *Life in California Before the Gold Discovery*. Introduction by Oscar Lewis. Palo Alto, California: Lewis Osborne, 1966.

_____. "Fremont in the Conquest of California." *The Century Illustrated Monthly Magazine*, 41 (February 1891): 518–525.

_____. "Address of John Bidwell to the Members of the Society of California Pioneers, November 1, 1897." Edited by Henry L. Byrne. *Quarterly of the Society of California Pioneers*, 3 (March 31, 1926): 9–29.

Brewer, William H. *Up And Down California in 1860–1864: The Journal of William H. Brewer*. Berkeley: University of California Press, 1974.

*Butte County, California: Illustrations*. Oakland, California: Smith and Elliott, 1877.

"Butte County." *Resources of California* (April 1888): 1–5.

Carr, Ezra S. *The Patrons of Husbandry on the Pacific Coast.* San Francisco: A. L. Bancroft, 1875.

Carson, Arenia Thankful [Lewis]. *Captured by the Mill Creek Indians: A True Story of the Capture of the Sam Lewis Children in the Year 1863.* Chico: A. Thankful Carson, 1915.

Crowder, D. F. "The Eventful Yesterdays: The Story of Early Chico." Chico *Enterprise*, 26 parts, 28 December 1917 to 28 January 1918.

Dow, Thomas K. *A Tour in America.* Melbourne, Australia: *Australasian* Office, 1884.

Gage, Helen Sommer. "Mrs. Bidwell as Her Friends Knew Her." In *Here is My Land: Sketches of Butte County, California.* Chico: Butte County Branch of the National League of American Pen Women, 1940.

Grabhorn, Jane, ed. *Pioneers of the Sacramento: A Group of Letters by and about Johann Augustus Sutter, James W. Marshall, and John Bidwell.* San Francisco: Book Club of California, 1953.

Gray, George M. "Reminiscences of the Life of General John Bidwell." 47 parts, (Chico) *Sandy Gulch News*, 28 April 1938 to 22 June 1939.

Green, Will S. "John Bidwell: A Character Study." *Out West*, 19 (December 1903): 625–634.

Hoffman, Ogden. *Reports of Land Cases Determined in the United States District Court.* San Francisco: Numa Hubert, 1862.

Hoopes, Chad L., ed. *What Makes A Man: The Annie Kennedy-John Bidwell Letters, 1866–1868.* Fresno, California: Valley Publishers, 1973.

Moak, Sim. *The Last of the Mill Creeks and Early Life in Northern California.* Chico: n.p., 1923.

Nunis, Doyce B., Jr., ed. *The Bidwell-Bartleson Party: 1841 California Emigrant Adventure: The Documents and Memoirs of the Overland Pioneers.* Santa Cruz, California: Western Tanager Press, 1991.

Ottley, Allan R., ed. *John Sutter's Last Days/The Bidwell Letters.* Sacramento: Sacramento Book Collectors' Club, 1986.

Parry, C. C. "Rancho Chico." *Overland Monthly*, 11 (June 1888): 561–576.

Potter, David M., ed. *Trail to California: The Overland Journals of Vincent Geiger and Wakeman Bryarly.* New Haven, Connecticut: Yale University Press, 1945.

Rawlings, Linda, ed. *Dear General: The Private Letters of Annie E. Kennedy and John Bidwell, 1866–1868.* Sacramento: California Department of Parks and Recreation, 1993.

Royce, Charles C. *John Bidwell: Pioneer, Statesman, Philanthropist: A Biographical Sketch.* Chico: n.p., 1906.

Sutter, John. *New Helvetia Diary: A Record of Events Kept by John A. Sutter and*

*His Clerks at New Helvetia, California, From September 9, 1845 to May 25, 1848.* San Francisco: Grabhorn Press, 1939.

Wickson, Edward J. "California Mission Fruits," *Overland Monthly*, 11 (May 1888): 501–05.

Wilson, S.G. "The Heart of the Sacramento Valley." *Overland Monthly*, 27 (February 1896): 185–203.

## Government Documents

Bidwell, John. "Annual Address." *CSAS, 1860*. (Sacramento: State Printer, 1861): 325–336.

———. "Annual Address Delivered at the Annual Fair of the Agricultural Society of the Northern District of California." *CSAS, 1864 and 1865*. (Sacramento: State Printer, 1866): 202–213.

———. "Annual Address." *CSAS, 1866 and 1867*. (Sacramento: State Printer, 1868): 419–436.

———. "Opening Address Delivered Before the Upper Sacramento Agricultural Society." *CSAS, 1869*. (Sacramento: State Printer, 1870): 318–322.

———. "California's Productive Interests." *CSAS, 1881*. (Sacramento: State Printer, 1881): 24–40.

California. Legislature. *Journal of the Assembly of California, First Session, 1850*. Sacramento: State Printer, 1850.

California. Legislature. *Journal of the Senate of California, First Session, 1850*. Sacramento: State Printer, 1850.

California. Supreme Court. *The People of the State of California vs. The Gold Run Ditch and Mining Company.* 66 Cal 138. Opening Brief for Appellant, March 27, 1884.

Conners, Pamela A. *The Chico to Round Valley Trail of Tears*. Willows, California: Mendocino National Forest, 1993.

United States. Congress. *Congressional Globe, Thirty-ninth Congress, First and Second Sessions.* Washington: 1867.

United States. Congress. House of Representatives. *Documents.* Thirty-Sixth Congress, Second Session, 1860. *Report of the U.S. Court of Claims, No. 257: Samuel Norris vs. United States, 1858.*

United States. Department of the Interior. Office of Indian Affairs. *Letters Received by the Office of Indian Affairs, 1824–1881: California Superintendency, 1849–1880.* National Archives Microfilm Publication, M-234.

United States. Ninth Circuit Court. *Edwards Woodruff vs. North Bloomfield Gravel Mining Company, et al.* 9 Sawyer 441 or 18F 753. Transcript, 26 volumes, Yuba County Library, Marysville, California.

United States. Department of War. *War of the Rebellion: A Compilation of the Official Records of the Union and Confederate Armies*, Series I, Vol. L, Part II, Serial 106. Washington: Government Printing Office, 1897.

NEWSPAPERS

*Butte Record* (Oroville)
*California Voice* (San Francisco)
*California Farmer* (San Francisco)
*Chico Courant*
*Chico Daily Enterprise*
*Chico Daily Evening Record*
*Chico Enterprise*
*Chico Enterprise-Record*
*Chico News and Review*
*Chico Record*
*Colusa Sun*
*Marysville Record*
*Michigan Messenger*
*Northern Enterprise* (Chico)
*Oroville Union*
*Pacific Rural Press* (San Francisco)
*Sacramento Daily Record*
*Sacramento Record Union*
*Sacramento Union*
*Sacramento Bee*
*Sandy Gulch News* (Chico)
*San Francisco Call*
*San Francisco Chronicle*
*San Francisco Occident*
*Weekly Butte Record* (Chico)

SELECTED SECONDARY SOURCES

Altrocchi, Julia Cooley. *The Old California Trail: Traces in Folklore and Furrow.* Caldwell, Idaho: Caxton Printers, 1945.
Azbill, Henry. "Bahapki." *Indian Historian*, 4 (Spring 1971): 47.
_____. "Maidu Indians of California: A Historical Note." *Indian Historian*, 4 (Summer 1971): 21.
Bancroft, Hubert Howe. *California Pioneer Register and Index, 1542–1848.* Baltimore: Regional Publishing Co., 1964.
Bates, Craig D. and Brian Bibby. "Collecting Among the Chico Maidu: The Stewart Culin Collection at the Brooklyn Museum." *American Indian Art Magazine*, 8 (Autumn 1983): 46–53.
_____. "Maidu Weaver: Amanda Wilson." *American Indian Art Magazine*, 9 (Summer 1984): 38–69.
Benjamin, Marcus. *John Bidwell, Pioneer: A Sketch of His Career.* Washington, D.C.: 1907.

Bidwell, Edwin M. *Genealogy to the Seventh Generation of the Bidwell Family in America*. Hudson, New York: n.p., 1884.

Bidwell, Joan J. *Bidwell Family History, 1587–1982*. Baltimore: Gateway Press, 1983.

Bleyhl, Norris. *Three Military Posts in Northeastern California, 1849–1863*. Chico: ANCRR, 1984.

Blocker, Jack S., Jr. *Retreat From Reform: The Prohibition Movement in the United States, 1890–1913*. Westport, Conn.: Greenwood Press, 1976.

Bousquet, Tim. "'Wiping Out the Red-Skins': A Look Back at Chico's Role in the Idaho Indian Wars." *Chico News and Review*, 12 January 1995: 16–19.

Boze, M. Jeanne. *The Nature of Bidwell Park*. Chico: n.p., 1991.

Buck, Solon J. *The Granger Movement: A Study of Agricultural Organization and its Political, Economic, and Social Manifestations, 1870–1880*. Cambridge, Mass.: Harvard University Press, 1913; reprint ed., Lincoln: University of Nebraska Press, 1969.

Carriker, Robert C. *Father Peter John DeSmet: Jesuit In The West*. Norman: University of Oklahoma Press, 1995.

Chan, Sucheng. *This Bittersweet Soil: The Chinese in California Agriculture, 1860–1910*. Berkeley: University of California Press, 1986.

Chang, Anita L. *The Historical Geography of the Humboldt Wagon Road*. Chico: ANCRR, 1992.

Clough, Frederick Stansbury. *The House at Fifth and Salem*. Chico: Quadco Printing and Stansbury Home Preservation Association, 1978.

Cook, Sherburne F. *The Population of the California Indians, 1769–1970*. Berkeley: University of California Press, 1976.

———. *The Conflict Between the California Indian and White Civilization*. Berkeley: University of California Press, 1976.

———. "The Epidemic of 1830–1833 in California and Oregon." *University of California Publications in American Archaeology and Ethnology*, 43. Berkeley: University of California Press, 1955.

Currie, Anne H. "Bidwell Rancheria." *California Historical Society Quarterly*, 36 (December 1957): 313–325.

———. "Bidwell Rancheria." Butte County Historical Society *Diggin's*, 4 (Fall 1960): 4–8.

Dana, Julian. *Sutter of California: A Biography*. New York: Press of the Pioneers, 1934.

———. *The Sacramento, River of Gold*. New York: Farrar and Reinhart, 1939.

Davis, Winfield J. *History of Political Conventions in California, 1849–1892*. Sacramento: California State Library, 1893.

DeLafosse, Peter H. *Trailing the Pioneers: A Guide to Utah's Emigrant Trails, 1829–1869*. Logan: Utah State University Press, 1994.

Delmatier, Royce; Clarence McIntosh; and Earl G. Waters, eds. *The Rumble of California Politics, 1848–1970.* New York: John Wiley & Sons, 1970.

Deuel, Charles H., ed. *Condensed History of Butte County, California.* N.p.: Gus R. Smith, 1940.

Dillon, Richard. *Fool's Gold: The Decline and Fall of Captain John Sutter of California.* Santa Cruz, California: Western Tanager Press, 1967.

_____. *Humbugs and Heroes: A Gallery of California Pioneers.* New York: Doubleday, 1970.

_____. *The Siskiyou Trail: The Hudson's Bay Company Route to California.* New York: McGraw-Hill, 1975.

Durkee, Frank B. "The Scar on General Bidwell's Forehead." Butte County Historical Society *Diggin's*, 23 (Spring 1979): 15–18.

Edmonson, Barbara T. "John Bidwell's Fifty Years on Rancho del Arroyo Chico." *Ripples Along Chico Creek: Perspectives on People and Times.* Chico: Butte County Branch, National League of American Pen Women, 1992. Pp. 41–74.

Egan, Ferol. *Fremont: Explorer for a Restless Nation.* New York: Doubleday & Co., 1977.

Fite, Gilbert C. *The Farmers' Frontier, 1865–1900.* New York: Holt, Rinehart and Winston, 1966.

Flynn, Ramona. "John Bidwell and Agriculture in Butte County in 1872." Butte County Historical Society *Diggin's*, 30 (Summer 1986): 38–48.

Fritz, Christian. *Federal Justice in California: The Court of Ogden Hoffman, 1851–1891.* Lincoln: University of Nebraska Press, 1991.

Gates, Paul W. *California Ranchos and Farms, 1846–1862.* Madison: The State Historical Society of Wisconsin, 1967.

George, Vivienne. "Chico, City of Trees: General Bidwell was Known as 'The Tree Man.'" Butte County Historical Society *Diggin's*, 19 (Spring 1975): 3–15.

Gillis, Michael J. "John Bidwell: Gentleman Farmer or Iconoclast?" Butte County Historical Society *Diggin's*, 36 (Summer 1992): 31–41.

_____. "John Muir and the Bidwells: The 1877 Mt. Shasta Expedition." Butte County Historical Society *Diggin's*, 37 (Winter 1993): 83–87.

_____. "John Muir and the Bidwells: The Forgotten Friendship." *Dogtown Territorial Quarterly*, 21 (Spring 1995): 4–5, 18–23, 26. Reprinted in *John Muir Newsletter*, 6 (Spring 1996): 1–6; and 7 (Summer 1997): 6–7.

_____. "The 1841 Trans-Sierra Route of the Bidwell-Bartleson Party," *Overland Journal*, 16 (Winter 1998–99): 21–29.

Giuliano, Pamela. "The Woman Behind the Myth" [Annie E. K. Bidwell]. In Megibow, Carol Burr; and Pamela Giuliano, eds. *Unstill Lives: Portraits of Northern California Women.* Chico: The Deering Endowment, CSUC #4 Regional Programs Monograph, 1981.

Guinn, James M. *History of the State of California and Biographical Record of the Sacramento Valley.* Chicago: Chapman Publishing Co., 1906.
Gudde, Erwin G. *Sutter's Own Story.* New York: G.P. Putnam, 1936.
Hafen, LeRoy and William J. Ghent. *Broken Hand: The Life Story of Thomas Fitzpatrick, Chief of the Mountain Men.* Denver, Colorado: Old West Publishing Company, 1931.
_____. *Broken Hand: The Life of Thomas Fitzpatrick: Mountain Man, Guide, and Indian Agent.* Denver: Old West Publishing Co., 1973.
Hardwick, Susan Wiley and Donald G. Holtgrieve. *Valley for Dreams: Life and Landscape in the Sacramento Valley.* Lanham, Maryland: Rowman and Littlefield, 1996.
Hartsell, Lynn. "Annie Bidwell, Elegant Pioneer." *Ripples Along Chico Creek: Perspectives on People and Times.* Chico: Butte County Branch, National League of American Pen Women, 1992. Pp. 161–172.
Harlow, Neal. *California Conquered: War and Peace on the Pacific, 1846–1850.* Berkeley: University of California Press, 1982.
Heizer, Robert F., ed. *The Destruction of California Indians: A Collection of Documents from the Period 1847 to 1865.* Santa Barbara, California: Peregrine Smith, 1974.
Heizer, Robert F. and Alan Almquist. *The Other Californians: Prejudice and Discrimination Under Spain, Mexico, and the United States to 1920.* Berkeley: University of California Press, 1971.
Heizer, Robert F. and Albert B. Elsasser. *The Natural World of the California Indians.* Berkeley: University of California Press, 1980.
*Here is My Land: Sketches of Butte County, California.* Chico: Butte County Branch of the National League of American Pen Women, 1940.
Higham, John. "The American Party, 1886–1891." *Pacific Historical Review,* 19 (February 1950): 37–46.
Hill, Dorothy J. *The Indians of Chico Rancheria.* Chico: Ka Ca Ma Press, 1978.
_____. "James John Morehead, 1828–1885: A California Pioneer." *Ripples Along Chico Creek: Perspectives on People and Times.* Chico: Butte County Branch, National League of American Pen Women, 1992. Pp. 127–149.
Hill, William E. *The California Trail Yesterday and Today: A Pictorial Journey Along the California Trail.* Boulder, Colorado: Pruett Publishing Company, 1986.
Holliday, J. S. *Rush for Riches: Gold Fever and the Making of California.* Oakland: Oakland Museum of California, and Berkeley: University of California Press, 1999.
Hornbeck, David. "Land Tenure and Rancho Expansion in Alta California, 1784–1846." *Journal of Historical Geography,* 4 (October 1978): 371–390.
Hunt, Rockwell D. *John Bidwell, Prince of California Pioneers.* Caldwell, Idaho: Caxton Printers, 1942.

_____. *California's Stately Hall of Fame*. Stockton, California: College of the Pacific, 1950.

_____. *Personal Sketches of California Pioneers I Have Known*. Stockton, California: University of the Pacific, 1962.

_____, ed. *California and Californians*. 5 vols. Chicago: Lewis Publishing Co., 1926.

Hurtado, Albert L. *Indian Survival on the California Frontier*. New Haven, Connecticut: Yale University Press, 1988.

_____. "'Hardly a Farm House—A Kitchen Without Them': Indian and White Households on the California Borderland Frontier in 1860." *Western Historical Quarterly*, 13 (July 1982): 245–270.

Hutchinson, William H. *California Heritage: A History of Northern California Lumbering*. Chico, Ca: Diamond National Corporation, 1958; reprint ed., Santa Cruz, Ca: The Forest History Society, 1974.

_____. *California: Two Centuries of Man, Land, and Growth in the Golden State*. Palo Alto, California: American West Publishing, 1969.

_____. *When Chico Stole the College*. Chico: Butte Savings and Loan Association, 1983.

Hutchinson, William H.; Clarence McIntosh; Pam Herman Bush. *A Precious Sense of Place: The Early Years of Chico State*. Chico: Friends of the Meriam Library, CSUC, 1991.

Jacobs, Margaret D. "Resistance to Rescue: The Indians of Bahapki and Mrs. Annie E. K. Bidwell." In *Writing the Range: Race, Class, and Culture in the Women's West*. Elizabeth Jameson and Susan Armitage, eds. Norman: University of Oklahoma Press, 1997. Pp. 230–251.

James, George Wharton. *Heroes of California: The Story of Founders of the Golden State*. Boston: Little, Brown and Co., 1910.

Jelinek, Lawrence J. *Harvest Empire: A History of California Agriculture*. San Francisco: Boyd and Fraser Publishing Co., 1979.

Jewell, Donald. *Indians of the Feather River: Tales and Legends of the Concow Maidu of California*. Menlo Park, Ca.: Ballena Press, 1987.

Johnson, Keith. *In Search of John Bidwell's Carriage House: Archaeological Investigations at Bidwell Mansion State Historic Park*. Long Beach, Ca.: Trustees of the California State University, 1988.

Johnson, Stephen; Gerald Haslam; Robert Dawson. *The Great Central Valley, California's Heartland*. Berkeley: University of California Press, 1993.

Kelley, Robert L. *Gold vs. Grain: The Hydraulic Mining Controversy in California's Sacramento Valley*. Glendale, California: Arthur H. Clark Co., 1959.

_____. *Battling the Inland Sea: American Political Culture, Public Policy, and the Sacramento Valley, 1850–1986*. Berkeley: University of California Press, 1989.

Killoren, John J. *"Come, Blackrobe:" De Smet and the Indian Tragedy.* Norman: University of Oklahoma Press, 1994.

Korns, J. Roderic and Dale L. Morgan. *West From Fort Bridger: The Pioneering of the Immigrant Trails Across Utah, 1846–1850.* Revised and updated by Will Bagley and Harold Schindler. Logan: Utah State University Press, 1994.

Kroeber, Alfred L. *Handbook of the Indians of California.* Berkeley: California Book Co., 1953.

Kroeber, Theodora. *Ishi In Two Worlds: A Biography of the Last Wild Indian in North America.* Berkeley: University of California Press, 1961.

Lenhoff, James. "The Day FDR 'Met' John Bidwell!," Butte County Historical Society *Diggin's*, 41 (Spring 1997): 3–5.

Levenson, Rosaline. "Chico's Jewish Residents and the Bidwells: Interactions and Relationships." Butte County Historical Society *Diggin's*, 33 (Summer 1989): 27–53.

———. "Bidwell's Relationships with Minorities: The Altruistic-Pragmatic Mix." *Ripples Along Chico Creek: Perspectives on People and Times.* Chico: Butte County Branch, National League of American Pen Women, 1992. Pp. 75–104.

Lewis, Donovan. *Pioneers of California: True Stories of Early Settlers in the Golden State.* San Francisco: Scottwall Associates, 1993.

MacGregor, Greg. *Overland: The California Emigrant Trail of 1841–1870.* Albuquerque: University of New Mexico Press, 1996.

———. "Traces of the Pioneers: Photographing the Overland Trail," *California History*, 70 (Winter 1991–1992): 338–351.

McDonald, Lois H. "Decade of Decision: John Bidwell's First Ten Years in California." *Ripples Along Chico Creek: Perspectives on People and Times.* Chico: Butte County Branch, National League of American Pen Women, 1992. Pp. 13–38.

———. "The Bidwell Family." *Ripples Along Chico Creek: Perspectives on People and Times.* Chico: Butte County Branch, National League of American Pen Women, 1992. Pp. 175–188.

McGie, Joseph F. *History of Butte County, 1840–1980.* 2 vols. Oroville, California: Butte County Board of Education, 1982.

McGowan, Joseph A. *History of the Sacramento Valley.* 3 vols. New York: Lewis Historical Publishing Co., 1961.

McIntosh, Clarence. "The Chico and Red Bluff Route: Stage Lines From Southern Idaho to the Sacramento Valley, 1865–1867." *Idaho Yesterdays*, 6 (Fall 1962): 12–19.

———. "Chico Normal, Teachers College, and State College, 1887–1962." Butte County Historical Society *Diggin's*, 6 (Fall 1962): 3–23. Reprinted as *Chico State College: The First Seventy-Five Years.* Oroville, California: Butte County Historical Society, 1962.

———. *Bidwell Memorial Presbyterian Church: Its First Century, 1868–1968*. Chico: n.p., 1968.

———. "A Brief History of California State University, Chico." Butte County Historical Society *Diggin's*, 31 (Summer 1987): 27–52.

McWilliams, Carey. *Factories in the Field: The Story of Migratory Farm Labor in California*. Santa Barbara, California: Peregrine Smith, 1971.

Magliari, Michael. "Populism, Steamboats, and the Octopus: Transportation Rates and Monopoly in California's Wheat Regions, 1890–1896." *Pacific Historical Review*, 58 (November 1989): 449–469.

Magliari, Michael, and Michael Gillis. "John Bidwell and the Indians of Chico Rancheria: Was He Their Protector—Or Their Enslaver?," *Chico News and Review* (March 2, 1995): 18–21.

*The Maidu Mechoopda Indians*. Chico: Mechoopda Indian Tribe, 1995.

Mansfield, George C. *History of Butte County, California*. Los Angeles: Historical Record Company, 1918.

Mathes, Valerie Sherer. "The Death of John Sutter as Seen Through the Letters of Annie and John Bidwell." *Pacific Historian*, 26 (Fall 1982): 40–52.

———. "Indian Philanthropy in California: Annie Bidwell and the Mechoopda Indians." *Arizona and the West*, 25 (Summer 1983): 153–166.

———. "Annie E. K. Bidwell: Chico's Benefactress." *California History*, 68 (Spring/Summer 1989): 14–25.

Meriam, Theodore. "Rancho Chico." Butte County Historical Society *Diggin's*, 4 (Fall 1960): 9–11.

Monaghan, Jay. *The Overland Trail*. Indianapolis: Bobbs-Merrill Company, 1947.

Moody, Ralph. *The Old Trails West*. New York: Thomas Crowell Company, 1963.

Munkres, Robert L. "The Bidwell-Bartleson Party: The Beginning of the Great Migration." *Journal of the West*, 30 (October 1991): 64–66.

Nash, Gerald D. "Stages of California's Economic Growth, 1870–1970." *California Historical Quarterly*, 51 (Winter 1972): 315–330.

Nevins, Allan. *Fremont, Pathmarker of the West*. New York: D. Appleton-Century, 1939.

Nordin, D. Sven. *Rich Harvest: A History of the Grange, 1867–1900*. Jackson: University Press of Mississippi, 1974.

Ogden, Annegret. "Love and Marriage: Five California Couples." *Californians*, 5 (July/August 1987): 8–19.

Ostrander, Gilman M. *The Prohibition Movement in California, 1848–1933*. Berkeley: University of California Press, 1957.

Owens, Kenneth N., ed. *John Sutter and a Wider West*. Lincoln: University of Nebraska Press, 1994.

Patera, Alan H. "The Chico Route to Idaho." *Western Express*, 40 (April 1990): 8–33.

Paul, Rodman W. *California Gold: The Beginning of Mining in the Far West.* Lincoln: University of Nebraska Press, 1947.

_____. "The Great California Grain War: The Grangers Challenge the Wheat King." *Pacific Historical Review,* 27 (November 1958): 331–349.

_____. "The Wheat Trade Between California and the United Kingdom." *Mississippi Valley Historical Review,* 45 (December 1958): 391–412.

_____. "The Beginnings of Agriculture in California: Innovation versus Continuity." *California Historical Quarterly,* 52 (Spring 1973): 16–27.

_____. *The Far West and the Great Plains in Transition, 1859–1900.* New York: Harper and Row, 1988.

Phillips, Paul C., ed. *Forty Years on the Frontier as Seen in Journals and Reminiscences of Granville Stuart.* Cleveland: Arthur H. Clark Co., 1925.

Petlock, Gerald. "Apricot Ventures: From Early Promise to Current Markets." Butte County Historical Society *Diggin's,* 33 (Spring 1989): 3–11.

Pisani, Donald J. *From the Family Farm to Agribusiness: The Irrigation Crusade in California and the West, 1850–1931.* Berkeley: University of California Press, 1984.

Prescott, Gerald L. "Farm Gentry vs. the Grangers: Conflict in Rural America." *California Historical Quarterly,* 56 (Winter 1977/78): 328–345.

Ramsland, Margaret. *Mary Bidwell Reed.* Chico: n.p., n.d.

_____. *The Other Bidwells.* Chico: Jensen Graphic, 1972.

_____. "Nopani: Unsung Heroine." *Butte County Bugle,* 1 March 1973.

_____. *The Forgotten Californians.* Chico: Jensen Graphic, 1974.

Rawls, James J. *Indians of California: The Changing Image.* Norman: University of Oklahoma Press, 1984.

Sandmeyer, Elmer Clarence. *The Anti-Chinese Movement in California.* Urbana: University of Illinois Press, 1939; reprint ed., 1973.

Shipley, William. *The Maidu Indian Myths and Stories of Hanc'ibyjim.* Berkeley, California: Heyday Books, 1991.

Shover, Michele. *Chico's Little Chapman Mansion: The House and its People.* Chico: ANCRR, 1981.

_____. "The Doctor, The Lawyer, and the Political Chief: In the 1850's of Butte County." CSUC *University Journal,* 19 (Winter 1982): 7–38.

_____. "Chico Women: Nemesis of a Rural Town's Anti-Chinese Campaigns, 1876–1888." *California History,* 67 (December 1988): 228–243, 289–290.

_____. "Sweet Memories and Bitter Moments: The Hom and the Lee Families of Chico." Butte County Historical Society *Diggin's,* 32 (Winter 1988): 71–91.

_____. "John Bidwell: A Reconsideration." CSUC *University Journal,* 35 (Winter 1990): 11–22.

_____. *Blacks in Chico, 1860–1935: Climbing the Slippery Slope.* Chico: ANCRR, 1991.

_____. "John Bidwell: A Reconsideration." *Ripples Along Chico Creek: Perspectives on People and Times.* Chico: Butte County Branch, National League of American Pen Women, 1992. Pp. 105–121.

_____. "Fighting Back: The Chinese Influence on Chico Law and Politics, 1880–1886." *California History,* 74 (Winter 1995/96): 408–421, 449–450.

_____. *Chico's Lemm Ranch Murders and the Anti-Chinese Campaign of 1877.* Chico: ANCRR, 1998.

_____. "John Bidwell: Reluctant Indian Fighter, 1852–1856." *Dogtown Territorial Quarterly,* 36 (Winter 1998): 32–56.

_____. "The Politics of the 1859 Kibbe Campaign: Northern California Indian-Settler Conflicts of the 1850s." *Dogtown Territorial Quarterly,* 38 (Summer 1999): pp. 4–37.

Slade, Martha. "Bidwell Hall For Ever." Butte County Historical Society *Diggin's,* 27 (Winter 1983): 79–97.

Stanley, Gerald. "The Whim and Caprice of a Majority in a Petty State: The 1867 Election in California." *Pacific Historian,* 24 (Winter 1980): 443–455.

Stewart, George R. *The California Trail: An Epic With Many Heroes.* New York: McGraw-Hill, 1962.

_____. *Good Lives: The Stories of Six Men and the Good Life That Each Won for Himself.* Boston: Houghton Mifflin, 1967.

Tea, Roy D. and Peter H. DeLafosse. "The First Wagons Across Utah: The Bidwell-Bartleson Party of 1841." *Overland Journal,* 12 (Winter 1994): 13–31.

Trussell, Margaret E. "Mexican Land Grants in Butte County." Butte County Historical Society *Diggin's,* 6 (Spring 1962): 2–32.

Tyrrell, Ian. *True Gardens of the Gods: Californian-Australian Environmental Reform, 1860–1930.* Berkeley: University of California Press, 1999.

Unruh, John D., Jr. *The Plains Across: The Overland Emigrants and the Trans-Mississippi West, 1840–1860.* Urbana: University of Illinois Press, 1979.

Weber, David. *The Mexican Frontier, 1821–1846: The American Southwest Under Mexico.* Albuquerque: University of New Mexico Press, 1982.

Wells, Harry L. and W. L. Chambers. *History of Butte County, California.* San Francisco: Harry L. Wells, 1882.

White, Thelma B. "The Many Facets of the Sacramento River." *Ripples Along Chico Creek: Perspectives on People and Times.* Chico: Butte County Branch, National League of American Pen Women, 1992. Pp. 191–212.

Williams, David. "California Democrats of 1860: Division, Disruption, Defeat." *Southern California Quarterly,* 55 (Fall 1973): 239–252.

Woods, Thomas A. *Knights of the Plow: Oliver H. Kelley and the Origins of the Grange in Republican Ideology.* Ames: Iowa State University Press, 1991.

Wooldridge, Major Jesse Walton. *History of the Sacramento Valley, California.* 3 vols. Chicago: Pioneer Historical Publishing Co., 1931.

Zollinger, James Peter. *Sutter: The Man and His Empire.* New York: Oxford University Press, 1939.

THESES AND OTHER UNPUBLISHED SECONDARY SOURCES

Book, Susan Wiley. "The Chinese in Butte County, 1860–1920." MA Thesis, CSUC, 1974.

Bourdeau, Larry Francis. "The Historic Archaeology of Cabo's Tavern, CA-BUT-712." MA Thesis, CSUC, 1982.

Brown, David R. "The History of Bidwell Bar, 1848–1856." MA Thesis, CSUC, 1969.

Cody, Cora Edith. "John Bidwell: His Early Career in California." MA Thesis, University of California, Berkeley, 1927.

Duim, Jon Aaron. "The Prohibition Party and the Election of 1892." MA Thesis, Midwestern State University, Wichita Falls, Texas, 1984.

Gabriel, Kathleen F. "James Lawrence Keefer, 1850–1901: An Ethnohistory Study of a Butte County Pioneer." MA Thesis, CSUC, 1981.

Goss, Virginia. "Annie Ellicot Kennedy Bidwell, 1839–1918." MA Thesis, California State University, Sacramento, 1981.

Haron, Nadzan. "Reception of Chinese Immigrants in California, 1848–1860." MA Thesis, CSUC, 1980.

Hislop, Donald L. "The Nome Lackee Indian Reservation, 1854–1870." MA Thesis, CSUC, 1975.

McKee, Dennis P. "A History of Bidwell Park." MA Thesis, CSUC, 1983.

Moore, Gail E. "History of Chico State College." MA Thesis, Oregon State College, 1939.

Paden, William Guy. "Bidwell's Route of the Sierras: A Field Study." MA Thesis, University of California, Berkeley, 1940.

Peery, Eugene R. "The Anti-Chinese Press in Butte County: A Study in Prejudice." MA Thesis, CSUC, 1968.

Schreiter, Pete. "John Bidwell: Annotated Bibliography." Typescript, CSUC, Meriam Library Special Collections, 1968.

Snelson, Ralph J. "An Annotated Bibliography on the Writings By and About John Bidwell." MLS thesis, San Jose State University, 1979.

Trussell, Margaret E. "Land Choice by Pioneer Farmers: Western Butte County Through 1877." Ph.D. Dissertation, University of Oregon, 1969.

Tubbesing, John. "Economics of the Bidwell Ranch, 1870–1875." MA Thesis, CSUC, 1978.

# Index

Achumawi Indians: 268, 278
Act for the Government and Protection of Indians (1850): 249-50, 251-53, 291-93
Agriculture: 151-52, 177-78; in Mexican California: 85-87, 89-90, 153-55, 178-79. *See also* fence laws, Rancho Chico
Aguas Nieves, rancho grant: 132 n 4
Ah Gow: 323
Ah Kun: 320 n 24
Ah Lee: 323
Ah Louey: 319-20, 320 n 24
Ah Sun: 318
Ah Wing: 318
Ah Yuen: 323
Alfalfa: 170-71
Allen, Benjamin F.: 329
Allen, Isaac: 272
Almonds: 163; on Rancho Chico, 137, 180, 181, 318, 319, 320, 321 n 30, 331
Alvarado, Juan: 75, 76
American Party: 204, 241-42
Anderson Fruit Company: 329-30, 331
Anderson, Robert A.: 261-64, 262 n 41, 265, 267, 269, 276-77
Antelope Valley: 35, 37
Antelope: 46, 59, 68, 87, 95, 154
Anthony, Susan B.: 18, 247-48
Anti-Debris Association: 118, 149
Arce, Francisco C.: 102, 113-14
Ashley, James M.: 190
Ashtabula, Ohio: 28
Atlantic and Pacific Railroad: 193
Atsugewi Indians: 268, 270, 278
Australian ballot: 242-43
Azbill, Henry: 279, 282

Bahapki: 256, 256 n 20. *See also* Mikchopdo
Baker, James: 54
Bancroft, Hubert Howe: 17, 261
Bartleson, John: 32, 37, 43, 44, 45, 57, 60, 61-63, 64-65, 69
Bartlett, Washington: 202
Bates, Craig: 14, 279 n 92
Bay, Harmen: 180
Beale, Edward F.: 104

Bear Flag Revolt: 77-78, 101-03
Bear Lake: 32
Bear River: 32, 34, 54-55
Bee, Frederick A.: 327
Belden, Josiah: 52
Belty, William: 61
Benjamin, Marcus: 20
Bermuda Grass: 170-71
Best, Daniel: 135
Bidwell, Abigail Benedict (father's first wife): 27-28
Bidwell, Abraham "Abram" (father): 27-28
Bidwell, Abram (nephew): 28 n 1, 336
Bidwell, Alpheus (brother): 28 n 1
Bidwell, Annie Ellicott Kennedy (wife): 18, 18 n 3, 72, 137, 141, 142, 150-51, 197-98, 202, 218-20, 224, 231, 256, 279-82, 310
Bidwell, Clarissa Griggs (mother): 27-28
Bidwell, Daniel (half-brother): 28 n 1
Bidwell, Elias (half-brother): 28 n 1
Bidwell, George (nephew): 28 n 1
Bidwell, Henry (nephew): 28 n 1
Bidwell, John: significance in California history, 17-19, 25-26; and Indians, 24, 249-83, 293-96, 300-10; issues Proclamation of Rules Made for Rancho Chico Indians, 281-82, 309-10; drafts Indian Legislation, 249-50, 251-53, 291-93; and Chinese, 24, 241, 311, 313, 316-42; founds city of Chico, 19, 24, 130; founds Chico Normal School (California State University, Chico), 19, 202; early years in New York, Pennsylvania, and Ohio, 27-29; moves west to Iowa and Missouri, 29; loses land to squatter, 29; schoolteacher in Ohio and Missouri, 28-29; overland emigration to California, 30-72 ; claims to be first white man to see Calaveras Big Trees, 39 n 23, 65-66, 70-72; jailed at Mission San Jose, 74; hired by John Sutter, 74-76; dismantles Fort Ross, 75, 92-93; manages Hock Farm, 76; acquires Rancho Ulpinos and Colusa Grant, 76, 99; fights in Micheltorena War, 76; taken prisoner at Cahuenga Pass, 76; explores and maps Sacramento Valley, 75-

76, 87-88, 93-95, 98-99, 100-01; joins Bear Flag Revolt, 77-78, 101-03; joins Fremont's Battalion, 78, 104-06 ; appointed *alcalde* at Mission San Luis Rey, 78-79, 106-08, 250-51; sails to San Pedro for help, 108-09; marches with Kearny and Stockton, 79, 111-13; takes Indian census, 80; drafts contract between Sutter and Marshall, 80, 115; builds Sutter residence at Hock Farm, 80; declines hand of Anna Eliza Sutter, 80, 114; and the Gold Rush, 115-27; opposes hydraulic mining, 117-18, 126, 149-50, 152-53; discovers gold at Hamilton and Bidwell's Bar, 116, 116 n 5, 120-22; develops Rancho Chico, 23-24, 130-51; opposes horse racing, 149, 172-73; elected to Constitutional Convention, 185, 205; in State Senate, 185, 205-06, 251-52; attends Democratic national convention, 187, 206-07; appointed Brigadier General in state militia during the Civil War, 187-89, 207-08, 209, 278; attends Union Party national convention, 189, 208; in Congress, 137, 148, 163-65, 178, 180-81, 189-97, 210-15; designs improved subsoil plow, 167-69; supports public irrigation, reclamation, and flood control projects, 173-77, 236-37; supports civil rights, Radical Reconstruction, and impeachment of President Johnson, 189-90, 190 n 14, 210-11, 214-15, 216-18, 225-26; coauthors California Land Act (1866), 191-92, 212-13; coauthors California and Oregon Railroad Bill, 192-93; supports efforts to divide Butte County, 195 n 26; promotes Chico and Humboldt Wagon Road and stage routes into Idaho, 194-96, 211-12; authors bill to expand Round Valley Reservation, 278, 304-05; runs for Governor (1867), 197-98, 210-11, 214-16, 218-23; courtship with Annie Kennedy, 197-98, 218-20; supports Cornelius Cole for U.S. Senate, 201 n 41, 229-32; elected president of the California Farmers' Union, 199; joins Grange, 199; runs for Governor (1875), 200-01, 203, 235-38; opposes Constitution of 1879, 201-02, 238; appointed University of California Regent, 202; appointed Normal School Trustee, 202; attends Prohibition Party national convention, 204; runs for Governor (1890), 204; runs for President, 204-05, 244-47; condemns Southern Pacific railroad monopoly, 224-25, 229, 231-32, 233-36, 237-41; calls for restrictions on immigration and naturalization, 204, 241-42, 247, 327-28; anti-Catholicism of, 204, 242; supports Australian ballot, 242-43; supports female suffrage, 202, 243-44, 245-46, 247-48; endorses prohibition, 204, 243-44; supports federal ownership of railroads, 202, 246-47; endorses federal income tax, 246

Bidwell, Thomas (brother): 28 n 1, 198 n 34
Bidwell-Bartleson Party: 32, 32 n 1, 43-45
Bidwell Mansion: 130, 142, 144, 144 n 23, 150, 281, 324, 332-33
Bidwell Park: 144, 148, 151
Bidwell Pass: 35 n 12
Bidwell's Bar: 116-17, 121-23, 129
Big Sandy River: 53
Bigler, John: 206
Billings, Frederick: 227
Bishop, A. W.: 265
Black Hills: 51-52
Black, Jeremiah S.: 200
Blood, Amos F.: 139
Bonneville, Benjamin: 34 n 10
Booth, Newton: 200 n 39
Boucher, David: 229, 230
Bowen, Thomas: 74
Boynton, Seth: 17
Brannan, Sam: 116 n 6
Breckenridge, John: 267
Breckinridge, John C.: 187, 206-07
Brown, Elam: 251, 251 n 9, 252
Brown, L.: 146 n 29
Bruheim, Joe: 93
Buchanan, James: 131-32
Buffalo: 48, 49-50, 52-54, 60
Burlingame Treaty: 313, 337
Burlington, Iowa Territory: 29
Burnett, Peter: 185 n 3
Burns, H. J.: 327
Bush, C. C.: 304

Cadwalader, Charles: 228-29

# Index

Cahuenga Pass: 76, 79
Calaveras Big Trees: 34 n 10, 39 n 23, 65-66
California and Oregon Railroad: 192-93, 211, 228-29
California Battalion: 78-79, 105-06, 108-10, 111-13
California cart: 83
California Land Act (1866): 191-92, 192 n 17, 212-13
California Land Commission: 131
California Pacific Railroad: 193, 213, 229
California State Agricultural Society: 118, 148-49, 172-73
California State Forestry Commission: 148
California Trail: 34-72
Camp Bidwell: 188-89, 196 n 27, 273-76. *See also* Fort Bidwell
Camper, Henry H.: 147 n 32, 182
Carpenter, Lemuel: 86
Carquinez Strait: 113-14
Carson River: 38
Carson, Christopher "Kit": 34 n 10, 77, 104, 105, 110
Carson, Moses: 76
Casaba melons: on Rancho Chico, 148, 165
Castro, Jose: 76, 77, 100, 102, 105-06, 113
Cattle: 170; in Mexican California, 76, 84-85, 154; on Rancho Chico, 132-33, 144, 170. *See also* hide and tallow trade
Centerville, Ohio: 28
Central Pacific Railroad: 192-97, 211-12, 213, 227, 228, 233, 239, 313, 321 n 32
Chalmers, Watson: 230, 231
Chico and Humboldt Wagon Road Company: 194-96, 211-12. *See also* Humboldt Wagon Road
Chico Anti-Chinese Association: 325, 327
Chico Anti-Chinese League: 329, 331
Chico Canning Company: 140
Chico Creek: 24, 76, 94-95, 129, 136, 148, 200, 232, 259, 271
Chico Normal School (California State University, Chico): 19, 202
Chico Roller Flouring Mills: 136, 160, 183, 271, 325, 327. *See also* Rancho Chico, wheat
Chiles, Joseph B.: 46, 53, 72
Chimney Rock: 51
Chinese: 146, 199, 200, 201-202, 204, 241, 262, 280, 311-42. *See also* farm labor

Civil Rights Act (1866): 190
Clark, John: 262 n 41
Clark's Fork, Stanislaus River: 38, 39, 64
Clements, Rodney: 256 n 21
Cleveland, Grover: 205, 241
Cochran, Rufus M.: 158, 308
Cole, Cornelius: 201 n. 41, 229-32
Colusa Rancho Grant: 76, 99
Conness, John: 187 n 7, 191-92, 193-94, 197, 212-13, 220-23, 226-27
Cook, Grove C.: 40, 66-67
Cook, Philip St. George: 106
Cornwall, P. B.: 229
Coyotes: 68
Crittenden, A. P.: 206
Crocker, Charles: 197 n 28, 229
Crocker, Edwin B.: 196, 197 n 28
Crossette, George: 238-39, 266
Curtin, Jeremiah: 258 n. 26, 308

Dairy: on Rancho Chico, 134, 144, 171, 318
Dardendelles Cone: 39
Dawson, Nicholas "Cheyenne": 41, 47-48
De Smet, Fr. Pierre Jean: 32, 33, 43, 45, 54, 55
Deer: 68, 87, 95, 154
DeHaven, W. N.: 229, 230, 232, 264
Delaney, Dan: 262
Dickey, William: 99, 116 n 6, 121, 131, 290-91
Dillon, Richard: 23
Disaster Creek: 38, 39
Dolly Vardens: *See* People's Independent Party
Douglas, Stephen A.: 186, 187, 207
Douglass, David: 251-52
Dow, Thomas K.: 15, 145
Dresbach, William: 161
DuPont, Samuel F.: 78

Earll, William: 340
Eddy, J. F.: 270, 272, 275
Edgarton, Henry: 238
Edmonson, Barbara: 23-24
Edmunds, James M.: 212-13
Elk: 68, 69, 87, 92, 95, 154
Emmons, E. J.: 325
Erie, Pennsylvania: 28
Estee, Morris M.: 340

Farm labor: Indians, in Mexican California, 85, 106, 156, 179; on Rancho Chico, 146, 181, 200, 256-57, 257 n 22, 24, 266, 308, 309-10, 319, 321 n 30; in American California, 270, 272; Chinese, in California, 313-14, 315-18, 318 n 18; on Rancho Chico, 146, 200, 280, 311, 313, 316-21, 328-33, 331 n 70, 338, 340; Whites, in California, 317-18, 321 n 28; on Rancho Chico, 315, 318-19, 320-21, 329-31
Farmers' Alliance: 204
Farmers' Union: 199, 233
Farnham, Thomas J.: 42
Farwell Rancho Grant (New Salem): 129, 132 n 4, 136
Farwell, Edward: 129
Fay, Caleb: 239
Fence laws: 133, 178-80
Field, Stephen J.: 212-13
Fillmore, Millard: 184, 186, 253
Fitzgerald, Edward H.: 298
Fitzpatrick, Thomas "Broken Hand": 32, 33, 34, 43, 44-45, 47, 48, 55
Flood Control and Reclamation: 174-77. See also irrigation
Flores, Jose Maria: 106-113
Flour milling: See Chico Roller Flouring Mills, wheat
Flugge, Charles W.: 95
Forster, John: 107
Fort Bidwell: 196, 196 n 27, 278. See also Camp Bidwell
Fort Hall: 32, 34, 55
Fort Laramie: 51
Fort Ross: 75, 85, 92-93, 95, 154, 284
Fort Tejon: 255
Foulke, L. M.: 230
Fourteenth Amendment: 190
Fremont, John C.: 34 n. 10, 65, 70-72, 77-79, 101-113, 206
Friedlander, Isaac: 199
Fruit: 162-63, 165; on Rancho Chico, 137-44, 165-66, 319-21, 321 n 27, 30, 329-30, 331, 333
Frye, Amos E.: 53, 259
Fur trade, trappers: 46-47, 48, 51, 53-54. See also Fitzpatrick, Thomas; and Robidoux, Antoine

Gantt, John: 76
Gates, Paul W.: 192 n 17
Gillespie, Archibald: 101-02, 105-10
Gillespie, George A.: 227
Gillis, Michael J.: 39 n 21
Gilroy, John: 84
Glenn, Hugh J.: 134-35, 136, 147, 159
Gold Rush: 115-127. See also hydraulic mining
Golden Canyon: 38, 63
Good, Harmon "Hi": 261-64, 262 n 41, 265, 267, 269-70, 275, 276-77
Gordon, Laura de Force: 341
Gorham, George C.: 197, 197 n 30, 201 n 41, 220-23, 226-27, 229-31, 233, 239
Graham, Isaac: 76
Grange: 199, 201
Grant, Ulysses S.: 189, 208-09, 226, 227, 233
Gray, Asa: 18, 141 n 21
Gray, George M.: 141 n 21, 147 n 32, 319-20
Gray, John: 49, 52, 53
Great Basin: 34, 35
Great Salt Lake: 32, 34, 35, 56
Greeley, Horace: 233
Green River: 32, 51-52, 53-54
Green, Talbot H.: 45
Green, Will S.: 20 n 5
Greenville, Ohio: 28, 29
Greenwood, Caleb: 76
Grizzly bears: 87-88, 90, 93-95, 98, 262, 287
Guill, John H.: 303
Gwin, William M.: 186, 207, 296

Haight, Henry: 239
Halleck, Henry W.: 80
Hansen, William: 334
Hanson, George: 270, 272-75, 303-04
Haraszthy, Agoston: 136
Harrison, Benjamin: 204
Harry, John: 332
Hartson, Chancellor: 227
Haskin, D. C.: 229
Hastings, Lansford: 95
Hayes, Rutherford B.: 18, 239
Henshaw, George: 43
Hensley, Samuel: 132 n 4, 187, 297
Hickok children, murder of: 265, 268-69, 276
Hide and Tallow Trade: 83-84
Higby, William: 192

Hock Farm: 76, 80, 93, 101
Hoffman, Ogden: 132
Holt, Benjamin: 135
Hooker, Ambrose: 273-74, 277-78
Hooker, Sir Joseph: 18
Hopper, Charles: 46, 57, 67
Horses: 44, 45, 54, 57, 58, 66, 67, 68, 69, 71, 85, 87, 92, 113-14, 149, 154-55, 171-73
Houghton, James F.: 213
Howe, I. D.: 330
Hoye Canyon: 35
Hudspeth, J. M.: 113
Huff, Dolores: 249, 249 n 4, 250
Humboldt River: 34, 34 n 10, 35, 55, 57, 60-61
Humboldt Sink: 35, 61
Humboldt Wagon Road: 277-78, 305-07, 318 n 19. *See also* Chico and Humboldt Wagon Road Company
Hunt, H. B.: 271
Hunt, J. C.: 147 n 32, 182-83
Hunt, Rockwell D.: 20-23, 21 n 7, 22 n 8, 9, 249
Hydraulic Mining: 117-18, 149-50, 152-53, 176-77

Idaho stage and wagon roads: 194-96, 211-12, 277-78, 305-07
Ide, William: 77
Immigration: 204, 241-42, 247
Income tax: 246
Independence Rock: 32, 52
Indians: along the overland trail, 34, 44, 45-46, 47-48, 49, 50, 51, 54, 55; in Sierra Nevada, 39-40, 65-67, 71, 283; in Mexican California, 69, 73, 85, 88, 93-94, 99, 101, 106-08, 109, 156, 179, 283-90; and gold rush, 116, 120-24, 284-85, 290-91; on Rancho Chico, 146, 181, 200, 249-51, 254-59, 265-67, 270-75, 279-82, 296-304, 307-310, 319, 321 n 30. *See also* Achumawi, Atsugewi, Farm Labor, Maidu, Mechoopda, Mill Creek, Paiute, Shoshone, Wailaki, Yahi, Yana
Ingalls, Rufus: 209
Irrigation: 148, 173-77, 236-37. *See also* flood control and reclamation
Irwin, William: 200, 203, 238
Ishi: 277

Jacobs, Margaret D.: 281 n 96
James, George Wharton: 20 n 5
Jason Springer and Company: 324
John, James: 40, 64-65
Johnson, Andrew: 189-90, 210, 225-26
Johnson, James A.: 238
Johnson, Reverdy: 212
Johnston, Albert Sidney: 207
Jones, Albert: 232
Jones, George F.: 232
Jones, Hayden: 324
Jones, Thomas: 53, 66, 69
Julian, George W.: 191-92
J. Z. Anderson Fruit Company: *See* Anderson Fruit Company

Kansas River: 31 n 1
Kearney, Denis: 199, 202, 204, 324, 325, 326-27, 341
Kearny, Stephen Watts: 79, 105, 110-13, 125
Keefer, James: 269, 270
Kelsey, Andrew: 66, 69
Kelsey, Ann: 37
Kelsey, Benjamin: 37, 41, 55, 57, 60
Kelsey, Nancy A.: 37, 54, 55
Kelsey, Isaac: 33 n 7, 47
Kemble, Edward C.: 116 n 6
Kern, Edward: 78
Kibbe, William: 268, 268 n 54
King, William: 147 n 32
Kingsley, Norman: 277
Kingsville Academy: 28
Kirkwood, William: 334
Know-Nothing Party: 186, 241
Kulmeh, Chief: 254

Ladenberger, Jacob: 147 n 33
Lafonso, Holi: 279 n 92, 282, 309
Larkin, Thomas O.: 83, 98, 102, 286
Lassen, Peter: 75, 76, 93-95, 100-01, 121
Latham, Milton S.: 207
Law and Order Committee of One Hundred: 325-26, 338-40
Lea, Luke: 293
Leese, Jacob: 78, 102
Lemm Ranch, murder of Chinese at: 323-24, 334-35
Lemm, Christian: 323

Levenson, Rosaline: 25 n 17
Lewis [Carson], Thankful: 271, 302
Lewis children, murder of: 271, 276, 302-03
Lewis, Donovan: 23 n 12
Lewis, Samuel: 271, 272
Lincoln, Abraham: 187-89, 208
Lindo Channel: *See* Sandy Gulch
Little Antelope Valley: 37, 38, 62
Little Blue River (Nebraska): 32
Livermore, Robert: 98, 154
Los Angeles: 79
Lovett, W. E.: 203
Low, Frederick: 197 n 30, 239, 306
Lucas, Robert: 29
Luccayan, Chief: 254, 279, 309
Lusk, Franklin C.: 24, 151 n 43, 334

Maidu: 254, 257, 259, 260 n 32, 265, 267-77, 280, 289-90, 300-02, 303
Mandeville, J. C.: 180
Marsh, John: 31, 40, 69-70, 74, 81-82
Marshall, James W.: 80, 115-16, 119-20, 127
Mary's River: *See* Humboldt River
Mason, Carnot Courtland: 233
Mason, Richard: 80, 125
Mason Valley: 35
Masons: 223-24
Mast, William: 51
Mathes, Valerie S.: 281 n 96
Matteson and Williamson Manufacturing Company, Stockton: 167-68
McCorkle, Joseph: 255, 293
McDonald, Lois H.: 13, 23
McDowell, Irvin: 189, 196, 278
McGee, John B.: 186
McIntosh, Edward: 85
McIntosh, L.H.: 340, 341
McKinstry, George: 116, 116 n 6, 122-24, 129
McRuer, Donald: 192
Mechoopda: 146, 151, 254, 256-58, 260 n 32, 265-77, 279-82, 296, 302-03, 319, 332
Meeks, Joe: 82
Merritt, Ezekiel: 76, 77, 79, 104
Mervine, William: 108
Mesa, battle of the: 79, 112-13
Micheltorena, Manuel: 76, 82
Mikchopdo: 256, 256 n 20, 257, 265, 267, 279-82, 300, 308

Mill Creek Indians: 258, 258 n 26, 261-62, 264, 265, 268-77, 303, 304
Mizner, Lansing B.: 227, 229
Moak, Sim: 188, 262
Moore, Robert: 186
Morrill Land Grant College Act: 148, 178, 213
Morton, Oliver: 231
Mountain lions: 92
Mt. Diablo: 40
Muir, John: 18, 70-72, 144, 150
Mules: 35, 44, 45, 46, 58, 66, 67, 68, 71, 85, 155
Mullan, John: 211
Murphy, Timothy: 87
Myers, Jacob: 288

Native Americans: *See* Indians
Neal, Samuel: 297, 308-09
Nesmith, James: 192
Nicolaus: 93, 123
Nome Cult: 255
Nome Lackee: 255
Nopanny: 279-80, 279 n 92, 308, 309, 319
Nordyke and Marmon Company: 160
Norris, Samuel: 299
Northgraves, William: 116 n 6, 121
Nye, Michael: 124

Oak: 69, 89
O'Brien, Patrick: 299
Ocampo, Francisco: 86
O'Farrell, Jasper: 76
Ogden, Peter Skene: 34 n 10
Order of Caucasians: 322-23, 333-34, 336
Oregon Steam Navigation Company: 194-95
Oregon Trail: 32
Oulton, George: 306
Oxen: 35, 44, 45, 46, 50, 53, 58-59, 61, 62, 63, 64, 71, 84, 155

Pacheco, Romualdo: 200 n 39
Pacific Fruit Packing Company: 331
Pacific Mail Steamship Company: 313
Paiute Indians: 61-63, 195-96, 268, 277-78, 305-07
Paradise Valley: 38
Parkinson, O. B.: 17-18
Patrons of Husbandry: *See* Grange
Patterson, Jacob: 265

## Index

Pedrorena, Miguel de: 108
Pence, Manoah: 260-61
Pence's Ranch: 271, 272-73, 274, 277
People's Independent Party: 199 n 38, 199-201, 203, 235-38
Perkins, George C.: 202, 230, 239
Petersen, Christian: 334
Peyri, Antonio: 107, 253 n 14
Peyton, Henry: 53
Phelan, Richard: 54
Phelps, Timothy Guy: 200-01, 203, 238
Phillips, Frederick: 269
Pico, Andres: 79, 106, 110-11
Pico, Pio: 76, 86, 99, 105-07
Pierce, E. D.: 307
Pilot Peak: 35 n 12
Pit River: 268, 278
Platte County, Missouri: 29, 31, 43
Platte River: 32, 33, 47, 48, 49, 50, 51
Point, Nicholas: 33
Populist Party: 204
Potter, John: 116 n 6, 121
Pratt, O. C.: 227
Pratt, Willard: 270
Preacher, Billy: 309
Prohibition: 200, 204, 243-44
Prohibition Party: 183, 204-05, 241, 244-47
Proudhon, Victor: 78, 102

Railroad passes: 193, 229, 234
Raisins: on Rancho Chico, 137, 165, 182, 318, 319
Rancho del Arroyo Chico: 116, 128, 129-51, 156-61, 163, 165-66, 169, 180-83, 188, 200, 254, 258-59, 265, 267, 270, 272-77, 279-82, 301-02, 311, 313, 318-22, 324, 325, 327, 328-33. *See also* alfalfa, almonds, Bidwell Mansion, Bermuda grass, casaba melon, cattle, Chico Roller Fouring Mills, dairy, farm labor, fruit, irrigation, Mechoopda, Mikchopdo, raisins, sheep, vinegar, wheat, wine
Rancho Ulpinos: 76, 99
Ranchos, society and culture of: 82-85, 90-92, 98
Reading, Pierson B.: 72, 104, 206
Reclamation: *See* flood control and reclamation

Redington, Alfred: 158
Reed, I.: 154
Ridley, Robert T.: 75, 92, 284, 289
Riley, Bennett: 125
Ripley, N. Y.: 27
Robidoux, Antoine: 31, 41-42
Rodriguez Flat: 38
Rogers, Edward: 53
Rogers, Justus: 17
Rolfe, T. H.: 116 n 6
Romaine, W.G.: 52, 53
Rosenfeld, John: 161
Round Valley: 255, 268, 270-71, 274-75, 278, 303-05
Royce, Charles C.: 20, 147-48, 148 n 34, 328-29
Ruby Mountains: 59

Sacramento River: 90
Sacramento Valley: 88, 93-95, 154, 285-89
Sahweeco: 308-09
St. John, John P.: 183, 241
Salmon: 90
San Bernardino: 237-38
San Diego, occupation of: 78-79, 105, 110
San Fernando, Mission: 76, 79, 113
San Gabriel, battle of: 79, 112
San Joaquin River: 69
San Joaquin Valley: 68, 87
San Jose, Mission: 74, 86
San Jose: 70, 74
San Luis Rey, Mission: 78-79, 87, 106-08, 137, 250-51, 253 n 14
San Pasqual, battle of: 110-11
San Rafael, Mission: 86, 87, 137
Sandy Gulch: 28 n 1
Sapling Grove: 31, 31 n 1, 32, 42, 43
Sargent, Aaron A.: 200, 201 n 41, 223, 229-32, 233, 340
Sauber, Halbert: 264, 264 n 43
Sawyer, Lorenzo: 118, 149
Schaeffer, James: 259
Scott's Bluff: 51
Seagraves, William: 147 n 32
Seaver, John: 147 n 33
Sebastian Indian Agency: 255
Secret ballot: *See* Australian ballot
Semple, Robert: 113
Sharpstein, John R.: 308

Sheep: 154, 171; on Rancho Chico, 132-33, 182
Sherman, William Tecumseh: 18
Shoshone Indians: 55-62
Shotwell, George: 33, 50-51
Shover, Michele: 13, 24-25, 253 n 14, 255 n 18, 257, 260 n 32
Sierra Flume and Lumber Company: 316, 322, 324
Sierra Lumber Company: 324, 329
Sierra Nevada: 35, 37-40, 63-68, 70-72
Silver King Creek: 38
Silver King Meadows: 38
Simpson, George: 51
Sinclair, John: 129
Size, John: 146 n 29
Slinkard Creek: 35
Sloat, John D.: 78, 105
Smith Valley: 35
Snake River: 32
Snodgrass Creek: 38
Society of California Pioneers: 17, 17 n 1
Soda Springs: 32, 33, 34, 54-55
Soosook, "Mike": 282, 309
South Pass: 32, 53
Southern Pacific Railroad and the Big Four: 182, 193, 197, 199-200, 211-12, 220-25, 229, 231-32, 233-36, 237-41, 311, 313. *See also* Cadwalader, Charles; California and Oregon Railroad; Central Pacific Railroad; Crocker, Charles; Crocker, Edwin; Gorham, George; railroad passes; Sargent, Aaron; Stanford, Leland; Towne, A.N.
Sperry Flour: 136
Spring Valley Water Company: 201
Sproule, Oliver: 146 n 29, 159
Stanford, Leland: 173, 187, 187 n 7, 188, 192-93, 223, 269, 270, 328
Stanislaus River: 38, 39, 64, 71
Stanton, Edwin M: 208
Starr, Augustus: 273, 274-75
Stevens, R. J.: 227-28
Stevens, Thaddeus: 189, 215
Stewart, George: 23
Stewart, William: 212
Stilson, Charles: 335
Stockton, Robert F.: 78-79, 104-13, 125
Stone, Elisha: 48
Sue Ung: *See* Ung, Sue

Sugar Pine and Lumber Company: 324
Sumner, Charles: 189
Sumner, Edwin V.: 207
Sutter, Anna Eliza: 80, 114
Sutter, John: 18, 72, 74-78, 80, 86, 92-93, 95-98, 99-100, 101, 102, 114, 115-16, 119-20, 127, 154-55, 206, 250, 253 n 14, 285-86
Sweetwater River: 32
Swift, Granville: 123

Talbot, Theodore: 105, 106
Temperance Reform Party: 200
Temple, Jackson: 150 n 40, 189
Thomes, Robert H.: 43
Three Knolls Massacre: 261, 262, 276-77
Todd, William L.: 103
Tonoco: 308-09
Towne, A. N.: 234
Townsend, John: 99-100, 124
True, Benjamin: 323
Tubbesing, John: 318 n 20
Turner, Joshua N.: 230
Tyrrell, Ian: 15, 144-45

Ung, Sue: 323
United Labor League: 330, 331

Vallejo, Francisca Benicia: 113
Vallejo, Mariano: 74, 77-78, 85, 102, 154-55, 192, 251-52
Vallejo, Salvador: 78
Van Voast, James: 266
Vigne, Louis: 86
Vinegar: on Rancho Chico, 144, 144 n 22

Wailaki Indians: 270
Walker Pass: 34 n 10
Walker River: 35, 62
Walker, Joseph Reddeford: 34 n 10, 39 n 23, 64, 70
Washington, Benjamin F.: 207
Weaver, James B.: 204-05
Wells, Michael: 272
Wells, Thomas: 271-72
Western Emigration Society: 31, 42-43
Weston, Missouri: 29, 42-43
Wesumto: 279 n 92
Wetherby, Ira: 277

Wheat: 133-35, 138-39, 162, 199; mechanization, 135, 158, 166-69; in Mexican California, 89-90, 92, 153, 155-56, 179; on Rancho Chico, 135-36, 147, 147 n 33, 156-61, 167-69, 181-83; flour milling, 136, 146 n 29, 147 n 32, 156, 160, 182-83, 259, 325, 327, 337. *See also* Chico Roller Flouring Mills
White, William: 325
Willard, Frances: 18, 243
Williams, Isaac: 86
Williams, John: 116 n 6, 121
Williams, Joseph: 33, 46, 47, 51
Williams, Richard: 33 n. 7, 47
Wilson, Amanda: 279 n 92
Wilson, Joseph: 212-13
Wilson's Gap: 35
Wine: 163-65; on Rancho Chico, 136-37, 163
Wo Ah Lin: 323
Wolfskill, William: 86
Wolves: 68, 90

Wong (Chinese servant): 332-33
Wood, George: 146 n 29
Wood, Joseph: 233
Woodruff v. North Bloomfield: 118, 149-50
Woodruff, Edwards: 118
Woods, George L.: 227, 335
Workingmen's Party of California: 199, 201-02, 204, 238-39, 324-25
Workman, Robert: 276
Wozencraft, Oliver M.: 254-55, 280, 296-300
Wright, George: 208, 269, 273, 278
Wright, Hank: 324

Yahi: 257, 258 n 26, 261, 275, 276
Yana: 257, 258 n 26, 267-77, 278, 304
Yang Tie: 318
Yee Kee: 322
Yosemite Valley: 34 n 10, 39 n 23
Young, Sandy: 233
Yummarine, Chief: 257 n 24